KINGDO**[**

Witnesses to

Mark (

In April 1945, when the Bergen-Belsen concentration camp was surrendered and handed over to the British Army, Canadian forces arrived on scene to provide support, to bear witness, and to document the crimes that had been committed there. They were overwhelmed, understaffed, and left without adequate supplies, equipment, or medicine. Their encounters at the camp were haunting, transformative experiences that forever changed their lives.

In *Kingdom of Night*, Mark Celinscak showcases the engagement of Canadian troops and other personnel at the Bergen-Belsen concentration camp, one of the most notorious sites in the Nazi camp system. The book brings together a series of gripping, often deeply moving accounts that demonstrate the critical relief work carried out by Canadians, whose role in the liberation of the camp has been largely overlooked for more than seventy-five years.

In addition, Celinscak presents biographical overviews for each Canadian featured in the book, not only highlighting some of their life-saving and humanitarian work but also revealing what ultimately became of their lives after the war. With stark and moving detail, *Kingdom of Night* depicts the gruelling efforts of these Canadians to assist the survivors of one of the worst crimes in history.

MARK CELINSCAK is the Louis and Frances Blumkin Professor of Holocaust and Genocide Studies and Executive Director of the Sam and Frances Fried Holocaust and Genocide Academy at the University of Nebraska at Omaha.

KINGDOM
of NIGHT
Witnesses to the Holocaust

MARK CELINSCAK

UNIVERSITY OF TORONTO PRESS
Toronto Buffalo London

© University of Toronto Press 2022
Toronto Buffalo London
utorontopress.com
Printed in Canada

ISBN 978-1-4875-0574-5 (cloth)   ISBN 978-1-4875-3259-8 (EPUB)
ISBN 978-1-4875-2392-3 (paper)   ISBN 978-1-4875-3258-1 (PDF)

Library and Archives Canada Cataloguing in Publication

Title: Kingdom of night : witnesses to the Holocaust / Mark Celinscak.
Names: Celinscak, Mark, 1978– author.
Description: Includes bibliographical references and index.
Identifiers: Canadiana (print) 20210307609 | Canadiana (ebook) 20210307617 |
ISBN 9781487505745 (cloth) | ISBN 9781487523923 (paper) |
ISBN 9781487532598 (EPUB) | ISBN 9781487532581 (PDF)
Subjects: LCSH: Bergen-Belsen (Concentration camp) | LCSH: World War,
1939–1945 – Concentration camps – Liberation – Germany. |
LCSH: Holocaust, Jewish (1939–1945) – Personal narratives, Canadian.
Classification: LCC D805.5.B47 C457 2022 | DDC 940.53/1853593 – dc23

This book has been published with the help of a grant from the Federation
for the Humanities and Social Sciences, through the Awards to Scholarly
Publications Program, using funds provided by the Social Sciences and
Humanities Research Council of Canada.

University of Toronto Press acknowledges the financial assistance to its
publishing program of the Canada Council for the Arts and the Ontario Arts
Council, an agency of the Government of Ontario.

Canada Council   Conseil des Arts
for the Arts   du Canada

ONTARIO ARTS COUNCIL
CONSEIL DES ARTS DE L'ONTARIO

an Ontario government agency
un organisme du gouvernement de l'Ontario

Funded by the   Financé par le
Government   gouvernement
of Canada   du Canada

MIX
Paper from
responsible sources
FSC® C016245

To Stephanie and Stacie

In memory of John David Rutherford

You were our liberators, but we, the diseased, emaciated, barely human survivors were your teachers. We taught you to understand the Kingdom of Night.

– Elie Wiesel

Contents

Illustrations

Figure 1. Joseph Podemski at Bergen-Belsen, ca. May 1945 (centre with his
hand on fence). Courtesy of Joseph Podemski Private Archives.

Foreword

I am a survivor of the Bergen-Belsen concentration camp, a horrifying site of abuse, neglect, and death. This book collects eyewitness testimony by our Canadian liberators. When British and Canadian forces first entered the camp in April 1945, they could not fully understand what they were witnessing.

Near the end of the war, Bergen-Belsen had become terribly overcrowded as prisoners were arriving from other locations across Europe. Josef Kramer, the former commandant of Auschwitz-Birkenau, oversaw this horrific camp. There was hardly any food or water. Every morning we awoke to see more dead bodies in our barracks. The crematorium was working all the time, but it was not enough. At one point I was tasked with dragging and pulling the corpses into ditches and pits. I remember that we had to take off our belts, put them around the necks of the dead bodies, and pull them into the pits. These are scenes that you cannot adequately describe.

Passing through the gates of Bergen-Belsen was as though life and time were suspended. We thought that it was the end of everything. I was fortunate that I did not get sick and was able to walk around and survive. There are some things that you cannot even remember what happened or how you managed to deal with these problems. A few days before our liberation we could sense that something was coming to an end. The night before our liberation we heard the big cannons and the bombs in the distance. We knew something had happened. We thought our liberators might soon arrive.

I remember the moment when I saw the first British tank coming into Bergen-Belsen. Soldiers were standing on top of it. They were looking around and they did not know where they were or what was happening. The camp was situated in a forest, very deep in the Lüneburger

Heide, which is a large woodland area in northern Germany. Our liberators looked at us in shock.

For many of us, thin, weak, and dishevelled, we did not celebrate or smile at our liberation. Many of us were crying. We had already lost so much. Any joy or celebration came later. Liberation was beyond our imagination, and I suppose we simply could not believe what was happening. A day before, we did not think that we would survive or be alive for another day. We must not forget that at the moment of our liberation, at the same hour when British and Canadian forces occupied Bergen-Belsen, people continued to die. Death was all around us even after liberation.

The first personnel who came into the camp were medics. They did not know what they were facing and were not fully prepared. There was no medication. They gave us the wrong food. They were not equipped to do anything. At that point, I believe there were about sixty thousand men and women in the camp. At the same time, there were pits and ditches with thousands of people in mass graves. Our recovery came slowly, and many people did not make it.

After liberation, some of us were transferred over to the German military complex next to the camp. Bergen-Belsen was in such a terrible state that there was a danger of a typhus epidemic. The British decided to evacuate everybody as soon as possible – and burned down many barracks – because it was too dangerous.

After the war I remained in the German military complex until the end of 1949. I stayed in the displaced persons camp where I had a job at the Jewish Agency, where we were mainly busy with educating and preparing people to go to Palestine, which after 1948 became the State of Israel. In 1950 I immigrated to Israel with my wife, whom I had met in Bergen-Belsen. After several years in Israel, I eventually immigrated to Canada and settled in Toronto with my wife and two children.

This book collects the accounts of Canadian liberators and relief personnel. While their hardships were nothing compared to our own, it is important to recognize the challenges they faced in helping us try to survive in the aftermath. These stories will help us remember the terrible crimes that were committed against the Jewish people and many other victims. Let us never allow such crimes to ever occur again.

Joseph Podemski, 1922–2021
Toronto, Ontario, Canada

Preface

The following collection presents the first-hand accounts of Canadians who were present at the liberation of the Bergen-Belsen concentration camp in April 1945 and beyond. The gripping, often deeply moving testimony demonstrates the critical relief work performed by Canadians who have been largely overlooked for more than seventy-five years. In their own words, it presents the responses of the men and women who helped assist the victims of one of the greatest crimes in human history.

This collection builds upon my book *Distance from the Belsen Heap: Allied Forces and the Liberation of a Nazi Concentration Camp*, the first to detail and examine the Canadian involvement at this notorious camp. This subsequent work brings together the voices of Canadian witnesses to the Bergen-Belsen concentration camp.

My research on this subject began in 2007 during my doctoral studies at York University in Toronto.[1] In those early days of inquiry, my objective was exclusively to explore how British military personnel responded to the liberation of Bergen-Belsen. It is a camp well known to have been liberated by the British Army. Indeed, in the United Kingdom, Bergen-Belsen occupies a distinct position in the remembrance of the Second World War. It was also the only major, still operational Nazi camp the British liberated during the war.[2] There have been films, books, articles, museum exhibits, and the like discussing the significance of Bergen-Belsen to the British people. It gives the country a direct link to the Holocaust. Accordingly, exploring how soldiers responded to the crimes provides insight into the importance of Bergen-Belsen to British history and reveals something about human nature when confronted with unimaginable suffering.

Therefore, and unlike previous studies regarding the camp's liberation,[3] the focus of my first book was solely on narrative. What did military personnel write when they encountered Bergen-Belsen?[4] What

words and metaphors did they use to document the scenes during the
camp's liberation and subsequent relief efforts? How did liberators
make sense of the horror, and what might this tell us? This was the
original plan for *Distance from the Belsen Heap.*

In 2007 when I began my initial research for this project, and upon
reviewing the camp's rich historiography, I detected several surprising
anomalies. For example, one of my earliest observations was that there
were a few conflicting accounts concerning the liberation of the camp,
and in particular, regarding the designation of the camp's liberators. In
short, what unit in the British forces liberated Bergen-Belsen? The first
description I came across stated that the 11th Armoured Division of the
British Army liberated the camp.[5] Knowing that an armoured division
comprised between fourteen and sixteen thousand military personnel,
I wanted something much more specific. The second source I reviewed
suggested that the 63rd Anti-Tank Regiment were the camp's "official
liberators."[6] A third account designated the 1st Special Air Service as
the liberators of Bergen-Belsen.[7] A fourth version named the 29th Armoured Brigade.[8] Meanwhile, a fifth source explained that personnel
from a regiment of the Royal Horse Artillery were the first to enter the
camp.[9] Five works of history offered five different accounts regarding
the camp's liberation. Why such a discrepancy among scholars?

These apparent inconsistencies would eventually lead to one of the
overarching themes of my research to date: liberation was both chaotic
and multifaceted. Indeed, when we broaden our view of Allied military formations in northwest Germany, it becomes evident that many
more units were involved at and came across Bergen-Belsen than have
been previously discussed. Indeed, thousands of Hitler's camps were
encountered by Allied forces during the last few weeks of the Second
World War. As the Allies moved rapidly through former Nazi-occupied
Europe, they came across numerous concentration, transit, labour, and
prisoner-of-war camps. Liberating forces frequently stopped at these
camps for a short while before moving forward. These were typically
frenzied, ephemeral moments in time.

I also began to grasp that, so many decades after the end of the war,
there was still much that we did not know about the Holocaust. What
does it mean to liberate a Nazi concentration camp? How might we de-
fine a liberator? Accordingly, and due to conflicting accounts over who
can be considered the definitive liberator of Bergen-Belsen, I felt compelled to re-examine the surrender and relief of this notorious camp in
Distance from the Belsen Heap.

Not long after this initial confusion, another issue arose. I searched
local archives in Toronto hoping to find material relating to the British

Army and the liberation of Bergen-Belsen. My first visit was to the Clara
Thomas Archives at York University, where I was completing my doctoral work. While they did not have any material relating to the British
and Bergen-Belsen, they had an impressive series of letters written by
a Canadian named Ted Aplin, an airman who, along with many of his
colleagues, became closely involved at the camp.[10]

I re-examined the secondary sources written about the history of
Bergen-Belsen but found nothing regarding any Canadian involvement
at the camp. In fact, Canadian forces were never mentioned in any of
the histories written about Bergen-Belsen. I then sought the advice of
experts in the country's military history, and the answer was always the
same: Canadian forces were not involved in the liberation of this or any
other Nazi camp – aside from a small site or two in the Netherlands.
And yet I wondered: what was Ted Aplin, a Canadian airman from
Toronto, doing at a camp liberated by the British Army?

As my research progressed, I continued to come across clues regarding some type of Canadian involvement at Bergen-Belsen. This generally came in the form of a name in a newspaper article, a reference in
a soldier's letter home, or a passing mention in an interview. To learn
more about this connection, I spent time working at Library and Archives Canada, Archives of Ontario, and the Canadian War Museum.
Unfortunately, these national and regional archives contained only a few
documents relating to the country's role at Bergen-Belsen. There was
certainly not enough material available in them to sufficiently explore
how Canadians – who were clearly involved with this camp – reacted.
If I found anything, it was simply more traces, such as a reference in
a letter home by a Canadian soldier telling his family that a colleague
encountered the horrors of Bergen-Belsen.

As I continued to gather documentary evidence, the name of one
Canadian often led to that of another, which often led to a few more.
Eventually, one name turned into ten and ten turned into hundreds.
However, names alone cannot tell a nuanced story. First and foremost, I was after eyewitness accounts by Canadian military personnel. Consequently, these national and regional archives did not reveal
the treasure trove of letters, diaries, and reports I was hoping to find.
I merely had a long list of names of Canadians who had some sort of
connection to Bergen-Belsen. What the precise connection was, I still
did not grasp.

By 2008, I decided to expand the scope of my initial project and explore how *both* British and Canadian military personnel responded to
the liberation of Bergen-Belsen. It was clear to me that the Canadian
angle would reveal an important, untold aspect of the story. However,

while the official archives offered hundreds of British responses, they revealed little about the Canadian involvement.

Therefore, I faced a scholarly dilemma. I was certain that Canadians were involved in the liberation and relief of the camp, yet I had little substance to answer my many questions. Why were so many Canadians at Bergen-Belsen? What roles did they play at the camp? How did they respond? I fumbled around in the dark, unsure of how things would develop.

Slowly and over a great deal of time, I built a substantial database of first-hand accounts produced by Canadian witnesses. As you will read in the following pages, this collection shares a small part of that database. While some of the documents ultimately came from national and regional archives, others emerged from private collections. Many of the sources were identified through sheer persistence and good fortune. Indeed, one clue often led to another until I located a considerable number of accounts. Ultimately, it was the kindness and generosity of people across North America, Europe, Australia, and Israel that helped shape my research and move it forward.

This book begins with an introduction to Canada's involvement in the liberation of Nazi concentration camps at the end of the war. It explains how Canadian forces became involved at the Bergen-Belsen concentration camp. This chapter is followed by a theoretical overview on reading narratives of real events. The accounts that comprise this collection include diaries, memoirs, interviews, letters, and other forms of expression.

The bulk of this work comprises the first-hand accounts of thirty-five Canadians who encountered the Bergen-Belsen concentration camp. Most arrived at Bergen-Belsen with Canadian forces, although a few were attached to the British Army at the time of liberation. A brief biographical sketch of each individual is provided, followed by the accounts themselves. Multiple accounts by the same individual are provided when historically significant. Several accounts have been condensed for reasons of space and to avoid repetition. An ellipsis indicates when an account has been condensed.

It is well-known that the Canadian government, like many of the world's states, did little to help European Jews.[11] This makes the Holocaust a part of Canadian history, albeit a shameful one. And yet, across the Atlantic, there was also a significant number of Canadians who became directly involved in assisting the victims of some of the Nazi regime's brutal offences.

This collection of witness testimony reveals the engagement of Canadian troops and other personnel at Bergen-Belsen. It thus remedies a gross misunderstanding regarding Canadian involvement in the liberation of the camps at the end of the Second World War. It acknowledges and demonstrates the significant relief work done by Canadians who have been largely overshadowed for more than three-quarters of century, bringing together, for the first time, a series of documents illustrating the life-saving efforts of Canadians during an appalling humanitarian crisis. In their own voices, it presents the work done by those who helped assist the victims of one of the greatest crimes in human history.

As witnesses to the Holocaust, these Canadians had a unique position of intimacy and distance, connection and alienation. Their responses are an amalgam of shock, sorrow, and shame. Canadians worked to complete their assignments, all the while preventing themselves, sometimes unsuccessfully, from breaking down emotionally or psychologically.

The Bergen-Belsen concentration camp was surrendered and handed over to the British Army. Canadian forces arrived on scene to provide support, witness, and document the crimes. They were initially overwhelmed, understaffed, and left without adequate supplies, equipment, and medicine. They were presented with an experience for which no one had been prepared or trained. In the end, their experience in the camp was a memory that remained, one that lingered and haunted. These Canadians had but only glimpsed the kingdom of night.

Acknowledgments

This work was conceived as I was revising the doctoral dissertation that became my first book, *Distance from the Belsen Heap: Allied Forces and the Liberation of a Nazi Concentration Camp* (University of Toronto Press, 2015). At the time I was the Pearl Resnick Postdoctoral Fellow at the Jack, Joseph and Morton Mandel Center for Advanced Holocaust Studies of the United States Holocaust Memorial Museum. My first book examined how British and Canadian military personnel responded to the liberation of the Bergen-Belsen concentration camp in northwest Germany. It explored the meanings, symbols, and metaphors offered in these often-riveting accounts.

As I revised *Distance from the Belsen Heap*, I recognized I had an opportunity to provide a platform to Canadians who have been largely overlooked for more than seventy-five years. Many of these accounts have never been read by a broader public. Indeed, I have been given permission to reprint letters, diary entries, and personal memoirs by servicemen and women that have been held privately for generations by families across Canada and in other parts of the world. I am grateful to them for allowing me and my readers the opportunity to glimpse what Elie Wiesel called the "kingdom of night." These gripping, at times harrowing, and often deeply moving accounts demonstrate the relief work carried out by Canadians at Bergen-Belsen.

This publication has received generous financial support. It has been published with the help of a grant from the Federation for the Humanities and Social Sciences, through the Awards to Scholarly Publications Program, using funds provided by the Social Sciences and Humanities Research Council of Canada. I am fortunate to have an endowed chair at the University of Nebraska at Omaha (UNO). Accordingly, funding has also been provided through the university's Louis and Frances Blumkin Professorship for Holocaust and Genocide Studies. I thank

Dean David Boocker of UNO's College of Arts and Sciences who provided me with a research release that allowed me to finally complete this project. I am grateful to the university's Department of History for allocating two graduate research assistants; my thanks go to UNO graduate students Derek Fister and Zane Jensen for their efforts in transcribing many of these accounts. Each transcription was met with my approval, and any discrepancies are mine alone.

I am fortunate to have worked closely with editor Len Husband of the University of Toronto Press for nearly ten years. His patience, guidance, friendship, and support have been critical for my first and second books. It has been an honour to have both works published by the University of Toronto Press.

A long list of talented and supportive colleagues have helped me with this project, including Sara Horowitz, Marlene Kadar, Suzanne Langlois, Carolyn Kay, and Richard Menkis, to name a few. I continue to receive support from colleagues at the United States Holocaust Memorial Museum.

Lastly, I must thank my family. My sisters have been a constant source of support. My parents demonstrate the importance of a work ethic, and I hope my efforts make them proud. In 2021, my wife and I welcomed a daughter into the world; they both fill my heart with joy and challenge me to be a better human being.

Bergen-Belsen: A Timeline

1935–1937	The Wehrmacht build an expansive military complex close to the village of Belsen, near the town of Bergen. Workers are housed in barracks in the forest south of the construction site. Initially 3,000 workers live in these units.
1937	The new military complex is completed, becoming the largest in Germany.
May 1940	The Wehrmacht use the workers barracks to house prisoners-of-war (POWs). Mostly French and Belgian military personnel are housed in what is called Stalag XI-B.
May 1941	Stalag XI-B is expanded to accommodate future Soviet POWs. The camp is renamed Stalag XI C (311) Bergen-Belsen.
July 1941	The first Soviet POWs arrive at Stalag XI C (311). Most live in the open, as the camp is still being constructed. Thousands of Soviet POWs die from illness and malnutrition due to poor living conditions, as well as abuse.
August 1941	A special selection of Soviet POWs occurs, including many Jews, who are transported to Sachsenhausen concentration camp and murdered.
April 1943	The Bergen-Belsen concentration camp is established. The SS Economic-Administration Main Office takes over control of part of the camp. SS Captain Adolf Haas becomes the first commandant of the Bergen-Belsen concentration camp.

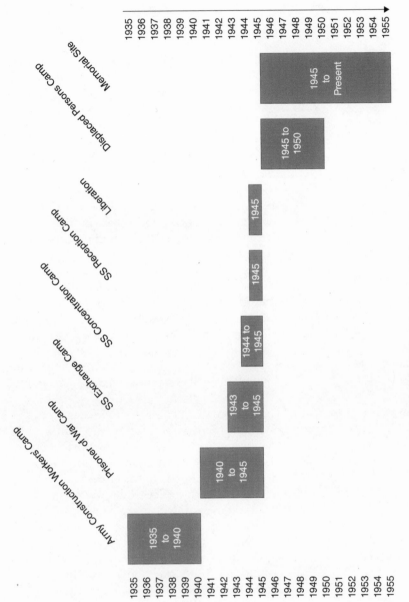

Figure 2. Timeline of the Bergen-Belsen complex.

July 1943	The first transport of Jewish prisoners arrives from Poland.
July-September 1943	The camp is divided into sections. The neutrals' camp houses Jewish citizens from noncombatant countries. The special camp contains citizens of neutral countries in Latin America who hold Palestine emigration papers. The star camp houses Jews whom the SS were willing to exchange for Germans interned abroad, foreign currency, or commodities valuable to the war effort. The prisoners' camp contains those previously held at Buchenwald and Natzweiler who were used to construct the internment Camp.
October 1943	Approximately 1,800 Polish Jews are deported from the special camp to Auschwitz-Birkenau and killed.
March 1944	Bergen-Belsen is redesignated as a recovery camp for prisoners from other concentration camps who are considered too weak or ill to work.
June 1944	222 Jewish prisoners being held in the star camp leave for Palestine in exchange for German citizens held on British territory.
July 1944	The SS establishes the Hungarian camp. Approximately 1,600 Hungarian Jews arrive in the camp that month.
August 1944	A women's camp is established to house women and girls transferred from other camps. Around 300 Hungarian Jews are sent to Switzerland in exchange for money.
December 1944	SS Captain Josef Kramer replaces Adolf Haas as the commandant of Bergen-Belsen. A second group of Hungarian Jews, approximately 1,300, is transported to Switzerland in exchange for cash payment.
January 1945	The POW camp at Bergen-Belsen is closed and is replaced with a large women's camp. One hundred and thirty-six Jewish prisoners with Central and South American papers are exchanged and leave for Switzerland.

February 1945   Thousands of prisoners are transferred to
                       Bergen-Belsen, and overcrowding becomes
                       a major issue. The death rate at the camp
                       continues to increase. In early February, Camp
                       Commandant Josef Kramer reports that 60–70
                       inmates die per day. By the end of the month,
                       400 people die per day. The camp crematorium
                       cannot handle the number of dead.

March 1945   Corpses are piled together, layered with
                       wood, and burnt in the open. Due to the sheer
                       number, the dead are no longer buried. Typhus
                       runs rampant throughout the camp. By the end
                       of the month, more than 44,000 prisoners are
                       being held in Bergen-Belsen.

6 April 1945   Approximately 2,500 exchange prisoners are
                       transported by train towards Theresienstadt.
                       The train was liberated by the Allies at
                       Farsleben near Magdeburg on 13 April
                       1945. Meanwhile, there are now over 60,000
                       prisoners at Bergen-Belsen.

8 April 1945   The railway infrastructure of the nearby town
                       of Celle is bombed by the Allies. Several
                       transports are hit and inmates flee. Along
                       with some of the general public, members
                       from the Schutzstaffel (SS), Wehrmacht, the
                       Volkssturm militia, police, and army search for
                       the escapees. This became known as the *Celler
                       Hasenjagd*, the "Celle hare hunt," the tracking
                       down of escaped inmates from the air raid. The
                       water supply at Bergen-Belsen has failed.

10 April 1945   German authorities are given an inspection
                       tour of Bergen-Belsen and are briefed by Camp
                       Commandant Josef Kramer on the conditions
                       in the camp. It is agreed that Bergen-Belsen
                       should be handed over to advancing British
                       troops.

11 April 1945   The British Second Army occupies nearby
                       Celle. Heinrich Himmler authorizes the
                       handover of Bergen-Belsen to the British Army.

12 April 1945   Colonel Hans Schmidt, an emissary from the
                       1st German Parachute Army, and Lieutenant-
                       Colonel Hans Bohnekamp, along with a

medical officer and a translator, cross Allied lines and are led to the British Army's VIII Corps' Headquarters at Winsen. Negotiations for the surrender of the camp began that evening between VIII Corps' chief of staff and the chief of staff of the 1st Parachute Army, Military Commandant Bergen.

13 April 1945   An agreement sets aside a neutral area of 48 square kilometres around the concentration camp and the military training grounds. Most of the SS guards stationed at the camp subsequently flee. Camp Commandant Josef Kramer and nearly eighty warders, both men and women, remain at Bergen-Belsen, along with 2,000 armed Hungarian guards.

14–15 April 1945   Allied forces are delayed from entering the camp by 48 hours due to fighting at the Aller River near Winsen and the village of Walle.

15 April 1945   British and Canadian forces arrive at Bergen-Belsen. The British Army assumes control of the camp.

April–May 1945   Thousands of dead bodies in Bergen-Belsen concentration camp are buried in mass graves. Many survivors are transferred from the camp to an emergency hospital set up by the British in the nearby Wehrmacht barracks. The survivors are given the status of displaced persons (DPs). To prevent the spread of disease, the British burn down many of the camp's wooden huts.

June 1945   The emergency hospital in the nearby Wehrmacht barracks is transformed into a displaced persons camp.

September–November 1945   The First Congress of Liberated Jews in the British Zone takes place in the Bergen-Belsen DP camp. A wooden monument to the Jewish victims is erected in the grounds of the camp. A British military tribunal tries 48 members of the Bergen-Belsen staff, including 37 SS personnel and 11 prisoner functionaries. Eleven defendants are sentenced to death, including Camp Commandant Josef Kramer.

12 December 1945	British military authorities execute Josef Kramer and his co-defendants.
June 1946	Bergen-Belsen becomes the largest Jewish DP camp in post-war Germany.
September 1950	The Bergen-Belsen DP camp is closed.

PART ONE

Historical Background

Canada, the Holocaust, and the Liberation of Bergen-Belsen

Until recently, studies of the liberation of Nazi camps were nearly absent from the ever-growing field of Holocaust Studies. As the field expanded, we came to know a great deal more about the origins of the Holocaust, the legal repression, resettlement and deportation, the camp system, methods of murder, resistance, and the death marches. Much less was known about the moment of liberation, and in particular the ensuing days, weeks, and months. By examining the immediate period after the Allies reached the camps, we can reveal the true complexities of liberation, as well as the challenges faced by both survivors and liberators in the immediate post-war period.

As a topic of study, liberation is important because the accounts offered by Allied military personnel at the end of the war were among the first attempts at a response to Nazi crimes by those not themselves victims of the camps. The stories that news organizations and military personnel told to the world helped sustain a vision of the Holocaust. Their impressions aided in the shaping of public perception of the crimes.

Moreover, narratives of liberation afford us a glimpse into how men and women both think and act when confronted by unimaginable suffering. Indeed, the accounts of Allied military personnel often push against the notion that liberation was somehow a joyous occasion, ending the survivors' miseries in the camps. The accounts in this collection help us understand that liberation was not a uniform moment in time; rather, it was a long, often trying process. For these reasons and more, the liberation of Nazi concentration camps is a worthwhile topic of study.

On the topic of the involvement of Canada's armed forces in the liberation of Nazi concentration camps, research has been nearly non-existent. For decades after the war, this was a subject largely ignored by scholars. This lack of research was clearly reflected during the 1998

Senate Subcommittee of Veteran Affairs hearings held to discuss the proposed Holocaust gallery in what was to be the new Canadian War Museum in Ottawa.[1] Academics, politicians, veterans, and others were invited to testify about the proposal. In the view of many who testified, the Holocaust held no direct connection to Canada and its military. Upon conclusion of the hearings, the plan for a Holocaust gallery in the Canadian War Museum was cancelled.

Recently, however, a growing body of research has explored how the Canadian government, media, military, and average citizens either responded to or encountered the remnants of the Holocaust. Indeed, new scholarship has shed light on the country's complex relationship with this dark period in history.

In the years following the Canadian War Museum controversy, a slew of research emerged that explores the topic of Canada and the Holocaust. For example, Franklin Bialystok's *Delayed Impact: The Holocaust and the Canadian Jewish Community* (2000) demonstrates how the remembrance of the Holocaust developed in Canada over time. The author reveals how the Holocaust became a significant part of Canadian Jewish identity. Likewise, Ruth Klein's edited collection *Nazi Germany, Canadian Responses: Confronting Antisemitism in the Shadow of War* (2012) examines Canada's complicated relationship with the Holocaust from a range of viewpoints. The work investigates how Canada responded to the unfolding of the Holocaust through its media coverage, community activism, and the world of literature as well as on university campuses.[2]

More recently, Richard Menkis and Harold Troper's *More than Just Games: Canada and the 1936 Olympics* (2015) highlights the history of Canada's involvement in the 1936 Olympics hosted by Nazi Germany. The authors relate how Canadian participation was about more than simply sport; it was also about nationalism and politics. Meanwhile, Adara Goldberg's *Holocaust Survivors in Canada: Exclusion, Inclusion, Transformation, 1947–1955* (2015) is the first comprehensive analysis of the resettlement experiences of Holocaust survivors in early post-war Canada. The author demonstrates how Canada's Jewish community both assisted and hampered the ability of Holocaust survivors to adjust to a new country.

Finally, recent research has also begun to detail the direct involvement of Canadians in the liberation of Nazi concentration camps at the end of the Second World War. In 2000, Cecil Ernest Law published the first full-length study of Canadian involvement in the liberation of a Nazi camp, titled *Kamp Westerbork, Transit Camp to Eternity: The Liberation Story*. Law details how the Canadian Army's South Saskatchewan Regiment liberated the Westerbork transit camp. In addition, Laura

Brandon, formerly of the Canadian War Museum, has written several articles on official Canadian war artists Alex Colville and Aba Bayefsky.[3] Both men encountered Bergen-Belsen towards the end of the war. They sketched and later painted the terrible scenes.

In 2015 my work *Distance from the Belsen Heap: Allied Forces and the Liberation of a Nazi Concentration Camp* was published. The book re-examines the surrender and relief of the Bergen-Belsen concentration camp in northwest Germany at the end of the Second World War. It explores how British and Canadian military personnel struggled with the intense experience of liberation; how they attempted to describe what they had seen, heard, and felt to those back home; and how their lives were ultimately transformed by the encounter.

A great deal of research has explored the involvement of America and British forces and their encounters with Nazi Germany's extensive camp system.[4] In contrast, much work remains to be done involving Canadian forces and their experiences with the Nazi camp network. The country's military personnel unquestionably helped end Hitler's regime and contributed to the liberation of prisoner of war, transit, labour, and concentration camps in German-occupied Europe. This collection aims to contribute to this growing field of study.

Canadian Forces and the Liberation of Nazi Camps

Aside from smaller labour and prisoner-of-war camps, the first significant camp Canadians came across during the Second World War was in the Netherlands. The two countries have a close relationship that largely stems from the war: the Dutch royal family took refuge in Canada; Princess Margriet was born in exile while her family lived in Ottawa; and Canadian forces led in liberating the Netherlands from Nazi occupation. Thus, it should be expected that Canadian forces first came across Hitler's camps in the Netherlands.

The first significant camp encountered by Canadian military personnel was Camp Vught, also known as the Herzogenbusch concentration camp. Located in the town of Vught in the southern Netherlands and established in 1943, it was one of the only concentration camps in Western Europe outside of Germany run directly by the *Schutzstaffel* (SS). During its existence, the camp held 31,000 prisoners and saw nearly eight hundred deaths.[5] Inmates included Jews, Roma, Jehovah's Witnesses, homosexuals, and political prisoners.

British and Canadian forces first encountered Camp Vught on 26 October 1944. Units from the 4th Canadian Armoured Division helped liberate the camp. It had been largely evacuated nearly a month before the

Figure 3. Canadian forces liberate the Westerbork transit camp. Beeldbank
WO2–NIOD, 12 April 1945.

Allies arrived, but when the Canadians appeared corpses still lay around
the grounds and a small number of inmates remained in the camp.[6]

During the war, inmates imprisoned in the Netherlands were frequently transferred from Vught to the Westerbork transit camp, the
second significant site liberated by Canadians. Located in northeastern
Netherlands, it was established by the Dutch government in October
1939 to hold Jewish refugees who had entered the country illegally.
From 1942 to 1944 Westerbork served as a transit camp for Dutch Jews
who were then deported to sites located throughout German-occupied Eastern Europe. During those two years, the Germans deported
nearly one hundred thousand Jews from Westerbork to camps such as

Auschwitz, Sobibor, Theresienstadt, and Bergen-Belsen.[7] In one of the final deportations, Anne Frank and her family were sent to Auschwitz.

On 12 April 1945 units from the Canadian 2nd Infantry Division liberated Westerbork.[8] The first troops to reach the camp were men from the 8th Reconnaissance Regiment, followed by troops of the South Saskatchewan Regiment. Canadians troops encountered approximately one thousand inmates at Westerbork, as the majority had already been deported. A few days after its liberation, First Canadian Army's senior Jewish chaplain, Samuel Cass, arrived and conducted a service attended by approximately five hundred survivors. Chaplain Cass called it one of his most dramatic memories of the war.[9]

Chronologically, while the Bergen-Belsen concentration camp in Germany was the next camp to be encountered by Canadian forces, the last camp in the Netherlands to be liberated by Canadians was in Amersfoort. In the summer of 1941, near the garrison town Amersfoort, the Germans converted Dutch army barracks into a transit camp. Initially, the transit camp at Amersfoort began deporting prisoners to places like Buchenwald, Mauthausen, and Neuengamme. The following year prisoners were sent from Amersfoort where they would ultimately end

Figure 4. Canadian forces liberate Amersfoort police transit camp, 7 May 1945. Beeldbank WO2–NIOD.

up in extermination camps such as Auschwitz and Sobibor. In 1943, Amersfoort was expanded and became what the Nazis referred to as a police camp. Between 1941 and 1945, Amersfoort held over thirty-five thousand prisoners.

As the Canadian Army pushed deeper into the Netherlands, on 19 April 1945 German staff fled Amersfoort. Under the watch of the Red Cross, the camp remained in operation for another three weeks. On 7 May 1945, the First Canadian Army arrived to officially liberate the camp. There were five hundred inmates still alive at liberation.[10] Amersfoort was initially administered by the 1st Canadian Division but was later transferred to the 3rd Canadian Division.

The Liberation of Bergen-Belsen

By the time Canadian forces arrived at Amersfoort, they had already encountered Bergen-Belsen, one of the most filmed, photographed, and discussed camps of the Second World War. The Bergen-Belsen concentration camp was a sprawling site located on the Lüneburg Heath in northwest Germany between the cities of Hannover to the south and Hamburg to the north. While it was initially constructed to house labourers, in 1940 the camp began to take in prisoners-of-war. By 1943, parts of the Bergen-Belsen complex had been converted into a concentration camp.

As a concentration camp, Bergen-Belsen imprisoned approximately 120,000 men, women, and children. In April 1945, at the time of its surrender, there were nearly 60,000 prisoners in the camp, and many were terribly ill. Of those still alive when the Allies arrived, the majority, more than 60 per cent, were Jews. The prisoners encompassed a vast array of nationalities, although most were Polish and Russian; women comprised slightly more than half of the inmates.

In Bergen-Belsen the death rate was extremely high. When it was surrendered, thousands of emaciated corpses were scattered around the campgrounds because the crematorium was overburdened by the sheer number of dead. It is estimated that between January and March 1945 35,000 people were killed, including sisters Margot and Anne Frank. The death rate continued to accelerate, and in the month of March 1945 alone 18,000 people died in the camp. In total, 50,000 people perished in Bergen-Belsen concentration camp prior to the arrival of Allied personnel. Disease and starvation were the primary causes of death.

During the late evening of 12 April 1945, and under the approval of Heinrich Himmler, Colonel Hans Schmidt, an emissary from the 1st

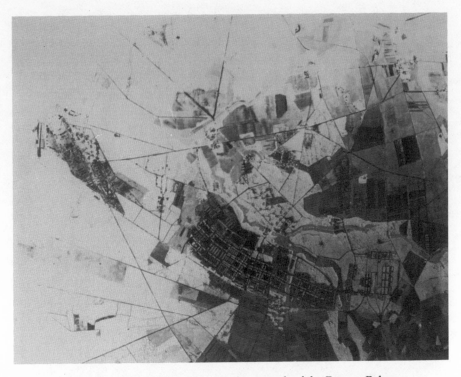

Figure 5. Aerial reconnaissance photograph of the Bergen-Belsen concentration camp area showing the village of Bergen. Image 743736, United States Holocaust Memorial Museum, courtesy of National Archives and Records Administration, College Park.

German Parachute Army, and Lieutenant-Colonel Bohnekamp, along with a medical officer and a translator, crossed British lines and declared that inmates in a nearby camp, Bergen-Belsen, were rife with typhus.[11] German representatives were then led to the VIII Corps' headquarters at Winsen. Negotiations for the surrender of the camp began that evening between VIII Corps' chief of staff (UK) and the chief of staff of the 1st Parachute Army, Military Commandant Bergen.[12] Signed in the early morning of 13 April 1945, the agreement set aside a neutral area of forty-eight square kilometres around the concentration camp and the military training grounds. This agreement, which was to last six days, subsequently led to instructions that the camp was to fall under the command of Lieutenant-Colonel R.I.G. Taylor, commander of the 63rd Anti-Tank Regiment, British Army.

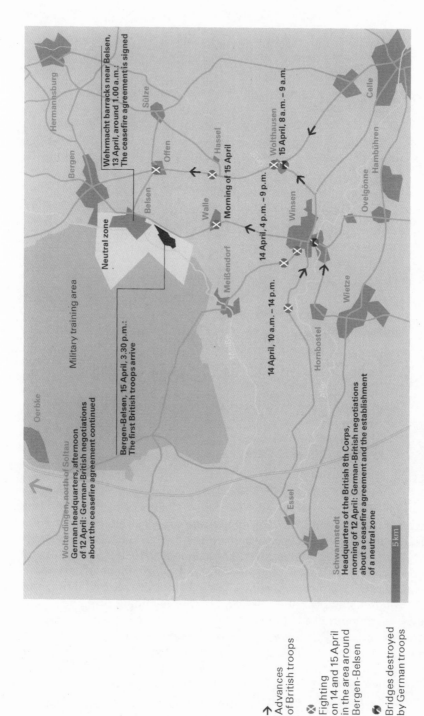

Figure 6. The advances of British troops towards Bergen-Belsen in April 1945. Berthold Weidner, weidnerhaendle.de.

Meanwhile, the negotiations and eventual agreement to surrender the camp affected military movements in the area. Indeed, word quickly spread that a concentration camp was in the area and that its inmates were terribly ill. In addition, later in the day on 13 April 1945, the majority of the SS guards stationed at the camp fled. Camp Commandant Josef Kramer and nearly eighty warders, comprising both men and women, remained at Bergen-Belsen, along with approximately 2,000 armed Hungarian guards.[13]

Men from 1st (British) Special Air Service (1SAS) entered Bergen-Belsen on the 15th and did so before the arrival of Lieutenant-Colonel Taylor and his assigned relief unit. The 1SAS was working with the 8th Parachute Battalion (UK), providing a reconnaissance screen. A detachment of 1SAS were patrolling the area for signs of any Allied POWs who were possibly incarcerated at the camp.[14] Along with this first British group to enter the camp was Lieutenant Keith W. MacLellan, a Canadian from Aylmer, Quebec, also with the 1SAS.[15] As the first Canadian to enter the camp, MacLellan has seen his efforts at Bergen-Belsen recognized by both the United States Holocaust Memorial Museum and the Canadian Jewish Congress.[16]

By the afternoon of 15 April 1945, Lieutenant-Colonel Taylor's 63rd Anti-Tank Regiment, Royal Artillery arrived in the neutral zone defined by the agreement. At shortly past 1500 hours, the leading party of Taylor's regiment, No. 249 (Oxfordshire Yeomanry) Battery, commanded by Major Benjamin Barnett, arrived at Bergen-Belsen. Meanwhile, the 11th Armoured Division bypassed the camp and drove towards Ebstorf.[17] Next, Lieutenant-Colonel Taylor ordered Captain Derrick Sington, then commanding No. 14 Amplifying Unit, and two non-commissioned officers (NCOs), Sergeant Eric Clyne and Lance Corporal Sidney Roberts, to enter the camp with an armoured car equipped with a battery of loudspeakers. Sington was instructed to announce that while the inmates were now free, due to the typhus outbreak, no one was permitted to leave the camp. Lieutenant-Colonel Taylor then became camp commandant.[18]

The first two days of British control of Bergen-Belsen saw several divisional units, detachments, battalions, and sections both enter and pass by the camp. It took nearly two days before substantial reinforcements arrived. In the intervening time, the 1st Canadian Parachute Battalion, which was part of the 3rd Parachute Brigade (UK) in the 6th Airborne Division (UK), had left Celle on 15 April 1945, on route to Eschede. The battalion had been coming across escaped POWs and refugees for the past couple of weeks. While travelling north from Celle, a company of the 1st Canadian Parachute Battalion arrived at the Bergen-Belsen

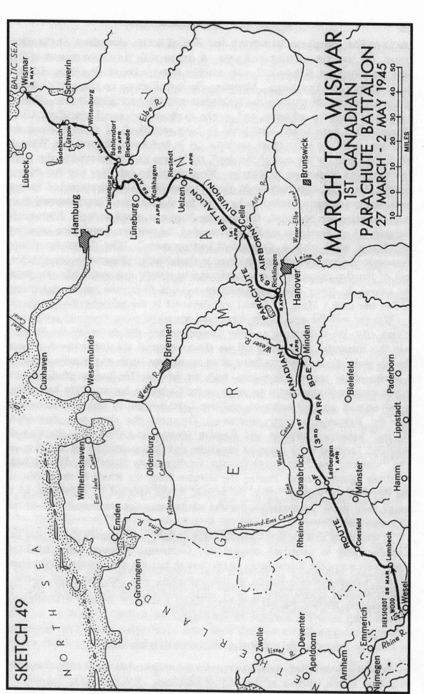

Figure 7. Sketch 49. March to Wismar, 1st Canadian Parachute Battalion 27 March–2 May 1945. Colonel C.P. Stacey, *The Victory Campaign: The Operations in North-West Europe, 1944–1945*. Published by authority of the Minister of National Defence, 1966.

concentration camp on the day of its liberation.[19] The convoy eventually stopped alongside the road next to the barbed-wire fence, south of the camp. A section of the 224 Parachute Field Ambulance (UK) was attached to the battalion, and a few of the men witnessed the appalling scenes at the camp.[20]

Some of the men from the 1st Canadian Parachute Battalion entered Bergen-Belsen to survey the scenes or to assist the prisoners, among them Lieutenant-Colonel Fraser Eadie, the battalion's commanding officer, and Captain Patrick Gerald Costigan, a medical officer. Costigan was among the first doctors to provide medical aid to the inmates in the camp.[21] He spent two days treating the ill in the camp before returning to his regular duties. Moreover, Sergeant A.H. Calder, Lieutenant Charles H. Richer, and Sergeant Mike Lattion of the Canadian Army Film and Photo Unit (CFPU), all of whom were with the 1st Canadian Parachute Battalion, entered the camp on 15 April 1945 and documented the scenes.[22] This makes the men from the battalion the first group of Canadians to arrive at Bergen-Belsen.

The following day, 16 April 1945, a smattering of reinforcements arrived at Bergen-Belsen. The 11th Armoured Division made available a hygiene section. In addition, Major A.L. Berney, a staff officer attached to VIII Corps (UK), was sent to 817 Military Government Detachment (UK), which had arrived the evening before, and was put in charge of general administration in Camp I.[23] Major Berney then took steps to arrange for the organization and requisition of various supplies from surrounding villages and towns. RCAF public relations officers Ron Laidlaw and Fred Hopkinson, along with Sergeant Joe Stone of 39 Wing (RCAF), also arrived at Bergen-Belsen on 16 April 1945 and recorded the terrible scenes.[24]

On 17 April 1945, 224 Military Government Detachment, under command of Major W.H. Miles, arrived at 1400 hours and established its headquarters in Camp I.[25] Squadron Leader John Proskie of the RCAF from Edmonton, Alberta, was immediately sent to 224 Detachment's headquarters, arriving the same day. An agricultural expert,[26] Proskie was put in charge of planning the collection and employment of resources from the local area. The monumental task of organizing food for the inmates was left almost entirely to Proskie and his lone assistant, a sergeant in the British Army. Later, on 19 April 1945, 904 Military Government Detachment arrived, to work under 224 Detachment, and was put in charge of Camp II.[27] On 26 April 1945, 618 Military Government Detachment also arrived.[28]

Allied photographic units arrived soon after the surrender of Bergen-Belsen. Visually documenting the dreadful situation at the camp

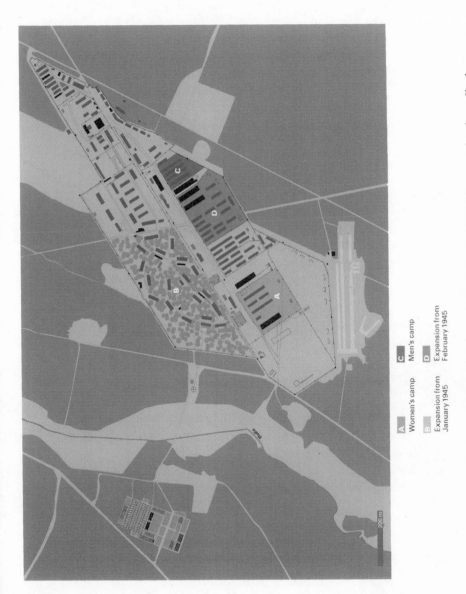

Women's camp

Men's camp

Expansion from
January 1945

Expansion from
February 1945

200 m

Figure 8. Bergen-Belsen concentration camp, 1945. Berthold Weidner, weidnerhaendle.de.

Figure 9. A convoy of the RCAF Typhoon Wing moving deep into Germany in the wake of the British Second Army passes through Celle near the Belsen horror camp. Image PL-43508 16/04/45. Department of National Defence.

became a preoccupation for many, even for personnel in non-photographic units. For example, numerous Canadian airmen took photographs while assisting at Bergen-Belsen. The RCAF's No. 5 and No. 6 Mobile Field Photographic Sections were stationed at an airfield in Soltau (B154), about twenty kilometres from the camp. A number of personnel from these sections, who went on several combined liberty runs to Bergen-Belsen on 3 and 4 May 1945, took a series of photographs of the terrible scenes at the camp.[29]

In addition to photographers, Canadian war artists, official and not, entered the camp. Three official war artists from Canada depicted scenes at the camp.[30] Lieutenant Alexander Colville, who worked with 3rd Canadian Infantry Division, was sent to the camp by Major A.T. Sesia and arrived on 29 April 1945.[31] Flight Officer Donald K. Anderson, attached to the RCAF's 127 Wing, arrived at the end of April or early May. Toronto-born Aba Bayefsky was with RCAF's 39 Wing when he arrived at Bergen-Belsen on 10 May 1945.[32] These individuals are well known for having depicted the camp, although there were other artists who also documented the scenes at Bergen-Belsen.[33]

Within a week of the liberation of the camp, and after survivors passed through the "human laundry," as it came to be known, personnel began moving the newly deloused survivors into an emergency "hospital" in buildings at the nearby Wehrmacht barracks.[34] Thousands of former inmates were treated at the emergency hospital. Later, once the numbers of patients subsided, the barracks reverted to provisional housing for survivors who no longer needed emergency medical care. Those still in need of treatment, and who could stand being moved, were eventually transferred to the German Military Hospital located a short distance from the main camp.[35]

By the end of April an advance party of the 9th British General Hospital arrived. They were soon joined by ninety-seven medical students from teaching hospitals in London, along with detachments from the British Red Cross Society. By the second week of May, 22 and 30 Field Transfusion Units as well as 35 Casualty Clearing Station moved into Bergen-Belsen.[36] On 16 May 1945 an advance party of the 29th British Hospital arrived. They were joined by the rest of the hospital staff a few days later.[37] At this time, the 29th British Hospital involved several Canadians, including Dr. Charles Sutherland Rennie, welfare officer and St. John Ambulance volunteer Elsie Deeks, and Doris Haines, who worked with the Queen Alexandra's Imperial Nursing Service.

After the arrival of the 35 Casualty Clearing Station on 14 May 1945, the remainder of the sick were transferred to the recently cleared German Military Hospital.[38] Initially, this military hospital became known as Bergen-Hohne or, more commonly, as Belsen Hospital. Later, it was renamed Glyn Hughes Hospital, after the humanitarian work of the well-known brigadier. It would soon become the largest hospital in Europe, housing over thirteen thousand patients.[39] The hospital was staffed by a mixed group including the medical students, Red Cross workers, and, controversially, German medical personnel – and yet staff shortages continued.

Canadian Lyle Creelman, who in early June 1945 was appointed chief nurse for the British zone of occupied Germany, became aware of staff shortages at the hospital.[40] Staff had been recruited from a variety of locations; indeed, nurses from a range of countries worked at Belsen Hospital, including at least six Canadians.[41] Personnel in charge of administrative matters were constantly looking for ways to ease nursing shortages, as well as deal with the large number of patients. Ultimately, in August 1945 the United Nations Relief and Rehabilitation Administration (UNRRA) formally took over Glyn Hughes Hospital.[42]

Military personnel continuously worked to ease the burden of the large number of inmates by transporting those who needed additional care out of the camp. Shortly after liberation, airmen from the RCAF's 437 Squadron, part of RAF Transport Command, not only flew inmates out of Bergen-Belsen but also flew high-ranking officials into the camp.[43] In addition, survivors from Bergen-Belsen, along with former prisoners from the POW camp at Sandbostel, were transferred to the No. 7 Canadian General Hospital, which had arrived at Bassum on 3 May 1945.[44]

On 4 May 1945, the RCAF's Nutrition Group, led by Wing Commander John F. McCreary, was sent from Epe, Netherlands, into Germany to examine the situation at Bergen-Belsen.[45] Accordingly, both of the RCAF Nutrition Group's Spearhead Survey Groups A and B arrived at the camp for inspection the following day. They surveyed the scene and completed a report. The groups were soon recalled, and on 7 May 1945 they proceeded in a convoy through Wageningen to Utrecht, establishing a base back at Bilthoven.[46]

As will be discussed below, numerous RCAF wings had air bases located in northern Germany during the spring and summer of 1945. A few of the wings were visited by British padres, both army and air force, asking personnel to assist at Bergen-Belsen. During the last week of April, British padre Leslie Hardman visited a nearby RCAF base requesting food and medical supplies, and the following day he received large lorry loads and jeeps carrying goods.[47] Reverend Louis Sanker, senior chaplain of the Second Tactical Air Force, also requested assistance and received numerous donations from RCAF's 126 Wing.[48] Most of the men from 39 Reconnaissance Wing visited Bergen-Belsen in early May, bringing along supplies, such as food, cigarettes, and medicine.[49] Likewise, 440 Squadron, 143 Wing, sent loads of supplies to the camp.[50] Furthermore, a number of personnel from these wings spent days working in the camp, assisting the inmates, acting as translators, and contributing to the overall relief efforts.

As the weeks after Bergen-Belsen was surrendered turned into months, additional units, groups, and battalions continued to move into the area, and many encountered the camp and its former inmates. In June, companies in the 4th Battalion of the Wiltshire Regiment (Duke of Edinburgh's) moved to new locations in Celle District.[51] Battalion companies arrived in villages such as Bergen, Garßen, Bostel, and Winsen. Later that summer, the battalion headquarters was moved into the former SS barracks in Bergen-Belsen.[52] The 4 Wilts, as they were known,

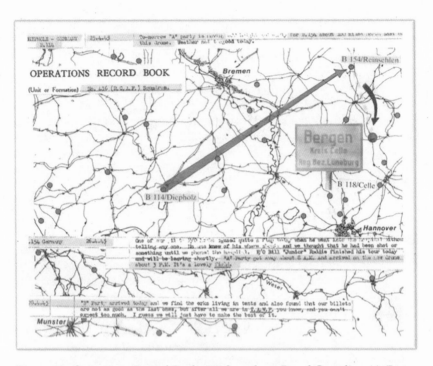

Figure 10. Operations Record Book, 416 Squadron, Royal Canadian Air Force.
Library and Archives Canada.

were unique in that the battalion included a cross-section of Canadian officers assigned through the CANLOAN program, including Lieutenant Wilfred I. Smith, who was a platoon commander.[53]

In early 1945 British and Canadian officials agreed to work together in the disarmament of Germany. Shortly thereafter, within 84 Group, RAF, a disarmament staff and wings were established. By mid-May 1945, 84 Group Headquarters was located at Scheuen, near Celle.[54] The unit was fully established at the end of the month. By this time, thousands of survivors from Bergen-Belsen had been transferred to hospitals in Celle. Soon, several men from 8402 (RCAF) Disarmament Wing, and one staffed entirely of Canadians, became intimately involved with the survivors, both in Celle and at Bergen-Belsen.[55] Men such as squadron leaders Ted Aplin and John W. Thompson and Sergeant Stanley Winfield, along with many other personnel from 8402 Wing as well as British personnel from 84 Group, went to great lengths to assist the survivors during the spring and summer of 1945 and beyond.

Military personnel were unprepared for what they were to find at the camp. When it was initially entered on 15 April 1945, the war continued. Consequently, supplies were limited, personnel were largely unavailable, and many resources were occupied elsewhere. Those who remained to work at the camp were left with monumental tasks.

The victims of Bergen-Belsen continued to die even after the camp was surrendered to the Allies. Between 19 and 30 April 1945 another nine thousand people died. The following month forty-five hundred inmates succumbed to illness, while in June four hundred more would perish. In total, approximately fourteen thousand people died in the camp after its transfer, nearly a quarter of the prisoners still alive when the British and Canadians first arrived at the camp. Allied control of Bergen-Belsen did not put an end to the misery and loss of life. While the situation slowly improved, the conditions in the camp remained grim even weeks after its surrender. Undoubtedly, the suffering weighed deeply on all involved in the camp's liberation.

The liberation of Hitler's brutal camp system occurred more than seventy-five years ago. The word "liberation" can summon images of freedom, elation, and camaraderie. The term perhaps even connotes intent and purpose, strategy and preparation; to liberate something or someone requires consideration and planning. Popular representations of the liberation of Nazi concentration camps often frame it as a jubilant event, one that brought an end to the suffering of the victims of the Holocaust.

However, liberator narratives are overflowing with shock, grief, confusion, disgust, and rage. Military personnel were horrified and deeply shaken by the scenes at camps like Bergen-Belsen. The diseased, emaciated survivors in striped prison uniforms appeared before them, moaning and crying in a variety of languages that many of the men could not understand. The camps grounds were covered with thousands of unburied corpses.

And yet the efforts of Canadian military personnel at camps like Bergen-Belsen undoubtedly saved many lives. Soldiers and medics repeatedly gave up rations, tended to the ill, and even helped bury the dead. They frequently put themselves at risk when working in close proximity – at times without adequate protection – to inmates with a wide variety of diseases, and many showed tremendous empathy and compassion towards the dying. Indeed, Canadians should be recognized for the life-saving work they provided to Holocaust survivors.

The ideas we have about liberation are often oversimplified. For example, the British and Canadians did not actively capture a camp like Bergen-Belsen. On the contrary, the German Army and the SS simply handed it over. The Germans recognized that Bergen-Belsen had

become a colossal humanitarian disaster, a place where typhus, typhoid, and other diseases were widespread. They felt that unless the
inmates were contained, they would infect the local German population and wreak havoc on a massive scale. When the Allies arrived at the
camp and saw the state of the inmates, they decided that while these
people would no longer be under German authority, no one was to be
released. Thus, the prisoners remained behind barbed wire.

For the survivors in camps like Bergen-Belsen, liberation does not
mean freedom in the way we normally use the term. Initially, the survivors were not given autonomy to leave the camp and go wherever
they saw fit. Instead, in the weeks and, for some, the months and even
years that followed, they continued to live behind the barbed wire in
these camps. When places like Bergen-Belsen became displaced persons camps, the survivors were still guarded – only by men in different
uniforms.

In the post-war period many of these camps could be unpleasant
places, especially for Jews. British officials at Bergen-Belsen refused to
recognize Jews as a distinct group, and thus Polish Jews were treated as
Poles, Hungarian Jews as Hungarians. Jews often discovered that they
now lived alongside people who had collaborated with Nazi Germany
or in some instances had even fought with the Germans, in German
Army uniforms. This led to serious tension, animosity, and in-fighting
between Jews and non-Jewish compatriots. Since there was generally
nowhere else to go, life could be rather grim, particularly for Jewish
survivors in Bergen-Belsen.

The liberation of inmates from Hitler's camp system was not an
Allied military objective during the Second World War. There was no
master plan to target and enter Nazi camps to save any victims. Indeed,
the discovery of the camps was generally inconsequential from the perspective of securing military goals.

Ultimately, it was the collective Allied victory in Europe that made it
possible for Hitler's brutal camp system to come to an end. While there
was no grand strategy put forward by any nation to rescue the prisoners of Hitler's Third Reich, the achievements of Allied forces in Europe
during the Second World War made it possible for such moments to
occur. Those still clinging to life in the camps were released from Nazi
tyranny because Allied armies liberated Europe and not due to any in-
tentional aim to end Hitler's camp system.

Taken together, the stories of both military personnel and Holocaust
survivors illustrate a salient point: liberation was a highly ambivalent
experience. For liberators there was a duty, both moral and military,
to help those in need, mixed with the shock and horror of the sights,

sounds, and smell of the inmates; there was a desire to document what they witnessed as liberators combined with the struggle to locate suitable words and metaphors. For the survivors, they understood that they were no longer prisoners of Nazi Germany. And yet large numbers would remain in displaced persons camps long after the war, learning that many of their friends and family had not survived what we now refer to as the Holocaust. Both survivor and liberator would contend with these profound experiences for the rest of their lives.

Reading Testimony

This collection brings together a range of personal accounts by Canadians who encountered the Bergen-Belsen concentration camp at the end of the Second World War.[1] It consists of a wide array of mediums, which include letters, diary entries, memoirs, wartime reports, interviews, and Senate testimonies as well as opinion pieces found in newspapers and journals. What they all have in common is the use of the narrative form: everyone presented in this collection attempted to make sense of their experience at Bergen-Belsen by expressing themselves through a story or chronicle.

Nonetheless, each account is unique: all contain distinct features. In particular, the genre in which each individual writes undoubtedly influenced his or her account. Consequently, it is important to recognize and understand the conventions of the genre employed by each writer. What advantages and disadvantages does each form contain? For example, how does a memoir differ from a letter? Why is a first-hand account of a real event, one with shortcomings or even errors, not a work of fiction? To better appreciate these accounts, it is necessary to consider the distinctions in reading different forms of testimony.

This chapter provides an overview of the complexity and nuance of narrative. It begins by explaining how several of the first-hand accounts presented in this work were collected and then outlines how a variety of sources help illuminate the history of the Canadian involvement at Bergen-Belsen. The next section reflects on the complex relationship between experience and narrative. How is language employed by individuals to represent experience? What is the value, and what are the limitations, of the autobiographical in the study of the past? I then assess the various forms and genres of the personal accounts presented in this work. The final section offers a meditation on the moral claims of these personal accounts.

Gathering Sources

Official state repositories are, of course, necessary and essential to re-constructing the past. However, several of the accounts that comprise this collection were not found in national or regional archives.[2] For example, in 2009 I came across the late Jean Bruce's *Back the Attack! Canadian Women during the Second World War, at Home and Abroad*.[3] Bruce drew upon letters, diaries, and personal interviews with women who played active roles as nurses, industrial workers, and volunteers during the Second World War. In the book she includes a brief account about Bergen-Belsen attributed to a woman named "Elsie Deeks," a volunteer with the St. John Ambulance. Unfortunately, Bruce provides no further details regarding this source. Was the account from an interview she conducted with Deeks, or did it come from a document written by the subject herself? In short, who was Elsie Deeks and how did she end up working at this dreadful camp in northwest Germany at the end of the war? These questions would lead me on a dizzying pursuit across both time and space.

Not long after reading *Back the Attack!* I discovered that the Jean Bruce fonds were held at Library and Archives Canada in Ottawa. Among other items, the fonds include oral interviews conducted by the author, some of which were completed during the writing of *Back the Attack!* Hoping that Bruce interviewed Deeks at some point, I visited the archive. However, no such interview existed in the fonds. I then turned my attention to archives overseas. Since Deeks volunteered with the St. John Ambulance, I conducted research at the Order of St. John and the British Red Cross Archives in London, England.[4] However, I found nothing relating to Deeks at either archive. In short, it appeared that national and regional archives did not have anything of substance regarding Ms. Deeks and her work at Bergen-Belsen.

Finally, in 2012, nearly three years after first coming across her name, I stumbled across an obituary in the *Winnipeg Free Press* that revealed that Elsie May Deeks passed away peacefully on 17 June 2005 at the age of ninety-five. In such instances, and if enough time had passed, I would attempt to contact family members in hopes of learning more. However, the obituary explained that Deeks never married, had no children and was predeceased by her siblings. Therefore, the chance of finding a living relative was low.

One of the last lines of the obituary stated, "Sincere thanks to ... staff on Tower 6 Deer Lodge Centre, for their care and compassion to Elsie over the past few months."[5] I contacted the Deer Lodge Centre, a long-term care and rehabilitation facility specializing in geriatric care and treatment of veterans in Winnipeg. Unfortunately, no one could recall any specific details to help me. Instead, they suggested I contact the newspaper to locate the author of the obituary.

Fortunately, staff at the *Winnipeg Free Press* informed me that while they did not know who wrote the obituary, according to their records it came directly from the funeral home. Ultimately, and on my behalf, the funeral home contacted the author of the obituary and let her know that I wanted to learn more about Deeks's life.

As it turned out, the author was a life-long friend and the executrix of the estate of Elsie Deeks. Convinced that my intentions were honoura-ble, the executrix shared the details of her friend. For most of their lives the two women lived near one another and remained close. Alas, one of the few aspects of Deeks's life that the executrix knew little about was her friend's wartime experiences in Germany. It was a topic that was always avoided. When I asked the executrix if Deeks ever discussed the war years with anyone else, she replied, "The only time she discussed the war was in the letters." Stunned, I asked, "What letters?" It was revealed to me that Deeks wrote letters regularly throughout the war to her family back in Winnipeg. When I enquired what happened to the letters, I was told that after her passing, all her wartime awards and correspondence were left to the executrix.

At best, I only hoped that the executrix would be willing to have the letters scanned and emailed to me. Instead, she agreed to send me these original documents by registered mail. Grateful, I thanked her and promised that I would take good care of the documents and return them as soon as they were reviewed.

A week later a package arrived from Winnipeg, and I was pleased to find a large pile of letters stretching over several months, as well as photographs and other items. In the letters, Deeks speaks vividly and movingly about her work aiding the survivors of Bergen-Belsen. As readers will discover in this collection, she describes in intimate detail the difficulty she and her colleagues faced working alongside such pain and suffering.

I digitized the letters and included their insights in what became *Dis-tance from the Belsen Heap*. I recommended to the executrix that they be preserved in an archive in order that future generations could ac-cess and learn from them. With her permission, and because of the fo-cus on the Bergen-Belsen concentration camp, I arranged to have the letters archived at the United States Holocaust Memorial Museum in Washington.[6]

The way in which I obtained Deeks's letters is merely one instance, repeated countless times, of how I built a large database of documents for my project exploring Canadian involvement in the liberation of the Bergen-Belsen concentration camp. I have received numerous personal accounts from people over the last decade. These important documents were often left sitting – waiting – in basements, closets, cabinets, shelving units, desks, boxes, under beds, and in storage. They were collected from lifelong friends of the writer, comrades in arms, neighbours, children, grandchildren, great-grandchildren. I was given access to rare, often never-before-examined documents relating to one of the twentieth century's most horrific crimes. All of this allowed me to reveal a long-ignored narrative in Canadian history.

Receiving rare documents from friends and family was not the only method I employed over the years. Listening to oral interviews also revealed clues that led to a greater number of important documents. For example, Toronto-born Shalome Michael Gelber was a field representative to the United Nations Relief and Rehabilitation Administration (UNRRA) and worked with the Joint Distribution Committee (JDC).[7] He spent months assisting the survivors at Bergen-Belsen. In an interview held at the Museum of Jewish Heritage in New York, Gelber mentions a scathing critique he wrote in the *New Statesman and Nation* concerning British policy in the displaced persons camp at Bergen-Belsen.[8] This was a document of which I was previously unaware. As it turns out, and due to the content of Gelber's missive, Kingsley Martin, the editor of the magazine, would not permit him to attach his name to the piece. According to Gelber, Martin's decision was a wise one: his account caused such a commotion that he claims it was referenced in debates in the House of Commons. In the interview, Gelber explains that he signed the piece as "Canadian Officer" and that it appeared sometime during the summer or fall of 1946. With these details available to me, I was able to track down Gelber's important piece "Are We Breaking Faith?" It gives a rare perspective on British post-war policy at Bergen-Belsen from someone who was once part of the Allied forces and was now working in the displaced persons camp. Accordingly, let us consider the value of these accounts.

Personal Accounts as Historical Sources

In writing about the past, evidence is essential. Without the benefit of traces from the past, the writing of history could not take place. Historical sources or traces are thus essential to the practice of history. Whenever there is an event or an experience, there will be a trace, an imprint, or a remnant of that event. That which remains in the form of a trace can materialize in written form, perhaps later housed in an archive, or as remembered, in the minds of individuals. Furthermore, people have a basic desire to narrate past experiences. Indeed, personal narratives are potential source materials for the historical researcher. While some historians view narratives of personal experience with doubt, quite often they become an indispensable source.

Historical researchers seek narratives not only to illustrate but also to substantiate specific interpretations of events. And yet historical narratives can never be definitive. The past is constantly being challenged, rewritten, amended, corrected, and supplemented. Indeed, the value of any historical account often lies in the recovery of a view of the past that had long been lost, forgotten, or even ignored.

For instance, until *Distance from the Belsen Heap*, Canadian involvement at Bergen-Belsen had never been fully detailed. Indeed, for decades following the war the Holocaust was not a significant part of public discourse or scholarly study in Canada. While hundreds of Canadians became involved at Bergen-Belsen, the vast majority have been ignored or relegated to a mere footnote in history books. Although official documents such as military reports, war diaries, and operations record books have noted, albeit sparsely, that Canadians assisted at Bergen-Belsen, it is often the abundant personal responses that offer a fuller, more detailed account of events. Perhaps the Canadian involvement had not been previously detailed because some personnel left their units to assist at the camp or were simply loaned to the British Army, and thus their participation was not formally documented. Nevertheless, the number of Canadian responses is immense. Therefore, how can we engage personal accounts in a serious, accurate, and attentive manner?

The work of Christopher Browning offers insight into how the historical researcher can employ testimony, first-hand accounts, in scholarly work. Browning has written numerous books that rely heavily on eyewitness testimony.[9] He is interested not only in the authenticity of an individual's testimony, but also in its factual accuracy. His methodology often involves gathering a sufficient mass of testimonies that can be weighed against one another.[10] When Canadians left their squadrons or units to assist at Bergen-Belsen, this was not always noted in the official operations record book or war diary, and thus when multiple accounts exist, experiences and encounters can be verified and corroborated with one another. Moreover, these accounts can be supplemented by records establishing the time and specific location of a battalion and unit. As the following chapter will reveal, for example, Royal Canadian Air Force squadrons, during the spring and summer of 1945, were scattered across the Lüneburg Heath. These squadron airbases were often only a few kilometres away from the Bergen-Belsen concentration camp.

Browning's approach involves looking at testimonies "not in the collective singular but rather in the individual plural, not collective memory but rather collected memories."[11] As is sometimes the case, when other historical sources are lacking, such as reports and personnel lists, a researcher must then rely on first-hand accounts or eyewitness testimonies. Nevertheless, personal accounts must be handled with the same scrutiny and analysis as any other form of evidence. Yehuda Bauer advises that "the principle should be that one testimony is interesting but not persuasive; two converging testimonies create a basis for consideration; ten converging testimonies are proof."[12] And while one can argue that even ten converging testimonies do not always offer incontrovertible proof, multiple accounts can be used to narrow the gap on empirical certainty. One must recognize and assess the problems that can arise from employing first-hand accounts in any study of the past, but this does not mean that first-hand accounts should be ignored.

Those cautious in employing personal narrative – such as autobiography, memoir, or other life-writing texts – in any objective study of the past often argue that it is because of the genre's perceived self-reflexive, unstable, fictive properties. Historians are concerned with the gap involving the past and its representation, or as Paul Ricoeur has expressed it, between "ce qui, un jour, fut."[13] Moreover, experiences, especially those involving particularly moving or crucial events, often motivate individuals to narration. People attempt to make sense of experience through language; our encounter with the world and with each other is often mediated through language. Accordingly, personal accounts can expose critical encounters, revealing what individuals both thought and understood at certain points in time. These texts demonstrate not only what was known, but also what *could* be known at a given time. An individual's actions can be better grasped when we consider how that individual perceived his or her role in history.

The way a historical event is remembered will inevitably be influenced by the responses to it. Historical researchers who ignore witnesses to an event, as Walter Laqueur notes, "however thorough their research and innovative their explanations, are missing one whole dimension."[14] Structure, style, substance, and strategy come together in shaping narratives of personal experience. What is needed, then, in any serious study involving first-hand accounts, is a narratological critique.

Experience and Narrative

Hayden White, a historian in the tradition of literary criticism, acknowledges that to focus on narrative is to think about the very nature of culture and about the spirit of humanity itself.[15] All narratives, to some degree, are dependent on culture. A narrative that recounts a real event can expose patterns of an individual's personal identity as well as something about their respective culture. Moreover, an individual does not remember in isolation. Sociologist Maurice Halbwachs observes that individuals evoke, distinguish, and focus their memories from the social framework of which they are a part.[16] In other words, individuals remember the past as members of a group. While narratives can be attributed to the individual, they are also socially and culturally determined. Being a subjective, internal aspect of human life, culture thus symbolically maps the external world. Individuals come to terms with themselves and their experiences as agents in history through culture.

The responses of Canadian men and women who encountered the Bergen-Belsen concentration camp during the spring and summer of 1945 not only reveal aspects of their own characters but, when collected, also reflect something of their viewpoints and communities. The testimony of Canadians offers a perspective on the way individuals both think and act when confronted with incredible anguish. Consequently, their encounters, which can be viewed as an event, can lead us to contemplate the narratives of that event. In other words, examining multiple accounts of an event can reveal the narrative practices and meaning-making patterns of members from cultural groups. The men and women who assisted at Bergen-Belsen did so both as individuals and as members of different nations and militaries, as well as from a multitude of cultures and communities.

Our encounter with an experience, and the way we represent it, is always mediated in some way through memory, language, or narrative. We comprehend our past experiences from a culturally and historically specific present. Barbara Kirshenblatt-Gimblett recognizes the importance of mediation to the understanding of any form of representation, stressing that we pay attention not only to form and content but also to the relations among creators, audiences, and critics as well as to the medium and genre.[17] Our vision of the past is much more than an isolated, personal act. There are significant layers to any vision of the past. We become subjects through experience, or, as Joan Scott suggests, "it is not individuals who have experience, but subjects who are constituted through experience."[18] As a subject, one's experience is shaped in terms of one's views of status and identity in society.

Language and narrative are fundamental to our relationship with experience. Edward Sapir demonstrates that people are "very much at the mercy of the particular language which has become the medium of expression for their society ... We see and hear and otherwise experience very largely as we do because the language habits of our community predispose certain choices of interpretation."[19] In other words, individuals are shaped by and subsequently draw from the culture or cultures they inhabit whenever they communicate. For example, doctors learn the languages, metaphors, and narratives produced by medical institutions; this medical discourse becomes a way doctors understand both themselves and their experiences. The stories they tell, the narratives they offer, are invariably shaped by these discursive domains.[20] But what exactly do narratives communicate? What can they reflect? The work of three scholars – Hayden White, David Carr, and Paul Ricoeur – provides insight regarding the value of narrative.

Hayden White considers that, to some extent, all forms of narrative are fictional. For White, a narrative is "always a figurative account, an allegory."[21] His work is significant because he reminded historians of the narrative dimensions of their work. Indeed, the *writing* of history certainly belongs to the genre of narrative. Accordingly, historical narratives share commonalities with fictional narratives, such as emplotment and the presentation of the temporal character of experience, though White recognizes that historians deal with events that are located specifically in time and space and that are clearly discernible, while imaginative writers can work with both real and imagined events.

White is at his most controversial when, moving beyond the similarities between the two, he assimilates history with fiction. He refuses to concede the difference between knowledge gained through historical research and the knowledge brought about by fiction. He calls historical narratives "verbal fictions, the contents of which are as much invented as found and the forms of which have more in common with their counterparts in literature than they have with those in the sciences."[22] For White, the very idea that the sequences of real events are contained in the narratives we tell is nothing more than "wishes, daydreams, reveries."[23] As a result, while historical narratives are still able to convey a form of truth, White views them as a type of fiction.

In well-known debates concerning historical objectivity and truth, historian Carlos Ginzburg confronted White in conferences in 1989 and 1990, and then again in print in Saul Friedländer's edited collection *Probing the Limits of Representation: Nazism and the "Final Solution"* (1992). Ginzburg charges White with absolute relativism and argues that even "just one witness" can move us closer to the reality of historical truth.[24] In an essay in the same volume, White looks for a compromise to this charge of "relativism." In the search for historical truth, White comments that, as accounts of factual events, "competing narratives can be assessed, criticized, and ranked on the basis of their fidelity to the factual record, their comprehensiveness, and the coherence of whatever arguments they may contain."[25] Thus, White concedes that historical events differ from fictional ones and that the former can be evaluated through documentation and records. Nevertheless, he insists that while narrative accounts can contain factual statements, they will also invariably contain poetic or rhetoric elements.[26]

Philosopher David Carr presents a differing view to White and one that unites life and narrative. While White emphasizes a discontinuity between life, its real events, and narrative, Carr stresses the continuity between them.[27] Theorists like White argue that historical and fictional narratives are distinct from the real world they claim to represent. This, they maintain, is due to the form of narrative itself. Narratives in this view are distortions of reality. Conversely, Carr considers narrative the principal way an individual organizes experience. While White insists that real events do not have an inherent narrative structure, Carr suggests that "narrative structure is not 'imposed' on anything. It constitutes the principle of organization for our action and experience ... it is the structure of our very being."[28] In Carr's analysis, real events, in terms of both experience and action, are narrative in nature. Therefore, narrative encompasses all human existence, in the way we experience time and in how we relate to one another.

According to Carr, historical and fictional narratives should be considered as "extensions and configurations" of reality.[29] Narrative is not then an exaggeration of reality, but an accompaniment to it. "[Stories] are told in being lived and lived in being told," he writes. "The actions and sufferings of life can be viewed as a process of telling ourselves stories, listening to those stories, and acting them out or living them through."[30] Our actions are based on the way we narrate our experiences and, consequently, our lives. Our relationship with time in our present draws its significance from the way we think of the past and the future. Thus, Carr wants us to grasp that narrative is at the core of who we are as individuals.

In his three-volume *Time and Narrative* (1985), philosopher Paul Ricoeur recognizes and integrates some of White's insights but, like Carr, stresses that life is not alien to narrative. In the debate between the discontinuous (White) and continuous (Carr) nature of narrative, Ricoeur appears to fall somewhere in between. His work highlights the connections between narrative and life, but he also acknowledges the differences. Thus, for Ricoeur, it is not a case of either/or; rather, it is a situation of and/ but in the contemplation of life and narrative. In other words, there are continuities and discontinuities between life and narrative.

A gap will always exist between the past as it happened and its representation in the present. Ricoeur acknowledges the possibility of narrowing this gap between narration and action in historical narratives. He emphasizes that there is a difference between discussing the past "as" it happened, to which the historian strives, and "as if" it happened, which is the domain of the imaginative writer. While historical narratives can never offer a completely precise account of the past, they are closer to the real world *as* it happened because they normally deal with claims that can be measured and verified. If it were otherwise, there would be no way to repudiate Holocaust deniers. "If we do not resolutely maintain the difference between history and fiction," Ricoeur insists, "[it] is an insult to the dead."[31] Therefore, while the two share commonalities, the intention of history is to offer a type of knowledge distinct from literature.

In addition, and like Carr, Ricoeur recognizes narrative as a part of our being, an element of our lived existence. "Time becomes human time," he remarks, "to the extent that it is organized after the manner of a narrative; narrative, in turn, is meaningful to the extent that it portrays the features of temporal existence."[32] Thus, narrative is the way individuals endeavour to comprehend the intricate relationship between time and life.

In response to Carr, Ricoeur does not place narrative, life, and history for that matter, on the same plain. Indeed, Carr's continuity thesis makes it difficult to claim that there are narratives that recount real events. Or as Richard Kearney succinctly puts it, "If *life, history* and *story* are placed on the same narrative continuum, how do we answer the revisionists that our narrative is not just *any* narrative but one which makes a claim to truth, which tells it as it really was?"[33] This presents a dilemma that also challenged White. In response to this predicament, Kearney points to what he calls a "trans-narrative truth" claim, something that would emerge from a "plurality of narrative interpretations."[34]

For a "trans-narrative truth," and drawing from the theories of both Carr and Ricoeur, Kearney offers three criteria to orient and anchor claims to historical truth. First, he points to "narratives referring back to prior narratives."[35] All historical narratives are mediated to some degree by narratives of witnesses to the events described. Historical researchers look to verify their claims with first-hand documents. What is more, personal narratives can, in turn, be measured and compared with other first-hand accounts of the same event. Kearney's second criterion is narratives corresponding with facts.[36] Personal narratives, stories of real events, need to be supported, wherever possible, with verifiable facts. For example, narratives that falsely claim there were gas chambers at Bergen-Belsen can be compared with empirical evidence, such as camp plans and maps, reports, and other accounts, which prove otherwise. Stories and empirical evidence are thus both essential in uncovering historical truth. Kearney's third criterion is what he calls the "thing," which is that which defies description and comprehension. More specifically, Kearney suggests that this brings forth a "move from a first-order reference to 'facts' and a second-order reference to 'life-stories' to a third-order reference to a reality deeper than words."[37] In the context of Bergen-Belsen and the Holocaust, this might mean somehow acknowledging the great challenge of adequately narrating a horror that defies any cogent, rational understanding.

The work of White, Carr, and Ricoeur helps us to appreciate the relationship between narrative, experience, and history. White's work illustrates the importance of narrative to the writing of history. However, as Ricoeur discusses, recognizing the importance of narrative to the enterprise of historical writing does not mean that history and literature are the same. As Sara Horowitz advises, "Without narrative, history becomes unknowable; but when narrative displaces history, the real events become inaccessible."[38] Ricoeur has gone to great lengths to show the ways history is distinct from literature. Carr's theory, which corresponds with some of Ricoeur's work, stresses the importance of narrative to all human experiences and suggests how narrative negotiates our way of being in and relating to time. Narrative is a record of our lived existence. I turn now to a review of the various forms personal narratives can take and that are available as source material for the historical researcher. For our purposes, the generic term "personal narrative" will be used in broad reference to the different types of accounts discussed below. Therefore, personal narratives are accounts – both written and oral – offered by participants who have first-hand experience of the events under discussion.

The Fictional, the Autobiographical, and the Historical

While many military personnel from the Canadian forces did not talk in any way about their encounters at the Bergen-Belsen concentration camp, hundreds did in fact discuss it. Thus, the historical researcher is left with a myriad of oral and written accounts. Some of the men and women documented their experiences as they were happening, while others waited years and, in some cases, decades before revealing their thoughts and feelings about the camp. It is thus important to recognize the time that has passed in the telling and the different forms taken in these written and oral accounts.

The personal narratives discussed in the following chapters can and should be classified as autobiographical or life-writing texts. The first-hand accounts concerning Bergen-Belsen that are available to researchers include primarily journals-diaries, letters, memoirs, and oral interviews. All can be considered life-writing texts and are examples of narrative in different forms. According to Marlene Kadar, life writing is "more or less" autobiographical and embraces narratives "by an author who does not continuously write about someone else, and who also does not pretend to be absent from the text ... life writing is a way of seeing."[39] Accordingly, life writing is a particular type of expression, distinct from both historical and fictional narratives, but sharing some commonalities with the two forms.

German philosopher Wilhelm Dilthey, in his work concerning historical methodology, underscores the significance of autobiographical writing for the study of culture and history. Dilthey considers autobiography as "the most direct expression of reflection about life."[40] He contends that autobiography is highly selective and that one's view of the past is inevitably influenced by the present. Instead of viewing this as a distinct weakness, Dilthey sees in it the potency of autobiography. "The person who seeks the connecting threads in the history of his life," he reveals, "has already, from different points of view, created a coherence in that life which he is now putting into words."[41] Through autobiography and other life-writing forms, the individual reflects on and evaluates the past, which can bring a meaning and coherence to it.

Like the historian who contemplates the past in a search for meaning, the autobiographer considers the events he or she has experienced in order to gain insight about existence. This can have implications for the historical researcher. Individuality and historical understanding depend on each other, and "therefore," Dilthey explains, "autobiography can, ultimately, widen out into a historical portrait; this is only limited but also made meaningful by being based on experience, through which the self and its relation to the world are comprehended. The reflection of a person about himself remains the standard and basis for understanding history."[42] For Dilthey, autobiography, like self-reflection, is an ongoing process. It is always incomplete, since the individual cannot remember his or her birth and will not be around to respond to his or her death. Nevertheless, Dilthey concludes that reflecting on the self is at the root of historical consciousness.

Dilthey's insights on autobiography have influenced a wide range of scholars. James Olney, who counts Dilthey as a source, insists that autobiography can offer knowledge of what a person has been or what they are now.[43] Rather than looking for names, dates, and places from an autobiographical account, Olney suggests that what we really seek is a "characteristic way of perceiving, or organizing, and of understanding, an individual way of feeling and expressing."[44] How did Canadian military personnel "see" Bergen-Belsen and its victims? What is being communicated in these innumerable accounts? Indeed, a writer reflecting on the self strives for coherence out of the instability and confusion of past events.

What is the value of autobiographical texts for the historical researcher? In *Artful Histories* (1996), David McCooey contends that autobiography is much closer to history than it is to fiction and thus can be a valuable source for historians. A major difference between fiction and autobiography is that the former cannot be empirically verified. "Autobiography, however, is an inherently discursive act of writing," McCooey remarks. "Like other forms of history, it is a form of testimony and as such it is not autonomous the way fiction and poetry are ... [it is] open to all the checks and limitations of testimony."[45] Since an autobiographer, like a historian, can lie or distort the truth, this is precisely what separates both genres from fiction. Consequently, McCooey underlines that, like historians, autobiographers become responsible for the points they make in their works.[46]

In *History, Historians, and Autobiography* (2005), historian Jeremy D. Popkin acknowledges some of McCooey's insights but also strives to distinguish autobiography from history. He agrees with McCooey that both history and autobiography aspire to shape the past into a comprehensible narrative;[47] as well, both claim to recount real events, and neither can be entirely absorbed as works of fiction. But he also sees important distinguishing characteristics between the two. He observes that autobiographies offer a distinct perspective concerning how individuals see themselves and grasp past experiences. As well, autobiography is not "bound by history's requirement for documentation and its emphasis on collective, as opposed to individual, experience, and since no autobiographer can tell his or her story all the way to the end, autobiography has an open-ended character that separates it from both history and fiction."[48] Understanding these differences is paramount for historical researchers who employ autobiography and autobiographical texts in their work.

Genres of the Autobiographical

Autobiographical or life-writing texts appear in a variety of forms and genres. Sidonie Smith and Julia Watson remind us that the term "autobiography" has been highly contested due to its broad historical reach and the sheer range of life-writing genres and practices.[49] For our purposes, an autobiographical text does not necessarily mean an autobiography. As Smith and Watson note, autobiographical or life-writing narratives are a "historically situated practice of self-representation" in which "narrators selectively engage their lived experience through personal storytelling."[50] Consequently, it is useful to briefly examine the conventions that diaries, letters, memoirs, and oral interviews typically follow.

Several personal accounts presented in this collection appear in the form of journal entries or diaries. Philippe Lejeune, who does not, incidentally, distinguish journals from diaries, has spent much of his career focusing on the practice of diary writing. His work has helped differentiate diaries from other forms of autobiographical writing.[51] Typically, entries in diaries appear chronologically and can demonstrate patterns of what people value in life. However, the reflections within often focus on specific moments in time. Moreover, as Sandrine Arons demonstrates, while diaries are generally unedited, diarists are often aware that their writings may be read posthumously.[52] Karl J. Weintraub comments that the diary is "governed by the very fact that a day has its end."[53] The diarist does not have the benefit of extended hindsight and does not know what tomorrow will bring.

In addition, the author of a diary often writes in the very moment that the events, which are being reflected upon, are taking place. Like letter writing and immediate eyewitness reports, the diarist often writes from the perspective that action can still effect change concerning the event being described. James Young highlights that this type of writing does not necessarily call out for "reflection or contemplation of the events' meaning (even as they suggested meaning) so much as they are demands for immediate action and justice."[54] Diary and journal entries, while generally written privately and without much consideration of outside sources, are thus more "faithful" in their recounting. It is then a document of "dailiness": a written record of the emotional reaction of an individual's everyday experiences. Furthermore, due to its proximity to the events being recounted, diaries can be restricted by inadequate or inaccurate knowledge of those events or by an idiosyncratic viewpoint.

Letters, like diary entries, are documents frequently written in the moment being reflected upon. Accordingly, opinions, thoughts, and feelings can shift widely over a collection of letters. Taken together, letters can reveal patterns of attitudes, thoughts, and feelings, not only about the self but also about others. As Robert McGill notes, letters are "both artifacts of existence and commentaries upon it."[55] The correspondence is generally, although not always, directed or addressed to someone else. Thus, there is often an intended audience in mind, and letters usually remain unpublished. In addition, letters are useful, particularly for the following chapters, in establishing the where and when from which the subject is writing.

Janet Malcolm observes that letters constitute the "great fixative of experience ... they are the fossils of feeling."[56] Thus, the fissure between experience and text is typically narrowed in letter writing. When a letter writer recounts a recent occurrence, the memory of the experience does not have the opportunity to ripen. As McGill explains, "a distinguishing feature of letters is their potential for proximity to the life-events they narrate – thus their conventional claim to be 'true' to those experiences. In this respect they share a close kinship with the diary form. The further convention of dating them foregrounds their occasional quality and confers upon them the status of events in their own right."[57] Of course, immediacy does not necessarily imply that letter writing will provide a closer image of the event itself. Nevertheless, letters do present the subject's initial responses, unrefined emotions, and prime thoughts.

In contrast, memoir writing is characteristically an edited narrative of an individual's past experiences. Memoirs are more frequently published than letters and diaries. There is often a larger gap between the event and writing in a memoir than, for example, in a diary or letter. A memoir is not, as Mary Jean Corbett posits, "an autobiographical text that tells a story about a centered self, but one in which the writing subject recounts stories of others and events or movements in which she and/or her other subjects have taken part."[58] Therefore, it is less "of the moment" and based more on lengthy retrospection. In addition, memoirists can employ narrative devices that are often associated with novelists, such as point of view, character, structure, and voice.

The memoirist has travelled beyond the experience being reflected upon and knows its outcome. The writer can consult historical sources, which might aid in understanding. For example, a Canadian soldier writing about Bergen-Belsen in a letter home or in a diary entry would not use the term "Holocaust," a word not commonly employed until the 1960s after the Eichmann trial. By contrast, the scope and conceptualization of the Holocaust would be available to the memoirist writing decades after the event. As Weintraub brings to light, "the fact once in the making can now be seen together with the fact in its result. By this superimposition of the completed fact, the fact in the making acquires a meaning it did not possess before. The meaning of the past is intelligible and meaningful in terms of the present understanding; it is thus with all historical understanding."[59] Memoirists bring with them facts, knowledge, and historical understandings not accessible at the time of the experience under consideration.

Oral accounts – also referred to as oral histories or oral narratives – which were once considered suspect and highly controversial, are now a widely used source for scholars. The eminent Holocaust historian Raul Hilberg had long been cautious and at times even critical of the use of oral accounts as evidence in historical research. In reference to establishing the historical record of Nazi policies and methods of persecution, Hilberg states that German documents were more reliable than post-war memories.[60] Over time, many historians have been willing to employ testimonies in their work, notably Christopher Browning, Omer Bartov, and Israel Gutman. Browning affirms the value of testimony in historical research if it is used carefully and met with critical analysis.[61] Any thorough historical account of the Holocaust requires a recognition and employment of the numerous oral accounts available.

Indeed, the number of oral accounts concerning the Holocaust is vast. While most oral responses concerning the Holocaust are rightfully survivor accounts, there are significant numbers of liberator accounts available. Moreover, they are among the first attempts at a response by those not themselves victims of the camps. Predominately, these accounts are conducted through the interview process. Thus, the interviewee and the interviewer both have a role in shaping the narrative of the account.

Henry Greenspan comments that oral accounts are not only oral history, but also oral psychology and oral narratology.[62] Even when a response departs from verifiable fact, it can still be a repository of meaning, revealing the teller's insecurities, thoughts, and feelings. Moreover, the accounts are not always only oral, but can also be visual, such as in video interviews. In these, the listener must focus not only on tone, cadence, and interruptions in speech but also be aware of visual cues, such as performance, gesture, and emotion. Julia Creet draws attention to the fact that gesture can be both a "historical act and a reenactment in the present."[63] Thus, oral accounts are quite distinct from diaries, letters, and memoirs, and yet each offers the reader or listener a meaning of some kind in each of the narrative's point, purpose, and direction.

Furthermore, oral responses can certainly be used as a historical source. Like any source, they must be examined on their own terms. Oral accounts should not necessarily be considered defective when compared to other sources. Written documentation, sources most historians regularly rely on, can certainly be susceptible to deception.

For instance, there is the well-known case of the Wannsee Protocol, whereby the minutes of the meeting discussing the annihilation of European Jews were distorted at the behest of SS-Obergruppenführer Reinhard Heydrich. At his trial, Adolf Eichmann testified to how the protocol was written and altered. His oral account ultimately revealed more of what was discussed at the meeting.[64] For many, the oral account exposed greater, more precise details than the written report. It is, of course, always possible that a letter or an oral testimony can be relied upon as one would depend on a formal report or document.

To summarize: the forms or genres examined above not only have disparate elements from one another, but also share similar qualities. Each form reflects on the past and can offer knowledge or information pertaining to that past. Nevertheless, the historical researcher must observe all sources with concern and a degree of scepticism.

The personal narratives in the following chapters can be used, to a limited extent, for their empirical value; but they are perhaps more valuable for the meanings and understandings they share about the past. As previously mentioned, when soldiers and medical personnel left their posts to assist at Bergen-Belsen, this was not always noted in official war diaries and reports; thus, multiple personal accounts can help empirically verify when and why groups of men or women assisted at the camp at certain points in time. Beyond what they empirically demonstrate, however, the accounts can also be relied upon for the patterns of meaning they exhibit. The final section of this chapter will consider what the accounts can potentially offer the researcher.

Empirical and Moral Claims in Narrative

The experiences of Canadian military personnel at Bergen-Belsen are not empirically knowable. Facts, names, and dates can certainly be verified, and some of the sequence of events emplotted in the narratives can be checked and assessed. However, what happened on the ground can never be fully revealed and detailed in any narrative; moments will be forgotten, discarded, or purposely ignored. Everyone who narrates his or her experience will select and reflect upon distinct parts, making connections to form patterns of meaning. Thus, we are left with parts empirical and parts representing a meaning or a moral. As Sissela Bok recognizes, "Autobiographical accounts constitute, in part, empirical and moral claims that individuals stake out about their lives and, in the process, about the lives of others they have known."[65] The men and women who shaped personal narratives in response to the situation at Bergen-Belsen did so for specific reasons. Some responded immediately, while others remained silent for decades until they were finally provoked to communicate.

In the understanding of life, and therefore of lived experience, Wilhelm Dilthey emphasizes three categories of thought: value, purpose, and meaning. He associates meaning with the past, value with the present, and purpose with the future.[66] When we look back on the past through our memories, moments emerge and become identified as patterns from which we draw meaning. The present is experienced through feeling, which we then value positively or negatively considering our subsequent realities. When we confront the future, our projective attitudes determine our purpose. Accordingly, since memory is a part of history and meaning relates to memory, then of Dilthey's three categories of thought, "meaning" is significant for the grasping of historical thought. Meaning embraces and arranges what we value and pursue in life.

These three categories of thought are certainly moral categories. Dilthey demonstrates how meaning could unite the different parts of life within its whole. He calls this the "connectedness of life."[67] Individuals grasp the meaning of past moments through their memory. The "connectedness of life," then, is equivalent to a life history. Accordingly, a life history is given its shape through narration. We survey and make judgments of events from our past through our narratives. Autobiography and autobiographical texts are thus communicative of one's historicity. In other words, the self grasps itself as it passes through history.

Narrative, as Paul Ricoeur puts forward, is the "first laboratory of moral judgment."[68] A narrative is always ethical or moral to some degree. Whenever a Canadian soldier sat down to write or speak to someone about his or her experiences at Bergen-Belsen, he did so from a particular point of view and for a specific reason. Accordingly, all narratives require some direction or motive for being given. The experiences at and observations about Bergen-Belsen were shared because the individual wanted the narrative to make a difference. The following chapters reveal what differences the narrators were trying (are trying) to make through their first-hand accounts.

For many of the Canadian military personnel working at Bergen-Belsen, the experience, in a variety of ways, changed them as individuals. Thus, the stories they told were not only about what happened, but also about what happened to them in the face of a momentous event. As Popkin notes, "Only narrative can resolve the paradox of how an individual or group can be seen as the same even as it changes over time."[69] As the following chapters will reveal, some personnel abandoned belief in god or religion, while others strove to become politically and socially active.

Others delved into philosophy or returned to religious school searching for answers. For some the horror was incorporated, repeatedly, in future works of expression. Thus, Bergen-Belsen became a turning point in their lives. For several Canadian personnel, memories of the war became organized as "before Bergen-Belsen" and "after Bergen-Belsen."

In *The Ethics of Memory* (2002), Avishai Margalit argues that acts of extreme evil can be defined as those that assault the very foundations of morality. Consequently, these assaults on morality should not be forgotten and ought to be documented.[70] In other words, crimes *against* humanity should be remembered *by* humanity. Thus, we are obliged to remember and, more importantly, to think to prevent deniers and revisionists from rewriting history with false accounts and to stop them from attempting to distort the collective memory. We see this responsibility from eyewitnesses to Bergen-Belsen in numerous examples. For example, in 1990 Lieutenant-Colonel Mervin Mirsky challenged Holocaust denier David Irving at a public lecture in Ottawa. For Mirsky, and for so many others, their stories (and photographs and films) serve to protect historical truth and counter revisionism.

It is also important to remember that individuals often belong to more than one group. As Carr remarks, "it is clear that many of the moral conflicts and dilemmas facing individuals have their origin in the individual's sense of belonging to different groups at the same time."[71] Indeed, the moral claims in the personal narratives under investigation often emerge from a sense of belonging to multiple groups. For example, Jewish chaplain Rabbi Samuel Cass of the 1st Canadian Army recalls when he met "our Jewish DPs" in Bergen-Belsen. He eventually became an intermediary between the survivors and the British Army. His narrative speaks from being a member of the group of survivors, as a Jew, while at the same time – as a healthy, well-fed chaplain in the Canadian Army – of not being one of them.[72]

Canadian military personnel successfully carried out their assignments of crossing the Rhine River and descending on the Lüneburg Heath. However, dealing with the atrocities at the Bergen-Belsen concentration camp was never something for which they could have prepared. Any vision or plan of how the remainder of the war would progress was immediately thwarted. "In life ... we are always under certain constraints," writes Alasdair MacIntyre, "we enter upon a stage which we did not design and we find ourselves part of an action that was not of our making."[73] To pass through the gates of Bergen-Belsen was, for all who experienced it, to enter upon a "stage" of extreme violence and inhumanity. How could the scenes at Bergen-Belsen be described? How could they be explained?

Many Canadian military personnel who attempted to describe or explain Bergen-Belsen felt overwhelmed by the horror. Even after months of intense fighting, and enduring all of war's brutalities, Canadian forces who entered the camp crossed into another realm and struggled with an assault on the senses. Countless witnesses repeated similar sentiments: Bergen-Belsen defied language and was simply beyond the mind's comprehension. Indeed, many encountered tremendous difficulties in finding fitting words to describe both the confusion they felt and the atrocities they witnessed. Yet this does not mean that their narratives are empty and without value. While they struggled to adequately *detail* and *explain* what they saw, their responses do *mean* something. Men and women took pen or pencil in hand, sat in front of typewriters or computers, retold stories to friends and family members, spoke in lecture halls or in front of television cameras, all because they had messages to share with audiences. Unearthing these messages illustrates the burden so many carried in relating what they had seen, smelled, touched, and heard. "The representation of history as a constructed subject," explains Suzanne Langlois, "makes possible the integration of all the sources that contribute to sustaining a vision of the past."[74] In the weeks before and after the end of the war in Europe, the stories that news organizations and military personnel told to the world helped "sustain a vision" of the Holocaust. Their impressions aided in the shaping of public perception of the crimes.

"Where, in any account of reality," White remarks, "narrativity is present, we can be sure that morality or a moralizing impulse is present too."[75] Moral claims bestow meaning on both the past and the present, as well as help guide future directions. Personal narratives that recount real events are an attempt to bring a coherence and sense to the mind. Those who wrote to remember and warn of the tragedy at Bergen-Belsen did so in the face of pain and death. The author of the autobiographical, McCooey insists, "writes not only to relive, but to confront death: his own and other people's ... Fictional characters die fictionally, people die in actual fact."[76] It is to this confrontation by Canadians at Bergen-Belsen that we now turn.

PART TWO

Testimony

Chapter One

Canadians Arrive at Bergen-Belsen

The Canadian military personnel who encountered the Bergen-Belsen concentration camp during the first few days of its liberation in April 1945 were often left incredulous. Personnel crossed into what survivor David Rousset has termed the "l'univers concentrationnaire." This was a situation in which moral and philosophical norms were often absent. Those still clinging to life wept openly, discharged excreta where they stood or lay, staggered partially unclothed and, in the most extreme cases, were unable to walk or speak. Accordingly, the soldier's perception of reality was greatly challenged, and often transformed permanently.

As Maurice Victor of the 1st Canadian Army explains in the following section, "[Y]ou couldn't tell the barracks from the outhouses. The stench ... was overwhelming ... It had to be seen, it had to be smelled, for anyone really to grasp what the camps meant."[1] Many military personnel remarked that it was difficult to acknowledge what was in front of them. The campground and barracks that surrounded the men were littered with dead bodies, garbage and excreta.

Thus, the interpretations of the first few days are teeming with astonishment, sorrow, confusion, revulsion, and anger. While Canadian personnel frequently drew from a reservoir of negative emotions, their responses demonstrate similar patterns of thought, language, imagery, and metaphors. Though each brought their own particular perspective to the experience, there is a discernible intersection in what was documented.

Indeed, the impression of Bergen-Belsen as a constant, a living entity that attached itself to those who entered the camp was something repeated by many military personnel. Alan Rose felt that his experience in the camp was not simply a memory that remained, but something more. "It's something which is physical," he says, "I mean, not

Figure 11. Survivors in Bergen-Belsen peel potatoes while behind them lie the corpses of prisoners who died before the liberation of the camp. Image 732615. United States Holocaust Memorial Museum, courtesy of Hadassah Bimko Rosensaft.

only mental in a sense ... In fact, it's like the colour of your eyes: They never change. The haunting quality of Belsen has never left me. It's not just lingering; it's extremely strong."[2] For many, the manifestation of the camp endured long after the war. Its sights, sounds, and smells hovered and returned at different points in time. Individuals often had no control over when these thoughts of the camp would revisit them.

In the end, the horror of Bergen-Belsen had a levelling effect: virtually everyone who entered the camp experienced some sense of shock or distress. Indeed, the intense feelings of disgust and dismay cut across religious, ethnic, gender, and professional lines. As the ensuing chapters will demonstrate, "time" had perhaps the greatest impact on an individual's response: either the point in time one entered Bergen-Belsen or the length of time one spent in the camp. In other words, the later one encountered the camp, the more humane the descriptors employed in their narratives. Likewise, the longer one spent in the camp, particularly after the initial few weeks, and the greater the opportunity to bond and communicate, the more likely the liberator would view the survivors as fellow beings. The following chapter documents the responses of Canadians at their most raw and candid.

~

RONALD FORD ANDERSON

1st Canadian Parachute Battalion

Ronald Ford "Andy" Anderson was born on 3 November 1922 in Toronto, Ontario, into a family of war veterans. Both of his parents served in the First World War. His father was a decorated veteran earning a Military Cross and Distinguished Service Order. His mother served as a nursing sister.[3]

Shortly after graduating from high school in 1940, Anderson joined the 2nd Field Company Royal Canadian Engineers. In 1941 he was sent overseas to England, where he became a troop sergeant and spent much of his time training to handle explosives and landmines. In 1943 he was granted permission to try out with the 1st Canadian Parachute Battalion.[4] His expertise in explosives helped secure him a coveted spot with the battalion. His training commenced at the RAF Ringway, a Royal Air Force station in Cheshire, England. In May 1944 Anderson joined the battalion at Bulford, a military camp on the Salisbury Plain in Wiltshire, England.

During Operation Overlord, when the 1st Canadian Parachute Battalion became the first Canadian unit on the ground in France, Anderson remained at Bulford. As part of a group of reinforcements, he joined the battalion in France seven days after the Normandy landings and remained with it throughout the rest of the war. He participated in the Battle of the Bulge and Operation Varsity, the latter being the Allied airborne assault over the Rhine River at Wesel, Germany.

On 15 April 1945, while travelling north from the German town of Celle, Anderson's platoon arrived at the Bergen-Belsen concentration camp on the day of its formal surrender.[5] The rest of his company arrived shortly thereafter. Though some personnel from the 1st Canadian Parachute Battalion entered the camp, Anderson was instructed to remain with his platoon at the front gates. Medics from the battalion and the 224 Parachute Field Ambulance were called forward to assist the sick and dying inmates. The experience at Bergen-Belsen gave Anderson nightmares throughout his life.[6]

After the war, Anderson returned to Toronto. He joined the Toronto City Police. In September 1949, as a young constable, he became one of the first responders to the great fire on the SS *Noronic*, a passenger ship that was destroyed in the Toronto harbour,[7] resulting in the deaths of more than one hundred people.

Years after the SS *Noronic* disaster, Anderson left the police department and studied traffic engineering. He worked for six different mayors in Scarborough over a twenty-year period. He also stayed active with his former battalion, and was at one time president of the 1st Canadian Parachute Battalion Association. On 3 November 2015, Ronald Ford "Andy" Anderson passed away due to complications from pulmonary disease, at the age of ninety-three years old.

Interview

It's ... somewhat disappointing to me to read in the history of the Second World War and so many authors have written [inaccurately] ... about those last days of the war when we were in Germany ...[8] When we got to the Elbe River ... We are given the task of breaking off from the American command, going under Montgomery, Second Army, Second British Army, to make a mad dash with the 6th Airborne Division ... leading the British Army [to] the Baltic to get to a ... place called Wismar, north of Hamburg, to establish ... a holding line to keep the Russians from advancing any further into the west to seize it.

So once we were across the Elbe the British Second Army assigned... a tank regiment of the guards and ... it was the Scots Guards with Churchill tanks [that] came down to join us on the other side of the Elbe. The Brigadier has said to me since the war [that] he knew that we were going to be making a last dash to end the war and he wanted the honour to go to his Canadians. So he said to the general commanding, "I want the 3rd Brigade to lead, I will lead it and I'm going to have the Canadian, 1st Canadian Battalion, leading the brigade because they've come the furthest to volunteer to win this bloody war and it's just about over." So that's what happened. The Canadians were ... selected to lead the brigade, which would lead the division trailing behind us and starting a mad dash away from the Russians and the 101st Airborne, which was headed for Austria, we were going to go up north of Hamburg on a line. So we mounted, we were given the support of Churchill tanks of the Scots Guards ...

Most of the history now that you read says that at this point the Scots Guards led this, or the ... British armoured brigade led this last dash ... Canadians are never mentioned at all. The fact is that ... it was the Canadians on the decks of these Churchill tanks, at the point of the advance all the way, with all kinds of thousands of troops behind us. And from the day we started leaving the Elbe heading up past village after village and ... town after town, the Germans were surrendering, flying white tablecloths and pillow cases from the windows surrendering. Also on the side of the road there were German companies and regiments laying their weapons down, no white flags or anything, but obviously out of it. But we moved and moved and the only thing that kept stopping us every once in a while was a roadblock in a village somewhere ... and we'd have to stop the tanks, get off, clear it up, get the Germans out of the way and then move on. So it was a matter of moving at a fair rate with these tanks and we're getting pretty close to the Baltic Sea ...

[On] the 15th ... of April [1945] ... I am on the lead tank with my platoon, the company behind me we're moving down at a fair rate, comfortable, on the Churchill tanks, we've passed a number of German emplacements that are deserted or abandoned ... suddenly we're coming across, on our right side, is a very heavily fenced area, a camp of some kind, barbed wire, heavily guarded or heavily enclosed ... and then in the distance you can see some guard towers poking up here. And I went, "What the hell is this?" [I] had no idea what it is. We kept moving, the tanks slowed down a little bit and we kept moving up and up, no sign of ... anybody except that I thought, "Oh this is a ... German camp of some kind." We get to ... the front main gates of this place and have no idea what it is but we had to come to a stop because the gates were open, big ... heavy wooden gates were open, there's an archway I remember but flowing out onto the ... the road ... are these individuals who are wearing striped clothing, some of them are even crawling and screaming and they're the most emaciated ... the vision is something that I can never erase from my mind. I can remember sitting on the front of this tank, Churchill tank, and the driver coming to a halt because he couldn't do anything else because the inmates of this camp, whoever they are, are throwing themselves in the road in front of the

Figure 12. Women survivors of Bergen-Belsen crowd together on the main
street of the camp to wait for food. A pile of victims' shoes is visible in the
background. Image 743803. United States Holocaust Memorial Museum,
courtesy of Hadassah Bimko Rosensaft.

tanks. And then they're clutching at the side where I, you know, where
my feet are and I'm ... sitting there, looking ... So ... eventually I get off
the tank and I'm looking in at these ... emaciated terrible characters,
people, crying and speaking in a variety of languages, although we had
people with me who knew Ukrainian and some Polish from Western
Canada they were not able to make much out of them except that they
were in desperate conditions ... and needed food and water and one
thing and another. So we were giving them water from the canisters
that were on the tank and then some of the guys started to throw off
the boxes of [K] rations, some of my men that then came up from the
other tanks ... behind me ... came up to see what the hell's going on.
These guys were starving, these people. So they started opening these
cans of [K] rations which ... was the wrong thing to do ... very soon,
within ... ten or fifteen minutes, with the whole brigade being halted ...
Colonel Fraser Eadie came up to me at the front tank and said what
the hell's going on? And then the Brigadier followed, Brigadier [James]

Hill came with his defense platoon ... and a couple of others and the medical officer ...

Anyway ... they said, "Stay here" ... but first, the medical officer said, "Don't, no more food, no more food, you're going to kill them, you're going to kill them. So take back any cans of bully beef or whatever you're going to give them, you know, don't give them any food. Water's fine. I'm going into the camp." So ... there's a group of about ten, two medical officers, a few medics, Brigadier Hill, Colonel Eadie ... They went in the gate and ... in the camp and I was told to stay right where I was completely. And then after about thirty minutes ... Colonel Eadie came out and said the Brigadier wants you to move, get the people off the front of the tank, talk to the tank commander here, we've got to bring up the Brigade headquarters with the medical unit. The 224 field ambulances are way back, ten miles down the road, but we're blocking the road, there's only room for one, one vehicle, so we want you to move. And I remember Fraser [Eadie] saying to me [that] the place is desperate, it's in a desperate situation, [and that] this is some kind of concentration camp. So I simply talked to the tank driver and the commander, who was a young officer, and I said, "We're holding up the brigade, the Brigadier wants the 224 field ambulance to come forward with more aid than we've got ... but ... we've got to move." So the idea was for us to move up to the next village and come to a halt until, until the rest of the brigade caught up with us.

Yes that ... [was] the first entry into Bergen-Belsen and it was done by ... the Canadian, the First Canadian Paratroop Battalion. Now mind you we were supported by the Guards Armoured Brigade of the British Second Army no question about it. But we were a lone battalion enveloped in the Second British Army and there's never been any mention of it.

Source: Interview conducted for the film *D-Day to Victory* (2011).

MERVIN MIRSKY

1st Canadian Army

Mervin Mirsky was born on 16 May 1914 in Ottawa, Ontario. His grandfather, Jacob, an immigrant from Mir, Province of Minsk in the Russian

Empire, was Ottawa's first rabbi. Mirsky's father, David, founded Pure Spring, a successful soda company. David and his wife, Sadie (née Vineberg), had three sons: Mervin, his twin brother John (often called Jack), and their eldest, Norman.

Mervin Mirsky attended the University of Toronto and Osgoode Law School, graduating with honours. He subsequently practiced law with his twin brother. Mirsky enlisted in the Canadian army the day the war broke out in 1939. He rose to the rank of lieutenant-colonel and ultimately received the Order of the British Empire (OBE).[9] During this time he met and married his English wife, Barbara.

In spring 1945, while stationed in the small town of Breda, Netherlands, Mirsky encountered a nun named Sister Catherine Pop. Under German occupation, she was hiding Jewish children.[10] He worked on behalf of Sister Pop and the children, procuring food, clothing, and other supplies. All of the children in Sister Pop's care survived the war. In 1957, Mirsky brought Sister Pop to Ottawa to meet his family.

After the war, Mirsky returned home, abandoned his law practice, and joined his father's company, Pure Spring. For a period, and in terms of sheer volume, Pure Spring outsold Coca-Cola in eastern Ontario.[11] Upon his retirement from Pure Springs, Mirsky returned to the legal profession, working with his son, Peter, for fifteen years.

Mirsky had long been haunted by his encounter with the Bergen-Belsen concentration camp in April 1945.[12] On 7 March 1989, Mirsky broke his silence when he confronted Holocaust denier David Irving at the Chateau Laurier in Ottawa.[13] Concerned for his safety, security guards escorted Mirsky to his car. After this incident, Mirsky regularly shared his experiences and his views on the Holocaust.

In the early 1970s, Mirsky became co-chair of a public campaign to raise millions to help create the Children's Hospital of Eastern Ontario. He was formerly the chair of the Ottawa Food Bank and helped create what became the Rockcliffe public library. He passed away on 24 June 2010 at the age of ninety-six,[14] survived by his children Peter, Phillip, Jane, Michael, and Brian as well as his ten grandchildren and six great-grandchildren.

Interview

I was a senior officer at Canadian Army Headquarters and we did not know of the execution camps, the torture camps, the Holocaust camps. We knew that there were some assemblies of Jewish refugees, but we had no idea about the Holocaust ... As we went further in and we discovered the Holocaust, by that time we were in the north of

Holland and I was on a reconnaissance across the Rhine ... we were looking to destroy the German camps that the Germans had been assembling over the winter. They were on the north side of Rhine the entire winter and we were on the south side. And our job was to find and destroy these tremendous dumps of ammunition and guns and so forth ...

It was during the course of my duties there when I was heading for Emden that I wandered, in a side road and I wandered into Bergen-Belsen. The camp had just been liberated the day before [15 April 1945] by the British army, and that's when I saw Bergen-Belsen exactly as it was ...

The first signs, we were on this side road, and I had the driver on the side of the jeep and this terrible smell, we didn't realize the smell of death, we were half a mile away, and when we approached the main gates, there were a hundred women in rags standing at the front, that got our attention, and the gates, and the British were just going in and out, we stopped and I went inside and saw what is so incredible, it's hard to say, the thousands of dead bodies and the smell and the effort being made to revive people that were half dead and a quarter dead. And during the, I gathered that during the day that I was there, there were 15,000 dead in piles all around that camp. An additional 15,000 people died in the week after I left, but I was just there the one day ... it was about the 16th of April 1945. It was about ten or eleven o clock in the morning [when I arrived] ...

[Bergen-Belsen] was entirely surrounded by quadruple wiring with towers all around it; it was completely designed for keeping people in, for sure. But once you got inside, they had all these big bunk buildings with three or four bunks high, and they were separated between men and women and so forth. And that, but what had happened was that they were starting to move the dead out of these buildings because of the effect on the other people there, so, there were dead bodies all over the place ...

When we left at the end of the day, there were two young people standing at the gate, they were astounded at the fact that they could walk out and leave. And I put them in the back of the Jeep, they smelled horrible, and I heard them talk and they were really incoherent ...

The first thing that I saw was all these people running around, that is the British soldiers trying to, and the next thing that I saw, what they did, they had a Hungarian regiment which was helping them supervise and they stayed and the British had these Hungarians and there is ... women involved in there as well, just pulling these bodies out of the buildings, stacking them up out front, then they had this bulldozer

Figure 13. Corpses in Bergen-Belsen. Image 730247. United States Holocaust
Memorial Museum, courtesy of Hadassah Bimko Rosensaft.

digging these pits. And apparently each pit was designed to hold 500
bodies and they were numbered ...

My feelings were how in the name of God could anyone treat people, human beings, like this. I was just astounded. And even though
Bergen-Belsen was that bad and the estimated dead at Bergen-Belsen
was 30,000 there were ... other concentration camps in Germany and
the German-occupied territories where the figures were even worse.
For example, at Buchenwald there was supposedly 70,000 dead,
and there was another further east 40,000 dead so when you start
taking these figures, mind some of these camps were small some of
them larger, you can quite easily see where the six million dead Jews
perished.

The inmates were in such desperate shape that they couldn't do anything to help. They were lying about slouched or lying about speechless

on the ground and they were of course worrying about what was going to happen to them because the thousands of the dead bodies that were passing by them on the way to these first pits, I think made a lot of them have serious concern if they could be saved. They were so close to death, so many of these people that they were really numb ...

I only spoke to two young [survivors]. As I left the camp at the end of the day, they must have been about 17 or 18 years old, they were standing at the gate astounded at the fact that they could walk out of the gate. So, I put them in back of the Jeep, they wanted to ride into the next village, and as I say the smell was awful ... I spoke Yiddish, I have a very slow command of Yiddish, I was able to make myself [understood] ... they could understand what I was saying, and visa-versa.

The British were doing a fantastic job, they had armed supervisors there, but the [work] was done by the very few Germans that remained, the German staff and then this Hungarian regiment there, 100s of these, they were doing the [work by hand] along with what remained of the original staff ... I think the Germans were so scared that they would be shot, that they were doing whatever they were told to do and doing in a hurry ...

The British were bringing in food by the truckload, but they couldn't possibly even feed, properly feed the pretty small part of the people that were rescued. The people are lying there hungry, getting hungrier, but I think within 24 hours, they were able to feed most of the survivors ... It was my understanding that there had been no food in the camp for weeks ...

There would be a pit about the size of a football field, say 100 yards, and about 40 yards wide. They had been dug. The British had bulldozers, the British would excavate these pits, they had these carts that you would use at a railway station to put bags on. They piled 40 to 50 dead bodies on one of these, bring it down to the edge and dump it into the hole.

I was amazed, I couldn't think that such a thing could possibly happen. It was beyond description. And beyond creditability. When I met up with my unit and told them about this, they couldn't believe it, they thought I was exaggerating.

They [were] mostly from Poland, Russia, Czechoslovakia, France, all the occupied countries unloaded their Jews to these concentration camps.

The thing that stuck in my mind was the age, all the elderly people had apparently died, and so the average age of those people there was probably in their 30s or 40s, as an average age. But there was no people

there over 60, or 65, very little of those, I think, they had all been ...
terminated and buried, before we got there. The rate of death in those
camps, even before the war was tremendous.

In all that training and by that time I had been five years in the Army,
we had not been prepared or told to expect anything like this. This was
a development that I don't think anyone in the Allied armies, the Americans, ourselves or anyone in the Allied armies were even expecting. They
had no more ideas, I've spoken to people who had been in the American army, and they tell me the same as what I say now, that they were
amazed at what they had uncovered with these concentration camps ...
And they saw exactly – and some were worse than Bergen-Belsen ... And
they saw exactly what I saw. With exactly the same reaction ...

I think my war experience had a very definite impact ... [on] my
sense of values. I think I took serious things seriously and light things
lightly. To use a terrible expression, I didn't make a fart sound like a
windstorm ... I think it did something [to my faith] because there was
a great many Jews have abandoned Judaism, but I never thought of it.
I think it did strengthen when I saw what happened in the Holocaust. I
think it strengthened my conviction. And I was very active in the Jewish community; I became President of the Jewish community for two
terms in the years when I came back. So, I took more interest in my
Judaism when I got back than before. I think that this saving of the Jews
and the threat to the Jews had a very profound influence on that ...

When I tell these stories, you see, any sensible people who'd never
been through it, it's pretty hard for them to accept. When I tell you that
I'm walking around in Bergen-Belsen stepping over dead bodies and
dead bodies all around me, it's hard to believe ...

I think the people of my generation, the Germans, have not been entirely relieved of their fascist past, and the reason I say this is that a
few years ago ... [I confronted] David Irving ... [He] was a Britisher
who became committed to the Nazis, because a Nazi didn't believe in
the Holocaust. He arrived in Canada about five years ago, and he was
sponsored by a little Ottawa Nazi group ... [and] they rented the Chateau Laurier for David Irving. I heard about the meeting and I went
there, and there must have been about three hundred people there of
which 180 were German people of that generation. And I was surprised
to the effect that when Irving finished talking, I went on the platform
and I told him that he's all [wrong], that I had seen Bergen-Belsen, and
for him to stand there and say there was no Holocaust. So that was
once. He came back a year later and had another meeting, and I stood
up at the second meeting and to cut a long story short, David Irving is
no longer able to get into the United States or Canada and he's banned,

so I killed that one. I think that was a result of my army experience that I reacted that quickly ...

I am concerned that the message of Bergen-Belsen and the Holocaust is starting to diminish. People, the old guys died who heard about it, the young people are coming up and they're being pushed into another direction, by the apologists, you see. And then it's incredible for them, so I feel we can't, as a Jew and as a Canadian ... [the] story of the Holocaust has got to be told and told, or it's going to die.

Source: Shoah Foundation Video Archive (Interview Code: 39023). Interviewed by Nancy Smith. Date of interview 22 February 1998.

ALAN ROSE

7th (British) Armoured Division

Alan Henry Rose was born on 28 October 1921 in Dundee, Scotland.[15] When he was six years old his family moved to London, England. According to Rose, his mother's family had been in England for more than three hundred years, while his father's had been in the country for about one hundred.[16] His ancestors were immigrants from Russia. He was raised in a modest, middle-class Jewish home.

Rose served as a tank commander initially in the British Eighth Army. He served in Italy and northwest Europe. As a sergeant in the 7th Armoured Division, on 15 April 1945 he and his men from 3rd/4th County of London Yeomanry encountered Bergen-Belsen. He called the experience a turning point in his life.

Upon returning to England, Rose became involved in the rehabilitation of Holocaust survivors. He also found himself caught up in the tumultuous political scene of the day. Following the release of interned fascists at the end of the war, far-right groups reformed. Rose worked vigorously to combat their messages. He also spoke out for the creation of the State of Israel. He eventually volunteered to serve in the Haganah, Israel's pre-state defence force during the 1948 War of Independence.

In 1952, he married artist Joyce Esther Dangoor, who was born in Shanghai, China, and was the daughter of Moshe and Sybil Dangoor.

In 1957, the couple immigrated to Canada. Initially, Rose worked for the Jewish Agency for Israel and for the forerunner of the Canada-Israel Committee. In 1970, he became assistant director of the Canadian Jewish Congress, and in 1977 became its executive vice-president. Rose worked for the Canadian Jewish Congress for nearly twenty-five years.[17] He was also a director of the Canadian Human Rights Foundation and Canadian Multiculturalism Advisory Committee.

Rose was the recipient of several awards and honours in his lifetime. In 1980, he received the United States Presidential Citation of Honor for his liberation of Bergen-Belsen. In 1987, he was awarded the Terezin Anti-Fascist Fighters Medal by the government of Czechoslovakia. In 1994, he received the Medaille Militaire de la Liberation from the Government of France. He was given the Samuel Bronfman Medal from the Canadian Jewish Congress for distinguished community service, while the World Zionist Organization awarded him the Jerusalem Prize. Finally, Rose was also awarded the Order of Canada, the highest award that can be bestowed upon a Canadian civilian.[18]

Alan Rose passed away on 18 July 1995 at the age of seventy-four after battling brain cancer. More than five hundred people attended his funeral held at Shearith Israel, the Spanish and Portuguese synagogue of Montreal. He was eulogized by various community and public leaders, and a message of condolence written by Canadian prime minister Jean Chretien was read during the service. Rose was survived by his wife, Joyce, and his sister Hazel Tovey of Israel.

Interview

I came from a very strong Jewish background in England, and by the beginning of 1943, I had reached an age where I had left school and got my matriculation ... And not being able to get to university at that time because of the difficulties of the war it was almost impossible, I decided to join up. I think my decision was prompted, first of all, because whilst nobody knew what Hitler was doing, we all knew what terrible things were happening in Europe. And I think that, to be honest about it, there was also some bravado of a boy of seventeen ...

[During the war] I had heard on the radio, on the BBC, that a concentration camp had been liberated in Europe ... I suspect it was Auschwitz or Treblinka, which was in fact liberated before Bergen-Belsen. One heard the horrors, but of course it was quite impossible to comprehend these horrors ...

We had no idea in those days what deportation meant. I mean, it was inconceivable to us still in those days. And you must remember I lived in a very small world: I lived in a tank, and I heard the BBC news every night. It was inconceivable to us to even think in civilized terms of such a thing happening ... But, at that time we had no knowledge of the gas chambers and the genocidal intention of the Nazis. At least, I didn't. I'm sure the Allied powers had. But I'm the very lonely soldier sitting in a tank with a very limited horizon ...

I was in the British forces. We took the town of Celle [in early April 1945]. The town of Celle is very close to Bergen-Belsen. In fact, the trains that came into Bergen-Belsen when they were sending people ... came through the town of Celle. I remember it had an open railway-crossing in the middle of it ...

We came into Celle after very hard fighting. The German rear guard was fighting very hard, and in Celle, as in all German cities once the German troops had disappeared, all the white flags came out. All the people putting bed sheets out. And we passed through Celle, I think it must have been ten o'clock in the morning, and the first indication that I had that there was anything like Bergen-Belsen was an incredible putrefied smell of human flesh ...

Just as it is very difficult for survivors to talk about this, it is very difficult for concentration camp liberators to talk about ... As we approached ... I saw ... piles of bodies ... One is so shocked that the reaction was unbelievable. I think that the shock made us all speechless ...

Perhaps [an] even greater shock [was that] we saw living skeletons walking towards us. These were people who had survived ... I saw a number of living dead walking towards me ... People started to come out of the huts and hiding. And there were literally hundreds of people, all crawling with lice. I remember that I had to, when we got to Hamburg, go to a delousing station. And, of course, when they recognized that they had been liberated as they understood, and it happened that I was a Jewish tankerman, you can imagine the scenes of emotion which were quite incredible ...

Some were lying [down]; others managed just to stand up. Others were in a half-reclining position. There was one woman who came up with a dead baby in her arms, who she had been suckling. I think it is quite impossible to describe. I mean the first one is of such shock, even after having seen battles and things of this kind, that it's impossible really to describe. I mean, it was sheer horror ...

They were so thin that they were indistinguishable from skeletons. They had no flesh on their bones. The children had bloated stomachs. They mainly had no hair ... I couldn't believe that anyone would have lived for another hour or two. So, our first thought after seeing them ... was to get out [as much] food as we had on the tank, which was very little,

Figure 14. Corpses lying amongst survivors in Bergen-Belsen. Image 13053.
United States Holocaust Memorial Museum, courtesy of National Archives
and Records Administration, College Park.

and give it to them. I don't know if it was such a good idea, because I
don't know if they were in a position to. I know doctors told me afterwards that they were so thin it was impossible to get an intravenous
needle into them ...

I had two or three thoughts. The first was that any German I would find,
I would kill him. There were no Germans around at that time. The other
thing was, when I began to look around and saw the magnitude of the
tragedy and the smell, I realized that it was something far beyond us ...

By that time, we were all absolutely emotionally drained, and then
two or three camp guards came over with their hands up and it was a
very strange situation because – I had discussed this with my squadron
commander, and he said, "Look, first of all, the British army doesn't
shoot people without trial. The other thing is it's terribly important that
there should be trials." It didn't cross my mind at the moment – I think
only inferentially, that this must be recorded for history, by trial. This
must be seen by the world. And the result was that although my crew
wanted to kill them – and would have killed any German – that we

decided to take them prisoner, and keep them away from the survivors, who even in their enfeebled situation, would have murdered them. Because we thought that one day, there should be a trial. Which indeed there was a year later. Now these were the only three people that I saw who were sort of well fed, middle-aged SS guards, who surrendered under our protection and were hanged, incidentally, by the British. I think the decision was a wise one ...

I had already got hardened to battle scenes. I had seen death and tanks blown up and people ... Battle is a pretty terrible thing. To see young boys with their stomachs blown off, men frying in tanks, and dead Germans; unfortunately, one becomes used to everything.

But there was no comparison between the horror of battle – which is horror enough – and the scene that we saw on April 15, 1945. There was no comparison whatsoever ... The difference is that in battle, there is the possibility that one side will survive with the other because they're equally armed. But, here you had a huge state machinery which had made it its business as only the Germans could, to degrade and humiliate, to starve and to torture people ... This is a scene from hell, which is totally and absolutely divorced from the horrors of war. Totally ...

It was indescribable. You can't describe it in any sense. No words in the English language that I could find could describe it. As [Winston] Churchill said, it was a crime beyond comprehension. I think the films show much more than I could ever adequately express.

The second thing is [that] one couldn't really believe that it happened. You close your eyes and you thought, "Is it really happening?" Could such a thing happen just across the waters from the civilized England that I knew? And most importantly, for me, was that virtually everyone in Bergen-Belsen was Jewish; I then understood the magnitude of the tragedy that had overwhelmed us ...

A month after liberation, I went back to Bergen-Belsen. It was my first leave, so instead of spending it in England, I spent it in Bergen-Belsen. It was an extraordinary sight because, first of all, all the camp had been burned down. All the bodies had been buried ... The remarkable resilience was that after about a month or six weeks, just after the end of the war, with the UNRRA [United Nations Relief and Rehabilitation Administration] there and the Jewish Relief people, that after the unfortunately many thousands of people had been buried, that there was life going on ... I mean, after all, it's an existential thing ... if my parents hadn't come to England ... and I had been in Russia, as my great-great-grandfather was before he came to Scotland, I would not have been sitting as a young British officer on top of a tank, and either I wouldn't have survived, or I would have been in Bergen-Belsen. So, I have a very strong sense of Jewish existential destiny, I think you could say. It had a meaning to me after that.

I found it very odd that when I came back [home] ... I was involved in the fighting against the Black Shirts, and in 1948, which I found even more distressing.[19] I was fighting for the State of Israel, which at the time was being blocked by the very British that had liberated Bergen-Belsen and was stopping Jewish immigration to Israel. I thought it was the blackest chapter in British history ...

[Bergen-Belsen] is something you remember until your dying day. It's something which haunts you. It's something which is physical. I mean, not only mental in a sense ... In fact, it's like the colour of your eyes: they never change. The haunting quality of Belsen has never left me. It's not just lingering, it's extremely strong. I have a very strong sense of what the Holocaust meant and the destiny of the British people ... What I saw has taught me that nothing compares to the Holocaust; and never will, I hope ...

I think that what it's taught me is a number of lessons. The first is that in a country like Germany, which was always cultured ... that the veneer of civilization is very thin. I mean, if this could happen in Germany in the centre of Europe, it could happen anywhere. The second thing is that, unfortunately, the impact of the Holocaust, both on Jews and Christians, is wearing off. Young Jews now view it as something terrible, but they view it in an historic aspect, in terms of history. I view it as something that happened to me. It's rather like the English talking about the great plagues, or the Americans talking about the Civil War or war of independence. It's now sort of part and parcel of history or hagiography. To me it's a real thing ... I think the other thing that we've learned is that those elements that created the Holocaust are still involved. The body politic might be much healthier now, but there's now a strong revisionist propaganda saying the Holocaust never happened and there are people who would like to do to us, in Europe and North America, what the Germans did to us ... So, the lesson that I learned in history, quite apart from the terror of the Holocaust, is that Jews are a besieged people, and I believe that in forty or fifty years' time, when I won't be around, I suspect that those who will be [reading these words] will also be besieged. That's the condition of being Jewish ...

I'm not one of those who regard myself as a liberator. It happened. Existentially, being Jewish, I was in the British Army, and just by chance, it happened. My unit, if you will, liberated Bergen-Belsen. The drive of the British Army was to destroy the Nazis, not necessarily to liberate camps. It just happened that this occurred in the course of the destruction of Nazi Germany. And it's important one should understand it in that context. Nobody was told in the British Army that the main task was to liberate concentration camps. The thrust of the propaganda, if you will, was that we had to liberate Europe and destroy Hitler. There is, I would suggest to you, a difference ...

It just happened in the course of our advance that we came across it. Nobody set out to liberate a concentration camp. So the word "liberator" is a misnomer, in a sense. Either we were all liberators or we were not liberators, but nobody specifically spent his or her time thinking, "how am I going to liberate a concentration camp?" First of all, we hardly knew that they existed. I didn't.

Source: Alex Dworkin Canadian Jewish Archives, HDPSV257-SV259: Transcript of Alan Rose Holocaust Documentation Project Interview (17 March 1982), Canadian Jewish Congress Records.

MAURICE VICTOR

1st Headquarters Army Group, Corps of Royal Canadian Engineers

The son of Jewish immigrants from what is today Belarus and Lithuania, Maurice Victor was born 5 May 1920 in Canora, Saskatchewan. His father, Ben, immigrated to Winnipeg in 1911, and after graduating from medical school in 1919 began practising in the town of Verigin, Saskatchewan. Victor's mother, Rose, immigrated to Canada as a child with her brother and sisters. The family eventually settled in Winnipeg.[20]

After high school, Victor was accepted into medical school. This was a significant achievement, as there was a quota system in place for Jews and East Europeans. In 1943 he graduated at the top of his class from the University of Winnipeg's Faculty of Medicine. His graduation was supposed to be followed by an internship, but the need for men to serve in the Canadian forces prompted Victor enlist in the army.[21]

Victor was commissioned as a lieutenant, trained at Camp Borden in Ontario, and then stationed at Canadian Forces Base in Shiloh, Manitoba. He was soon sent overseas as a member of the Royal Canadian Army Medical Corps. He served in the European theatre and rose to the rank of captain.

At the time of his encounter with Bergen-Belsen, Victor was attached to the 1st Headquarters Army Group, Corps of Royal Canadian Engineers.[22] On 6 August 1945, he was posted to the No. 12 Field Dressing Station, Royal Canadian Army Medical Corps. For his wartime efforts, he was decorated by both the Canadian and Dutch governments.

After the war Victor accepted a senior internship at Winnipeg General Hospital. After completing his internship, he went to Salt Lake City to train in hematology. In 1948, he decided to specialize in neurology and obtained a residency at the Harvard Neurological Unit in the Boston City Hospital. In 1951 he joined the staff of Massachusetts General Hospital and began to teach in the department of neurology at Harvard Medical School. In 1957 he was elected to the American Neurological Association.

In 1962, he became a professor at Case Western Reserve University and the director of the neurology department at Cleveland Metropolitan General Hospital. In 1986 Victor retired and was appointed Distinguished Physician of the Veterans Administration at White River Junction, Vermont, and professor of medicine and neurology at Dartmouth Medical School in Hanover, New Hampshire

Victor's impact on the field of neurology is noteworthy.[23] He is the author of numerous books and more than two hundred scientific articles, and made major contributions concerning the effects of alcoholism on the nervous system and their treatment. His *Principles of Neurology* (co-written with Dr. Raymond Adams) became a widely used textbook on diseases of the nervous system. He also trained over thirty neurologists who were subsequently elected to the American Neurological Association.

Maurice Victor passed away on 21 June 2001 at the age of eight-one. The cause of death was metastatic prostate cancer. At the time of his passing, he was survived by his wife of forty-four years, Dr. Betty Banker Victor, and his son, Dr. Benjamin A. Victor.[24]

Interview

I had a ringside seat for [the Allied invasion of France] with part of the army that made its way through France, Belgium, Holland and into Germany. And as we penetrated deeper into occupied territories, we saw first hand what Nazism was all about. It was an experience we could not possibly have prepared for.

I have racked my brain since then, trying to remember what we did know about the horror in Europe, back in the warm safety of North America. In the early Thirties, when fascism began to make political inroads in Europe, and to raise echoes among its Canadian and American followers, my father and some of his friends organized the Jewish Anti-Facist League in Winnipeg. They worked to arouse public opinion about the menace; they organized a boycott of German-made goods; they brought in prominent speakers, both Jews and non-Jews, to address public meetings. This was at a time when the leadership of the Jewish community still insisted on soft-pedalling the danger, attempting a sort of quiet diplomacy with the Canadian government. My parents and their activist group clashed with some of their own friends on the issue – there were some deep and painful divisions. We were certainly aware, then, of what was happening to the Jews of Europe, but psychologically, few of us were prepared to accept the unprecedented scale and savagery of the annihilation.

I can remember on one occasion, before I left for overseas, my father's coming back from a meeting of some sort. He had heard an address by a Jewish refugee from Germany who was now trying to alert communities across the continent to the magnitude of the Nazi depredations. As my father walked into our pleasant, happy house, the look on his face was simply indescribable. He had known death and sorrow in his lifetime, but never tragedy of that nature. Ordinarily a man who loved to talk, he could only say now that what he had heard was unimaginable – and could not be doubted. People in general, I think, had no way of understanding just what was happening, not even people closely connected with Jewish life. We knew when we joined the army that Hitler had to be defeated, but we had to come face-to-face with Hitlerism before we understood.

I was the physician in a field dressing station, a forward unit with a group of engineers. My driver was an average sort of Canadian, not well educated, who had no idea of what the war was all about. When the English or French irritated him, he grumbled that he would just as soon be fighting the "limeys" or the "frogs" as fighting Germans. We were attached to a British division when we drove our jeep into Bergen-Belsen, a relatively small hellhole in relation to Auschwitz and Buchenwald and the others, getting there just twenty-four hours after the camp was liberated ...

And for the first time, for both me and for my driver, the absolute comprehension of what had gone on struck us with full force ... you couldn't tell the barracks from the outhouses. The stench of the dead and dying was just overwhelming; cadaverous people were literally stacked up like cords of wood in rows, some of them still squirming. It had to be seen, it had to be smelled, for anyone really to grasp what the camps meant. My driver knew now, for the first time, what the war was really about.

There was no more talk of fighting the English or the French or Germans indifferently. For both of us, what we were doing here, far from home, had finally crystallized. It is unfortunate that those who deny the Holocaust couldn't be taken back in time to relive its agony.

When the war was over I found myself in Germany, but my revulsion against Germans was so intense that I could not bear to be among these people. In fact, the entire Canadian army was soon withdrawn to Holland and eventually we were repatriated.

Source: Gutkin and Gutkin, *The Worst of Times*.

LEO HEAPS

1st (British) Airborne Division, Special Air Service

Leo Heaps was born on 17 July 1922 in Winnipeg, Manitoba. His father, English-born Abraham Albert Heaps, was a former member of Parliament for Winnipeg and one of the leaders of the Winnipeg general strike of 1919. Abraham Heaps unsuccessfully lobbied the Canadian government to accept Jewish refugees fleeing Nazi persecution.

Leo Heaps attended Queen's University, the University of California, and McGill University. In September 1942 he enlisted in the Canadian forces at the rank of private. As part of the CANLOAN program, he volunteered to serve with the British Army.[25] By May 1944 he was attached to the 1st Dorsetshire Regiment as a captain.[26]

Heaps took part in the invasion of Normandy. He was with British troops when they discovered the bodies of thirty-five Canadian prisoners of war killed by the Germans. He was wounded two weeks after the invasion of Normandy, and upon recovery participated in the Battle of Arnhem. Heaps was captured by the Germans on 24 September 1944 and sent to Germany by train, but escaped near the Dutch border; the Dutch underground helped him return to Allied lines. He documented these events in *Escape from Arnhem: A Canadian among the Lost Paratroops*, which was a runner-up for the 1945 Governor General's Award for non-fiction.

Heaps spent the last six months of the war working with the Dutch underground. Known as "Heaps jeeps," a squad of jeeps would gather intelligence behind enemy lines.[27] He was awarded the Military Cross for his work with the Dutch Resistance, and it was during this time that Heaps encountered the Bergen-Belsen concentration camp.[28]

After the war, Heaps assisted Jews in the 1948 Arab-Israeli War, helping the army in the establishment of mobile striking units. Whilst there he met his future wife, Tamar. In 1956, during the Hungarian Revolution, Heaps led a special team to transport refugees across the border. In the late 1970s, he organized relief supplies during the rescue of the Vietnamese boat people.

Heaps is the author of twelve books, including two on the Arnhem battle. He was part of a contingent of forty Canadian veterans who returned to Arnhem in 1994 to mark the fiftieth anniversary. Heaps passed away the following year, in 1995, after battle with an illness. He was survived by his wife, four children, and eight grandchildren.

Memoir

During my stay in Germany the role we were told to play was hindered by the lack of sympathetic people on the land; which made it necessary to advance with the forward elements of our troops. It is of one particular day in Germany that I would like to write about now. On this day I witnessed a sight so horrible and unbelievable that in later times it was difficult to conceive in memory the things I actually saw.

We had been advancing east in central Germany one day in April and had been warned of a German concentration camp in the area. A little later we came upon the barbed-wire perimeter which surrounded it, and upon a huge enclosure of planks rimmed with more strands of barbed-wire. Troops had evidently been here before us, for signs saying "Beware of Typhus" were everywhere. I noticed on the side entrance that Hungarians were on guard. We went in the entrance with our jeep. The Hungarians were very servile. They had been employed by the Germans to do the duty guards. We passed through another gate and we were in the main part of Belsen. The sight I saw made me suck in my breath.

Lying all over the ground there were bodies, thin and emaciated. There were thousands of them. They looked as thin as dried leaves. Some people were crawling on their bellies past us, others were relieving themselves anywhere. The faces of the people were shriveled and were drawn like tight sheets of paper about shrunken skulls. But it was the eyes of the children which frightened you. Small, dark eyes that seemed almost to have disappeared back into the recess of the brain. Their eyes were duller than mist and as transparent. No one paid any attention to us. There seemed to be no German guards inside the camp.

As we passed some of the people tried to raise their faces upward in ugly grimaces. They were trying to smile at us. Most lacked the strength to look up.

It was difficult to tell the dead on the ground from the living. If a body quivered, you knew it was in the last stages of life. If it remained still for an hour or more, it was sure to be dead either from typhus or starvation.

I saw two tiny, wasted figures carry a third out of a hut and lay it down upon the ground. You could see this happening every few minutes.

A little distance away another wizened figure was pushing a wheelbarrow. Inside was the remains of what was a boy. He lay crimpled like dust in the bottom of the wheelbarrow, and his big, swollen head would wobble freely in protest as the wheelbarrow jogged along.

Each figure that walked, stumbled along with the weariness of the living dead, plodding along through hell. Each step was filled with terrible agony.

Everywhere the dead lay rotting, and every now and then a live man would lie down to die beside his dead mate.

We passed one of the huts where the people lived. The stench of diseased life was overpowering. It engulfed you. We had to move away. But we could see people lying side by side, across and over one another and nude on the floor.

If hell has a counterpart, it was here.

We passed the great pits where the dead, like twigs, lay stacked upon the dead. There were countless thousands in the pits.

On the edge of the camp the more recent arrivals lived. They lived in family groups, with almost always a woman who cooked in charge. What they cooked, I don't know.

It was a huge camp. Some men say there were as many fifty thousand people in the camp. Others say no one will ever know how many lived and died there. I saw some of our soldiers in rubber suits spraying and decontaminating the shacks.

I stopped and spoke to a corporal. He told me they had arrived a few hours before and had immediately put the SS women and guards in the camp jail. The Commandant, a Major [Josef] Kramer, was kept in special solitary confinement. I visited these people. When I saw them, they were craven and very servile. Only last night, out of sheer brutality, they had shot fifteen helpless inmates dead.

I looked at these beasts, who had once been men. They winced and withdrew into the shadows of the cell. No matter how degraded they had forced, by starvation and indignity, the people of the camp to become, the SS guards had reached by their own crimes untouchable

Figure 15. Shackled and under guard, Josef Kramer, formerly the commandant of Auschwitz-Birkenau killing centre and Bergen-Belsen concentration camp, awaits his fate. He was later hanged for his crimes. Image 743791. United States Holocaust Memorial Museum, courtesy of Hadassah Bimko Rosensaft.

depths of degradation. These men were the untouchables. They were fed on crusts of black bread and three slices of bully beef a day. They were all stripped to the waist and stank of sweat.

Outside an old white-haired lady looked up at us and said, "Please give me a cigarette. Don't be angry if I ask. Don't be angry." She was beyond thinness.

We gave her all we had. Habit had made her expect a beating where she should have received kindness. Who knows from what home she had been dragged, what luxury of age she had been denied, what wealth had she been stripped of? And now she was reduced to this.

Everywhere it was the same. Here in a cesspool of disease and filth the best brains of the country lay rotting, the best men stewing in their own juices – professors, clergymen and ordinary people ...

I saw the incinerators where the dead and the living were burned. And then I saw where the red cabbages grew out of the fertilization of human ashes. It was appalling to think that human beings had calculatingly designed this camp to destroy their own kind.

Everything I saw here was scientifically designed to degrade intelligent human beings, by indignity and starvation, to the state of beasts ... The number that died must be replaced by the same number of new arrivals. The Nazis had succeeded. They had reduced the inmates to the state of beasts.

At the main gate a medical officer stopped us. I stripped and sprayed from head to foot with anti-typhus powder. Then I dressed again.

At the main gate we met a very pretty Hungarian girl. She was also an inmate but was in much better health than the others. She spoke English fluently and was acting as an interpreter.

She told me that she had been studying physics in Hungary, but during the war had been forced, because of anti-Semitic decrees, to study economics. She had obtained her degree. And when the Germans had taken complete control of Hungary, she had been pressed into service with one of the labor gangs. Here the food was almost sufficient to live on, and with what she could get by bribing the guards, she had managed to keep her health. Two weeks ago, she had been brought to Belsen. Her great crime in life was that she was Jewish. There was no malice in her voice as she spoke. She seemed to have infinite tolerance for others. Only her eyes told of intolerable loneliness.

We watched the inmates in their striped pajama uniforms trying to move from one hut to another. They would wobble a few feet, then stop, then wobble again and stop, until they reached the next building. Here they would pause for rest, completely exhausted. The distance between two huts could not have been more than ten feet.

"Some food is being brought in now," she said. "Perhaps some of the people will be saved. Already the dead are being separated from the living and the doomed from those who will survive. Those who are not diseased and able to walk are to be moved as quickly as possible to another camp."

The girl told me how much crueler the SS women were than the SS male guards. And how she had used her feminine wiles to secure food from the guard who supervised her hut.

Her fiancé was in Hungary. He was all she had left in the world, and she was clinging desperately to the hope that he still lived, and they would someday meet again. This girl was only twenty-one years of age.

Stimpson, the driver of my jeep, had just finished being deloused. We said goodbye to the girl and left. Stimpson is a plain, good-natured Canadian from the west. He is hardened to the ways of war, and he has seen a great deal of the privation and suffering in Europe. But that night as we drove Stimpson kept repeating to me, "You know, people who treat other people like that can't be human. They *can't* be human."

Stimpson was right.

We could not eat anything that evening.

And the last thing I saw before my eyes that night was the ghoulish picture of the dead who walked alone in hell.

Source: Heaps, *Escape from Arnhem.*

Letter

Holland
27 April 1945

My dear dad,

I received yesterday your very welcome letter which had been waiting around several days for me. I am very glad to hear that Collins publishing company may publish my book.

Dave [Heaps] is somewhere fairly deep in Germany at present.

I have just returned from central Germany. The people are sullen and afraid. They are all a miserable lot.

About central Germany I saw two days ago one of the worst sites I have ever seen. It was called the Belsen concentration camp. The sights I saw in the camp were unbelievable. It consisted of Germans, Hungarians, Poles, many Jewish, many political prisoners.

The bulldozer was burying thousands of starved, typhus ridden corpses. People were coming out of their filthy quarters and falling down dead in front of me as I walked through. No one had any energy to walk a few yards for food ...

But the worst site of all were the German SS women and men who guarded the camp. They beat and shot the poor people daily. There was no sanitation nor water for the prisoners.

It was such a colossal sight of inhumanity to men and women that you would not quite believe what you saw with your eyes.

Many more will die, but work is being done every day to ease the situation.

I may go to London in a few days.

Affectionally,
Leo

Source: Ontario Jewish Archives: 2014-8-8. Heaps family fonds – 1932–1945.

Chapter Two

Documenting the Horror Camp

Canadian war artists and photographers attempted to document the suffering they witnessed in the Bergen-Belsen concentration camp, while being sensitive to not exploit the dead and the ailing survivors. Those who felt compelled or who were formally assigned to portray Nazi crimes in the camps were confronted with serious moral and ethical demands. Visually documenting the scenes in the camp, through photography and other forms of artistic expression such as painting, drawing, and sketching, was a considerable undertaking and often a stylistic, moral, and aesthetic challenge. When photographers directed their cameras and artists opened their sketchbooks, they did so among sights, sounds, and smells that they had never before experienced or conceived possible. Many felt the weight of appropriately and accurately representing the brutal conditions of the inmates inside the camp.

Photographers and war artists were thus faced with a situation that assailed the senses and that they felt duty-bound to record. "I saw what I cannot yet believe," remarked Canadian artist Henry Abramson in a letter home reprinted below. "My mind, my emotions indeed my whole being could not accept, could not begin to grasp what my eyes saw, what my ears heard. How shall I start to explain?"[1] Many recognized that their assignment was an important one, but some felt the challenge of working in their respective mediums. The experience at liberation was momentous for all involved. It affected their personal lives and often transformed the way they viewed their modes of representation in the future.

As the horror was so extreme, Canadian war artists and photographers also struggled with striking a measured balance in their depictions of the dreadfulness. "[M]y painting of the Belsen thing," recalls official Canadian war artist Alex Colville, "I think it was a failure. It's inadequate."[2] The suffering, stench, and gloom in the camps were extreme, and to amplify the horror would lead only to distortion.

The following pages present the accounts of several Canadian war artists and photographers who attempted to depict and interpret the liberation of Bergen-Belsen. How does one visually represent the terrible crimes of the Holocaust? In the following pages, artists and photographers explain how they understood their responsibilities and the ways in which they struggled with their respective modes of representation.

RON LAIDLAW

Royal Canadian Air Force, Public Relations

Ron Laidlaw was born in 1920 in St. Mary's, Ontario. His career in journalism began in 1937 when he started working for several newspapers as a freelance reporter and photographer. He soon joined the photography department of the *London Free Press*.[3] In 1941, he enlisted in the Royal Canadian Air Force, becoming a public relations officer. He supplied pictures from Cherbourg, Caen, the liberation of Paris and, while in Copenhagen, Victory in Europe Day. In Copenhagen Laidlaw met his future wife, a local woman named Vibeke Probst who was the daughter of a prestigious commercial and studio photographer.[4] In November 1945, the couple married.

Laidlaw's encounter at Bergen-Belsen occurred on 16 April 1945. He was one of the first Allied photographers to enter the camp, travelling to Bergen-Belsen with fellow Canadians Fred Hopkinson and Joe Stone. All three men took photographs of the horrible scenes in the camp. Laidlaw was invited into the camp's headquarters, where he witnessed the detention of the commandant of Bergen-Belsen, Josef Kramer, as well as the infamous warden, Irma Grese.

After the war, Laidlaw returned to the *London Free Press*. In 1948, the paper ran a photograph of Adolf Hitler from 1940 when, after the fall of France, he toured Canada's dramatic First World War memorial at Vimy Ridge. Previously unseen by the Canadian public due to government censorship, the photograph was part of a collection that Laidlaw found and absconded with from an airfield darkroom not long after the Allies forced Hitler's armies out of France.[5]

In 1953, Laidlaw was asked to set up the newsroom for the newly founded CFPL television station (C-Free-Press-of-London). He became the station's news director, a position he held until 1985 when he retired. Under Laidlaw's guidance, CFPL Television became one of the first Canadian news stations to expand to thirty-minute and, later, to hour-long newscasts. It was also the first private station to convert to colour broadcasts and to charge a premium rate to advertisers who sponsored a newscast. CFPL Television later became the first private Canadian television station to computerize its newsroom.

In his honour, the Radio-Television News Directors Association of Canada (RTNDA Canada) bestows the Ron Laidlaw Award, which is given to the station offering the best continuing coverage of a news story. Ron Laidlaw passed away in 2008 at the age of eighty-eight.

Memoir

On the last morning of a Rhine area bomb damage assignment I was on the way back to camp ... I was out of rations and more importantly out of film. Out of sorts I think too – the damn dysentery and troublesome molars in the main. I knew the press camp had been in a fluid state for several days due to a forest fire of some kind near them, it had suddenly moved on. I didn't know where but it was easier to find [RCAF] 143 Typhoon Wing. I could always find a bunk there. Suddenly I am in the town of Celle – just north east of Hanover – it seemed untouched by bombs. There weren't many military vehicles.

Quite by chance I ran into [a] new P/O – like me – Fred Hopkinson (Hoppy) and Joe Stone, a photo Sergeant from 39 Reconnaissance Wing (RCAF). They had just found out that a concentration camp was nearby and late "yesterday afternoon" had been seized by a British tank squadron. We took off ... immediately ... the three of us. The camp is BELSEN ...

[The] horrors, scenes and smells and awfulness are still vivid in my memory – still indescribable with my limited writing skills. I am sure the smell will never be erased. I captured a bit of what we saw on film – I had nine exposures left on the rollei and no rolls in a pocket ... I was told by a tank sergeant left behind when the tank company pressed on that I was the first allied photographer into the camp.

This is what I wrote home, "And you say the Germans don't seem to be as bad as we make them out to be. Nuts. You would have been sick for weeks after I saw about 5 women die while I helplessly watched them. There were thousands of bodies in the pits. Piles of naked bodies stacked outside a building that had a sign saying it was a hospital and

Figure 16. It was impossible for all Canadian airmen to see the horrors of Belsen and to therefore recognize the enemy's incredibly cruelty, so these pictures were taken to prove it. The airmen are Sgt. Joe Stone, of Saint John, NB, who headed the photographic section of the RCAF Typhoon Wing in Germany, and P/O Fred Hopkinson of Dunneville, Ontario, a motion picture cameraman with the RCAF Film Unit in Germany. Image PL 43511, Department of National Defence.

there was no way that it was. There were people around tiny fires. They didn't seem real. A foot or so away were naked and shrunken bodies. Dysentery to end all dysentery and no, repeat NO sanitary arrangements in the camp at all ..."

They say memory works like a film. I didn't have much film and my damnable memory is full of editing splices! I think we must have been shocked out of our minds. In fact, I know we were!

There are however some "scenes" of which I have vivid recall. The total indifference of the poor souls we encountered, I'm sure they didn't know that the suffering there would soon be alleviated. They were free.

But it was too late. Every living inmate we saw that day, I am sure would die. They were beyond help.

The most compelling memory and with it the stench that always returns when I see a photograph was of the huge pits filled with rotting and naked bodies. A couple of British tommies were forcing German guards to put more of the stacked bodies into the pits – as I recall there were two maybe three pits. If a guard paused to be sick he was pushed down into the pit with the other bodies and had to scramble. It was a living hell.

Right close to the pits was a huge pile of boots and shoes. Hoppy was dreadfully sick and was continually throwing up ...

There was a little sparse woods ... and dozens of apparitions of living beings were trying to make little fires. Almost everyone was defecating continually ... The sight inside [the makeshift hospital] was of bunks reaching to the ceiling and bodies lying all over ... on the floor, half out of bunks. And always there [were] those wide open staring eyes ... I had less than a full roll of film in the rollei. A thousand rolls would not have captured the horrors of Belsen ...

I was invited to go into what I suppose was a headquarters building and in there were the important prisoners, the camp commandant, the notorious Josef Kramer, and in another room, Irma Grese, who later was to be known as the most brutal of female Nazi guards anywhere.[6] Of course I didn't know their names then – just that they were the camp's top authorities.

I vividly remember looking through a tiny window into their temporary cells. Kramer was pacing back and forth in shirtsleeves. Dark and unshaven. And in another room, this big blond with a hard but maybe still attractive face puffing on a cigarette. Later I found out that she was only 21...

I don't remember leaving the place but I do know I had found our press camp that evening ... and I was desperately trying to get my photos out to London HQ ...

It will be 60 years since that day. I won't forget it ...

Less than one month later, the hostilities ceased. In that time, several Typhoon pilots I knew were killed. The Germans did not give up easily.

Source: Private collection of the Laidlaw family. Memoir was written circa 2005.

FRED HOPKINSON

Royal Canadian Air Force, Public Relations

Fred Hopkinson was born on 17 October 1916 in Dunnville, Ontario.[7] He married Frances Jennie Hines, also from Dunnville. The couple had three children. After war broke out in Europe, Hopkinson enlisted at Hamilton, Ontario, on 8 June 1940 as a general duties airman.[8] He was tasked to perform whatever tasks were required that were not covered by other professional trades. On 12 December 1940 he received training as a photographer and throughout 1940 and 1941 received additional training in that craft.

Hopkinson received still more training at the No. 6 Service Flying Training School, where his rank was leading aircraftman. He was posted overseas from No. 1 "Y" Depot on 11 February 1942; his occupation was listed as a "photographic officer." He mostly did public relations work. Eventually, Hopkinson worked as a motion picture cameraman with the RCAF Film Unit.

On 16 April 1945, along with fellow RCAF public relations officer Ron Laidlaw and Sergeant Joe Stone of 39 Wing, Hopkinson entered the Bergen-Belsen concentration camp. The men took several photographs of the scenes. A few days later Hopkinson wrote a letter home to his wife about the experience.

Hopkinson was sent for repatriation to Canada on 13 December 1945 and retired on 21 January 1946. Little is known about his life after the war.

Letter

I just arrived back in camp after three days in the centre of Germany where I had some very interesting experiences. One of which was a visit to [Bergen-Belsen]. When we first went in the gate the Major in charge of the camp took us to a building where they had quite a few SS men and women held as prisoners. They were very arrogant looking individuals but they seemed to be quiet enough as the boys were keeping a good eye on them. From there we went on our own. Joe Stone and Ronnie Laidlaw were with me. We walked through the gate and the first thing we saw was bodies of men, women and children; all along the side of the road was the same. The stench was terrible but I was so determined to see what these camps were like I took another breath and went on. There were thousands of people in there and they all looked like death itself. The Germans hadn't given them anything to eat and they were all dying from malnutrition.

Figure 17. Sgt. Joe Stone, who was in charge of the photographic section on the all-Canadian Typhoon Wing in Germany, peers down into this horror pit of human bodies brutally murdered, starved to death, or victims of the dreaded typhus at Belsen. Stone stepped into the picture at the request of the RCAF cameraman just to prove that this sight was real. Image PL-43509 16/04/45, Department of National Defence.

We kept walking and came to a huge pit where they were dumping the dead. It is indescribable but I will do my best to picture it for you. The pit was about fifty feet long, twenty feet wide and twenty five feet deep. There were bodies of men, women and children, all naked and really piled up. The pit was full of them. The wrists and arms on the bodies weren't any bigger than a good sized broom handle. Some of the bodies were turning black but some were still life colour as they had only died a day before. The guards make the S.S. men and women gather up the dead and put them in the pit. We left there and started to walk toward the women's enclosure when we saw another pile of them so we took another look. Some of these bodies still had straps on their wrists where they had been hung up by the Germans. We could see welts across the backs of some of them. I'm taking pictures of all this mind you and so are Ronnie [Laidlaw] and Joe [Stone]. We have some gruesome pictures of ourselves standing near these bodies. We took these pictures because we know that when we start telling about this we are going to have to have proof or we wouldn't be believed. As we were going into the women's enclosure we could see more bodies so we steered clear of them as we had our share of that. You can imagine what conditions would be like in a place with no toilet facilities and the majority of them with dysentery.

The people have lost all sense of pride and decency. As we walked there were women relieving themselves by the side of the road. They just went on with their business but still took time out to wave and give us a smile. I met a Polish Jewess who could speak a few words of English. She had only been there a few months but had been through plenty in those months. She showed us her arm where the Germans had tattooed a number on her with electric needles. Under the number was a triangle that marked her as a Jew. All the people in the camp were tattooed in the same way. She took us along the road to a place that was called a hospital. While we were on our way we noticed a woman helping another one along the road. The one woman was moaning and crying. We asked the girl what was the matter with her and she told us the woman was dying and would die in the night. If they waited until the next day they would have her dead weight to carry so they were taking her while she could still stand up (she died before we left the camp).

All these people are suffering from typhus. We went into the so called hospital and were stopped dead. The room was about sixty by forty feet and there wasn't room for another body on the floor. Yes! On the floor! There were women and children dying. We could nearly see them die. They didn't have any clothes on and just had a blanket over them. One or two of the women tried to rise up and motion to us to come over to

Figure 18. P/O Fred Hopkinson of Dunneville, Ontario, a motion picture operator with the RCAF's No. 1 Film Unit in Germany, turns a wry look to the camera in front of a pile of bodies, ruthlessly murdered by one way or another at the Belsen horror camp. Image PL-43510 16/04/45, Department of National Defence.

them but they would just fall back on the floor. One woman did sit up and as she did the blanket she was using for a cover fell away. She was nothing but skin and bone and not very much of that. All of them were moaning and groaning. Even that was enough to make our stomachs turn inside out. As we came out another door we saw more naked bodies lying along the ditch. They were piled in tiers of three and the line stretched for about fifty or sixty feet. The girl told us that the bodies had been cleared away from there the night before and that these were the bodies of people who had died through the night and that day. While we were standing there, two women carried out the body of a little girl and laid her on the pile with the rest.

The only exercise these people get is to walk around the yard. They are not allowed out yet as there are plenty of cases that are going to be weeded out in time and sent to another camp to be looked after. They walk around where all these bodies are and think nothing of it. Death means nothing to them; they have seen so much of it. One girl told us her mother and sister had died just a day or so before and you would think she was telling you the time of day, she was so calm about it. It took us four hours to look the camp over and then we didn't see everything; but it was enough for me.

There are quite a few prison camps in that part of Germany and a lot of them had just been freed the day before. The highways were packed solid with Dutch, Belgians, Poles, and Russians etc. They are all making their own way back. They have their belongings in anything they can find. Some have baby carriages, wheelbarrows, small wagons and some are fortunate enough to have farm wagons complete with a horse. They just go into a field where the farmer is ploughing and take his horse away from him. When we pass them on the road they give us the old "V" sign and thumbs up. They are a sorry looking lot but are happy just to be free again.

Source: Private Collection of the Laidlaw family. Letter dated 20 April 1945.

~

AL CALDER

Canadian Army Film and Photo Unit

Al Calder was born circa 1919. He went to school in New Westminster, British Columbia. In high school, he developed a passion for photography and was president of the school photography club. After graduation, he worked as a schoolteacher. In 1940 he enlisted in the Canadian forces and was assigned to a few positions. At one point he worked as a disciplinarian. Ultimately, he wanted to become paratrooper.[9] He was trained at the Canadian Forces Base Shilo in Manitoba.

Calder was sent overseas with the 1st Canadian Parachute Battalion as a member of its Intelligence Section. At the end of 1943, an opportunity arose for Calder to work as a photographer. He took his training at Pinewood Studies in England, and upon completion became a member of the Canadian Army Film and Photo Unit. After his training he was loaned back to 1st Canadian Parachute Battalion. It was six months before the invasion of Normandy, and there was little for him to do at that time. As a result, he was sent all over the United Kingdom to cover such events as Field Marshal Bernard Law Montgomery conducting troop inspection at Aldershot and to photograph a commando unit in Scotland.

As a corporal, he crossed the channel two days after the initial Normandy landings with the 1st Canadian Parachute Battalion. Calder replaced photographer David Reynolds – one of the first Allied photographers to land during the invasion – who had been injured in the line of duty. He participated in Operation Varsity and the crossing of the Rhine.

While with the 1st Canadian Parachute Battalion, Calder arrived at Bergen-Belsen on 15 April 1945, the day of the camp's formal surrender.[10] Along with Lieutenant Charles H. Richer and Sergeant Mike Lattion, Calder documented the scenes at the camp and sent the material back to Canadian Military Headquarters. Calder remained at the camp for one harrowing day before moving on to Wismar. Little is known about Calder after the war.

Interview

[The liberation of Belsen] was recorded … I took a lot of pictures [in] Belsen, the concentration [camp] with all of these people in utterly emaciated conditions … We were there and I took some of those photographs … [This experience] is one I hate to even think about; something that you could never put into a picture, hit us. The sounds that came from these people: whimpering sounds, utter misery, unbelievable conditions. In the barracks they would have bunk … beds and so on and these did not have mattresses on them. The floors … were two feet thick in human excrement. The other thing that you can't record is the unbelievable stench … like walking through a toilet, the people dead, dying, sick … sick, to the point where their bodies were just simply rotten. And those are the things I can never forget, never.

Anybody who has ever had this experience … Well, I know with myself, I couldn't eat any kind of food for more than a week afterwards. I couldn't face anything to eat. The minute I looked at food I would start to wretch and throw up. That's the effect it had on me.

We were attached to the British. Being photographers we carried passes signed by General Eisenhower: we could go anywhere, any battle zone, any place that we thought there was a picture to be taken. As I said, we were attached for our food and so forth to a particular unit. But our privilege was to go wherever there was action going. It was very interesting for us, because we had a lot of freedom, we could take a lot of side trips and do things.

We went over [to Bergen-Belsen] to see what it was all about … That was one of the more horrifying things. I was glad I didn't see that much of it. What I saw was enough. It seemed like ages, but it was just a single day ... There were many other photographers there ... they would get in on this for their own intelligence reasons. They wanted a record of this. There were other British photographers there ... All of our stuff automatically went back to CMHQ [Canadian Military Headquarters] and, in turn, it was censored, if it was necessary, before they released it to anybody.

Part of what we were doing was for the record: and every aspect of this was important. Whether they were going to use this in a newsreel or anything ... that was one half of our business. And the other was to record this for history. And these are the things that they want. They want everything about it. And that was part of it ... Whether I thought anyone would want it or use it or not ... If it interested me, I took it. And some of those films I hope I never have to see, really. I never want to see them again ... I've tried, in fact, over the years to push some of those things out of my mind ...

Source: Library and Archives Canada, R5642-0-2-E, interview with Al Calder by Dan Conlin (23 September 1986), Dan Conlin Fonds.

~

ALEX COLVILLE

Official War Artist, Canadian Army

The son of a Scottish emigrant father and Canadian mother, David Alexander Colville was born on 24 August 1920 in Toronto, Ontario. When Colville was nine years old, the family moved to Amherst, Nova Scotia. He attended Mount Allison University in Sackville, New Brunswick, majoring in fine arts.[11] Upon graduation in 1942, he married the painter and poet Rhoda Wright and enlisted in the Canadian Army, being assigned to the infantry.

Before he departed for overseas in 1944, Colville's first son was born. Colville was sent to Europe and in 1944 was made a war artist. He was initially attached to the Royal Canadian Navy for their landings in southern France; then as part of the 3rd Canadian Division he served in France, the Netherlands, and Germany. He was sent to document Bergen-Belsen by the Canadian High Commissioner to Britain and arrived on 29 April 1945.[12] After spending three days at the camp, Colville made his way to Wismar where the 1st Canadian Parachute Battalion – who had encountered the camp two weeks prior – had been resting in billets. In 1945, at war's end, he returned to Canada to turn many of his European sketches into paintings. In 1946 he began teaching at Mount Allison University, a job he held until 1963 when he resigned. He continued to teach and held visiting positions at the University of California, Santa Cruz, and in Germany. In 1973, Colville and his wife moved to the latter's hometown of Wolfville, Nova Scotia. They lived and worked in the house that Rhoda's father built and in which she was born.

Colville was largely a figurative painter. He developed an international following for his work, which was known for its psychological elements. In 1965, he was commissioned by the government to design commemorative coins for Canada's centennial. He also represented Canada at the 1966 Venice Biennale and was made an Officer of the Order of Canada. In 2003 he received the Governor General's Award in Visual and Media Arts.

The works of Colville, celebrated by many as Canada's "painter laureate," are held in several major international collections, including the Museum of Modern Art in New York, the Musée National d'Art Moderne in Paris, the National Gallery of Canada in Ottawa, and the Centre National d'Art et de Culture Georges Pompidou in Paris.[13]

The Colvilles were married for seventy years and had four children. Colville's wife, Rhoda, died on 29 December 2012. Alex Colville passed away seven months later of a heart condition on 16 July 2013 at his house in Wolfville. He was ninety-two years old.

Progress Report

1) On 1 Apr I completed "Crocodile" and worked on "PW Cage," both subjects which I had sketched the day before. We moved to HEERENBURG late in the day. On 2 Apr, a day of showers, I worked again on "PW Cage." The rain continued the following day; we moved to LAAG KEPPEL. I drove north toward ZUTPHEN on 4 Apr, but after having rather a narrow escape from shelling, returned to LAAG KEPPEL, where I sketched a Baily bridge. Divisional Headquarters moved again in the afternoon. On 5 Apr I drove around in the rain looking for prospective subjects, but found none, so worked on a new composition of "PW Cage." The next day I finished this work before we moved to a new area in the afternoon.

2) The weather cleared on 7 Apr, so I went into the Northeast part of ZUTPHEN, which had just been cleared and sketched "Liberated Street." We moved again the next morning; in the afternoon I pained "Medium Gun," with 10 Med Regt R.A. On 9 Apr I completed

"Liberated Street," then went to Corps where I replenished my stock of art materials. The next day I made a drawing of an AA site – and SP Bofors and crew. The following day I made a pen and wash drawing near DEVENTER, "Dead Paratrooper." This subject gave me a tentative idea for a large oil composition. On 12 Apr I went to 1 Heavy Regt, R.A. where I made some sketches. That afternoon we moved to a new location south of RAALTE. Early the next morning I saw a beautiful, although very fleeting, subject: The H.L.I of C. [Highland Light Infantry of Canada] advancing over a misty field on Wasps and carriers. I made a number of very quick sketches which I embraced the next day in a large watercolor, "Infantry Advancing." On 15 Apr Divisional Headquarters moved twice – first to MEPPEL, then to a location near HEERENVEEN.

3) On 16 Apr I drove to LEEUWARDEN and was very moved by the enthusiastic reception given to us by the people of FRIESLAND. I did a small sketch on this theme of "liberation," and later a large watercolor drawing. I feel, however that neither of these are successful to me, the watercolor is too fixed and limited [a] medium for what I wanted to express. I went to the Q.O.R. of C. [Queen's Own Rifles of Canada] on 18 Apr, and sketched PW being marched along a road near BOLSWARD. I did a large pen and wash drawing from these sketches on the following day. On 20 Apr I drove to the eastern end of the causeway, South of HARLINGEN, and painted "Desolate Landscape." This was an excellent subject; and there was a beautiful maritime greyness in everything with the sun a yellowish blur behind high fog. I was interrupted by a heavy rainstorm, but finished this work the next day.

4) We moved on 22 Apr to WINSCHOTEN. I began a watercolor of a late evening effect in Headquarters, which was in a municipal park. On 23 Apr I made a large drawing of three armoured cars of "A" Sqn, 7 Cdn Recce Regt (17 D.Y.R.C.H.), pulled off the road awaiting further orders. On 24 Apr I made some sketches of Regina Rif marching, then completed "Headquarters in Evening." The following day I made numerous sketches of infantrymen doing assault boat training. I found a good subject in NEUWE SCHANS on 26 Apr but was unable to sketch it as we moved that afternoon to a wood near BUNDE. That evening I was informed by Maj. A.T. Sesia that I would be going to the concentration camp at BELSEN to do some sketching.

5) I therefore left HQ 3 Cdn Inf Div on 27 April and drove to HQ First Cdn Army where I reported to Major E. Harrison (now Lt. Col). My instructions were to spend several days sketching BELSEN, then, if possible, to visit 1 Cdn Para Bn, 6 Brit Airborne Div, then under command 18 US Airborne Corps. The necessary arrangements were made, and on 28 Apr I drove to HQ 2 Brit Army, near SALTAU and reported

Figure 19. Official war artist Alex Colville working on his painting *Bodies in a Grave, Belsen*. From the private collection of the Colville family.

to the D.A.D.P.R. at the Press Camp. Here I was given a letter of introduction to the Governor of the concentration camp. On 29 Apr I drove to this camp at BELSEN, saw the authorities there, and was dusted (as protection against typhus) and set up camp in a nearby barracks. That afternoon I visited No 1 concentration camp. I will make no attempt to describe the conditions there, as they have already been adequately described by others. The subjects were not the sort which can be executed expressively at the time, on the spot. I felt that I would get the most out of this visit by making sketches, then returning to these sketches at some later date and painting compositions from them. On the first day, I made a drawing of some women, dead from starvation and typhus, lying outside one of the huts. While I drew, the group of bodies was added to as more people died and were feebly dragged out of the hut by the inhabitants, who were themselves more dead than alive. On 30 Apr it rained all morning. In the afternoon I began a watercolor of one of the huge open graves, with the camp in the background. I finished this the next morning. That afternoon I made a drawing of bodies lying in a grave. These were soon obscured by other bodies which were being thrown from the back of a truck. On 2 May I decided that I had done all I could do in the concentration camp, and that I would try to visit 1 Cdn Para Bn. I therefore drove to the Forward Press camp, 2 Brit Army, at LIMEBURG where I saw another D.A.D.P.R. Here I was introduced to a Public Affairs Officer of 18 US Airborne Corps, and on 3 may I followed him to his Corps HQ at HAGENOW. I was given the location of 6 Brit Airborne Div, and drove to WISMAR, on the BALTIC SEA. I reported at the Div HQ, then proceeded to B.H.Q., 1 Cdn Para Bn who were also at WISMAR. I met the CO and was billeted. The next day, 4 May, I started a large drawing at the airport which was being guarded by "B" Coy of 1 Cdn Para Bn. Unfortunately, most of the troops were in billets resting, so that subjects directly connected with the Cdn Bn were few. On 5 may there were showers all morning and heavy rain in the afternoon; I therefore decided to start back to HQ First Cdn Army. I drove to HAMBURG, and spent the night with 53 (W) Div. On 6 May I arrived at HQ First Cdn Army, where I again reported to Lt Col E. Harrison. On 7 May I drove to HQ 3 Cdn Inf Div, at AURICH. Throughout this whole trip I was treated with the greatest cordiality and hospitality by British, American, and Canadian units and formations. Everything that could possibly be done to help me was done. I only regret that I visited 1 Cdn Para Bn at such an unfortunate time, when all the fighting had ceased, and they were resting in a rather uninteresting setting.

Lt D.A. Colville

Source: Library and Archives Canada: MG30, D 292, R2111-0-5-E: Progress Report by Lt D.A. Colville (1 April–7 May 1945).

Interview

Some years after [the war] I remember reading an English paper that said that what one felt was regret and shame that one didn't feel worse … Vincent Massey was the High Commissioner in London, and the Second British Army had just overrun the first German concentration camps and he wanted one of the war artists to go. This major called me and said, "I want you to go to Belsen," and I said, "yes, sir," that's what you did, so … I went.

We were there for two days and lived in a little pup tent. I can remember that there were still about three hundred people a day dying of typhoid. There were open graves with five, six, seven thousand bodies in them and still open. Bulldozed graves. Bodies were being thrown in off trucks. But there were still people dying all the time and I can remember standing between the rows of tarpaper barracks that you see pictures of ... the place had been overrun by British troops and so it was British medical corps who were trying to cope with this.

We had to have anti-flea and louse powder as soon as we arrived to get in. We had to put this inside our clothes and our caps so that we wouldn't get bitten by bugs of this type.

I was standing there, looking down between the row of huts, and I see two medical guys carrying out a beautiful, naked young woman. She was in or on a grey blanket – I don't know if she was dead; she was probably still alive. But the incongruity of this was just bizarre.

But mostly what you feel is that – I remember a character and I – we ate supper that first night we were there; we were hungry as we would be on any day. So we cooked on a gasoline stove and life goes on and you get into your sleeping bag at night and you go to sleep ...

Source: Robert McLaughlin Gallery, Oshawa; Alex Colville interview with Joan Murray, 18 December 1978. Alex Colville, artist file. Joan Murray artists' files.

Interview

Major Sage just said to me, "The High Commissioner to Great Britain suggested a Canadian war artist should go and record this, I'm sending you." So, I just said "Yes" and went back to [the] Division, and my driver and I took off.

They told me when I was there, I think it was the 30th day of April, or the first day of May, there were still 200–300 people dying every day. Typhus and so on ... People drove up with a big flat-bed truck and there were bodies and they were throwing them off the flat-bed truck into this huge grave. I did a watercolor of some of those big pits.

We have naïve ideas about the central innocence of people; one has to be able to somehow encompass the idea that there can be absolute evil. You look at a photograph of a four-year-old French Jewish girl, who's been sent to a camp in Germany to be killed. You can't say that this is not evil. That the person doing this doesn't mean any harm. The things that happened there are almost beyond comprehension.

I did a drawing of two or three women lying there dead, which was a good drawing, but then I tried to do a painting of it, my painting of the Belsen thing, I think it was a failure. It's inadequate. This is not my kind of material. Some people have got some kind of sense of what was happening from the stuff I did of Belsen. But basically, I think I was the wrong guy for the job in a way.

Figure 20. Alex Colville, *Dead Women, Belsen*, pencil on paper, 12 × 19, 12143.
CWM 19710261-2052. Beaverbrook Collection of War Art, Canadian War Museum.

Figure 21. Alex Colville, *Bodies in a Grave, Belsen*, oil on canvas, 30 × 40. CWM
19710261-2033. Beaverbrook Collection of War Art, Canadian War Museum.

I was there, I think about three days, so I thought, "Well, I've done all I can do here," so I'll leave. So, we took off. [I] wonder "Am I an exceptionally callous person?" You know[,] unfeeling, almost inhuman. Of course, you feel badly about it, but you're not ruined by it. The human capacity to survive bad experiences is greater than most people think. I think most people underestimate their capacity to do this. You know we can deal with a lot of bad stuff.

Source: Portraits of War (DVD).

DONALD K. ANDERSON

Official War Artist, Royal Canadian Air Force, 127 Wing

Donald Kenneth Anderson was born on 6 June 1920 in Toronto. He received special arts training at the Danforth Technical School and between 1938 and 1940 studied at the Ontario College of Art. From 1940 to 1941 he worked as a commercial artist, during which time he painted a large landscape mural in the No. 1 Training School in Toronto.[14]

In April 1941, Anderson enlisted in the Royal Canadian Air Force. He initially trained to work as a radio mechanic but was later reclassified to general duties. At RCAF Headquarters in Ottawa, Anderson was assigned to the Art Section of the Directorate of Public Relations. On 10 August 1944, Anderson arrived in England. His approach to his war art was to "select, establish a mood, and record."[15]

While in London, Anderson was part of RCAF Overseas Headquarters. During the autumn of 1944 he was assigned to work with No. 6 Group, Bomber Command. Finally, on 11 December 1944 Anderson was sent to Europe. He was assigned to the RCAF's 127 Wing, which consisted of 403, 416, and 421 Squadrons. He served in Belgium, the Netherlands, and Germany.

As the need in the camp was still so great, in late April or early May 1945 Anderson was part of a group of men who brought food and supplies to Bergen-Belsen. While he carried a camera with him, he refused to take photos of the scenes, as he felt it was like "infringing on other people's privacy."[16] After the initial shock, he sketched many of the scenes he witnessed. Ultimately, he completed only one painting of the experience that is now held in the Canadian War Museum.

In the post-war period, Anderson continued to work as a commercial artist. He worked in Montreal for twenty years before moving back to Toronto, where he was employed mostly in advertising. He received a lifetime achievement award in 1990 from the Canadian Association of Photographers and Illustrators in Communications. Upon retirement he lived in northern Ontario. Donald Anderson passed away on 11 May 2009 near Toronto.

Interview

[In my early sketches of Belsen one] can see the initial shock … I like to draw but look at that, that's just pure shock. You'd think I was drunk or something. Then the people, and a woman come up to me and said, "that her friend was dying," and I think I did a little sketch there of her and she asked, "would I come and help?" I had two cameras. I wouldn't take any photographs. It was like infringing on other peoples' privacy. It was like, going up to a coffin and taking a photograph. There are some things you do and some things you don't do. That's the way it affected me. I was in there for three days.

The tractor had just pushed the bodies in there and I recall, one thing about that was when the tractor was pushing the bodies in I thought how fortunate it was such sandy soil. These two chaps here were grinding up coal to eat … because they felt that the carbon would settle their stomachs. I think there was something like 500 a day dying then and my big impression there was a major in the British Army, a doctor, a great big tall guy, he had a lot of test tubes going and he was doing something in the camp and I thought what a great guy this is and I've always felt that somebody should have recognized this man because he'd moved his office right in the camp. As we went in, the first thing that happened was that you were sprayed with DDT right down your back, all over the place and each night I destroyed my uniform.[17]

We brought in more food and the great thing about this a few years ago the chief Rabbi from Israel was in Toronto and he wanted to know who these Air Force people were, Canadians who were in Belsen and no-body said a word and I thought that's wonderful that's real class because you don't stick your chest out about something that you're supposed to do, that you should do and you do it for humanity I guess … I didn't think of them as Jews or anything else just people.

[It was the worst thing I saw in the war] … I haven't thought much about it because it's right off the emotional scale. I don't relate to it. It's something that, thank God if you thought about this sort of thing or related to it or you were a little bit paranoid or psychotic you'd be

Figure 22. Donald K. Anderson, *Belsen*, watercolour, 31.9 × 56.4. CWM
19710261-1309. Beaverbrook Collection of War Art, Canadian War Museum.

mentally ill. No, it didn't – it was just too great to be absorbed so I forgot about it for years.

The only time that I was having lunch in Montreal, and I noticed the man behind the bar had his numbers on his arm and I said, "What camp were you in?" and he said "Belsen," and I said, "Oh, yes I was in there," and he said, "Oh, I remember I remember you bringing food in."

We were told to bring the food in, but we had to keep the people away from the food because the juices for instance had to be watered down and no chocolate, don't give them any chocolate because you'll kill people with this. It's hard to believe how deadly sick people were and I remember one weird incident it seemed to be not much to think about was this old woman and I mean old, bent over, … and she was carrying some sort of little pot. I think it was a shell casing that was cut in half and along came a man, a younger man and grabbed the shell casing off the old lady and he had a white cross on his back, painted on his back, he was classified as a Christian I suppose and he took the casing off the old lady because they were very valuable things if they could get a potato peeling they boiled it you see and along came a man hit this other man who was practically dying on the side of the head took the pot off him and gave it to the old lady again and I though boy oh boy, people reduced to fighting over a pot.

Figure 23. Artist Donald K. Anderson, with sketchbook in hand, stands in front of a downed Luftwaffe airplane, April 1945. The Robert McLaughlin Gallery.

...
I think it was important. I think this could happen again.

There were two or three people from [my unit] ... a couple of drivers, somebody else and myself, just a nondescript group who decided we'd go and bring some food in. We had three trucks and I think we did it, for three days. People were starving they needed food so what do you do, you grab the parcels that the people have, and we took all that stuff and handed it over.

Source: Robert McLaughlin Gallery, Oshawa; Donald Anderson interview with Joan Murray, 23 June 1981. Donald Anderson, artist file. Joan Murray artists' files.

~

ABA BAYEFSKY

Official War Artist, Royal Canadian Air Force, 39 Wing

The second of four children of a Russian-born father and a Scottish-born mother of Polish descent, Aba Bayefsky was born 7 April 1923 in Toronto, Ontario.[18] His father – a linotype operator at the *Hebrew Journal* – and mother moved the family, in 1925, from a predominately Jewish neighbourhood to a mainly gentile area of town. Consequently, Bayefsky was confronted with a great deal of antisemitism growing up.[19] These early hardships would remain with him for the rest of his life.

During his teenage years, Bayefsky received instruction at the Children's Art Centre in the Art Gallery of Ontario.[20] In 1937 he enrolled in the Central Technical School in Toronto where he studied under Carl Schaefer, Charles Goldhammer, and Peter Haworth. Recognizing his emerging talent, and to support the young artist, in 1941 the Children's Art Centre hired Bayefsky as a junior instructor. Concurrently, he joined a cooperative of socially conscious figurative painters called the Studio Group.

The following year, in 1942, Bayefsky enlisted in the Royal Canadian Air Force, initially assigned to air traffic control. While stationed in Portage La Prairie, he submitted a painting for a competition open to all Commonwealth air force personnel. His watercolour won first prize, which led to Bayefsky's appointment, in 1944, as an official Canadian war artist. He was commissioned as a flying officer and was sent to London.

Figure 24. Aba Bayefsky, *Remembering the Holocaust*, oil, 167.7 × 121.7. CWM 19970112-001. Beaverbrook Collection of War Art, Canadian War Museum.

Bayefsky soon found himself in northwest Europe, where he was assigned to depict airborne operations. In early May 1945 he was sent to 39 Wing (RCAF) at Lüneburg, which was part of the Second Tactical Air Force. When Bayefsky learned that Bergen-Belsen was located nearby, he made his way to the camp. His first visit occurred on 10 May 1945; the Toronto-born artist had turned twenty-two years old only a few weeks before.[21] Stunned and horrified by the scenes, Bayefsky returned to the camp a week later, 17 May 1945, and then for a third and final time on 10 June 1945. He completed a series of drawings and sketches. After the war, he was assigned to a studio at the Hunt Club in Toronto, where a fire destroyed his Belsen sketchbooks.[22] Ultimately, nine official images relating to Bergen-Belsen were submitted by Bayefsky.

In 1947, he returned to Europe to study at the Académie Julian, an art school in Paris, after receiving a scholarship from the French government. Newly married, he and his wife, Evelyn, travelled throughout France and Italy. Bayefsky visited displaced person camps in both Paris and Milan, documenting what he witnessed.

Eventually returning to Canada, in 1957 he became an instructor in fine art at the Ontario College of Art (now the Ontario College of Art and Design University). This position lasted until 1989. From 1967 to 1978 he also taught a popular drawing class at Hart House, University of Toronto. He was a member of the Canadian Society of Graphic Art, the Canadian Group of Painters, and the Royal Canadian Academy of Arts. In 1979 he was appointed to the Order of Canada.

Throughout his career, Bayefsky would return to the topic of Bergen-Belsen and the Holocaust. Regarding his encounter with Bergen-Belsen, he declares, "It was the determining factor in everything I have done since."[23] Indeed, the camp and the Holocaust have been a source for much of his future oeuvre, particularly his set of works entitled *Epilogue*, a forty-one-piece collection.

The work of Aba Bayefsky is held in the Canadian War Museum, the Art Gallery of Ontario, Yad Vashem, and in countless private and public galleries. His work has been exhibited in Toronto, New York, Chicago, London, Tokyo, and India. Bayefsky passed away on 5 May 2001 at the age of seventy-eight. He was survived by his wife, three children, and five grandchildren.

Interview

... When I became a war artist, I was given a pass which allowed me all sorts of flexibility ... And I went to the Second Tactical Air Force, which [included] the ... Reconnaissance Wing, which was very close to Belsen.[24] And that's how I got to Belsen ...

[People] knew about these camps. The horror is difficult to say. You know that you don't really believe that this is going on. When you see the camp, then you understand it more completely ... And when you see the pits ... with bodies ... just stacked up ... I mean, what can you say about it? ...

While I was in Belsen, I met someone called Ted Aplin.[25] Now, Ted was someone I happened to know ... in Toronto. And he was a Squadron Leader ... [a] very intelligent and sensitive man. And there was a lot of [art] work around, done by the inmates [of Belsen]. I remember there were several trunks of this material with music, drawings, writing ... little things that the inmates had been doing. And I decided to go to London to the High Commissioner who was Vincent Massey, at the time, and ask him to get this material out before somebody took it. And that it really should be circulated to show what was going on there because it was extremely interesting. You know the young people, the drawings, just fascinating things ... a terrible condemnation of what was going on in the camp. And so he [Aplin] and I discussed it and I got a flight to London ... [I] went to the High Commissioner's ... [and his secretary] ... wouldn't let me see Massey. And he told me, in no uncertain words, that this was none of my business. You know, this is a political thing, and [I'm] just an artist ...

That was it. So when I got back, the stuff has been taken by somebody and what I heard was that it had gone to Sweden ... So we lost it ...

[After seeing Belsen there] wasn't very much point of my drawing airplanes any longer. That's part of it, you know. I'm a war artist for the air force. Therefore, that's what I should be doing. Now I did this on my own ... when I went to Belsen, when I saw what was there. But in the meantime everybody expected airplanes flying over or flying under or whatever ...

Most of the war artists did pictures which said nothing about the horrors of the war. You know, they did pictures of a tank ... But, the things were limited in context. I mean there's nothing, the human side of it had disappeared. Or never appeared, for that matter ...

I think most people or many people saw [war] as some kind of adventure. And that was it. You know, without really thinking how it came about, what the consequences would be, where they really played a part in this war, you just knew that there was a war, and you were going to be called up one way or another, and you joined the service and just built up friendships with people, and that was it. And you just went and did whatever you were supposed to do. And there weren't too many people that I know who thought very deeply about the war. We just knew that there was a war on, and that it was your duty to fight whatever ...

Figure 25. Aba Bayefsky, *Belsen Concentration Camp Pit, 1945*, oil, 91.6 × 121.8. CWM 19710261-1394. Beaverbrook Collection of War Art, Canadian War Museum.

I think when people saw Belsen – and I'm sure it applies to all the camps – they knew what war was about. I mean, that was really war. That may have applied if you were in a brigade of some kind, where you were actually fighting, you know, and people were dying and were being wounded, and in that situation you would probably understand, you know, you'd think a little more [about it and say,] "what am I doing here, how did I come to be here, and who are these people who are, you know, killing us, and we're killing them." But certainly in Belsen … I mean it was such a sort of horrible experience that there wasn't any room for camaraderie. It was just a vicious spectacle. And you had to react on that level. In fact they went out into the town and got the townspeople to come … And they didn't want to … but they had to … and everybody [was] weeping and crying and … [saying,] "I never knew anything about it," and "It wasn't me," and … that kind of thing …
If at the end of the war, anti-Semitism ceased and became a thing of the past – and you would think that after everything that had happened that it would have just disappeared – then I could, possibly … [have

Figure 26. Aba Bayefsky's photograph of mass graves at Bergen-Belsen. Photo Archive, Yad Vashem.

Figure 27. Aba Bayefsky, *Belsen Concentration Camp – Malnutrition No. 2*, charcoal, 35.2 cm × 51.9. CWM 19710261-1392. Beaverbrook Collection of War Art, Canadian War Museum.

Figure 28. Aba Bayefsky, *All Quiet on the Western Front*, oil, 127.3 × 101.8. CWM 19970112-002. Beaverbrook Collection of War Art, Canadian War Museum.

said,] "OK, that was the war and that was the war, and it's over with." Except that it didn't happen that way, you know, for the Jews it was the beginning of trying to find their homeland. And you know I've often sort of thought about that. The intensity of it even after the war.

[They say] "It'll never happen again" ... So that's the part that sort of brings me into where I simply have not been able, I didn't have the luxury, I don't have the luxury of forgetting that, and you know every so often I turned my skills, whatever they are, to trying to say something about it. And I simply think, you know, the older I get, the less time I have, the more I believe that art should say something. It has to say something meaningful ... The human side of it was largely ignored – I won't say forgotten, but ignored is, I guess, the right word for it. And yet all these experiences ... is a human experience.

Source: Library and Archives Canada, R3940: C.M. Donald Interviews Aba Bayefsky (1995–1996).

HENRY S. ABRAMSON

Artist, Royal Canadian Air Force, 39 Wing

Henry S. Abramson was born in 1922 in Montreal, Quebec.[26] He studied at Baron Byng High School, an English-language public high school in Montreal. Baron Byng featured a predominately Jewish student population and was immortalized by writer Mordecai Richler in several works. Abramson subsequently studied at the École des beaux-arts de Montréal, which was incorporated into the Faculty of the Arts of the University of Quebec at Montreal.

Prior to the war, Abramson worked at the *Montreal Standard* in its rotogravure department. In 1943 he joined the Royal Canadian Air Force and in 1944 was posted overseas to 39 Reconnaissance Wing. He landed in France a few days after the Normandy landings. In May 1945, he visited Bergen-Belsen and decided to paint what he witnessed. An image he created appeared in 39 Wing's *Flap* magazine in August 1945.[27] He also photographed the scenes and wrote letters back to family in Canada about the experience. At the end of the war, he was discharged while in Britain.

In the post-war period, Abramson was selected by the Committee for Education Overseas, under the chairmanship of Vincent Massey, to study in Paris. As part of a cultural project initiated by the French government, Abramson was awarded a scholarship to study at the École des Beaux-Arts, Musée du Louvre, where he worked with modernist painter Fernand Léger.[28]

While in France, Abramson married fellow Canadian Anita Elkin. An artist and teacher, Elkin was from the Notre-Dame-de-Grâce neighbourhood of Montreal in the city's west end. She was studying at the Academie Julien and Academie La Grande Chaumiere in Paris at the time. While they were living in France their daughter, Ronney, was born.[29] The couple also had a second daughter, Rayanne.

Upon his return to Montreal in 1950, Henry Abramson founded and directed the Waldorf Galleries and Clayart Studios with his wife.[30] He also directed the Galerie de Montréal with Yves Lasnier. He later taught the history of aesthetics of film and creative photography for twelve years at Dawson College, and in 1985 he became an adjunct professor in the Faculty of Fine Arts at Concordia University in Montreal.

In the 1980s Abramson became known for having developed "kine-morphic imagery," a new photographic system.[31] In Greek *kine* means "movement" and *morph* means "form." The technique attempted to capture movement and the transformation of forms through time and space. This new system was demonstrated publicly for the first time at his exhibition "Transmutations" in 1987. An artist, teacher, and inventor, Henry Abramson passed away in 1991 at sixty-nine years of age.

Letters

Germany. May 4th 1945

Dearest Dad,

To-night, May 4th 1945, will go down in history as one of the most significant dates in our lives. Certainly one of the most significant of the war against Germany. To-night, we heard, over the A.E.F. radio the electrifying news that hostilities in our sector will cease as of 8:00 A.M. double British summer time tomorrow Saturday, May 5th 1945.[32] Humiliating un-conditional surrender for the once proud German monsters that so murderously spilled good human blood all over Europe. The butchers that murdered men, women, and children by the hundreds of thousands, without the slightest qualms or conscience.

To you, dear father, far away from the actual scenes of crimes so foul, so hideous, this may sound like a newspaper exaggeration. Believe me, everything you have read or seen about the German beasts, every story, no matter how insane it may appear is true! Even the wildest nightmare, the craziest imagination cannot possibly exaggerate the wanton cruel atrocities committed here.

This afternoon I saw for myself. I saw what I cannot yet believe. My mind, my emotions indeed my whole being could not accept, could not begin to grasp what my eyes saw, what my ears heard. How shall I start to explain? How can I put it all together to make it sound true?

II

I am writing you this letter to-night because I cannot sleep. I've got to get it off my chest. Above all I want to impress you and anyone you come into contact with, with the facts. If there is even the slightest shred of doubt amongst them it must be removed. I know, dad, that you are a solid citizen. I have always admired and respected your judgement and sound common sense. The best any of us can do, out of ordinary human decency, out of respect to those thousands upon thousands of innocent victims of Hitler barbarism, is to know and understand the brutal truth. I feel that our censorship has been relaxed sufficiently now, to allow me to stick to the facts.

At the moment, we are in Northern Germany, not very far from Hamburg. This morning, a special run was authorized by our officers to take some of us to see the notorious German concentration camps at Belsen. (You've read the accounts in the papers). We had the opportunity to see at close range, and examine Germany's greatest war-time industry – murder! In many ways we were prepared for this experience, but the actual contact with the scenes themselves left us all speechless and completely horrified.

Belsen camp is a fairly large place, covering a number of acres of German soil. It leads off the main road past a sign that says "Forbidden area, you will be shot for trespassing," in German. The first impressions that one gets are rather inoffensive.

III

The road leads by a number of paved streets called "Bismarck Strasse" and "Rommel Strasse" and a few other "heroic" names. One can see well-spaced groups of two story barracks, very similar to the ones back home on airfields and permanent army set ups. This is where the gentlemen and ladies of the S.S. lived and ate, played tennis and indulged in various other activities. For real amusement, of course, and good clean fun, they used to go a little way further along the road that leads into the woods. These woods were carefully cultivated to conceal certain "military" operations that took place a little way up the line. Some of these trees were planted not very long ago, but they have developed beautifully, nurtured by blood and bones. Human blood and bones. Nothing but the best for these Germans.

As one goes a little deeper through the road marked "Verboten, lebens gefahr" [Danger, keep out] the place begins to lose the appearance of a pleasure resort for holiday makers. You see first, barbed wire, black and heavy, and with barbs every few inches. The fence system is very unique. There are two fences. The inner fence, composed of barbed wire and steel girders is about ten feet high. It curves inwards at the top. The outer fence, about seven feet beyond is composed of the same material but is not quite so high, only about seven feet.

IV

In the center of the system of fences is an interwoven network of the same German barbed-wire. The total result is characteristically thorough and effective. All around this section of the camp (a vast area) at regular intervals and as far as the eye can see, is a series of wooden observation towers regularly spaced at about fifty yard intervals. Each tower was equipped with a powerful searchlight, telephone and probably expert machine gunners. On the walls of these towers, also on some of the fences and doors below were repeated the word "PST," the German equivalent of "SH" in English. The Germans used many poster ideas similar to ours. This one is supposed to caution people to silence; but when you looked across the camp from one of these towers and then saw the letter "PST" your heart cried out with pain. The Germans had the nerve to make a secret of their monstrous crimes.

What we saw of the camp itself had to be seen through the barbed wire, because the camp is quarantined and the danger of typhus is great. This camp was operating no more than ten days ago. There are signs of the Germans trying desperately to cover up their activities at the last minute, but it would take hundreds of years to wipe away the pain and agony the torture and terror that were contained in this hellhole. We passed great stacks of mattresses and clothing being burned because they were contaminated with disease.

V

Now came a sight I shall never forget. A sight so horrible that it cannot be described. Through the heavy smoke of the burning piles of refuse, through the nauseating smell of dung and rot, there came a terrifying procession. About fifteen men dressed from head to foot in a uniform as gruesome as death, green hoods they wore, their hands were covered by large fabric gloves and their feet in oilskin boots. These men drew a large, low wheeled cart. (I shudder when I recall the squeaking of the wheels and the way the heavy load shook from side to side as they pushed the cart up to the edge of a large pit.) Behind them came British 2nd Army men and the hard looks on their faces, the way they shouted at the workers and poked them with their guns made it quite clear how they felt.

Figure 29. An untitled painting depicting the dead in one of the pits at the Bergen-Belsen concentration camp by Leading Aircraftman Henry S. Abramson of 39 Wing, RCAF. Used by permission of Ronney Abramson for the estate of H.S. Abramson.

The men pushing the carts, I found out later, were German Wehrmacht specially brought in to help clean the place up. Apparently the SS people (those that lived after our troops got through with them), were forced to dig graves and bury the dead. Some of the swine committed suicide, others went crazy so now they're using the Wehrmacht.

The cart came to a halt at the edge of the pit and the men were ordered in threatening voices to get busy. A tarpaulin cover was removed and the sight that met our eyes made the blood run cold in our veins.

VI

Bodies, human bodies, withered and shrunken to the bone. Hundreds of them, piled carelessly one on top of the other like guts in a slaughterhouse. We found out later that all those terrible bodies had

Figure 30. A mass grave in Bergen-Belsen concentration camp. Image 32072. United States Holocaust Memorial Museum, courtesy of Arnold Bauer Barach.

lived only twenty-four hours earlier, and yet they were shrunken down to about nothing. Arms and legs as big around as broomsticks. Systematic and scientific starvation, part of the German "higher culture."

We have seen death before. We have seen people die, have seen plenty of corpses (this is to be expected in war) many of us have become used to it; but this was absolutely shocking and devastating. As we began to grasp what was going on we looked around and realized what vast mass-production machine of murder stretched out before our eyes. We could see about ten or fifteen covered graves behind this fresh one. There are thousands of bodies in each one. Think of it! Imagine, if you can, what this means! Remember this when you talk about the war and discuss these things with people. Don't allow the skeptics to dismiss it as propaganda. It's not propaganda, it's the brutal terrible truth. Your son has seen it with his own eyes, tell them that!

Source: Used by permission of Ronney Abramson for the estate of H.S. Abramson.

Germany. May 4th 1945.

Dearest Norm:

To-night, I will find it impossible to sleep. The scenes I witnessed this afternoon, the stark brutal truth that met my eyes are impossible to describe in words. Indeed, an entire new language, a completely revised set of human emotions would have to be created to make these things understandable.

We were taken, this afternoon, to visit the notorious German concentration camp at Belsen. You have probably seen the newspaper accounts of this place; but no newspaper could possibly give you a real picture of the extent to which these maniacal barbarians have gone. No cattle have ever been slaughtered as methodically and in such great numbers as real live human beings, men, women, and children of all ages, have been in this unbelievable horror camp on poisoned German soil. The men with me are still burning with anger. If there was anyone among us who didn't believe the stories about the Germans, if there was a single simple minded softie amongst us this morning, there isn't one to-night. No human being could see the hideous results of German Fascism that we saw this afternoon and remain indifferent. No, I think that if we could lay our hands on just a few German SS and Wehrmacht men, there wouldn't be one amongst us who would hesitate from killing, not with a gun, but with his bare hands. Death is too sweet a gift for these absolutely inhuman cannibals. They have committed the most hideous and sadistic crimes in all history.

II

I am writing to you to-night, dear brother, because I have been thinking about you constantly this last time. I miss you very much kid and I am very much concerned about your future. Ma writes me that you fit my grey suit. You must have grown tremendously since I left. I can hardly wait to see you. The thirteenth of May will be your fourteenth birthday; (no, I haven't forgotten) last year I had just landed in England and I couldn't do very much about it. This year however, I want to send you all my best wishes and all my deepest love, and I hope that I will be around to celebrate your fifteenth birthday together with you and the rest of the family. I am sending you a parcel containing a few odds and ends that I picked up in my travels. I know it won't get there in time for your birthday, indeed it is questionable whether it will get there at all. At any rate, I tried, so let me know if

Figure 31. A sketch of an untitled Belsen painting by Leading Aircraftman Henry S. Abramson of 39 Wing, RCAF. Used by permission of Ronney Abramson for the estate of H.S. Abramson.

the stuff shows up. It isn't much, but anyway, it's from me to you with all my love.

I started this letter off on a pretty grim note. This I did with a purpose, I hope you don't mind. In a few days you're going to be fourteen years old, and, to my way of thinking, that makes you a responsible human being. In other words, you are supposed to know the score. I don't know what you have been doing with yourself, what you read or how you are getting along with your studies. You'll have to write and tell me all about these things. However, for now, let me explain a few things I have seen and learnt over here in Europe, particularly in the last few months. Things which will affect your life and mine, for years to come.

Source: Used by permission of Ronney Abramson for the estate of H.S. Abramson

Chapter Three

Relief Measures

For the Canadian relief personnel who entered the Bergen-Belsen concentration camp during the spring and summer of 1945 the experience was enormously difficult, one that ushered in a variety of personal and professional challenges. Initially lacking staff, supplies, equipment, and facilities, personnel frequently had to improvise and adopt roles they had never previously performed. And while the physical decline of the inmates stunned them, it was often the perceived moral and social collapse that so disturbed many of the relief personnel. "[S]ome of the inmates turned to cannibalism," observed agriculture economist and squadron leader John Proskie of Edmonton, "and thereby the dead helped sustain life for the living until food again was made available after liberation."[1] For most personnel, the situation was entirely unprecedented.

Canadians performed a variety of roles in the aftermath of the liberation of Bergen-Belsen. Their tasks were demanding, and some suffered greatly because of the work: dysentery, isolation, depression, and feelings of inadequacy were common. And yet the work needed to be done. "My men were extremely compassionate," remembers Mathew Nesbitt of the Royal Canadian Air Force, "and we had discussed immediately upon entering the camp, that this is no time to show emotion, the job was to find the living, ... bury the dead, and feed the people who could eat. So whatever emotion we had, we tried to hide very much. Our job was to just save the living."[2] Indeed, most accepted their assignments willingly, working with the resources they had around them.

Relief personnel confronted a multitude of people with diverse languages, religions, and cultural backgrounds, most of whom had endured years of abuse and neglect. They thus had to deal with language limitations and unfamiliar cultures in addition to untrained staff responding to mass starvation and illness. Timely, tough decisions had to be made.

Initially, not everyone was given adequate care, as there were not enough personnel and supplies. Thousands of inmates died, and this weighed heavily on all involved. German military personnel were employed, much to the great dismay of the survivors. The work of the relief personnel was vital, and while thousands died, many more thousands were saved.

This chapter demonstrates the wide range of issues that Canadians had to contend with daily while providing care in the camp.

~

JOHN PROSKIE

Squadron Leader, Royal Canadian Air Force

Military Government, 224 Detachment

Born in 1906 in Edmonton, Alberta, John Proskie dedicated his life to agricultural science.[3] In 1934 he graduated with a bachelor of science degree from the University of Alberta. He remained at the university and, in 1937, received a master's degree from the Department of Political Economy. Upon graduation, Proskie became associated with the Dominion of Canada's Department of Agriculture Research and Economics at the University of Alberta. Three years after the outbreak of the Second World War, he enlisted in the Royal Canadian Air Force.

He rose to the rank of squadron leader, and on 18 April 1945 assisted at the recently surrendered Bergen-Belsen concentration camp, having arrived the previous day.[4] Due to his expertise as an agricultural economist, Proskie was responsible for planning the collection and employment of resources from the local area. The monumental task of organizing food for the inmates was left to Proskie and his lone assistant, a sergeant in the British Army.[5] The two men surveyed the surrounding area, visiting local farms and foodstocks to gather the necessary supplies. In one week, Proskie delivered 40,000 pounds of fresh meat, 65,000 pounds of onions, 1,000 pounds of strawberries, and 13,000 pounds of rhubarb to the camp. Conditions slowly improved at Bergen-Belsen, and Proskie's efforts helped save countless lives. He remained at the camp for several months.

In the post-war period, and due to the world's sugar shortage, he was assigned to survey the sugar beet stocks in the British Zone of Germany.

His efforts ensured that enough seed was planted from the 1947 crop.[6] Upon receiving an honourable discharge from the air force in 1946, Proskie accepted a contract with the British Foreign Office. This led him to become involved in one of the first major international crises of the Cold War, the Berlin Blockade. Proskie organized and administered the supply and distribution of food during the Berlin Airlift. His efforts helped restore economic balance to the sectors of Berlin under Allied control.

After his foreign service, Proskie returned to Canada to work for the Department of Fisheries and authored several books on the Atlantic fishing industry. He retired from the Department of Fisheries in 1970 after twenty-one years of service. In retirement he developed an interest in philately.

Proskie passed away in 1993 after a short battle with an illness. In 1994 his sister, Rosalie Rector, established the John Proskie Memorial Scholarship at both the University of Alberta and the University of Ottawa.[7] The scholarship is offered to promote financial assistance and encouragement to graduate students studying agricultural economics.

Report

This report sets out the food positions at BELSEN camp and takes into account other factors on which food is dependent ...

BELSEN Concentration Camp together with the Wehrmacht Panzer School is situated in Kreis CELLE. This organisation is divided into two concentration camps and the panzer school. Camp No. 1 at present contains 40,500 and Camp No. 2, 17,500 inmates. The Hungarian Garrison is stationed in the panzer school and is made up of 2,506 soldiers and 281 members of their families. Therefore the total population at present is roughly 61,587 living. In addition to this there are approximately 3,000 dead bodies at Camp No. 1, which are gradually being buried. This number is increased by about 500 new deaths per day. To the living population about six births are added per day.

The population of over 60,000 persons represents the population of a modern sized city where people market, procure, cook and feed themselves. Even under these conditions and with a normal population a fairly intricate and organised marketing agency must be in force to have food flowing in. In this case, however, you have a sub-normal population and all the inmates are a liability as far as feeding themselves, processing food, cooking and distribution is concerned. There is little wonder, then, that chaos and uncertainty exists in this reshuffling and readjusting stage.

The population in Camp No. 1 is particularly intricate in the pattern of personalities. One can see dead bodies here and there on the one

Figure 32. The airmen, P/O Fred Hopkinson of Dunneville, Ontario, and Sgt. Joe Stone of Saint John, New Brunswick, are looking at the tattoos. In the background is a heap of bodies, all of which have died from typhus and malnutrition. PL-43516 16/04/45, Department of National Defence.

hand and on the other robust and healthy looking individuals. The dead bodies and the living seem to be intermixed, for the living use the dead as pillows at night and in the daytime a place that is convenient to sit and eat their rations. There apparently is little concern and no marked line drawn between the living and the dead, for those who are alive today may be dead tomorrow. In fact, during the critical stage of the food in this camp, some of the inmates turned to cannibalism and thereby the dead helped sustain life for the living until food again was made available after liberation by the BLA [British Liberation Army].

The inmates of these camps are naturally overjoyed at being liberated and on being questioned about food ask that certain types of food be provided. For example, the Central Europeans ask for foods that normally make up their diet, others have demands which they feel will quickly restore them back to healthy life, and so on. For example,

Figure 33. Soup being carried by the inmates. In the background is P/O
Fred Hopkinson, a motion picture cameraman with the RCAF Film Unit in
Germany. PL-43515, Department of National Defence.

a Polish woman asked for buckwheat so that she could make herself a
little "Kacha," others want sauerkraut and potatoes, still others "gris."
In fact the demands are so great and the individuals choices are so
limited that for the present they must carry on sustaining rations.

The clothing situation is also very poor and there are those that are
almost wholly naked and others are fully clothed and in good clothes.
However, the proportion that have sufficient clothing is very small
and the majority could do with a complete outfit.

The security of the camp at present is uncertain and there have
been three murders in three days. There has been a tendency for the
population to split into groups and take sides, and in some cases resort to force. Further problems may be expected with security. There
is no doubt that, among the good and reliable, this camp contains
the sweepings of Europe, including German criminals, in addition
to political inmates and Jews who are here simply because they are
Jews.

Official records indicate that 17,000 inmates died in March of this year. Crematorium was used for burning the dead bodies. The population was kept up by bringing in new inmates, who, on arrival, were stripped of all their belongings and clothing and told to get into rags which were left after the dead were cremated. At present a loot of 24 cases of watches has been uncovered. How much loot was taken away, hidden, or distributed to the German population no one knows, but it must have been great.

The cooking and distribution systems within the camp are not altogether satisfactory. One case may be cited in Camp No. 1 which prepares food for 15,000. They need 2 ½ complete cookings for one meal and if breakfast is started at 7 in the morning the last is not served until 11:30 the same morning. At present two meals are prepared daily, but the whole process is too slow.

It is reported that about 25% of the inmates in No. 1 Camp have dysentery or other stomach troubles and individuals are asking for special food in order to stop these troubles. None or very little medicine is available for this. This presents a great problem in nutrition and there are no specific foods available in such quantities that can be prepared to correct their digestive troubles.

Out of all this chaos and confusion some sort of order is gradually appearing here and there, but it is apparent that it is too early to affect complete co-ordination and control. The armed forces have tackled the job willingly, co-operatively and with enthusiasm and a good job has been done all round and many lives have been saved although the people are still dying, but the death rate has been reduced. Many more deaths can be expected and no force, no matter how strong, can stop it at present. In other words a certain proportion of population must be written off because it is beyond any hope of being saved.

Source: National Archives, London, WO 219/3944A: Belsen Concentration Camp by J. Proskie (22 April 1945)

~⌣

MATTHEW NESBITT

Royal Canadian Air Force, 126 Wing

Born Max Nezgor, Matthew Nesbitt was born on 20 September 1913 in Toronto, Ontario. His parents were Jewish immigrants from Odessa,

Russia. His father, Tovia Nezgoraski, worked as a foreman in a construc-
tion company in Toronto. His mother, Deena (née Green), was a home-
maker. Nesbitt had a brother and four sisters.[8]

The family was observant, and Nesbitt's father was the president
of the local shul in Toronto. When his father died, Nesbitt dropped
out of high school. He began working for Saturday Night, a general
interest paper and, later, magazine. A competitive baseball player,
Nesbitt later moved to Detroit to play for the Hudson Motor Car Company team.

When war broke out, Nesbitt was playing baseball in Seattle,
Washington. According to his personnel record, he enlisted in the
Royal Canadian Air Force on 8 May 1941 in Toronto. He worked as
a physical training Instructor and initially held the rank of temporary
sergeant. Nesbitt was eventually assigned to the RCAF's 126 Wing.
He saw action in the European theatre and was with the wing when
he assisted at Bergen-Belsen.[9] He was discharged on 26 February
1946.

After the war, Nesbitt returned to Toronto and had a difficult time
adjusting to civilian life. He eventually immigrated to the United
States, first to Detroit and then to the Atlanta metropolitan area.
He worked in the furniture business for six years before entering
the floor-covering business for the next twenty-five years. He was
then involved in teen pageants before getting into the office-supply
business for ten years, after which when he sold his business and
retired.

Upon retirement, Nesbitt volunteered to work with senior citizens,
athletes with a range of disabilities, and children battling cancer. He
was a member of the White House Advisory Council for the Elderly and
the Georgia Commission on the Holocaust, and also worked with the
Anti-Defamation League.

In the late 1970s Nesbitt met Dr. Fred Roberts Crawford, an air
force veteran and director of Emory University's Center for Research
in Social Change. Crawford founded the "Witness to the Holocaust"
project in 1978 with the objective to refute the claims of Holocaust
deniers.[10] Later the project grew to also document and analyse the
long-term effects of the Holocaust. Nesbitt was interviewed twice for
the project. Thereafter, he was a tireless public speaker, sharing his
experiences during the war and his encounter with the Holocaust. He
regularly gave lectures at high schools, academic conferences, com-
memorations, memorials, and to public audiences across the United
States.[11] Matthew Nesbitt passed away on 22 August 1999 at the
age of eighty-five.[12]

Interview

I was in the Royal Canadian Air Force. I enlisted in the latter part of 1939. I was playing [base]ball on the West Coast when war was declared, I went to Toronto, Canada and enlisted in the Royal Canadian Air Force, and I spent six and a half years in the Air Force.

While we were in Germany, one night the Commanding Officer asked me to come to his office immediately, which I did, and there in his office was a Padre who was sobbing hysterically, uncontrollably, and we couldn't make out exactly what he was saying, but he kept saying "Belsen, Belsen, they are dying like flies. You must go there and save them." And we didn't know what he was talking about, at that point we had never heard of a death camp before or a concentration camp. And finally, when the MO, the Medical Officer, settled him down, he started to tell us about what he called the concentration camp.

So, we gathered together two doctors, two nurses, thirteen men and myself, and we left at dawn the next morning with three trucks of food, medicine and whatever we could get our hands on and went down to Belsen. Well, about two miles from Belsen we smelt an odor that we can't describe, it was very, very heavy [and] as we got closer to the camp the odor became stronger. This odor was the smell of decaying bodies. The dead were lying in the streets, in the bunks and nobody had bothered to bury them. And the disease was rampant in the camp, there were people walking around with open, dripping sores.

The first thing, we all experienced the same thing including the doctors and the nurses, was complete horror and disbelief. We couldn't believe that what we saw was actually what we saw. Then was anger and there was grief for the people in there. And it was unbelievable, I mean we could not [believe it] even when they sent us back to England for three days and put us in the hospital to recuperate, because we had worked for 96 hours around-the-clock, without food or sleep or anything, we were completely emotionally and physically exhausted, until help came three days later. We looked at each other and we said, "We know we are in the hospital, but did we actually see what we saw?" Such inhumane things. Bodies all over the place rotting like animals. We didn't believe it for a while. I know it to be true, but still sometimes I think back when I'm talking that "Did it really happen?" Of course, it did, I have a picture and the documents, but how could one person do this to another? I have a picture of two babies that were killed, one must have been about eight months old, one must have been two years old, they weren't satisfied to just kill the kids, they had to break their legs before they killed them. Does that make sense?

Figure 34. Close-up of a female survivor with bandaged face. Stuart A. Rose
Manuscript, Archives and Rare Book Library, Emory University.

We just couldn't believe what we saw then. The first thing we had
to do was get the German guards, there were 800 guards there to
help us find out who was living and who was dead. The only way
we could tell who was alive and was dead is because if we shook
them, vigorously and they didn't move, they were dead, and we
had the carts to take them out and stack them up on the street and
then have the German trucks come by, pick the bodies up. We had
dug a big grave, a mammoth grave and we tried to keep count of the
bodies, about 1000 at a time, and put them in this mammoth grave
and cover them with lime and dirt and bulldoze the dirt back over
the grave.

Some of the people had starved to death in their little bunks because
they were too weak to get out of their bunks. Some people were living
right next to bodies on either side because they were too weak to get up.
When I walked into one hovel there the odor was just overwhelming,
here I saw in the corner of one of these so-called barracks, a little girl
and a little boy, and a man and a woman were all defecating and urinating all together in the same corner and just sitting in it. I mean they
were completely dehumanized.

Figure 35. Female camp guards bury corpses of prisoners in a mass grave. Stuart A. Rose Manuscript, Archives and Rare Book Library, Emory University.

I asked one of the inmates there, who seemed to be in better shape than the others, "How could you possibly let this happen to you?" He says "Well, if you will recall Germany at that particular time was one of the most cultured and civilized nations in the world, and we didn't believe that this could possibly happen to us."

[When I speak to young people today] I take my pictures along. Then I start speaking on the Holocaust, what happened, how it happened, why it happened, and why we should take every step we possibly can to see that it doesn't happen again. And I allow them to break in with questions at any time of my lecture at any time at all. And then I know on occasions, when I have been supposed to be speaking for an hour, I'm there for two hours afterwards, they gather around asking questions and then some of the kids I've seen on many occasions just crying, tears coming down their [faces] they had no idea, and I have letters here that would just break your heart, from the kids that said, "I never realized that human being could treat another human being so inhumanly." They don't understand how the Nazis could be so savage. They don't understand that. But now when I get through talking to them and the letters I receive, it's made a whole big difference. Now they realize some parts of the Holocaust, of course they don't know all of it; I try to give them the facts and the figures. And the reception I've received in every instance is very, very gratifying particularly the letters ...

It can happen at anywhere, at any time. It is our moral obligation, not to forget and to remember always, that it did take place, and to be aware and alert and to expose the racists, the hate-mongers, and all these groups that foster hatred. That's our moral obligation to the future generations.

Source: Interview with WGST Radio, Atlanta, GA, 18 April 1987.

Interview

At the time of the liberation of Belsen, I was approximately 32 years of age ... And none of us were aware of anything such as a concentration camp. We had never heard anything ...

The night prior to our going to Bergen-Belsen, there was a Jewish Padre, who came into our unit, and he was crying so much and emotionally upset that our commanding officer couldn't make head or tail of it. So the Padre being Jewish, the C.O. [commanding officer] called me and said he wanted me to try to find out what he was talking about. We calmed him down a little bit, and then he continued to say that there was such a place[,]Bergen-Belsen, about 20 miles away from us, and they are in need of food and medical supplies, and could we help them? At that particular time, the military was moving in such a manner that the C.O. had to ask for volunteers, rather than tell certain group to go. So, he asked me if I would command the unit of volunteers. So I picked up about fourteen volunteers, who included doctors or somebody who was familiar with medicine who could help save lives, and we started out very early the next morning with a truckload of food, medical supplies and went right down to Belsen. Well, when we got down to Belsen, there were 800 as I believe, SS and Hungarian guards (both men and women still in the camp) ...

Prior to even distributing the food ... was to make sure we used the guards to separate the living from the dead, from the huts, because first of all, if we are going to save anybody, we had to know who was alive and who had to be buried. So, we made arrangements with the commanding officer for us to use all of the guards to find out who was alive and who was dead. The only way you could do that was to go into each individual hut and shake whoever was on that little slab ... If they didn't move, they were dead. If there was any movement,

Figure 36. Piles of decomposing corpses of prisoners in a field. Stuart A. Rose Manuscript, Archives and Rare Book Library, Emory University.

we pulled them out and put them into a different section of the hut ... We instructed the guards to take the dead and pile them up outside in the so-called streets, at which time there were other guards who went by with trucks and I have pictures that I took myself showing the guard taking the bodies from the pile and putting them into the truck, at which time there were so many bodies that we had to have a mass grave. To dig a big hole with bulldozers when they were available and cover it up, and put lime on it. And that we intended to have the German guards do, both men and women. So, when I first saw the camp, the stench was beyond description, the camp itself was beyond description. The people were walking around without any idea where they were going, they were absolutely in a daze; one little girl came up to me and without any emotion whatsoever ... she said "My mother just died" and turned around and walked away just as if death was an everyday occurrence, and of course it was. But the conditions there ... it is awfully difficult to describe it, because I don't think ... Actually a picture can describe it, but words probably couldn't do it justice ...

We baked practically a truckload of bread the night before, and then the way we got the food for the inmates was voluntary contributions from the men who had received parcels from overseas, because we, ourselves, in our camp, were moving so fast that we didn't have adequate food. So they very kindly consented to contribute all of the extra things they had. And the smell of the bread caused an almost small riot when we drove into the camp, but rather than use the guards to control the people, we used the inmates who were coherent to control the people. Because, you could see that the inmates who were coherent, the first thing they wanted to do – after they had eaten – was to get revenge, and we didn't want a blood-bath in that camp at that particular time. So this took a little bit of diplomacy, and persuasion.

My men were extremely compassionate, and we had discussed immediately upon entering the camp, that this is no time to show emotion, the job was to find the living and to save and bury the dead, and feed the people who could eat. So whatever emotion we had, we tried to hide very much. Our job was to just save the living. But, as far as my commanding officer was concerned, I had no instructions. And there were no instructions he could give me, because he had never been there, and he didn't know what the situation was. So, we did what we thought we had to do, and we did it on our own, and apparently it was the right thing to do ...

We knew that we should not give them too much at one time. So, again, the coherent inmates came into play at that particular time. We put the responsibility of the welfare of the other inmates, somewhat upon their shoulders too. And we told them, we are here to save them, not to kill them. So, let us just give what we think they ought to have, and then we had a couple of nurses and a couple of doctors who offered help, but of course, it wasn't enough.

The living quarters for them was just beyond belief. They just had enough room to lie flat, they couldn't even turn around during the night, if they had to or wanted to in their sleep. Just enough room to lie there and nothing else. And ... the conditions we found there for example, the sanitary conditions were just. .. well, there just weren't any. Some of the people had lost complete respect ... and I went into one of the huts or barracks as they called it, and here is a man and a woman urinating and defecating in the corner, and everybody is talking and they pay no attention. Their self-respect had been stripped. And they were just walking around in a state of shock, and had no feeling, and no concern, just waiting to die ...

[Afterwards people] were reluctant to discuss it, because they felt that even though they had been there, and did what they did, which

Figure 37. Dysentery with no facilities at Bergen-Belsen. Stuart A. Rose
Manuscript, Archives and Rare Book Library, Emory University.

was great, they didn't know how anybody would believe the conditions they would describe because it was beyond a human comprehension without actually photographic evidence. So, of course they were
touched, and we all got a leave after that. We went away ...

I wouldn't say [we were] unable to cope with it, but we had to watch
our men pretty closely too, because of the emotion that could be cultivated there, and there was one instance where my right hand man
almost went out of control when he had detailed some of the German
guards, or Hungarian guards, to pick the bodies up and put them in the
truck. He was smoking a cigarette, and I remember this very vividly,
and one of the guards, the German guards on the truck, saw him flick
his cigarette butt away, and wanted to get off the truck and pick up the
butt. The last thing my man wanted to give these people was anything
at all. And when he saw that, he made a move toward his pistol, and I
was there, and I said, just hold it, let's don't start anything. We've got a
job to do, and that's the only instance I had with my people where they
might have gotten out of control.

... This situation could have been prevented, and as said before
when they have the same situation here [in the United States], although

everybody thinks that it is impossible, but they thought the same thing in Germany. They thought it was impossible. In other words, it can't happen to us ... it can only happen to "them." This is a bad attitude to have. I believe that people in Germany, more or less, brought it upon themselves; sure I feel sorry for them and hope it never happens again, but I believe the people themselves can prevent these things from happening if they have the courage to do so and will speak out and nip it in the bud before it gets a good hold on the nation. Any nation, whatever it may be ...

I believe we have an obligation to ourselves, we have an obligation to our fellow human beings, and again this goes back to education. I believe that if we have enough people who went through this thing and say what they saw, they can go out and talk to the people. This would make a big difference in the years to come ... We could stop these people from saying "it can't happen here." They said that in Germany and it did happen ...

Source: Special Collections, Woodruff Library, Emory University. Interview by Ruth Scheinberg (7 August 1980).

SAUL STEIN

Royal Canadian Air Force, 126 Wing

Saul Stein was born on 7 April 1916 in Montreal, Québec. He grew up speaking English, Yiddish, and French. His parents were immigrants to Montreal from Vilnius. His father, Richard, was a tailor who passed away when Stein was just an infant. As a widow, his mother, Sarah, raised six children. Stein never finished school as he had to work to help sustain the family.[13]

The family attended synagogue regularly, and Stein went to Hebrew school. Prior to the war, he worked in a mail-order house in Montreal. In 1941 Stein enlisted in the Royal Canadian Air Force. He was trained in St. Thomas and Toronto, Ontario, and later in Brandon, Manitoba. In 1942 he was sent overseas to Bournemouth, England, and was assigned to 126 Wing of the Royal Canadian Air Force, servicing aircraft as a mechanic.

In June 1944 Stein arrived in France with 126 Wing and was stationed at Bény-sur-Mer. The wing later moved to Belgium, the Netherlands, and then finally into Germany. In April 1945, as a leading aircraftman, he entered the Bergen-Belsen concentration camp with four colleagues.[14] They brought food into the camp. Stein wrote a letter to his family back home in Montreal about his encounter with the camp. After being stationed in Germany, he returned to England, where he was discharged.

Stein returned from overseas in 1945. In 1948 he married Pearl (née Zuker), daughter of Louis Zuker, a prominent Zionist. He and his wife had two children, a daughter named Rea and a son named Sheldon. The couple opened a shoe store called Styne's in Saint-Laurent, a borough of Montreal. Upon his retirement, Stein attended synagogue every morning as Judaism became central to his life. He passed away in Montreal on 27 November 2003 at the age of eighty-seven.

Interview

The first I heard of [Belsen] was when this Jewish Chaplain from Britain came in [to our squadron] ... he was looking for all kinds of food, [to see] if we had any, and for some help, which we [later] organized. He wanted to get enough food to come and feed these people – what you call survivors – I don't know if they were survivors at that time because they were just lying in the gutter in Belsen.

So, we collected a lot of parcels that we had received from home; usually the Baron de Hirsch were sending parcels all the time to some of the veterans overseas ...[15] [We collected] chocolate, cigarettes, and all kinds of food, salamis and things like that. So we took it and they couldn't eat it anyway, how could they, they were skeletons. We took it in trucks and it was maybe an hour's ride or so [to the camp]. We had our flight lieutenant with us, so there was no problem getting into the camp ...

We drove into this camp and the first sign we see said "Danger: Typhus." And then when we got in there we had to be deloused on the account of whatever was going on there ... There were [Hungarian] guards [present], and when I walked in, I still remember this: a beautiful woman [dead] in the gutter ... [legs] like a skeleton. It shook me up. I walked through some of the barracks, I had these [Canadian] fellas with me – I wouldn't walk alone ... the dead lay along the gutter ... The other sad part of it is when you see those other German prisoners-of-war picking up those bodies, one with the leg and the other with the head, and just throwing them on the truck as if they were a bag of flour or something ... They put the bodies on a truck and dumped them into a pit. They had to clean up that camp. They picked them up from the gutter; they made [the Germans] do it with their bare hands. They

picked them up by their legs, by their hands, and just threw them up on
the truck and then dumped them in the pit – what else could you do?
You couldn't bury them [individually]. It made me feel shook up, quite
a bit. But, I was just a kid.

The camp smelled [terrible]. Human bodies were lying on the ground
[rotting]. There were people [still alive] in the barracks. You could see
them sticking their heads out, pleading to get them out of there. And
that was up to the army to get them out of there. I had nothing to do
with that. Like I said, I just looked at them. I couldn't do nothing for
them ...

We had to take [the supplies] back. We couldn't eat it or anything because it was coming from the camp because [the survivors] couldn't eat
it. So, there was nothing for them to eat. They hadn't eaten maybe for
many years [with any regularity] ... [The authorities] told me that [the
food] wasn't going to do them any good because they are just a bag of
bones and whatever was left of them, so they couldn't give it to them.

From what I understand, it wasn't only Jews [in Bergen-Belsen].
There was French, some from Holland; it was a mixture, it wasn't all
the Jews ... [The rest of the men I was with] took [the experience] more
or less like I did: when we came out of there and when we discussed it
when we got back to [our] camp. I was glad that they came to the camp
with me. I was glad they got to see what was going on there. They
were really shocked .... I am pretty sure [the people from the surrounding area] knew about the camp. If they were close by, they must have
known ...

We went in, we looked around, saw what was going on and we did
our job and we came out – that's all. There was nothing else we could
do ... I spoke to a lot of the other [Canadian] boys there [about it when
I got back to base] ... and they felt just as bad as what I was describing
to them. [And when I returned to Montreal] I showed pictures [of the
camp]. It was very easy, you didn't have to convince these people what
it was all about because they knew what was going on; it was in the papers. They found it very interesting when I was talking about to them
and telling them about this camp.

I am not here [telling my story] for the glory of it. I don't want no
publicity. I am telling you the facts: what I was doing, where I was,
what I saw. Things like that, you know? That everybody else should
know about it.

I can honestly say that I am not the least bit sorry that I joined [the
RCAF] voluntarily. What I saw sort of [shed light] on what went on at
that particular time of the war. So, I came out of there with a lot of experience. And it's still with me. I cannot forget about it. It still comes back

to you: what you saw, what you did. And the fact is that you were able to come back and talk about it.

Source: USC Shoah Foundation Video Archive (Interview Code: 54699). Interview by Richard Hancox. Interview date: 3 June 1999.

Letter

Somewhere in Germany – April 30, 1945

Dear Brothers and Sisters,
I am writing this letter to each and every one of you at home and also my friends. After what I have seen and experienced yesterday has left me completely heartbroken. It is something that will forever remain in my mind. As you know the Allies are overrunning Germany today and as they pass on they are liberating concentration camps and prisoner of war camps. This is what I want you to know[,] that your brother Saul was the first Canadian Jewish boy to enter a concentration camp filled with Jews. It was also the first concentration camp the Allies liberated.[16] The name of the camp [is Bergen-Belsen and] it is one of the largest the Germans had. It is a long story how I got to know this camp. I do not expect to derive any publicity from this but I will only give you a few facts about this camp.

After three and one half years I have finally found out for myself what I am fighting for, to liberate our own Jewish people and other nationalities. Our Jewish padre from 2nd T.A.F. came to see us Thursday night and the first thing he said to the Jewish boys [is] that he needs help. He described the picture to us but after a while broke down. We gave him whatever food we had and he left for the camp to feed a few people. The next day we made a collection of food, candy, and cigarettes from our wing. The donations were tremendous and everyone gave what they had with their full heart and soul. It took myself, our Protestant padre and another Jewish lad to collect all the donations with my section's truck. By the time we got through the truck was loaded and it was impossible to pack in any more. In the evening the padre came back from the concentration camp and I showed him all the stuff. He was surprised to see how well response was from the wing.

The next morning we left for the camp. My boss and another lad from the office came along. They wanted to see what the inside of one of these places looked like. When we arrived there we had to wait a while before we could unload the food. Before entering the camp we had to be deloused with a spray gun as the place was full of lice. There was also a danger sign of "Typhus" which you know is a very dangerous disease but we all had inoculations against it.

While waiting the Jewish padre showed us around the camp. I have never yet seen so many people in all my life in one camp. There were dead bodies sprawled outside wherever we walked. Those who are living look practically dead and everyone is starving from hunger. The army is trying their utmost to clear out the camp and get them to hospitals. The main problem is food and medical supplies. I cannot begin to describe to you how grim the picture is. We have got to do something for these people immediately as they are dying like flies. Our own people must help them. I never [dreamed] that one day I would see such horrible scenes. I can't believe how there could be such a fanatic race as the bloody German people. The greatest pleasure I had in the camp was to see German prisoners load the dead and believe me the army is working the ass off them. This is just a few of the things which I can tell you, but when I get home I am going to see what I can do to help them. If only more people would see this camp they would realize how they were tortured by the Germans. I never slept all night thinking of that camp.

You were told all this [by] your brother who is there to see all this and who was the first one to visit a concentration camp. Kindly relate all this to Micky and see whether he can write an article in the "Y" Beacon. Cheerios for now and the best of luck. Hope to see you all soon.

Saul

Source: Montreal Holocaust Memorial Centre Archives, 2000.10.10, Saul Stein letter (30 April 1945). Gift from Saul Stein.

~

LYLE M. CREELMAN

Chief Nurse, British Zone, UNRRA

Considered by many to be Canada's most influential nurse in the twentieth century, Lyle Creelman helped elevate the standards of the profession both at home and internationally.[17] Born in 1908 in Upper

Stewiacke, Nova Scotia, Creelman was raised in the fishing community of Steveston, British Columbia. After earning a teaching certificate from normal school, she spent three years as an elementary school teacher, then earned a degree in nursing in 1936 from the University of British Columbia. Upon graduating she took a position as a nurse in Cranbrook before finding employment with the Metropolitan Health Committee in Vancouver.

In 1938 she was awarded a Rockefeller Fellowship to attend Teachers' College at Columbia University. She completed a master's degree in 1939, specializing in public health nursing administration. Returning to British Columbia, Creelman was appointed director of public health nursing with the Metropolitan Vancouver Health Committee. She also became the president of the Registered Nurses Association of British Columbia.

In 1944 Creelman joined the United Nations Relief and Rehabilitation Administration.[18] She was first stationed in England but was then invited to become the chief nurse of the British Zone in occupied Germany. Her main task was to organize nursing services in the zone, a complex assignment that was necessary to take care of some of the millions of displaced persons across Europe.

Contending with the nursing issues at Belsen Hospital (renamed Glyn Hughes Hospital) became a primary occupation for Creelman. Staff were recruited from a variety of locations. Indeed, nurses from a range of countries worked at Belsen Hospital, including at least six Canadians. Muriel Knox Doherty, principal matron at the hospital, frequently came into conflict with Creelman, often over the latter's employment of German nurses, particularly for the care of Jewish patients.[19] Perhaps as a result of the heavy criticism, Creelman went on to pioneer specialized nurses' training programs in the British Zone, assisting and teaching young women in displaced persons camps so that they could provide their own medical care to those in need.

After two years of working overseas, Creelman returned to Vancouver and to the Metropolitan Health Committee. However, she was granted an immediate leave in order to serve as the field director of an extensive study of public health services in Canada, which was being conducted by the Canadian Public Health Association. Along with Dr. J.H. Baillie, in 1950 Creelman co-authored what became known as the "Ballie-Creelman Report," a landmark study that "fundamentally influenced the provision of public-health care in Canada and functioned as the central reference for the preparation of public-health professionals in Canada."[20]

Creelman later became a nursing consultant in maternal and child health in the then recently established World Health Organization (WHO).

In 1954 she became the WHO's chief nursing officer, a position she would hold for fourteen years. Following her retirement in 1968, Creelman was commissioned by the WHO to study maternal and child health services in Southeast Asia.[21]

She was the recipient of numerous honours, including the Medal of Service of the Order of Canada (1971), the Canadian Centennial Medal (1967), and honorary doctorate degrees from both the University of New Brunswick (1963) and the University of British Columbia (1992). Lyle Creelman passed away on 27 February 2007 at the age of ninety-eight.

Diary

On Thursday [July] 19th we left for Belsen. A very nice drive up. Did a rapid survey. Found Dr. [T.B.] Layton conducting a mastoid clinic for Belgian students![22] There were 162 patients in the large room in the Round House. Nursing very poor. We have visited three times since. Dr. Layton muddles things with the military. Miss Doherty is not much better.[23] Worried too much about the small details. Got from her the number of nurses she wanted, and started to send out signals for them. Have managed to secure 14 for her but they are certainly slow in coming forward. Also the American Zone opened up and all the nurses seemed to go there from Granville. When we were there last Sun. we went through the Hospital. The military have been doing a little bit of re-organization at the last moment before they hand over to us. There has been no seg-regation of patients, T.B.'s mixed in with all the rest. The Q.A. [Queen Alexandrea nurses] have not done a very good job. Have shown no interest. The work is done by 117 German and Latvian nurses who sleep in a large attic room over one wing of the hospital. [They] are really prisoners but conditions are terrible for their living. If a little more con-sideration is shown to them I am sure they will respond and will carry on the nursing job with very little supervision from us. Miss [Doherty] says she wants 20 nurses but I think she will find she can manage with 11 or 12 at the most. That is for the hospital. When our activities expand we will have to have more staff. There are reported to be 500 pregnant women and girls in the camp of 14,000 people. It is hard to know whether this is an under or over-statement. I went through the maternity hospital which was reported as being very deplorable. It was not nearly as bad as expected and in this Miss Stenhouse agreed with me.

The trouble is people expect modern standards. True the babies were in the same room with their mothers, were wrapped in much too many clothes, but those are the customs of the people. Also the Roumanian woman Dr. took the babies in her arms and loved them, but

Figure 38. Lyle Creelman, right, with the matron at Belsen Hospital, Muriel
Knox Doherty. UBC 117.1 / 65p, University of British Columbia Archives.

perhaps that is not as bad as we think. Incidentally she is said to run a huge abortionist business. She was forced to kill some 5,000 babies at A—? the terrible horror camp.[24] After coming through such an experience one could hardly expect her to be very normal. Dr. Wheatley arrived last Sat. just when Sir Raphael [Cilento] was most discouraged following his discovery of some of the things Dr. Layton had done. Five nurses also arrived on Sun. so we came away feeling much more cheerful. Had a lovely trip back. – On our return from our first trip to Belsen we were escorted by Major [William A.] Davis of the Rockefeller Found. Typhus Commission. He took us to call on a lady friend of his who had been a typhus patient in Belsen. She was supposed to be a Hungarian Dr. Was also a journalist. Had Major Davis completely fooled. Just the other day she wrote a letter to Sir Raphael asking for a job with UNRRA. On the way home we got stuck in the mud in one of the diversions off the Autobahn. Had to be pulled out by the jeep. Sir Raphael told the story several times in the mess and was called over the coals for being out with me unarmed! He has since obtained a revolver. The next day Major Davis took me to tea at the Major's mess. Always intended to return but never had the time.

... Our next visit was to Munster near Soltau. The M.O. [medical officer] of this team was a Frenchman, Dr. Bianquis and the nurse, Miss Lazecko. She was rather unhappy in her team. The camp population had been greatly reduced recently and she felt there was not sufficient work to do. The French doctor was not very energetic and I had the impression that the initiative in the whole program had been taken by the Nurse. Arranged for Miss Lazecko to be transferred elsewhere following her leave. Went on to Belsen that evening where we were joined by Sir Raphael. At that time the three nurses mentioned were the only English speaking nurses of 30 Corps and I had hoped that they would all be of the caliber for Supervisors. It turned out that none of them were. Miss Inglis was subsequently transferred to Belsen and has now resigned. Miss Lazecko, having returned from her leave is now in Belsen and will be available for another hospital position should one develop ...

Source: University of British Columbia Archives: Lyle Creelman Fonds, Box 2-2: 1944–1945 Record of Service with UNRAA.

Report

UNRRA HQ.,
H.Q.,

B.A.O.R.
10th October 1945
To: Dr. Phillips, Chief Medical Officer
From: Miss Creelman, Chief Nurse
Subject: Nursing Personnel for Belsen-Falling Bostel

1 Belsen Hospital
The present UNRRA nursing staff at this Hospital, including the
Matron, numbers 13. This represents a reduction of four during
the period since UNRRA has taken over the Hospital. At first a
considerable amount of organisation was necessary in the nursing
programme. The German nursing staff, of which there is now 134,
(only 19 of whom are untrained nurses), has greatly improved, and
we can at any time exchange unsatisfactory members of this staff, by
arrangement with Miss Heaney of C.C.G. There are also ten Latvian
nurses, only two of whom are unqualified.

On Sunday, October 7th – the bed state of Belsen was 380.

It would seem that the nursing staff is very high at this Hospital
in relation to conditions existing elsewhere, even though it is rec-
ognised that Belsen Hospital must receive special consideration
in regard to staffing by UNRRA personnel. It is recommended
therefore:

a The present staff of UNRRA nurses be reduced to 8 (including the
  Matron)
b The post of Assistant Matron be abolished. This post was never
  made officially but has been in effect since the programme started.
c That the matter of further reduction be left open for consideration at
  a later date.

1 Belsen Camp – 21,000 D.PS.
For the development of the Public Health Nursing programme in
this Camp, it is recommended that –

1 Three UNRRA Public Health nurses be appointed, one of these
  nurses to be in charge.
2 The nurse in charge under the direction of the Chief Nurse of the
  Zone, to plan the Public Health Nursing programme in accordance
  with medical policies and to select sufficient D.P. qualified nursing
  personnel and assistant nursing personnel, as are needed.
3 If sufficient numbers of such D.P. personnel are not available, the
  following procedure be adopted:

a Transfer of such personnel from other situations where there may be
an excess number.
b The selection and training of suitable personnel.

Source: United Nations Archive, S-0408-0043, File 3: Nursing Personnel for
Belsen-Falling Bostel by Lyle Creelman (10 October 1945).

Article

LONG before VE-Day (May 8, 1945), which marked the end of the war
in Europe, it was recognized that there were many problems of peace
which must be dealt with on an international basis, and preferably by
an international organization.

The most urgent of these was the task of caring for the millions
of people of many nationalities who had been displaced from their
homes by actual war; had fled before the enemy; had been offered the
alternative of compulsory work in Germany or starvation; had been
the victims of political or religious pressure; or had been part of the
huge deliberate transfer of populations that, particularly in Poland
and the Baltic States, had been carried out for political reasons. For
all these people there was the problem of immediate relief, necessary
rehabilitation and, ultimately, repatriation. For some there was no possibility of repatriation, and to the problem of relief and rehabilitation
had to be added the possibility of resettlement, temporary or permanent, in some hospitable land.

The United Nations Relief and Rehabilitation Administration –
UNRRA, as it soon came to be called – was set up to undertake this
gigantic task, and, immediately upon the unconditional surrender of
Germany, it was called upon to provide as rapidly as possible spearhead teams, complete units, and later specialized services to aid the
army. These were finally to be welded into a semi-independent, co-
operative agency. The earliest members were in operation even before
the fall of Germany, striving to do whatever could be done among
the masses of refugees, displaced persons, and hordes of allied and
enemy civilians who literally in millions crowded the roads of western
Germany.

There has never been any accurate estimate of the total number of
displaced persons at that time in this area, but figures of from six to
eleven millions have been quoted, and undoubtedly the truth lies between these – nearer the upper than the lower figure. All had suffered
much in mind and body. They had been uprooted from their homes,
and did not know if they would ever live to return or, indeed, if there

would be a free homeland to which they could return. Many were separated from their families and often ignorant of their fate or only too
well aware of it. Most of them were wretchedly ill-clad, hungry and
deprived of all sources of regular food.

It was into this massive and somewhat terrifying confusion of people and problems that I was asked by the UNRRA chief medical officer
in the British Zone in Germany to accompany him as chief nurse (June
11, 1945). My immediate reaction, when asked to organize the nursing
service of UNRRA for the displaced persons operation in the British
Zone of Germany, was an eager desire to accept the job, and a great
happiness at having some small part in this tremendous undertaking.

Getting Ready

The inevitable delays associated with the collection of the necessary
office staff, equipment and, above all, transport; the many formalities
that had to be dealt with in respect of passports, travel orders, and all
the essential but irksome red-tape associated with visiting what was
still an enemy country under immediate military guard, occupied
a month. Finally, all was ready, and the chief medical officer, and I,
a secretary, two drivers, and two new cars proceeded from London
to Purfleet, boarded an Army LST and set out in convoy to cross the
Channel – rendered dangerous just then by a heavy storm in the
North Sea which had caused thousands of mines to break loose and
float along the ocean fairways.

At a snail's pace we crossed the Channel, and made a landing at the
ruined harbour of Ostend. What a thrill to set foot for the first time on
the continent of Europe; but what a tragedy to behold the bombed and
ruined buildings of that well-known port! Then came all the orderly
disorder of disembarkation and, in an hour or so, we were driving towards Brussels where already, the Belgians, freed from the nightmare
of years of occupation by the enemy, were spreading an air of resolute
gaiety through their streets and cafes.

In Germany

Special road maps with marked and numbered routes leading from
Brussels in Belgium to Bad Oyenhausen in Germany, the centre for the
moment of the HQ of the 21st Army Group, BLA, offered alternative
routes to our destination. We chose the one that ran through Louvain –
scene of massacre and destruction in 1914 and later – across the Dutch
border and on to Hatert, Nijmegen, and Arnhem, across the Rhine into

Germany through Emmerich and Bocholt to Munster, and then by
way of Rheda, Bielefeld, and Herford to Bad Oyenhausen.

At Hatert we had our first opportunity of meeting a large group of
UNRRA people waiting, in what had formerly been a prisoner-of-war
camp, for allocation to their various posts. Nijmegen had a particular interest to me as a Canadian for in the early morning (we spent
the second night there) I walked through the debris of the terribly
bombed streets to see the important bridge which the Canadians had
so gallantly and successfully defended. It was a curious sensation
to be actually in Germany, and to see the tremendous destruction of
towns like Bocholt, hardly more than a mass of rubble; the notices on
trees, fences, and so forth, warning of bombs, giving stern orders and
prohibitions in English and German and, occasionally, ending with the
grim words "Penalty – Death." In spite of its ruined houses and heaps
of broken bricks, it was difficult to imagine that this beautiful farming
country, where women, children, and a few men were working in the
fields and harvesting the crops without the aid of machinery and farm
animals, had so recently been the scene of the most savage fighting in
the world.

As we proceeded, the devastation became even more intense. I shall
never forget the drive through Munster, which was the first major city
en route and which, being an important railway centre, had been a
special target for the R.A.F. They had certainly done their job well! At
Rheda we joined one of Hitler's famous highways – the autobahn –
leading from Cologne to Berlin, and on that beautiful surface quickly
reached Bad Oyenhausen to report for duty.

Establishing Headquarters

It is not necessary to tell the story of the establishment of our headquarters; the collection of information relative to conditions in the field;
the locating of our personnel already on duty there; the winning of the
confidence of the military authorities who were in sole command; and
attempting always to carry out a constructive and co-operative program. Eventually, by much hard work and by the great administrative
skill of our Zone Director, Sir Raphael Cilento, who had originally gone
out as chief medical officer, opposition was overcome and a sound
administrative structure gradually took shape. On November 27, 1945,
an agreement – the first in the three zones and the one on which agree-
ments in the French and American Zones were subsequently based –
was signed between UNRRA and the Commander-in-Chief and
Military Governor of the British Zone of German – none other than

Field Marshal Montgomery. In this agreement, responsibilities of the Occupation Authorities and UNRRA respectively were, for the first time, set out on a mutually satisfactory basis.

The British Zone of Occupation in Germany – one of the four into which the country was divided – comprises the northwestern and central western parts of Germany from the Danish border south to Cologne, and from the Dutch and Belgian borders eastwards as far as Lubeck in the north and Helmstedt in the south (Gottingen is in the British Zone and Cassel in the American). It covers an area about the size of England without Wales. Situated in it are the great coal-mining areas and the former centres of German industry. The area was said to contain some twenty-two million Germans, and when the war ceased there were over three million displaced persons in this British Zone alone. At the time of our arrival the number had fallen to 860,000 who were scattered over the country in nearly four thousand camps within approximately eight hundred "assembly centres."

Assembly Centres

The distribution of these camps was largely an accidental matter. In the early stages, units of the British Army, seizing towns and bringing under control every German area, had "frozen" all collections of displaced persons and had attempted gradually to assemble these into larger and larger groups. Within a few months, with UNRRA assistance, there were 210 of these assembly centres, comprising slightly more than 800 camps and, within a year, they had fallen to a total of 160, of which UNRRA controlled directly 104. UNRRA teams as they reached the Field – and 250 had been sent for most urgently – were allocated each to a small army unit and worked under the direct control of the responsible officer, whether he was a colonel or merely a lieutenant. They had, at the beginning, no contact at all with other UNRRA units and no relation to the headquarters unit. Correction of this situation was one of the first requirements.

Each team consisted of a director, various administrative and clerical officers, a doctor, a nurse, a welfare officer, supply officers, cooks, etc., with such increases as were necessary depending upon the number of displaced persons under the care of each team.

The refugees and displaced persons – DPs, as they were called – were collected in the assembly centres and might be as few as 1,500 or as many as 20,000. Naturally enough, the shelter provided was inadequate from the standpoint of room space, sanitation, and warmth, but, considering that the occupation authorities were also responsible for housing their own troops and for providing shelter for the thousands of German refugees who kept pouring into the Zone from the east, the accommodation provided was the best available. In this, as in many other instances, the occupation authorities did magnificent work under great difficulties.

Many of the assembly centres were established in what had formerly been German barracks. These were undoubtedly best from the point of view of sanitation, ease of administration, and general living conditions. Psychologically, however, the effect was not good for, necessarily, thousands of people were crowded together under conditions all too similar to those they had experienced during the war as prisoners or forced laborers. The crowded conditions also contributed to the spread of airborne and parasitic diseases, to which further reference will be made later. On the other extreme, there were numbers of centres consisting of many scattered camps quite long distances apart. One assembly centre, for example, contained nineteen camps, the furthest of which from north to south were twenty-five kilometres apart and the furthest from east to west were sixteen kilometres apart! While the objections of overcrowding and concentration camp conditions were not present, lack of transport made delivery of supplies and administrative supervision extremely difficult. A very few centres were established in German villages, which had been taken over completely, or almost completely, by the DPS themselves. This was, of course, the most natural set-up, because programs could be developed precisely as they can in any village community. The disadvantage in this type of assembly centre was that people were so comfortable and so well cared for that they hesitated to leave such surroundings even to return to their homeland, since the homeland itself had become an unknown and distant country.

Immediate Problems

The immediate problems were three in number. The first and most urgent was to meet the threat of epidemic diseases; the second was to take over from the army some of its responsibilities in respect to displaced persons, really a civilian job; the third was to build up a proper administrative structure to which the army could, with confidence, hand over these responsibilities.

Danger of Epidemics

As mentioned above, overcrowding and poor sanitation, a gross lack of equipment and hospital facilities, and insufficiently trained junior personnel made airborne and parasitic diseases continual threats. Typhus, typhoid fever, diphtheria, scarlet fever, skin diseases – particularly scabies – tuberculosis, and venereal diseases were all of major importance; epidemics of typhoid and typhus were sweeping some areas; diphtheria of a very fatal type had been prevalent at the end of 1944, and it was feared might again become dangerously common. Scarlet fever was already beginning to show itself. Scabies was prevalent owing to the scarcity of soap, the great difficulty in obtaining ointment for treatment, and the crowding that provided great numbers of cases, all of which prevented immediate treatment and so permitted continued reinfection.

The first attack was made upon the typhus situation, particularly in those areas that constituted the border with the Russian Zone. Since European typhus is a louse-borne disease, the chief measure for control was the use of DDT. As it was impossible to control the movements of DPs, it was necessary to see that on every arrival and departure they were treated by dusting. Though the work was very imperfectly done, there is no doubt that it kept the incidence of typhus to a minimum, and prevented the epidemics which might so easily have occurred.

There were no facilities for immunization against scarlet fever, and it ran its course, but immunization against diphtheria and typhoid was started early. It was felt that if from one-third to one-half of the susceptible portions of the community were successfully immunized, no epidemic would result, or, if cases did occur, they would "smoulder" in the community rather than "blaze." This proved to be the case. Since the main period of typhoid incidence was in the spring, inoculation against this disease was made secondary to diphtheria, but the routine of typhus, diphtheria, and then typhoid was not always as clear-cut as this sounds.

Flying squads had been sent into the area earlier for the purpose of picking up wandering DPs and bringing them to assembly centres or, if necessary, to hospitals or feeding stations. This plan was very soon exhausted by the fact that the DPs were cleared from the roads, and the flying squads became of great value in the immunization campaign. Many team doctors and nurses had little knowledge of, or interest in, the public health aspects of the medical care program and often, as a result of their inertia, and also owing to the difficulty of obtaining supplies, the initiative in immunizing was taken by the flying squads. Finally, they were charged to deal directly with this situation, the squads being reorganized and each being provided with a doctor and two medical attendants. They visited the assembly centres and, with the assistance of the team doctor and nurse, demonstrated the method and gave the first series of inoculations. A follow-up visit was made later to see that the program was continued, and to give any necessary assistance.

Hospitals and Sick Bays

The second part of the program – taking over responsibilities from the army – consisted (1) in taking over the Belsen hospital and, ultimately, several other activities; and (2) in establishing proper medical facilities and sick bays in all assembly centres, with a gradual building up towards larger installations in the central sites. A sick bay had to be set up in each centre, sometimes more than one if the camps making up the assembly centre were far apart. One of the major difficulties was the lack of transport and the consequent slowness in receipt of supplies. Each UNRRA team went out equipped with a certain quantity of supplies, but these did not stretch very far in the setting up of sick bays and clinics. The military government and the officers in charge of the various units were very generous if they had supplies on hand. The DPs themselves had secret sources of information, and were quite adept at providing the necessary items of equipment and drugs. No questions were asked as to the source!

From the sick bay, anyone who was really ill was sent to the nearest German hospital, in which a certain number of beds were reserved for DPs and were kept under the supervision of the UNRRA personnel. All maternity cases were supposed to be hospitalized in this manner, but frequently the baby was well on the way before the doctor or the nurse was notified.

In the early days there was a great reluctance to report illness because of the fear of hospitalization. The cruel circumstances of the war had given the word "hospital" a dread significance to many of the DPs. It was only because of their confidence in the health worker and her explanation of the fact that by reporting the first sign of illness the need for hospital care might be averted, regular treatment facilities were ultimately established.

The British Red Cross Society had five hospitals caring for displaced persons, and, by arrangement, some hospitals – known as "DP hospitals" – were established and staffed almost entirely by DP personnel. The standards of medical and nursing care in some of the latter were adequate, but, in many, conditions were really alarming. It was very difficult to assess the qualifications of the so-called nurses, and in some hospitals probably not more than one or two of the "nursing" staff had ever had any form of professional training.

The first major activity taken over from the army was the Glynn Hughes Hospital at Belsen, the notorious Nazi concentration camp which became known throughout the world as a byword for atrocity. When this camp was liberated in April, 1945, there were thousands of sick and dying persons, and the magnificent work done by British Army doctors and nurses, and particularly that of Colonel Glynn Hughes for whom this hospital was renamed, is well known. The hospital had been established at Belsen in the building which had formerly served as a hospital for German officers. It was a 500-bed hospital, containing at the highest occupancy 900 patients; at the time it was taken over by us it had 690 patients. It was staffed by German doctors and nurses, under the supervision of British officers and nursing sisters. It was a condition of the transfer that the German staff should be retained, and that the UNRRA doctors and nurses would act in a supervisory capacity. There were 7 German doctors and 134 German nurses, of whom 119 were fully qualified. This hospital had a greater number of nurses per patient and a greater proportion of qualified nurses to unqualified nurses than any other hospital I visited in Germany. The care given the patients was of good quality, but Belsen had acquired a notoriety that caused it constantly to be a subject of criticism. One must, in all fairness, say a word of praise for these German nurses, who gave excellent nursing care to the displaced persons under conditions which at times were most humiliating and most difficult. There was much criticism from many sources of the continued use of German personnel but, apart from the fact that this was the basis upon which the hospital had been transferred, it was not possible to obtain a sufficient number of qualified DP personnel in spite of the many statements made claiming that "hundreds" of qualified nurses were available. The very fact that it was the first large UNRRA responsibility made it necessary to maintain the highest possible standard under existing conditions.

Repatriation of DPs

The general objective of the whole program of UNRRA in Germany was the repatriation of displaced persons and, although resettlement for those who were unwilling to be repatriated became necessary, an extensive and successful drive was made early in 1946 to send home as many DPs as were willing to go. Army trucks were provided to take them and their luggage to the trains. By train they proceeded to one of the two transit camps established – either Lubeck, whence they went by boat to Gydinia in Poland, or Hesslingen, thence by train through the Russian Zone of Germany into Poland.

From the assembly centre to the transit camp the nurse had an important part to play in the repatriation program. To begin with, she was responsible, under the supervision of the doctor, to see that all DPs were dusted with DDT powder; that they were free from communicable disease; and that no person obviously ill was included in the group. The nurse also had to be sure that the mothers had adequate supplies of food for infants and young children. Each train carried about twelve hundred DPs and one nurse and two nurse aides travelled to the transit camp with each train group. The nurse took with her a first-aid kit and an emergency maternity kit. Although no woman more than six months pregnant was permitted to be included in the departing group, it was sometimes found that if the husband was going the expectant mother managed to sneak into the repatriation train! At all rest stations and feeding halts the nurse and her assistants travelled the whole length of the train, checking especially on the condition of mothers and young babies. This service was greatly appreciated by the DPs, who felt that there was someone who was taking a real interest in their welfare until they left the tragic soil of Germany. The Flying Squads, it may be mentioned, serviced the feeding halts, and also provided a small dispensary for the distribution of medical necessities. At the transit camp at Lubeck, or Hesslingen, there was a waiting period of from twenty-four hours to several days. Here a well organized nursing service was provided to care for them while in camp and to meet in advance the possible needs for the remainder of the journey. After the transit camps, UNRRA personnel relinquished the care of the DPs to their own countrymen and were permitted to accompany them no further.

Many Nations

I cannot conclude without mentioning the nursing representatives of other organizations working in the British Zone. The British Red Cross Society, while working under the sponsorship of UNRRA, was responsible for the administration of a certain number of assembly centres and, as mentioned previously, controlled a number of hospitals for the care of DPs. The principal matron of the British Red Cross Society and all her staff were most capable and co-operative colleagues. One of the centres for the nurse aide course previously mentioned was located in the Red Cross hospital at Darup. There, the staff, in addition to providing facilities for instruction, took a very great personal interest in the DP girls, an important contribution both to their instruction and their rehabilitation. Attached to the Control Commission for Germany (British Element) were two principal nursing advisers, whose responsibility it was to help rebuild the Germany nursing services. As UNRRA nursing adviser, it was my privilege to establish a Nursing Advisory Committee, of which the principal nurses of these two organizations were members. From them much helpful advice was obtained in various aspects of the nursing programs and they kept us informed also of developments in their own services – there was, in fact, a mutual interchange of information that was most valuable.

Since I left Germany, the policy of turning over as much as possible of the work of the nursing service to the DP nurses and nurse-aide personnel has been continued, and the reduced staff of UNRRA nurses has acted more and more in supervisory and administrative capacities. In some small measure, we hope and believe, this has enabled many of the displaced persons to escape the sense of frustration which was so apparent among them, and to undertake something constructive not only to themselves, but something that permitted them to contribute quite obviously and satisfactorily to the welfare of their own groups. We hope, also, that what they have learned professionally will be of value to them when they return to their homeland or settle ultimately in some new country and that, on the bases that have been established, they will continue to build further.

For the UNRRA nurses from the many countries represented, this unusual experience, which we trust need never be rejected in human history, has been, indeed, a most gratifying and interesting one. It was an opportunity to give service to people in dire need, and it was most satisfying to see the immediate results of one's personal work under circumstances of such urgency. In addition, the contact with nurses and other professional workers from the various countries, and the study of their standards and methods was most stimulating – it was an opportunity, indeed, to examine and revise one's own methods. Further, as a Canadian, I am glad to be able to say – as I think it should be said – that there was great satisfaction in realizing that the professional standards in our own country are second to none in the world.

Source: Creelman, "With the UNRRA in Germany."

JOHN W. THOMPSON

Royal Canadian Air Force, 8402 Disarmament Wing

John West Thompson was born on 8 May 1906 in Mexico City. His American-born father and Mexican-born mother married in 1900 and had six children. During the First World War, Thompson and his older brother were sent back to the United States to live with their paternal grandmother and to continue their education. They attended Palo Alto Intermediate School and later Union High School.[25]

In 1924, Thompson attended Stanford University. Upon graduation, in 1928 he enrolled in the medical program at the University of Edinburgh in Scotland. He received a clinical appointment in psychiatry in Edinburgh and then took on research positions at Harvard and Massachusetts General Hospital, where he studied physiology.

In 1940, in support of the war effort, Thompson moved to Canada to study the physiology of emotions and breathing patterns of pilots under stress. He subsequently enlisted in the Royal Canadian Air Force. In January 1944, he became medical liaison officer of the Joint Services Medical Intelligence Organization.

Thompson was sent overseas as part of the 8402 Disarmament Wing, where his job was to evaluate German aviation equipment. While based in Celle, Germany, Thompson encountered the Bergen-Belsen concentration camp. He treated the survivors of the camp for several months. He also interrogated Dr. Fritz Klein, who worked at Bergen-Belsen and had conducted experiments with mescaline and Rutenol while stationed at Auschwitz. Thompson's experiences at Bergen-Belsen became a turning point in his life.[26]

In September 1945 Thompson was assigned to the Field Information Agency Technical (FIAT) research group. Their goal was to secure military, scientific, and technical intelligence. Thompson and his team called attention to what he deemed medical war crimes and collected documentation regarding medical experiments ordered by Heinrich Himmler and others.

In December 1945, Thompson informed the British War Crimes Executive at Nuremberg that a significant number of doctors in Germany were involved in unethical research. The "Doctors' Trial" at Nuremberg, influenced by Thompson's research and persistence, was held between December 1946 and August 1947. Twenty-three German physicians and administrators were tried for their participation in war crimes and crimes against humanity. Ultimately, sixteen of the doctors were found guilty and seven were sentenced to death.

In the 1950s Thompson lived at Eau Vive, a Catholic religious and educational retreat near Paris. He worked for United Nations Educational, Scientific and Cultural Organization (UNESCO). In the late 1950s, he moved to New York to train psychiatric residents at Albert Einstein College of Medicine.

In 1965 Thompson vacationed in St. Thomas, one of the U.S. Virgin Islands, where on 18 August he drowned while snorkeling. He was fifty-nine years old.

Letter

Dear Karl,
It was a balm to receive your letter and to hear of mum. I need so much to hear of such things in order to maintain some grip on myself and on humanity itself. I am working with the people liberated from a concentration camp at Belsen. Can you imagine what that means? I myself have seen 8,000 women: typhus, starvation, despair. Oh God! God! Give me strength to carry on. I work among them from seven in the morning until far, far into the night. Sometimes my strength gives way and I must fall exhausted on the straw with them. Still I lose each day 20–30. I have scarcely any drugs. The patients are still on the most meagre of food supplies. More than half have open tuberculosis – there is no space to segregate them! I bring the shadow of a smile to some poor suffering one. I feel encouraged but then I turn and see thousands of others and I need to call on every nerve of courage to continue. It requires courage, Karl. So much courage. Does this sound ill-becoming? I am far too tired to be critical of my own statements. All I know is that I can scarcely stagger from one end of this barn to another. Lying all about here are these people: their eyes watching each of my movements as though they expect that one of these movements would magically bring them food or relief. There is no magic for you my poor brethren. You must suffer and I must suffer with you. I shall try to find your friend but it is difficult, so difficult.
God be with you.

John

Source: Provided courtesy of the Karl Stern Archive at the Simon Silverman Phenomenology Center, Duquesne University, Pittsburgh, PA. Letter written ca. June–July 1945.

Speech

It would certainly be invidious of me to attempt to point out ... [the] moral implications of [the] Holocaust. It seems to me that it is a matter for each individual to decide and to come to terms with it, within the configurations of his own conscience.

Many times, since those dark days in Bergen-Belsen, I've been asked either to speak about it or to write about it, and as you see today, I've been ... utterly unable to put down anything in words. And when I find myself speaking to you, I find myself in a curious paradox, because I believe that what has happened is unspeakable, incommunicable. And I've often quoted, and I'll quote again, the only person who seems to me to have said something pertinent about that whole episode in the history of man. It comes from a review of a book written by a person who himself was an inmate in Auschwitz. He said, "The experience of the Holocaust in Europe defies language and leads to a mystique of silence or to madness itself."[27] The experience cannot be communicated, not truly communicated, one knows it only from within, where knowledge becomes an obsession. Survivors refrain from speech because they no longer believe in words. And there's the trap. One wants to communicate what happened and yet, in the very attempt one is defeated.

There is something happened there in Germany which was dark and black. It fell completely outside the human expectations of behavior; it's a point if I might say utterly outside the human curve. And I think this is the difficulty of facing it as such, something which, cannot be understood. Try as we might, we have to face simply its horror. Now, I've been taken to task and told that I'm evading, perhaps I am, perhaps that's the way of protecting myself. But I can only tell you what I have experienced, not in the factual episodes which would fall far short of what happens inside.

There is some terrible thing which we need to face and in trying to explain it, I failed. But only approximating it and I emphasize approximating it, I think it has something to do with the utter destruction, atomization of trust. When such things happen that vital element of the human being, to trust, vanishes, and subsequently, the individual in some sense has lost his biggest possession. Whoever who has lost trust has nothing more to lose. And it is those experiences, which happened in Germany, which go to the very root of trust and after that few can trust themselves and fewer still can trust others. It's a cancerous growth that starts in one social setting and finds its way into every tissue of the social structure.

I know that one has to study this by every means possible, but somehow, as I hear the facts being stated I'm aware of deep irony, that those
who have been destroyed, have to prove that they've been damaged. If a
person were to be exploded into atoms, by some high-explosive, would
the question be relevant "was the person damaged?" And have we the
knowledge to know how these now atomized pieces relate to one another? This dreadful symphony was written in a strange and alien key
and we've heard about the attempt on the part of some of the people
in Germany who defend themselves by denying it. We all must use, or
may be tempted to use one or another form of denial. And I somehow
sense, and I hope my colleagues, will not take this in any way as a criticism, but I somehow sense this terrible key in which that symphony
was written, is being transposed into a more familiar key. The attempt
is being made to translate what is utterly untranslatable, into something
which is more comfortable. That individuals who have been hurled into
that torrent, should drag themselves out and then be asked "were you
injured?" There are some things it seems to me, which must be instanta-
neously and immediately recognized, and not the subject of discussion.
Injustice is one. Unless we can bring ourselves to see that immediately
and not throw it into the realm of wonderment, I think we're lost. Unless
we can respond in some immediate way, to what is patently present, but
against which we are apt to defend ourselves, then this defense process
will continue, and the dark forces will have their way.

I think that we're all subject to the very same thing that happened in
Germany, however much we wish to deny it. That it happened there is
true, but that it's happening everywhere is also true. I had a long, two-
year debate with one of the accused at Nuremberg. This was a written
debate and I thought it was significant that with daily interchange it finally evolved that where he and I differed was that he attributed a finite
value to a single human being. Unless we live in such a way that we can
honestly say to ourselves that the single individual has infinite value; that
we are prepared to do everything possible to correct injustice to a single
person, I think the trend will continue until another Holocaust arrives.
We wait, and wait, and wait, until there are four, five, six, seven thousand
and millions being destroyed and then when we decide to act it is too
late. I don't think this is a question of Germany and concentration camps,
it is a human question and the answer to it does not reside, as I see it,
in physiological, biochemical, or anatomical studies. The answer resides
within ourselves, each one, and until we can stand in the middle of the
night and face that darkness and not lose trust, unless we can do that, I
see no hope for the future. But I believe that we can if we determine to
do so.

Source: John W. Thompson, speech at 1965 conference on the Holocaust. From the Tony Schwartz Collection, Library of Congress.

~

ELSIE MAY DEEKS

St. John's Ambulance Brigade

Elsie May Deeks was born on 7 May 1910 in Winnipeg, Manitoba, to parents Walter and Mary. Except for the war years, she lived her entire life on Ashburn Street in the west end of Winnipeg.[28] She had a sister, Beatrice, and a brother, Walter, who passed away in infancy. In her youth, Deeks went to Isaac Brock and Daniel McIntyre schools. She attended St. Patrick's and St. Jude's Anglican Church, where she remained a member throughout her life. Upon graduating high school, she was employed at Eaton's department store. Deeks worked at the camera counter, while her sister, Beatrice, worked in the stationary department.

During the Second World War, Deeks took leave from Eaton's to serve as a Voluntary Aid Detachment (VAD) worker with the St. John's Ambulance Brigade, an organization that has long provided first aid and emergency medical services around the world.[29] She was assigned as a welfare officer and attached to the 29th British General Hospital,[30] along with several other Canadians. Her team arrived at Bergen-Belsen in May 1945. In her letters home, Deeks notes that many of the haunting images in the camp could not simply be forgotten, including emaciated inmates, the worn-out crematoria, and the mass graves. According to Deeks, who suffered a bout of bronchitis while working at Bergen-Belsen, living conditions for some Allied personnel were dismal. Since so much of the camp was decrepit and unlivable, personnel from the 29th General Hospital were forced to sleep outside in tents, lying on top of sleeping bags and mattresses on the cold, damp spring ground as there was no room for cots. Deeks spent seven weeks working at Bergen-Belsen before being transferred to Hannover.

She returned to Canada in 1946, working briefly at St. John's College. She ultimately found employment with the Canadian federal government working in Indian Health Services. She retired in 1975. Deeks was a supporter of the arts in Winnipeg, including the Winnipeg Symphony Orchestra and Manitoba Theatre Centre. In addition, she was involved with the Federal Superannuates and the English Speaking Union. She was a lifelong member of Beta Sigma Phi Sorority, an organization that exposes women to social, cultural, and educational issues, which were unavailable to many at the time.

Deeks lived independently for much of her life.[31] She remained unmarried and had no children. In 2004 she moved into the Deer Lodge Centre in Winnipeg. She passed away the following year, 17 June 2005, at the age of ninety-five.[32]

Account

You could smell Belsen seventeen miles away. It was a peculiar odour, on the wind. The Germans had been burning bodies, but there were thousands and thousands of bodies decomposing, and they hadn't had time to cremate them.

I went into Germany from Belgium, as a welfare officer with the 29th British General Hospital, a 1,200-bed hospital. We were sent to Belsen in May 1945, just as the war ended. I was the only Canadian V.A.D.

When we got into Belsen, we were not allowed in for a week, until the British Army had removed all the bodies and burned the camp. Sometimes they said they couldn't tell the dead from the living.

When we were allowed in … I witnessed the burial. The bodies were put into pits dug by German prisoners of war, they were laid out, and lime was put on top of them. When we went in to the camp the Army made us wear hip waders, because of the ash – there was so much of it – and because of the vermin. We had to be hosed off whenever we left the camp.

The prisoners all wore pyjamas. It was a long, long time before I could look at a pair of blue-and-white striped pyjamas again. One of our jobs was to collect clothing for the prisoners. Harrods of London was what we called the clothing depot.

We lived outside the camp, under canvas, and to begin with there were two hundred of us, nurses and physiotherapists and V.A.D.s in one huge marquee. There was no room for our cots. We put our mattresses down on the canvas floor, and our sleeping bags on top. But the wet came through the canvas floor. It rained for four days after we arrived, poured down as if it would never stop. When the sun did come out, you could see the steam rising from this huge marquee. Later, though, we moved into tents, four girls to a tent.

We were at Belsen for seven weeks. First we had to segregate the prisoners, the dying, the T.B. [tuberculosis] cases, and those who were still healthy because they hadn't been there for very long. We put them into barracks which had been occupied by the Germans.

Quite a lot of the children had T.B. and a number were border-
ing on mental cases. I still worry about the children – a child always
remembers.

Source: Bruce, *Back the Attack!*

Letter

10/6/45
Belsen Camp
Germany
29th Br Gen Hosp
B.L.A

Dearest Dears,
I don't think I am blood thirsty at all because these people were terrible the treatment they gave these poor Jews & the way they chose to
kill them such [as] starvation supposed to die within 6 months slow
starvation it is a rather horrible death and the [living] quarters they
had were frightful & only the very strong lived there were some ten
thousand unburied dead lying around Camp 1 when our boys came in
the Germans sent out an S.O.S. because it got beyond even the S.S. so
they let us (softies that we are) come & clean it up our boys came in &
took over as an advanced party even passed through the enemy lines
to do it and they did a wonderful job believe me. Enough of that to get
back to yesterday.

We were invited to the Air Port [party in] Celle pronounced Cella I
met some very nice Canadians but we met so many I can't get all their
names straight mostly intelligence men and Liaison officers but it was
a lovely party the refreshments were grand and the drinks were very
nice [the] fruit Punch Had a whisky base but quite nice & had chunks
of cherries & Pineapple quite a treat believe me which we enjoyed the
most. Then we had the largest dishes of ice cream that I have ever seen
since I last had ice cream … I felt like I was back in Canada with a lad
from Hog Town on one side of me & a RAF on the other but very nice
company I came home in a jeep all the boys I know seem to have jeeps
terrible breezy things and I had a cold so John wrapped me up in his
big trench coat and I wore his beret I bet I looked funny.

We have to be armed here all military medical & BRCS [British Red
Cross] personnel have to go out armed that is the men & we can't go
out without an armed guard because the cracked pots around here get
into the forest & take pot shots at anyone or any things so we always

have revolvers around but we do have a very nice social life and we are joining a club called The Belsen Officers Club. It will open officially on Wednesday we expect unless something happens between now and then as far as we know they are going to have meals & dancing so it should be fun.

Our work is endless we are trying to get food suitable for these poor souls ... Hope we get some the cigs are quite a problem here. We can't give out many because we have some 8000 patients so imagine trying to give them out we haven't even received a 1000 T Brushes yet as the problem is really terrible but we will muddle through I hope & get it all straightened up soon but the Senior M.O. are mostly in 1st Group and if they get discharged soon it will be terrible because they are just beginning to know their patients and I think they would like to see the job finished but I don't think ever will neither will we as far as I know because it is endless.

Well no more space. So heaps of love
Lovingly,

Elsie May xxxx

xxxx

oooo

Source: United States Holocaust Memorial Museum, 2012.367.1, Elsie Deeks collection.

JOHN F. MCCREARY

Royal Canadian Air Force, Nutrition Group

Born in Eganville, but raised in both Arnprior and Sudbury, Ontario, Dr. John F. McCreary received his medical training at the University of Toronto. From 1935 to 1939 he was affiliated with the Toronto General Hospital and the Hospital for Sick Children. This was followed by two years as Millbank Research Fellow at Harvard.[33]

Dr. McCreary enlisted in the Royal Canadian Air Force as a flying officer. In 1942 he was promoted to the rank of wing commander and was appointed to the position of consultant to nutrition in the RCAF.[34] He completed studies on various topics, such as the palatability and

nutritional value of airmen's rations. His immediate team consisted of
Squadron Leader Dr. Hugh Branion and Warrant Officer J.R.F. Sauve.
In 1944 Dr. McCreary was seconded to the Supreme Headquarters
Allied Expeditionary Force (SHAEF). He took part in a mission to con-
duct clinical surveys of children in various concentration camps across
northwest Europe. The team spent time in France, the Netherlands, and
Germany.

On 4 May 1945, the RCAF's Nutrition Group, led by Dr. McCreary, was
sent by SHAEF from the Netherlands into Germany to examine the situation at Bergen-Belsen. Accordingly, both of the RCAF Nutrition Group's
Spearhead Survey Groups A and B arrived at the camp for inspection
the following day. They surveyed the scenes and completed a report.
Dr. McCreary took several photographs to document the situation at the
camp.[35]

In 1945 he was discharged and returned to Toronto. Dr. McCreary
went into private practice of pediatrics. In 1951 he moved from Toronto
to Vancouver to become professor and head of the Department of
Pediatrics at the University of British Columbia. He was also the pedi-
atrician-in-chief of the Vancouver General Hospital's Health Centre for
Children. Moreover, he consulted at hospitals across both Vancouver
and Victoria and for the British Columbia Department of Health.

In 1961 he served as a member of the Canadian delegation to the
United Nations Conference on Health Services to Underdeveloped Countries held in Geneva, Switzerland. In the mid-1960s, McCreary was president of the Association of Canadian Medical Colleges, an organization
he led for three years. He also served as chairman of the Queen Elizabeth II Fund for Research on Diseases of Children, in addition to other
duties.

McCreary received the centennial medal award of the Government
of Canada, the Canadian Paediatric Society's Ross Award, and the
Duncan Graham Award of the Royal College of Physicians and Sur-
geons of Canada in recognition of his contribution to medical education. He was granted honorary degrees by Memorial University of
Newfoundland, the University of British Columbia, and the University
of Toronto.[36]

John McCreary died suddenly on 14 October 1979 at his home in
Gibsons on the coast of British Columbia. He was sixty-nine years old.

Speech

... I should like to go on and say a few words about concentration
camps. The concentration camp I would like particularly to speak

about is Belsen. As you know, Belsen is a political concentration camp, a place where the Nazis put people who did not adhere to the Nazi ideals in their own country or in Occupied countries. They were people whom the Nazis feared had sufficient influence in their own countries that they might do a good deal of harm to the Nazi cause. These people were by no means the riffraff in the country. They were brought to places like the Belsen Concentration Camp and there interned. Belsen was situated in a relatively uninhabited part of Germany. It was a large camp in terms of the amount of acreage it covered. It was barbed wire enclosed, of course, and inside the barbed wire were dozens of huts similar to the 35 man huts we used in our Services, but instead of 35 men in each hut, the Germans put anywhere between 200 and 600 people in each of these dwellings. These people were fed always in the same way – twice a day – a large tureen of watery potato soup which was pushed in through the open door at either end of the hut. Every individual was equipped with a tin mug and it was his own responsibility how much of this material he obtained before it ran out. The people able to survive long periods in the Belsen Concentration Camp were people with tremendous will to win through and tremendous physical endurance to fight their way up to the soup tureen and obtain three or four cupfulls. This was at the expense of their fellows, because after they were there a few days nobody thought of anything else or anybody else and in that way some of them retained their physical well-being.

When the Army went into the Concentration Camp nobody had any idea how many had been there. The Germans asked for a 48 hour truce. They stated that they wanted to mend the fences [and] bury the dead.

They did neither of these things but they did destroy every record available in the Camp of who the occupants were. It turned out later that there were something like 50,000 in the camp at the time the British Army entered.

For the purpose of simplicity I am going to try to divide the people into three main groups. The first group and those best off were people either in the camp for a long period of time and who had tremendous physical endurance and who had been able to maintain their physical and mental state on the inadequate food which they had received, those people required only a little special feeding for a relatively few days or weeks and were able to go back home.

The second group, unfortunately also quite large, were a group of people who had deteriorated physically but not so far that they could not be returned on the Bengal Famine mixture which was fed to most of the occupants of the camp and was made of skimmed milk powder,

Figure 39. Wing Commander John F. McCreary, right, and an unidentified
colleague stand before one of the mass graves at Bergen-Belsen, 5 May 1945.
Courtesy of the Vancouver Holocaust Education Centre, Robert Krell fonds,
98.006.001.

flour and sugar and is a singularly easy thing for people not eating to
be able to digest.

The second group were those able to take that, and keep it down,
and gradually gain strength. Unfortunately, they had been so disturbed mentally by so long a period in the camp that their mental
return was far from as rapid as their physical return. When we saw
the people in the camp they were lower in any sense of the word than
any domestic animal one could imagine. They had lost their ability
to see. They had of course no idea what their names were. They had
no idea where they came from. They didn't know how long they had
been there. They were simply mute. They were people whose only
noise was a high pitched cry. There were thousands of these people
and they represented the most disturbing sight to be seen in the Belsen
Concentration Camp.

It looked for a long time as if there was absolutely no hope of any return to normal of this group. However, a very short time ago Sir [Jack]
Drummond was over in this country from England and he had been
back to some of the places where the people were being treated a few

Figure 40. Mass grave at Bergen-Belsen, ca. April–May 1945. Courtesy of the Vancouver Holocaust Education Centre, Robert Krell fonds, 98.006.002.

months ago and he said that after about a year of treatment with good food and quiet surroundings, when these people had long since been returned to their prewar physical state, they began to get a glimmer of normal intelligence.[37] As soon as the glimmer began to return very rapidly they returned toward normal and the great bulk of the people by that time had been discharged back to their own homes, knowing where they came from and knowing their families and taking up their prewar status in life again.

The third group was the group that was too far gone to take even the Bengal Famine Mixture. The group who as soon as they attempted to take any food lost it almost immediately. Most of these people died in the month following the taking over of the camp by the Allies.

… [The] common graves of which you have seen many pictures in the newspapers … represents the number of people picked up one morning who had died in one night during the month after the Allies had taken over, people for whom absolutely nothing could be done.

We have often heard the expression, "skin and bones." That expression didn't mean very much to me until one actually had an opportunity of seeing these people who had died in the Belsen Concentration Camp but it actually is true. People do deteriorate until there is nothing left but skin and bone and some of the people shown in the common grave are in that state.

... [The] concentration camps ... meant complete and utter tragedy for every individual who was involved.

Source: John F. McCreary, "The Conditions of Civilians in Western Europe at the Conclusion of the German Occupations," *The Empire Club of Canada Addresses,* Toronto (27 February 1947), 228–44.

~

JAMES ERNEST THOMPSON

Royal Canadian Air Force, 437 Transport Squadron

James Ernest Thompson was born on 19 January 1922 in Bowden, Alberta, and grew up on a farm near Buffalo Creek. He attended high school in nearby Innisfail. The day after he graduated from Innisfail High School he enlisted in the Royal Canadian Air Force. He served in the air force from 1941 to 1946, participating in the European theatre. His brother, Willard, served in RCAF Bomber Command.[38]

The Royal Canadian Air Force's 437 Squadron was established on 4 September 1944 at Blakehill Farm, an airfield in Wiltshire, England. Utilizing Dakota aircraft, 437 Squadron was a transportation unit. Thompson was a pilot with 437 Squadron when he first encountered the Bergen-Belsen concentration camp during the spring of 1945.

According to the squadron's Operation Records Book, Thompson's squadron made at least six trips to Bergen-Belsen between 25 April and 29 April 1945. The squadron generally flew from their base in Nivelles, Belgium, to Bergen-Belsen and then onto Lille, the northern tip of France, before returning to base.[39]

While in Belgium, Thompson met his future wife, Rita, in Brussels, where they were later married. After his discharge in 1946, Thompson and his wife returned to Bowden. In the post-war period Thompson both farmed and worked at the Bowden Refinery. Later on, he owned and operated the Refinery Shell gas station. Lastly, he worked at the Bowden Institution until 1984, when he retired.

Thompson had a lifelong love of flying. In 1960, he helped found the Innisfail Flying Club. According to his obituary, Thompson was a "quiet, private man ... [who] was a gifted mechanic, machinist, welder and carpenter. He was meticulous and paid great attention to detail."[40] He and his wife Rita had twelve children.

James Ernest Thompson passed away on 27 February 2005 at the age of eighty-three. He was survived by twenty-five grandchildren and eleven great-grandchildren. He was interred at Bowden Cemetery.

Interview

I got woken up about 3:00 AM one morning. I was living in a tent in Belgium, on an airport that was just a field, I had to go to get to Brussels real early, get some people there and take them to Germany. And they didn't tell us what we were going to they just told us where we were going, latitude and longitude and that was it. The people we picked up in Brussels were pretty high-ranking people, military people, doctors and so on.

Anyway, we landed in a field northeast of Hannover, Germany, a grass field, and a lot of barracks and small [unclear] things. There were two other airplanes, landed at the same time as the plane I was flying, they were English troops. And it turned out to be [the Bergen-Belsen] concentration camp ... So, I went in with the first bunch, I went in the gate, I went in with doctors and so on, there were bodies all over the place. None with any clothes on, just skin and bones. There were some of the inmates trying to gather them up and stack them in piles. I went into one of the barracks and ... [I was] unable to breathe in there, just jammed-packed and as dark as can be. And about half of the people in there were dead.

They lined up the guards who were on that end of the camp, and had them standing to attention there, they were all women. And they were pretty healthy-looking women, they sure looked different than the people lying on the ground. The commander of the camp was away, when he arrived back the next day, they grabbed him too. We loaded up a load of these people, the ones that, I think they picked out people that were for some reason, they wanted to talk to them. They wanted to get them out of there, get them medical attention and talk to them. They were underground or military people. I remember we loaded one on that was taller than I was, and he weighed ninety pounds.

We flew them back to Lyon, France, to a hospital there, the next day we did the same thing, we did the same thing for a couple of three days, then they stopped it when they found out it was a typhus epidemic.

A lot of the concentration camps, when they got something like that, they [the Germans] just let them die, it was cheaper than gassing them or whatever, a cruel thing to do. They shut the water off, people hadn't had water for quite a few days, and it was a pretty horrific thing. I went back there later on when they were burying the people, bulldozers, big trenches – open trenches, and they were making the German army, military do the actual burying. Burying the bodies. It's quite a horrific experience. The sad part of it was I told that to a few people, when I first got back and nobody believed it. And up until just recently, nobody believed it. I wouldn't say nobody, but a lot of people hadn't believed it.

That was Belsen.

Source: Thompson Family, Private Collection, James Ernest Thompson interview.

Chapter Four

Eyewitness Testimony

Aside from those who performed approved, authorized roles at Bergen-Belsen, hundreds of other Canadians also descended upon the camp, often without official permission from authorities. Thousands of Canadian soldiers, airmen, medics, and the like were working and fighting in and around the Lüneburg Heath where the camp was located. As news broke about Bergen-Belsen and military personnel became aware that this infamous concentration camp was located nearby, scores of individuals and small groups made their way to the site.

Some Canadians came to bear witness to a significant crime in history, while others appeared out of basic human curiosity. Indeed, throughout the spring and summer of 1945, Canadian personnel repeatedly made private, independent excursions to the camp, often in small groups while on leave or during time off. These journeys increased after the unconditional surrender of the armed forces of Nazi Germany. In addition, and not long after the camp's capitulation, large groups of military personnel from the surrounding areas were organized by authorities and brought by bus to take guided tours of Bergen-Belsen to have numerous eyewitnesses to the crimes.

Perhaps more than any other camp liberated at the time, Bergen-Belsen was a major news story, as it made international headlines and was presented in numerous forms of media. In a letter to his daughter, Allan Ironside of the Royal Canadian Air Force wrote, "The papers are full of atrocity stories and one never knows what to believe and what may just be propaganda. The camp we saw today was real and was no propaganda."[1] The importance of witnessing was a driving force for the visits of many Canadian military personnel. In the camps, they were able to find a reason or confirmation for why the war needed to be undertaken and, for the Allies, had to be won.

This chapter presents the eyewitness testimony of Canadian military personnel in the weeks and months following the handover of the Bergen-Belsen concentration camp. What did the crimes at Bergen-Belsen demonstrate to outside observers? What stories did those observers emphasize and what do these stories ultimately signify? How and to whom did they assign blame? Finally, what prompted Canadian personnel to discuss and describe the horrific crimes in the weeks, months, years, and even decades after the war? What did they hope to achieve by speaking out? Thus, the subsequent section touches on the themes of shame and remorse, culpability and complicity, punishment and revenge.

∼

LARRY D. MANN

Royal Canadian Air Force, 39 Wing

Born Louis Libman, Larry D. Mann was born on 18 December 1922 in Toronto, Ontario. His parents, Charles Libman and Rose Steinberg, were Jewish immigrants who came to Canada from Ostrowiec Świętokrzyski, Poland. The family was largely secular, and Mann never had a bar mitzvah. Growing up, he recalls facing a great deal of antisemitism in Toronto.[2] He attended Oakwood Collegiate and Vaughn Road Collegiate.

In 1941 Mann enlisted in the Royal Canadian Air Force. He was initially assigned to No. 419 Bomber Squadron as part of No. 3 Group, Bomber Command. He was later transferred to the 39 Reconnaissance Wing, where he was employed as an instrument technician. He worked on aircraft throughout the war. He visited Bergen-Belsen in May 1945 with other Jewish personnel.

After the war, Mann was stationed in Lüneburg, Germany. As part of the occupation forces, he helped start a newspaper and radio station for Allied troops.[3] When he returned to Canada, Mann changed his name from Libman and began working as a disc jockey for CHUM radio in Toronto.[4] In 1949, Mann moved to WHAM in Rochester. Less than a year later he returned to Toronto to begin work in television.

His break came as a regular on Let's See (1952–53), a broadcast on CBC Television. He often worked opposite a puppet known as "Uncle Chichimus," to the amusement of audiences. Mann was also a frequent guest on *Wayne and Shuster* during the 1950s and was featured in several well-known television commercials in Canada. In the 1980s he appeared as "The Boss" in a series of Bell Canada spots.

Mann acted in numerous feature films such as *The Sting* (1973) and *In the Heat of the Night* (1967). He also frequently appeared on television in such programs as *Gunsmoke, Bewitched, Hogans Heroes, Green Acres,* and *Hill Street Blues*. He also did voice work for animated shows; he was the voice of Yukon Cornelius in the 1964 Christmas stop-motion animated television special *Rudolph the Red-Nosed Reindeer*.

Mann's brother, Paul, was an acclaimed film and theatre actor, earning two nominations for the Golden Globe Award for Best Supporting Actor in Motion Picture. Larry D. Mann passed away on 6 January 2014 in Tarzana, California.[5] He was survived by his wife, Gloria; his four sons, Ron, Jeff, Danny, and Richard; and three grandchildren. At his funeral, and in lieu of flowers, donations were requested to the Variety Club International, a children's charity, and the United States Holocaust Memorial Museum.

Interview

There were Protestant and Catholic padres [in our] squadron, and I don't know how it happened, but I became very friendly with the Roman Catholic padre, who at that time was a Squadron Leader, whose name was Norman Gallagher. And when he came back home he became a bishop. My wife and I went to visit him in Ontario, Canada. And I don't know why, a lot of Jews and Protestants alike went to Father Gallagher's services. And he geared the services so that they were practically non-sectarian; you could have been a left-handed Episcopalian, it really didn't matter to him. And his sermons were pretty gutsy stuff. And I guess I learned as much about life from him as I did from anyone else ... At one time *Readers' Digest* did a series called "The most unforgettable character I've ever met" and I think he would qualify, with me, as the most unforgettable character I'd ever met. He was just an exceptional man.

He didn't think that Catholicism was any more important than anything else, than Buddhism. He thought that all of us were here for a purpose, but that none of us should feel superior to another. He believed in the goodness of Man, he believed in kindness, he believed in fair play, and he didn't see what was wrong with him playing in a crap game and having a couple of drinks. He was a realist, he was one of the most honest people I'd ever met in my life, and he was the right guy for me to meet at the right time. And I remember years later, his assistant called me and said, "Father's getting low." And so, Gloria and I took off a couple thousand miles to go see him. And he greeted Gloria as though he'd known her all his life. And over his fireplace he had a Star of David, which had been made out of a couple hundred little squares, about two inches square, and it had been smuggled out of Auschwitz. That's who he was. He was special. I look forward to meeting him if we end up in the same place.

It wasn't until we got into Germany that I saw the beginning of what Nazism was all about. After we crossed the Rhine in ... March of '45, and we came to a, driving along the road and a man waved us down, at this time there were displaced persons everywhere. They were all over the place. They didn't know which way to go; people were trying to get back to Poland, but how? Trying to get back to Russia, but how?

They looked like they had been on a real bad diet, wearing rags, sometimes impromptu shoes, now and again you would see them wearing good German Army boots, and you knew where those came from. [One time we came across a man who] motioned to us to "come." It was at a railway crossing ... And there was a field nearby and he scraped away at the ground and we saw a hand sticking out and he motioned to us – the whole field was like that. So, we went back to the squadron, told the CO [commanding officer], told him what [happened, we] got a bunch of guys and a couple of truckloads of fellas with shovels, went back to the spot and they unearthed 158 bodies without trying. They didn't unearth them fully, just a little, and then he said ... since it was getting ... dark and the prognosis was rain, "Let's get about ten trucks, go into town and get all the people, all the civilians, men women, whatever's there and bring 'em out here." And that he did. He gave each person a shovel and said, "Start digging."

Most of them were crying or bringing up. I don't know if any of them had been privy to this information, or they knew anything about what was going on, what was going on in this particular case was it was obvious that the German Army had commandeered the train because they were running short of rolling stock, so they just took out what was in there, it happened to be a bunch of people on their way to a concentration camp, shot them and stuck them in a field.

That was the modus operandi if you are running short of rolling stock. What you do is empty what you got, there was no other reason to do it. Because that wasn't a camp, it was a "nowhere." It was a crossroads, and that was the beginning ...

I remember being at an airfield called Celle, and Father Gallagher came to see me, and said, "Do you smell what we smell?" And what you could smell was nine-and-half miles away; it turned out what we were smelling was Bergen-Belsen ... We had been told there were such things, but we had no idea what they were ... What's a prison? If someone says it's a prison camp, what's in your head about a prison? Jimmy Cagney in jail, you know what I'm saying? That's prison; there is a guy here and a guy there, very orderly. That's why we weren't prepared for what we saw when we got to Bergen-Belsen ...

We all smelled it. But prior to that, there was a report through Intelligence, that there was a slave labor camp they said. And so, Father Gallagher decided to look into it. And he rounded-up a bunch of guys he thought would be interested, and it turned out to be all the Jewish kids in the squadron, plus others. And we grabbed food and took off and I went to Bergen-Belsen, you couldn't get in the front gate because there were bodies piled up like cordwood against the front gate. We got around the back. The British Army had gone through there with the Canadian Forces and just kept right on going.

I would say hundreds of bodies were piled up against the gate, the walls, on the ground, we hadn't seen the pits yet. Only 5000 to a pit. Not more, not less. If it was open, they didn't have their 5000 yet. And I went in. I killed a lot of Jews that day I guess ... by feeding them ...

I didn't think that a body could function with that little on its bones. I saw walking skeletons, I guess. And you know, it was almost impossible to tell the age of a person. I know there was, at one point I thought there was a young man, 16 or 17, turned out he was 30. Which is amazing that he had been able to live that long, of course I don't know when he was taken prisoner. But how anybody could survive that, and we had some relatives. My wife had several relatives who survived that, I don't know how they survived that, and came out if it. I have a friend Bob Clary who survived that. And, it's quite amazing, that people who were wandering around that camp, dazed, unbelieving, a lot of them were already out of it and didn't know it, you know? And it wouldn't be hard to lose your mind with those surroundings. In those bunks, with people relieving themselves on to you, and you couldn't move, and you were doing the same to the person under you. It's hard to believe that people would do anything for a piece of bread.

The remnants of life is what I saw ... There were a lot of pits, and there were a lot of pits open with bodies in them, skeletal, there were a lot of people wandering around, I've no idea how many were actually saved, but I know they were treated. And the interesting thing is, in treating them, the doctors were on fresh ground. It wasn't like they were being treated for whooping cough. They were on fresh ground. There had not been any treatment of this kind given to people who needed that kind of help. It didn't exist. And so, a lot of people died who shouldn't have died because no one knew really how to help them ...

[In the barracks] there were many tiers of bunks, and dark, and dirty, and smelly, and full of bowel movements, the smell of urine, the smell of puke, you mix it all together and it's not too pleasant. And the very thought that someone could allow people to live like that and considered themselves member of the human race, how people could allow things like that to exist, I will never fathom ...

The women were hardcore, I can tell that. The women guards, I don't know where they, how they raised those. They were just imbued with the madness of Nazism, and there was nothing you could say or do to convince them that they had done anything wrong. In light of everything that was around.

I was stunned. I was, I was a young kid really, I was twenty-three, twenty-two, what the heck did I know about life? I learned a lot that day and the few days that followed. I was out of it. That's the only way I can describe it. I was in another sphere. I was completely out of myself. I was filled with hatred. Because to me at that moment, at that day, at that time, I didn't see that there couldn't possibly be one German who wasn't responsible. Of course, I was so wrong. But, you understand what I was saying about that time. It was ... to this minute, in my life, if I see a German and he's anywhere near my age, the question I most want to say is "Where were you during the war buddy, and what did you do?" And life can't go on like that. And yet, maybe that's the Jewish perspective ...

I spoke Yiddish fluently thanks to my grandmother who even though she didn't prepare me for school [by teaching me English,] she prepared me for Bergen-Belsen. I don't know whether I am eradicating things from my mind, subconsciously or consciously, but I'm suddenly in one location at that camp. Some pits over there and the gate out here, and the way to get out and get back to the airfield because I can be of no use here. And I do remember saying "Nobody is ever going to believe this in a million years, I'd better take some pictures."

We gave the [inmates] chocolate bars, Spam, crackers, that wasn't very clever. But I didn't know any better, I thought we were doing something pretty good. Day two, we quit, we were told. The smell was still there when we got back to the airfield. It followed us all the way back.

Jewish or non-Jewish, [we] became a different breed [after Belsen], there was a lot of things happen that shouldn't have happened, as a result of having seen that ... Going on "hunting trips" to hunt Germans. I know a lot of people that did that. It's very difficult to explain the feeling that comes over you, the change that comes over you, it's like a little kid saying "Why I'll ..." You get so filled with horror, hate all mixed up and it doesn't make sense. You mean people were actually able to do this to other people? ...

[I changed my surname in] 1948. The reason I remember is that was when my son was born, and he had to have his name changed too because he was born a Libman. And I went to have my name changed for, they didn't ask, but it's in your mind for several reasons. First of all, it wasn't a time, I don't think it was a time when Jews were openly welcome, and my brother had chosen the name Mann, because it was the end of Libman. So, I figure, well, if it's good enough for him, it's good enough for me ...

I had just finished being in a war and seeing what I had seen, experiencing what I had experienced, and my wife and I got married and went on a honeymoon. And we went to a place called Sainte-Adèle-en-Haut which is outside of Montreal; I don't know about 50–60 miles north of Montreal. The owner of the radio station I worked at said, "You're going on a honeymoon? I know a great place for you to go to. Phone them [and] make reservations." So, I did. And we went there, swung into the parking lot and as I did there's this sign and it said "pas de Juifs." And Gloria said, "What's that sign say?" I said, "We are not allowed to park on that side," but "pas de Juifs" means "No Jews Allowed." And it struck me, as completely out of synch with what had just happened in my life. It struck me as being out of synch with Bergen-Belsen. It struck me as being out of synch with a kid from Canada who'd gone to do his bit in the war and come home and be met with "Oh no you don't." It was like African-Americans coming back and facing signs that said "Coloured – White" And we stayed there on our honeymoon for a week. I went back in the hotel and I said to the manager who was still standing there, "I have to tell you something. I have a suggestion of how you can make your guests more comfortable." He said "Really? You tell me anything, I'll be glad to do." I said, "Take down the sign in the parking lot because anyone who is Jewish, is not going to be feeling comfortable, and I'm Jewish and so is my wife." "Oh, well that's not my fault; the owner it is his fault because that's the way he makes the rules." I said, "Well you tell the guy that makes the rules that I'm a radio announcer and I'm going back to Toronto, and I have a program where I discuss anything I want. And the first thing I'm going to discuss is that sign and your hotel." And I went back, and I did it. And I felt great. And they called, and they were going to have a lawsuit and the owner of our radio station, who was not Jewish said "You do that, and you will probably put yourself right out of business." That was the last we heard of it ...

When you see how fragile a life is, how fragile life itself can be, I think you have to realize, that this fragile life, needs care, needs nurturing, and how you go about living your life, is not just your business. Because you influence others by everything you do, by everything you say and if you let your thoughts be known, by everything you think.

So, if you present a world of double standards, the message gets read wrong. If you brag to your kids how you cheated on your income tax and try to teach them to be honest citizens, it doesn't work out too good. If you try to teach your children not to hate and talk of what disgusting people there are around you, and how you dislike them, it's not going to work. I guess it comes down to: I want my children and grandchildren to be honest, to live life with a mirror. Look at yourself: is this what you want them to be? That's it.

Source: Shoah Foundation Video Archive (Interview Code: 48192). Interview by Hilary Helstein. Interview date: 10 November 1998.

LEO VELLEMAN

Royal Canadian Air Force, 39 Wing

The son of Jewish immigrants from the Netherlands, Leo Velleman was born in 1917. During the Second World War, Velleman served with 39 Reconnaissance Wing of the Royal Canadian Air Force, which specialized in aerial photo reconnaissance. Velleman contributed to the Wing's *Flap* magazine. When a group of his colleagues visited the Bergen-Belsen concentration camp, he wrote about the experience in *Flap*.[6]

After the war, Velleman married and a daughter was born. In 1952, Velleman would remarry. His second wife, Dora, had also been married previously and had three children. The new family lived together as one. In addition to three daughters and one son, the couple would go on to have fifteen grandchildren and thirteen great-grandchildren.

Leo and Dora Velleman became world-renowned puppeteers. In 1950, the family moved to Toronto. Their company, Canadian Puppet Festivals, was featured at Expo 67 and toured across Canada and Europe several times. They also worked in television in both Canada and the United

States. *Planet Tolex* (1953–54), a children's science fiction television series that aired on CBC Television, was created by the couple.

The Vellemans employed hand and rod puppets and, while dressed in black, often appeared on stage.[7] They were also educators, employed as puppetry instructors by the Ontario Ministry of Education and community colleges. In addition, Canadian Puppet Festivals trained countless apprentices.

In 1975, the Vellemans moved to Nova Scotia to form the Leading Wind Puppet Theatre. In 1977 the Union Internationale de la Marionnette (UNIMA) awarded the couple a Citation for Excellence in the Art of Puppetry. Their impact on puppetry was significant. Leo Velleman passed away in March 2009 at the age of ninety-two.[8]

Article

In such camps as Belsen lies the answer to why we fought the war. These pits of rotting, emaciated corpses are the logical product of the process of Fascism which in Germany was called Nazism.

For the last twelve years the German people have been led by a deliberate campaign of propaganda. Starting from the most trivial beginnings a process of self-centred intolerance and perverted nationalism was developed until a whole nation could stand by calmly while millions of other human beings were slowly starved, tortured and then slaughtered as efficiently as possible. The Germans who objected to such treatment of other human beings soon found themselves behind the barbed wires of the concentration camp with the very ones whose rights they had tried to uphold. The Germans who remained passive preferred to accept the new order and identified themselves with it because they were afraid to do otherwise and they believed that they had something to gain in this process of expansion of the Third Reich.

To further the growth of greed and callousness of a whole people the leaders of the German nation exploited every possible avenue. Particularly for the young, they exalted ruthlessness and racial prejudice. Such a system made the concentration camp possible.

The enemies of Germany were those who by accident of birth or circumstance were unacceptable to the perverted philosophy that claimed an exclusive nationality and the future of the human race for the German. These victims of the concentration camps were not soldiers, but civilians who were the pawns in a gigantic plan to destroy the races and creeds that stood in the way of world domination. The first to go were those who spoke for freedom and humanity. Those who died in the camps across Germany in the past ten years were the soldiers of democracy as surely as we are.

The Germans have had to pay – and pay dearly – for their willingness to accept a whole system of false values and debased ideals. Their towns have been levelled and their people have died by the tens of thousands before the monstrous creed of Fascism was smashed. Belsen stands as a terrible warning to the people of the whole world.

If we do not wish to see this war fought in vain we must make sure that we will never allow the seeds of prejudice and intolerance to be sown among us. Time will tell if the Germans have learned the lessons of Belsen. We must make sure that we have learned that lesson also. It will take unwearying vigilance and clear thinking to make sure that this does not happen again anywhere – ever.

Source: Velleman, "Belsen."

ALLAN IRONSIDE

Royal Canadian Air Force, No. 5 Mobile Field
Photographic Section

Allan Ironside was born in 1908 in the township of Puslinch in south-central Ontario.[9] When he was a teenager, his family moved to Toronto. Ironside attended Jarvis Collegiate but did not complete high school. He married and shortly after the birth of his daughter, Nancy, his wife passed away. Upon his wife's request, his daughter was placed into the care of his parents. During the Depression years, Ironside travelled in search of employment.

He worked for a commercial directory in Toronto and a newspaper in Montreal. In 1932 he moved to Orillia, Ontario, where he found employment in a shoe store. At this time he lived at the YMCA, worked as a volunteer fire fighter, and created a map of Orillia in his spare time. He soon met his second wife, Carolyn, and in 1935 the couple moved to Toronto.

By 1939 Ironside was producing audiovisual aids for schools in Ontario and Quebec while working for the Associated Screen News of Montreal. When war broke out, Ironside enlisted in the Royal Canadian Air Force and was assigned to the Joint Air Training Plan, working in aerial reconnaissance. In 1944, he received a posting to the European theatre as an officer commanding a mobile field photographic section, which was attached to 39 Wing, RCAF. He saw action in the Netherlands, Belgium, and Germany. During his time overseas he wrote letters to his daughter about his experiences.

In the post-war period, Ironside found employment with Standard Oil of New Jersey. For the company his task was to air-map sites in countries such as Columbia, Ecuador, and Peru. He later worked as an administrator in Venezuela. In the 1950s he was transferred to Iran, where he managed an international oil consortium. He opted for early retirement in 1962.

Upon retirement, he and Carolyn settled in Washago, a small community located north of Orillia. Ironside became active in the community of Orillia, supporting those with visual and hearing impairments. He also became involved in the Orillia Historical Society, the Simcoe County Historical Association, and the Ontario Historical Society.[10]

Ironside was known for his expertise in public lore and became a popular speaker on local topics. He wrote a column for a weekly newspaper, the *Wednesday Nighter*. He also wrote the Orillia Historical Society's monthly newsletter. Some of these writings appeared in his book *Anecdotes of Old Orillia*.

After the passing of his second wife, Carolyn, Ironside married Dr. Elsie Hoffman Crawford, director of the Huronia Regional Centre. Allan Ironside passed away in 1992. A scholarship was established in his name and is given to outstanding students of history attending an Orillia school.[11]

Letter

May 4/45

As usual, I have not made much progress in getting this letter finished. Last night I had to go out to try to locate a unit which was on the move and from which we draw some of our supplies, and I did not get back until after 11, so no chance to write.

Today I took a truckload of chaps to visit a nearby concentration camp [Bergen-Belsen], which we captured two weeks ago. I'm going to enclose a couple of pictures of it and tell you a little of what I saw so that you know it first hand what sort of things have been going on in Germany. The papers are full of atrocity stories and one never knows what to believe and what may just be propaganda.

The camp we saw today was real and was no propaganda. From the entrance could be seen large barracks, like at Trenton and Rockcliff.

However, when we drove on past there, we came to barbed wire en-
tanglements surrounding wretched little hovels, where over 45,000
prisoners were housed. These were about 70% Jews and came from
Germany, Poland, Russia, Czechoslovakia etc. When we got it, nearly
15,000 had died in the last 6 months and they were dying at the rate
of 500 per day. There are still nearly 300 per day dying there. Into
buildings which should accommodate less than 100 as many as 1500
had been crowded. They were so tightly packed that they could move
neither hand nor foot and had to answer the calls of nature just as
they stood. Vermin of all sorts overran the place and soon typhus was
raging. They got little or no food and those who were not carried off
by typhus were starved to death. SS troops, male and female, were
in charge. The SS men used to take the women out and use them for
rifle practice aiming at their breasts. The SS women applied torture to
the men prisoners. Quite often, babies were born there, and when this
happened, the guards would tear the babies apart – wrenching arms
and legs out – in front if their sick mothers. There was no medical or
dental attention. It was simply [a] systematic brutal plan to extermi-
nate Jews and other enemies of the Glorious Reich. Great graves lie
around the fence marked thus "Grave #1 – approx. 1000" "Grave #2 –
nearly 5000" "Grave #3 – quantity unknown."

When captured, our troops put 57 SS men to work burying those
who lay everywhere dead. In a week, only 50 SS men were living and
the authority stepped in and sent in a lot of German prisoners to do
the work as our men could not control themselves as they saw evidence of SS brutality and were killing the men responsible.

We stood and watched the dead bodies being hauled into grave #11
just like sacks of potatoes, about 400 wretched starved skeletons with
arms and legs that flapped around like rag dolls, as they rolled them
into the huge communal grave. Try to imagine looking at 400 dead
people at once. Dead from filth, starvation and typhus. The stench
was such that you could taste it and had to keep spitting it out. So far
gone, are the remaining prisoners that they can't take food and with
the typhus, the camp is sealed and probably another 10,000 will die.
The ones who they hope to save, are removed to another part of the
camp, and the rest were just sitting around without hope or expression awaiting death. I talked to them (some spoke English) and to
their guards who are now British soldiers looking after them. This is
a first-hand story and is true, so you will know what to say when you
hear people say that atrocity stories are just newspaper talk.

I am sending you 5 pictures. Two of the graves I saw them filling. I
took a couple as well but didn't have fast film and haven't had them

developed yet. It was raining when I was there, and these were taken the day before. This is a horrible story, but I thought you ought to know how thankful we all should be that we live in Canada.

Well I must hurry on, as I don't want to tell you too much and have your mind dwell on it. It is still raining here; it has rained everyday now for 9 days with the sun shining for only a couple of hours, twice in that time. Our tents are getting very cold and damp, but I am warm in my little bed. It could more correctly be called a sleeping bag; for I have the blankets all wrapped around to keep the cold out and I have to insert myself in feet first.

Must say good night, my little girl. I am gaining a lot of experience these days and it makes me fonder of my wife and family. Don't worry about me at all, I am completely healthy and safe and don't have any bad dreams at night. Heaps and heaps of love to you and all.

Your fond,
Daddy

Source: Sarah and Chaim Neuberger Holocaust Education Centre, Toronto, Allan Ironside Collection. Permission courtesy of Dr. Nancy Ironside.

KING WHYTE

Public Relations Officer, Psychological Warfare Division (SHAEF); 1st Canadian Army

King Whyte was born in 1911 in Montreal, Quebec, and raised in Winnipeg, Manitoba. In the 1920s he moved to the United States, finding work in Cincinnati, Ohio. He later wrote an outdoor column for the *Toronto Daily Star*. He had a great passion for news media, and in particular radio and television. In 1939 he moved back to Winnipeg where he worked for the CBC.[12]

When the Second World War broke out, Whyte joined the Canadian Army. In 1941 he was sent overseas to work in public relations. In 1943 he was transferred to the Psychological Warfare Department of the Supreme Headquarters Allied Expeditionary Force (SHAEF),[13] where he continued to work as a public-relations officer. After completing his assignment, he became a war correspondent for Radio Luxembourg, which served as the voice of SHAEF. While overseas Whyte regularly wrote letters home to his wife, Canadian singer Dorothy Alt. He encountered the Bergen-Belsen concentration camp in April 1945 and revealed his shock to his wife in a series of moving letters.[14]

After the war, in 1946, Whyte returned to Canada. He soon became known as the country's foremost outdoor writer and telecaster.[15] *The King Whyte Show*, which aired on the CBC from 1955 to 1962, was a popular fifteen-minute program that featured interviews with a variety of guests, including hockey great Maurice Richard, on such topics as outdoor sports, hunting, fishing, and boating. Following *Hockey Night in Canada* on Saturday evenings, the program had a large audience in both Canada and the United States. At the time of his death, it was the second-oldest program sponsored on CBC-TV.

In the post-war period, Whyte worked tirelessly on behalf of war veterans. He arranged dinners and events for veterans in hospitals. Fans of his television program would often donate fish and other game for these special dinners. At Sunnybrook Hospital in Toronto one evening, more than 1,400 servicemen were treated to a dinner of goose, deer, moose, beaver, trout, pheasant, and partridge.[16]

On 26 June 1962, at the age of fifty-one, King Whyte died of a heart attack in Laurentide Park, Quebec, where he was preparing film for his television show. At the time of his death he was with Louis-Philippe Gagnon, Quebec's deputy minister of fisheries, and Jacques LaRoche of the CJRL radio station in Quebec City.[17]

Twenty years after his death, his wife located Whyte's wartime letters and photographs in a trunk in the basement of her east-end Toronto home. One of Whyte's daughters, Maureen, organized and edited his wartime correspondence, which included poems, pictures, articles, and briefs. The collection was first published in 1996 as *Letters Home, 1944–1946*.

Letter

April 24, Somewhere in Germany

Tonight, I am a different man. I have spent the last two days in Belsen concentration camp, the most horrible festering scab there has ever been on the face of humanity. It was so horrible that I'm not going to tell you of it. I still cannot bring myself to write my reports to Radio Luxembourg. It makes me sick to my stomach even to imagine the smell, and I want to weep and go out in the streets and kill every Nazi I see when I think of what they have done to those countless thousands of people.

You have seen pictures in the paper, but they cannot tell the story. You have to smell it and feel it and keep a stern look on your face while your heart tears itself into pieces and the tears of compassion drench your soul. My God, that there should be such suffering on the face of the earth. I have seen hundreds of people dying before my eyes. I have seen filthy green corpses used as pillows for the living. I have seen forty thousand people living and dying amongst their own fetid offal. They are dying faster than they can be buried. For most of them food is absolutely no use. Their stomachs will not take it – they vomit or have dysentery and it goes right through them. All over the camp, both men and woman squat wherever they happen to be. There is no latrine and it is almost impossible to walk around without stepping in filth.

An American medical officer in charge of the Allied Typhus Commission told me that any one of the cases in the camp would put any hospital in the United States into a flap.[18] I had to be sprayed with powder even my hair and beret before I could enter the place. It is a sinkhole of pestilence. The SS guards were left behind at the camp when the Germans retreated. They are burying the dead. I will leave it to your imagination – the love the Tommies have for them.

I could write you like this for hours my darling, but I said I wasn't going to tell you of the things I have seen. Only, in the years to come if I am suddenly sick on the street it will be because some smell has wafted to my nostrils which my stomach remembers from Belsen.

Figure 41. Main road from watch tower, Belsen concentration camp, April 1945. Photographer: King Whyte. Laurier Military History Archive MG-0003-1-11.

... I expect that I will only be here for another week and then it will be back to Luxembourg for reassignment. It will be good to go back to Luxembourg where I can get a good bath and put on a fresh uniform and get into my feather bed. I am lucky and I know it.

I do wish this letter wasn't like this darling, but you are the only one I can tell my thoughts to. I couldn't help thinking of your mother and father. If they were living in Europe they would have been in such a place.

I took this one [figure 41] from the steps of one of the watch towers and it shows part of the main road through the camp. Most of the bodies have been taken away from the main road but if you look closely you can still see some lying around. The fire hoses brought the first pure water into the camp that these people have had for many months. The buildings were the ones in which they were herded. Twenty-two people slept in the same amount of space allotted to one British solider in the barracks. The ambulance is hauling away a load to the hospital about two miles distant.

Figure 42. Some of the thousands of bodies at Belsen concentration camp, viewed from one of the "lagers," April 1945. Photographer: King Whyte. Laurier Military History Archive MG-0003-1-11.

This [figure 42] is from inside one of the "lagers" [meaning "camp" or "warehouse"] looking out onto the main road. In the foreground are just a few of the thousands and thousands of dead lying about the place.

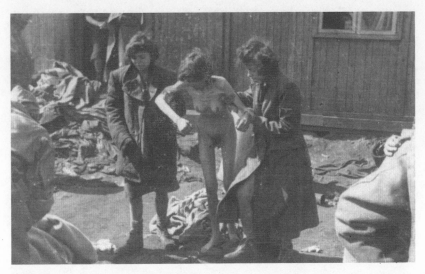

Figure 43. A young girl suffering from typhus and malnutrition is helped by her sister and a friend, Belsen concentration camp, April 1945. Photographer: King Whyte. Laurier Military History Archive MG-0003-1-11.

This girl [figure 43] is suffering from typhus and malnutrition. She was too weak to walk and is being helped by her sister on the left and her friend. The drill was that typhus people were taken out of the huts, stripped of their clothing because it was diseased too, wrapped in a blanket and taken away in an ambulance. They were washed at the hospital on a table especially built for the job and were then put to bed. The girl incidentally is only nineteen and had spent five years of her life in concentration camps. She was one of those whom they believed they could save so you can imagine what the majority of those who had typhus looked like.

These are the German SS troops hauling away the people they killed [figure 44]. These men were the guards at the camp and were taken when we liberated it. They are, of course, just a few of the several hundred. You will recognize your old man standing there. This sort of thing was so usual that nobody paid any attention to it whatsoever. Only when some of the guards were getting beat up did they stop and look. A few moments later the SS man on the left caved in. He was beaten up and then thrown on the top of the corpses in the truck until he came to. At the time they were dying much faster than they could be picked up and carted to the pits.

Source: Laurier Military History Archive MG-0003-1-10-8a. Whyte, Maureen (2 of 2).

Figure 44. SS troops load bodies on to a truck, Belsen concentration camp, April 1945. Photographer: King Whyte. Laurier Military History Archive MG-0003-1-11.

CARL REINKE

Royal Canadian Air Force, 126 Wing

Carl Reinke was born circa 1905. He was educated in Hamilton and later attended and graduated from the University of Toronto. He subsequently spent two years at Osgoode Law School. Early in his career, he found employment in the newspaper industry in Toronto. He then moved to Ottawa, where he worked as a correspondent for four years in the Parliamentary Press Gallery.[19]

During the war he was first employed at the National Selective Service (NSS) and was executive assistant to director Elliot M. Little. The NSS was established by Prime Minister Mackenzie King in 1942 and was designed to employ men and women in the Canadian war effort. It alleviated the labour shortage the country was experiencing. He also worked as chief of the news and picture division of the Directorate of Public Information.[20]

Reinke later enlisted in the Royal Canadian Air Force as a flying officer. He was trained at Lachine, Quebec, and was assigned to an administrative post at Air Force Headquarters in Ottawa in the Directorate of Manning. At the RCAF training centre at Domain D'Estrelle, Reinke received his commission to the rank of pilot officer.

Towards the end of the war, Reinke arrived on the continent as part of the RCAF's Historical Section in London. He was soon attached to the RCAF's 126 Wing. On 1 May 1945 Reinke, along with the wing's Monty Berger, Gordon Panchuk, and Bob Francis, travelled from their airfield at Wunstorf to the Bergen-Belsen concentration camp.[21] Reinke kept a wartime diary and documented this encounter.[22] He later wrote "Fighter Wings on the Continent," which explained RCAF command and structure.[23]

After the war, Reinke settled in Montreal. He worked briefly with a Quebec paper company before transferring to the Public Relations Department of Canadian Industries Limited. In 1948 he and his former air force colleague, Monty Berger, helped found the Canadian Public Relations Society. He also served as chair of the Public Relations Committee of the Welfare Federation of Montreal.

In later life Reinke became a business executive, working for the DuPont Company of Canada, as well as being named chair of the Community Chest Division of the Canadian Welfare Council. Carl Reinke passed away on 22 July 1992 at the age of eight-six.

Diary

May 1 1945 – Wunstorf
Had a glimpse of Belsen concentration camp today – but it failed to make my blood curdle after having read and heard so many gruesome details about the place. I had also deliberately steeled myself for it, to prevent any outward reaction if possible. I guess one simply ceases to be surprised or shocked after a time, which is perhaps a kind of [a] tragedy in itself.

Monty Berger ... was taking some medical supplies up, so Bob Francis, another [intelligence officer], [Gordon] Panchuk and I went along for the ride. I had earlier intended moving to 143 Wing today.

We went up in a newish Opel car which had been requisitioned from AMG. En route, the now customary stream of DPs and ex-POWs. A couple of clusters bravely bore great red flags, this being May Day. We also saw a car bearing a red hammer-and-sickle in front, though, we could not tell if it was an official Russian car. There were the usual groups on bicycles, driving a horse and cart, or just dragging a four-wheeled cart. We saw Poles going West and Poles going East, which seemed to sum up the current confusion and lack of control and direction for these wandering millions. In the daylight all is calm and orderly with them, but one hears suggestions of different conduct at night.

At Belsen, 18 miles north of Celle, we visited only one of five [sub] camps. The Hungarian guards who had helped confine those pitiful creatures for the Nazis are still doing the same thing – for us! Not very surprisingly, they are meticulous about saluting visiting officers. The British Army is in charge of the place. There must be a very severe manpower shortage.

We first met a Jewish lady, Canadian, who took us to the "dusting room" in the HQ building. This involved having DDT (anti-bug powder) squirted down your neck, before and after, down your trousers, before and after, over your hair, in your cap, and up your sleeves. We looked like millers.

There we strolled down the avenues, somewhat hurriedly since we lacked official approval. The plain grey streets might have been on any military establishment, judging by their outward appearance. First a group of elderly civilians, very dejected, with shovels, waiting to march somewhere. (It was just 1:30 pm). These we were told were burying the dead. The SS guards who had been doing this under the control of Tommies, had been unable to "take it" any further and were all ill – and quite understandably. The authorities had tried to make German POWs do it, but they had raised legal objection and been upheld. So German civilians had been ordered to continue the ghoulish job of loading the stinking corpses on carts, unloading them into great pits and burying them.

We walked by a kitchen from which the stronger inmates were carrying big buckets of soup or stew to the huts, two were on each bucket.

Inmates lounged around the barbed wire fences boxing off their huts from the road. They were heavily clad most wearing winter coats and all sorts of other paraphernalia (!) to keep warm, though the sun warmed the chilly air. They looked dumbly with lifeless gaze, scarcely interested in anything going on around. They were surprisingly well fed looking, though their faces were pasty and dead looking. Some were woefully thin and emaciated.

Then between two huts we saw a dozen-odd scrawny corpses on the ground, some nude, the rest partially covered with some cloth. They were like skeletons with skin over them, in all sorts of positions.

"Those have died since [the corpses] were picked up this morning," the Padre explained. They had been carried out from their huts by the others.

We saw ambulances carrying many away from these huts. The ambulance staffs wore khaki coveralls which covered everything but their eyes, nose and mouth. They were removing Typhus cases to the hospital camp.

We looked in several huts. In some great improvements had been made in 10 days and some women seemed [to be] mingling with the men. Then a hut which could not have been cleaned up. The three-tier wooden bunks were almost all filled with men, simply numbed, paralyzed by disease and starvation of slow kind. They lay on the floor in overcoats or bundled in their beds, unaware we were looking in. They were only half alive in the most literal sense. Outside the door it said Enteritis. Whatever the causes whether of accumulated filth or decomposing humans, that hut had a sickly fetid stench which one could never forget. But the men in there were incapable of interest.

We walked around some other huts. A rosy-cheeked girl walked by, interestingly, oblivious of the open, unscreened latrines a few feet away being used by men. The very idea of having latrines was an innovation of the past week. Men and women had unselfconsciously lived like primitive animals squatting where and whenever so inclined.

A barbed wire fence separated two huts. We walked out to the road. A man was lying across the path. We looked closer. He was sprawled out mouth and eyes wide open – but dead. The translucent, waxy skin over the emaciated frame told the story. The glassy stare of the starving is not too different from the starved!

Before their "liberation" (!) the inmates were periodically thrown a few loaves of bread and given some watery soup. In the frantic scramble the strong got the food. In short, it was the survival of the fittest. Some were still fit.

As the inmates can be cleaned up, de-loused and accommodated elsewhere, they are being moved. Thousands of course, go to the hospital camp, many far past help.

The camp Padre told us he buried 100 this morning. Only two of those hundred were even identified! The rest didn't know who they were or were beyond being articulate long ago.

Then there were a couple of signs in the HQ ready to be placed.

Grave 5, Approx. 800, April 1945

Grave 8, Approx. 5000, April 24, 1945.

A nice round figure, 5000. Mostly Russians and Poles with a high percentage of Jews.

Throughout the camp there was a pungent smell, like an incinerator, only worse. This was from the filth from the huts being burned mainly.

Only a few seemed to be wearing the pajama-striped uniforms of the concentration camps, though we had seen more along the roads, some on men who could certainly not walk far, but wanted to drink in their freedom.

In a group of women pushing a cart, one incongruously was wearing a good Hudson seal coat. The women generally were segregated often huddled over [a] little gypsy-like fire by their huts, their few spare garments hanging on the barbed wire to dry.

But today they announced that the Americans had reached Dachau, which was notorious even before the war. It is supposed to be the worst yet, at least in the west.

The radio and press bring only a mass of rumors about Himmler's further peace maneuvers. The States apparently had a false and short-lived peace celebration last Saturday night.

The papers today also carry pictures of Mussolini's undignified end, complete without strutting or balcony scene: he and his mistress were shot, then hung by the heels from a service station roof. A dozen other henchmen were also written off.

The San Francisco meeting continues, but progress is unspectacular and even dubious.[24] The States sponsors Argentina but draws objection from Molotov who says Argentina has certainly no more democratic government than the provisional Polish gov't – which the States refused to admit. So, the deadlock seems to grow.

The local looting by officers and airmen goes on unabated. One ... got himself six radios. An officer brought in eight good cameras and was going back with a haversack for more! So, it continues with and without waving a revolver.

A RAF F/L [Royal Air Force flight lieutenant] is acting as military governor of a nearby town and had all cameras confiscated. Imagine who took the pick! Others had the rest for the asking. War breeds law-lessness even among the normally law-abiding.

At 10:26 pm tonight, Admiral Donitz announced over German radio that Hitler died this afternoon and that he was Hitler's successor.[25] He said the war would continue. At the same time, it was stated that Count Bernadotte had returned to Stockholm ... without seeing Himmler.[26] So, the question is what has happened to him.

Source: Department of National Defence, Directorate of History and Heritage, Ottawa: 87/241: "War Diary of Flight Lieutenant Carl Reinke, RCAF."

FRANK SNOWSELL

Royal Canadian Air Force, 39 Wing

Frank Snowsell was born on 15 May 1908 in Cirencester, a market town in east Gloucestershire, England. His parents, Edwin and Felicia, immigrated to Canada in 1911 when Snowsell was three years old. The family settled on a farm in Sedgewick, Alberta, before moving in 1925 to another farm in Kelowna, British Columbia.[27]

Snowsell attended the University of British Columbia, graduating in 1932 with a bachelor's degree in history; he would later earn a master's degree. Upon graduation he entered the teaching profession. In 1933 he married Chelta Reid of Kelowna, a recent nursing graduate at Vancouver General Hospital. The couple was married for seventy years and had five children and six grandchildren.

During the Second World War, at the age of thirty-one, Snowsell volunteered to serve in the Royal Canadian Air Force, where he was assigned to the Intelligence Division. He served in the Aleutians campaign and saw active duty in France, Germany, and Denmark. Snowsell was with the RCAF's 39 Reconnaissance Wing when he encountered the Bergen-Belsen concentration camp on 1 May 1945, two weeks after its liberation. He travelled to the camp with Protestant padre Ross Cameron.[28]

After the war, Snowsell returned to the teaching profession. Over the years he taught in Rutland, Armstrong, Victoria, Prince George, Squamish, West Vancouver, Simon Fraser University, and Kamloops before retiring in 1970. He also coached high school soccer, basketball, and softball.

Snowsell's mother, Felicia, was involved in politics. She was an activist for the United Farmers of Alberta and later joined the Co-operative Commonwealth Federation (CCF). Likewise, Snowsell represented the former electoral district of Saanich in the Legislative Assembly of British Columbia in 1953 as a CCF member. He ran for re-election in 1953 and 1956 and was defeated both times.[29]

In 1965, he was elected president of British Columbia's New Democratic Party (NDP). In 1968, he was the NDP candidate in the Capilano federal riding; he was unsuccessful in his bid. In 1985, he published *Road to Ruin: The Path of the United States Foreign Policy, 1945–1984*. He was well known for sharing his opinions through letters to newspapers. The *Kelowna Capital News* once called him the greatest correspondent in their paper's history.[30]

According to his obituary, Snowsell was an "avid reader, writer, bridge player, gardener, world traveler, camper and social activist."[31] Frank Snowsell passed away at Kelowna General Hospital on 16 August 2003 at the age of ninety-five.

Letter

I visited the concentration camp at Belsen, a grim area of moor with stunted pines surrounded by a double fence of barbed wire with coiled barbed wire between the fences. Great signs warned "Typhus Danger" and we were unable to gain admittance. But we drove the jeep all around the fence, stopping frequently, and saw all we wanted to see.

Among the pines were long wooden huts and shelters built of canvas, old tents, or odds and ends. The camp stinks, not the rich odor of dead men, but the sticky, rancid fetid odor which tastes as well as smells. Among the trees German civilians and members of the Wehrmacht are at work burying the top surface and spreading clean sand. A British Tommy stands guard. Scattered around among the trees and workers and on the little slops in the sun are bundles of rags which move. Three are lying in the sun just beside the fence, they are women.

In front of one of the shacks a three-ton truck with four wheeled trailer is standing. From the building men in anti-gas clothing are carrying bodies in blankets and dumping them from the blankets onto the trailer and truck. The bodies bear no relation to anything human. From the back of the blanket the legs dangle and drag on the ground

like two sticks. The truck and trailer are loaded well above the sides
and turn around right in front of us. There is no semblance of anything human in the load. One body on top of the trailer stands out.
It lies face down naked, bent over the load, the bare rump a narrow
wedge pointing upward, the legs, sticks.

Two women come out of the shack and oblivious of guards and
working men lift up their skirts, revealing hip bones with no rump,
backsides from which all flash has gone, and relieve themselves. They
stagger back to the shack bent double. There are latrines dug since we
took over, but only the stronger get that far. Two more women are in
one of the latrines. Three men walk past the fence in front of us. They
turn their grey faces in our direction but there is no expression at all in
the faces or the eyes. The skin is like dirty grey cloth stretched over the
facial bones.

The guard comes over to talk. The people in the camp of are all
nationalities and from all walks of life. The well to do have been the
worse sufferers. The German civilians had no idea, he tells us, that
conditions in the camp were so bad. Those working under his guard
are often ill and many of those forced to visit the camp are nauseated.
To many of the inmates our help has come too late, they are unable to
digest the food we supply, there is no hope for them but in death. He
tells us that the gypsies and the peasants imprisoned in the camp have
fared better, able to do with less and look after themselves better than
the wealthier groups.

On the hill just inside the camp not far from the buildings are the
graves great holes in the hillside dug by bulldozers, there are several
fresh dug awaiting their quota. Each filled grave has a sign with its
number, the date and the amount of bodies. The sign on number 1
grave says, "5000, April 1945." Another No. 2, 2000. Not one grave
has less than 1000 bodies. Two signs read, "No. 9, number unknown,"
"No. 10, number unknown." Number 11 is now being filled. Two German soldiers in full anti gas clothing drop the bodies from the truck
and trailer into the grave. At one time there were 60,000 prisoners in
the camp, they have been dying at the rate of over 500 per day.

German civilians are clearing one building, forking rags and filth
out of the windows, rags and filth in which living and dead had been
rolled together; men women and children. The living stripped the
clothing from the dead and wrapped themselves and their children in
the rags against the cold. There was no fuel and the dead were dead
and not bad company in the cold weather.

The wall is out of one shack, the floor is feet deep in rags, straw
and filth. A great pile is smoldering with terrible smoke and stink. A

German civilian pokes at it and it breaks into flame. We climb into one of the guard towers where the SS troops used to keep guard. The entire camp is below us. Four adults carry a pail of water between them into one of the shacks. At the door of one shack four women are cooking over a tiny fire. They pay no attention to anything. Two Mustangs fly low across the camp, only one raises her head. The stink of the camp rises to the top of the towers. There are very few people moving around the camp besides the Red Cross workers and guards. Most of the inmates stagger as they move bent almost double. It is impossible to guess at the age of most of them.

The grave digging bulldozer goes past with four or five children riding with the driver. They are shouting and laughing. The guard told us that the adults had given the children the best they had. The children paid no attention to the bodies or the graves.

Further up the road is the convalescent camp where those cured of typhus and of no danger as a source of infection are taken. It is an establishment of rather fine-looking buildings formerly, I believe, an SS barracks. At first, in the camp, the SS men captured were used to bury the dead, but as the guard told us, the mortality rate among the SS men was too high. The guards made them do everything on the double and fed them only turnips, the same diet as they had fed the prisoners. Now the camp is cleaned up by Wehrmacht and German civilians.

Frank Snowsell
39 Reconnaissance Wing, RCAF (Intel)
C 11 6 88

Source: University of British Columbia Archives, D805.G3 S66 1945a: Bergen-Belsen by Frank Snowswell (1 May 1945). Permission courtesy of the Snowsell family.

⌒

GORDON PANCHUK

Royal Canadian Air Force, 126 Wing

The son of Ukrainian pioneers, Gordon Bohdan Panchuk was born on 8 February 1915 in Meacham, Saskatchewan. In 1934 he attended a teacher training institute in Saskatoon, where he joined the Ukrainian Greek Orthodox Church of Canada and became active in the Canadian Ukrainian Youth Association. He also received a Bachelor of Arts degree from Sir George Williams University and a Master of Arts degree from the University of Montreal. Between 1935 and 1939 he was a teacher and later principal at Yellow Creek High School in Saskatchewan.[32]

In 1939, Panchuk enlisted in the Royal Canadian Air Force and trained as a wireless operator at the University of Saskatchewan. His training continued in both Toronto and Montreal before he was sent overseas in 1941. While stationed in England, Panchuk helped establish the Ukrainian Canadian Servicemen's Association in London, acting as its president for three years.

When he arrived in Europe, Panchuk held the rank of leading aircraftsman, and he worked in the Intelligence Section. He took part in the Allied landings in Normandy and saw action in Belgium, the Netherlands, and Germany. He travelled to Bergen-Belsen in May 1945 with personnel from 126 Wing, bringing parcels from Canada to the survivors of the camp.[33]

For his actions during the war he received several decorations, including an Order of the British Empire (MBE). He was discharged from the air force in June 1946 at the rank of flight lieutenant. After the war, Panchuk became involved in the rehabilitation and resettlement of European refugees, particularly Ukrainians. He was one of the founders of the Central Ukrainian Relief Bureau in London and became its first director.[34] He also helped establish the Association of Ukrainian Soldiers in the Polish Armed Forces, which later became the Association of Ukrainians in Great Britain. He and his wife, Anne Cherniawsky, spent seven years in England doing relief and social work.

Panchuk returned to Canada in 1952 and began working as the head of the Ukrainian Section of the Canadian Broadcasting Corporation's International Service. In 1955 he began teaching high school in Montreal, a job he would keep until his retirement in 1980. In 1967 he received the Order of Canada for community work

After his retirement he became rector of the St. Petro Mohyla Institute in Saskatoon. He continued to work on behalf of Ukrainian Canadians and was active in the Ukrainian Canadian Veterans' Association, the Ukrainian Museum of Ottawa, and the Canadian Foundation for Ukrainian Studies. In 1983, he published his memoir *Heroes of Their Day: The Reminiscences of Bohdan Panchuk*. Gordon Panchuk passed away on 20 June 1987 in Montreal at the age of seventy-two. He is buried in the St. Volodymyr Ukrainian Cemetery in Oakville, Ontario.

Senate Testimony

It is not my intention to deal with a long-term policy of immigration, as it was not our intention to urge a long-term policy during the war. We are quite prepared, and glad to leave these things to people much more fitted and capable to do them. I only want to plead very briefly, the case of a people that I saw, that I met, and that I left as recently as three weeks ago. The case is not only important for them, not only urgent for them, but it is most important, and most urgent for us in Canada.

I first met the Ukrainian refugees seven days after D-day. I was very fortunate in that I was one of the first Air Force officers on the beach – that includes both the Royal Air Force and the Royal Canadian Air Force. I was one of the first two officers – the other was a fellow officer from Montreal, who landed on the beach. We were sent there to prepare the base from which our fighters flew. I was very fortunate in that I was serving with a Canadian Wing, 126 Wing, which had the highest score of enemy aircraft destroyed in the war. The first refugees I met were mostly French, Belgian, and every type you can imagine. I was most amazed, it was something I never expected – that among those people were Ukrainians. They were people who had been evacuated by force by Germans to work in German factories, and in German bases all throughout the German occupied territory. At the very first opportunity they had, they deserted, and joined the Free French Forces, and at the first opportunity they came across, and helped us. Months before we landed they helped to make arrangements for our landing. One of the most famous units that served with the Free French was Taras Shevchenao, which is now serving in the French Foreign Legion. The refugees were sent away to many places. Some were evacuated to England, and some were used in Army and Air Force units. Again, it was my fortune to be able to speak Ukrainian and a little French in my dealings with people. I was able to deal with them very closely.

It was the same as we continued on our way up through Belgium and Holland and after we eventually crossed the Rhine on our R-day. It broke the hearts of all that saw the long streams of people pushing carts, pulling little wagons, and carrying their belongings – mothers, husbands, wives, and children – making a general exodus westward. When we asked them why they were moving, they tried to explain. Some could not, and some would not. They all felt that only by going westward could they reach freedom and privileges they had all dreamt of, and which had been denied them. They were all hopeful of meeting British forces, and the American forces, and I was very proud to hear them say that over and above everything else they wanted to meet the Canadians. Canada herself has built up a reputation unequalled in the world. No nation, with all due respect to England and the United States – no nation has ever exceeded the respect and prestige which Canada has there. No soldiers were treated better anywhere in the country – in France, in Holland, and even Germany – than were the Canadian soldiers, and I hope we treated them as well and were successful to some extent in justifying ourselves. It was only because of that I want to present their case.

I underline the subject not as a Canadian officer, but as a Canadian citizen who has been away from Canada for five years, and as a citizen who has come back to his country. I was born, raised and expect to die in Canada. I expect my children will live here, and I want to try to do everything I can to make this country, and the country of my children, the best country in the world.

When I met the refugees, I saw many hordes of struggling humanity coming along the road, and they often blocked our passage, often interfered with our military operations. We all felt one and the same thing – if there was only something we could do for them – if we could move them back into the wilderness of Canada, to open it up. They are willing to work. If there was only somewhere they could be set up and develop along the lines of freedom it would be worthwhile. It was my privilege to work with them, and to talk with them, and to learn what could be done, and what should be done, for them.

It was also my privilege to help the military government and UNNRA organize camps. This I did as a side-line when I was free from ordinary service duties. I was privileged in knowing two languages and being able to talk to them. The first camp was at Wentorf near Hamburg.[35] At Unterless there were forty Ukrainian girls.[36] I was able to have conversation with them. Major Hodginson was the Military Commander in charge there. We said we were going to Belgium to celebrate Easter with a Ukrainian feast. They were amazed that such a thing was possible and that such a thing existed. It was the same story in all the camps in the British zone, and the American zone.

I would like now to give you a brief picture of the camps as they are now. The camp at Heidenan, near Hamburg, had several Ukrainians.[37] In six months they had organized fifteen institutions in the camp itself. It is a completely self-supporting unit. They have built a church – converted a barn into a church. They have built a beautiful theatre, organized a kindergarten for one hundred and twenty children, they have a high-school, and university for adult education. They are completely independent, and completely self-supporting, and, as all the military people dealing with them know, they are a very industrious, and very self-reliant people. It is not only my opinion, but the impression of other army people who were dealing with them. Major Shadwell, of the British Army was in charge of the camps at Kiel. One of my most treasured souvenirs of the war is a picture of the church built there. Those people did not know how long they would be there – a week, three weeks, six weeks, a month, or six months. The first thing they did was to build a church. On that church there is a beautiful cross made of glass with electric lights to illuminate it.

The Ukrainians in Germany were forced to wear these tags to distinguish them from other slave laborers, in the German mind, they were not from the same political station. It was the only identity that they were of the "lower" category and did not belong to the ordinary German population. They were to wear them everywhere they went. If a German was inside a restaurant, they would have to immediately evacuate it. If they were in a restaurant, and a German came in, they would have to get up and leave. The girls continued to wear them, not knowing that they were free to take them off. On one occasion when we said they did not have to wear them any more they replied they did not understand.

I could read an extract from a letter from a Canadian in UNRRA, who writes as a Canadian of British origin, and who was in charge of a camp of 2,000 people. He says that any country who has these people will be a really lucky country. We appreciate the fact that we need industrial workers, agricultural workers, domestic laborers, and people who can really fill in those places which are empty in Canada. If we do something to help these people enter Canada I think it would be an accomplishment worth while ...

In every camp the people are self-reliant. If they require shoes they have their own cooperative shoe repair shop to do it for them; if the pots need mending there is a cooperative pottery that will look after them. Their every effort is to fill the needs that we have not yet been able to supply through UNRRA or the military government. They have started printing their own publications. They manage to beg, borrow – or scrounge, as we say in the service – everything they can to establish a printing press. I have among my souvenirs a sample of their newspaper printed in the camps. It is the Easter edition of "The Echo" published in a Ukrainian (stateless) DP camp in Heidenan, Germany. I do not think I could dwell too much on their industry

and how they support and manage themselves. There is no end to
the confirmation of this fact that can be received from any UNRRA
people or the military government staffs who have to do with these
people.

So not to take up more of your time may I in conclusion briefly say
that I feel strongly, as every service man who served overseas, that
Canada needs more men. Certainly, our population is much too small.
But in the selection of these immigrants we must always emphasize
quality; we want men of integrity and with respect for themselves and
others. Men who love their homes and country and who know their
duty and strive to do it. I have no doubt we all agree that is the type
of person we want. If we want such citizens they are at our disposal; if
we do not take them, somebody else will.

At one time our wing, 126 Wing, was stationed only six miles from
the concentration camp of Belsen. Flight Lieutenant Berger, of Montreal Squadron Leader Field, who was the equipment officer of our
wings, and myself organized a relief unit for Belsen. We took medical supplies and food from parcels from Canada to Belsen for people
of whom you have heard, and whom you have read. I found, much
to my surprise, something I didn't expect – something I didn't know
existed. There was at least thirty per cent of the prisoners in Belsen,
Ukrainians. Kosarenko Kosarewych, the writer, was a prisoner of
war there, and at the time I saw him he weighed forty pounds. He
is one of those I would recommend to come here. He is now one of
the DPs in Hamburg. I personally saw Kosarenko Kosarewych in
Hamburg, and I left him all the parcels I received from Canada, so he
would have something to eat while convalescing there. There is one
other argument often presented with which I am not in agreement,
that of the SS division.[38] That division is not an SS division but the
Ukrainian Straight Shooter Division. That division is in the camp
at Rimini, and there are about ten thousand in the division.[39] They
are known to the British authorities, the British Foreign Office, the
British War Office, and the British Provost Corps. Those people are
not even considered by the British as SEP, which means surrendered
enemy personnel, even though they marched 150 miles to lay down
their arms before our present Governor General. That is a division
which has never been in the SS, never served in the SS, and one
certain truth of that is that every man serving in the German army,
in the SS, had a tattoo under the left arm. Our Intelligence and the
American C.I.C. [Counter Intelligence Corps], who are I think, as
good an authority as can be found on that, knows about that. I think
the British Intelligence, the British Provost Corps, and the American

C.I.C. are as good an authority, if not better, than the people in
Canada who have not been overseas. This division has never been
in the SS, never served in the SS, and if you wish information about
that, it is known to the British Foreign Office, and the British War Office. The British government generally knows about it.

Source: Testimony of B. Panchuk, Senate of Canada, "Proceedings of the Standing Committee on Immigration and Labour" (29 May 1946).

Chapter Five

Displaced Persons Camp

For survivors at camps like Bergen-Belsen, liberation does not necessarily mean freedom. Initially, the survivors were not permitted to leave the camp. Instead, in the weeks and, for some, the months and even years that followed, they continued to live behind the barbed wire in the camps. When places like Bergen-Belsen became displaced persons camps, the survivors were still guarded – only by men in different uniforms.

Among the survivors at the camp were scores of orphaned children. Their situations often captured the attention of Canadian personnel working in or nearby the camp. "The question is what is to become of the remaining [orphans]," explained Stanley Winfield of the RCAF, "They have neither homes nor families – they have nothing!"[1] Accordingly, several personnel from the Royal Canadian Air Force rallied around the children, organizing picnics and other activities. A few others, like Winfield and his colleague Ted Aplin, explored the possibility of arranging adoptions.

In the post-war period, DP camps often posed great challenges for survivors. Bergen-Belsen became the largest displaced persons camp in Germany. Survivors were faced with a lack of food, inadequate accommodation, and limited medical equipment. In October 1945, in an effort to protest against the poor rations and supplies in the camp, a hunger strike was called in Bergen-Belsen. It was not until the summer of 1946 that the food situation and the accommodations improved in the DP camp.

If a survivor was healthy enough, why not simply leave the camp? Within weeks of their liberation, many non-Jews did return home. So, too, did Jews from Western Europe. The situation was quite different for Jews from Eastern Europe. For many of these survivors, returning home was generally unthinkable. The fear of antisemitic attacks and the haunting memories of what happened to their family and friends made this an unrealistic prospect.

Many survivors wanted to leave Europe in pursuit of a life in a new Jewish state. However, Britain had long maintained a policy of limiting Jewish immigration to Palestine, which they had done throughout the 1930s. The British argued that the interests of the region would be better served by maintaining an Arab majority. In essence, paradoxically, the British saved Jews by liberating them from the concentration camps but then re-imprisoned them in the immediate post-war period.

The following pages explore the involvement of Canadians at the displaced persons camp at Bergen-Belsen (officially named the Hohne Displaced Persons Camp). What assistance could Canadians offer to survivors in the post-war period? Their responses touch on topics such as immigration, adoption, the situation in Palestine, and the creative and spiritual life in the DP camp.

STANLEY H. WINFIELD

Royal Canadian Air Force, 8402 Disarmament Wing

The youngest of four brothers, Stanley Harold Winfield was born on 16 August 1923 in Calgary, Alberta. His father, John Joshua (J.J.) Weinfield (1879–1985), immigrated to Montreal in 1886 from Zbarash, Austria.[2] He was the first Jewish graduate of the Montreal College of Pharmacy and was a pharmacist for much of his working life. In 1911, he married Sophia Sereth of Calgary, and the couple settled in her hometown and had four sons; Stanley was the youngest.

In 1941, Stanley Winfield joined the Royal Canadian Air Force, serving in Newfoundland, England, and north-west Europe. He was assigned to 8402 Disarmament Wing with the rank of sergeant; their assignment was to neutralize the Luftwaffe in north-west Germany. The headquarters for 84 Group was located near Celle, and therefore near Bergen-Belsen.

In June 1945 Winfield's colleague, Squadron Leader Ted Aplin, visited the nearby camp for the first time.[3] Deeply moved by the encounter, he encouraged Winfield to make a trip to the camp with him. While initially reluctant, Winfield ultimately toured Bergen-Belsen and later became closely involved in helping the survivors. He assisted Aplin in using the armed forces postal service to help survivors contact family and friends outside of Germany. In addition, the two men helped to organize goods collected overseas to be distributed at the camp. Winfield also took part in picnics with the children of Bergen-Belsen. Above all, Winfield concerned himself with the future welfare of the children at the camp.[4]

After the war Winfield studied at the University of British Columbia, earning a degree in law in 1952. He began his legal career with Allstate Insurance before going into private practice. He later served as both chief counsel and special counsel to the Insurance Corporation of British Columbia.

Winfield maintained his ties to the military during his legal career. He was associated with the Canadian Intelligence Corps and later became president of the Canadian Military Intelligence Association. He was the director and secretary of the Churchill Society of British Columbia, where he administered its university scholarship program. In 1996 and 1997 he was appointed to the Canadian delegation sent to Bosnia and Herzegovina to oversee elections.[5] Between 1969 and 1979 he served on UNICEF boards and committees. In 1977 he received the Queen's Silver Jubilee Medal.

In his later years he was active in the Vancouver Holocaust Education Centre. He donated his wartime effects to the centre's archive, as well as his recorded testimony. He firmly believed in the importance of Holocaust education. Stanley Winfield passed away on 14 August 2011, two days before he was to turn eighty-eight years old.[6]

Memoir

In February, 1945, I was stationed with an R.C.A.F. Unit in Peterborough, England, at which time I was selected to serve with the Allied Control Commission (Air) and I proceeded to London in March to attend a four week course, the aim of which was to prepare the candidates with a knowledge of the historical and psychological foundations of Germany, the German Airforce organization and methods of disarmament and control with particular attention paid to the attitude to be adopted by disarmament personnel towards the military and civil population of Germany once victory was attained. I completed the course in April and on May 12th, 1945 I was flown to Airport B 106 at Enschede, Holland ... Squadron Leader Ted Aplin was in charge of our small party and our destination was Celle, Germany. On crossing the Dutch-German frontier into Germany, I felt that I was entering a land of the dead – the same feeling that I had when I went into Germany the first time when my destination was Meppen. As we traveled further into Germany, we became oblivious to the tremendous damage in the towns, countless blown bridges, etc., but noticed with very profound interest the attitude and reactions of the former "super race." When passing us or other Allied troops, they either looked to the ground, sideways or straight ahead. Some just stood at the side of the road, watching in a sort of a stupor while endless streams of Army vehicles of all types and descriptions rolled by. "Could this really be happening to us?" was what their stunned expressions seemed to say. However, there were a few whose hostile looks betrayed their emotions and made me realize that I was in Germany and not just passing through some town that had been struck by a hurricane or some other act of nature.

... According to General Montgomery's regulations, we were forbidden to speak or to have anything to do with them. This did not bother me in the slightest, although I felt it was a ridiculous policy but to Squadron Leader Aplin the sight of these children reminded him of his own youngsters and he remarked how he would feel if the boot was on the other foot. I cannot say that I did not agree with his point of view insofar as non-fraternization with the youngsters was concerned. The non-fraternization regulations were in part: "you must not have anything whatsoever to do with German nationals and this includes smiling or speaking or giving gum or chocolate, etc. to any child regardless of age." As concerned, this is absolutely correct, but I certainly cannot see what good effect such an order would have on a three or four year old child who doesn't know what the hell it's all about anyway. As a matter of fact, the only possible reaction that he or she at that age would get would be to look on anybody in an Allied uniform as something very closely associated with the devil himself and in time would hate all Englishman, Canadian or whatever. Not a very good way of re-educating the future German nation to our way of life in my opinion. However, orders are orders, and I don't feel like spending a couple of years in "the digger" for giving little three-year-old Gretels a piece of chocolate even though she might remember when she became a little older that one of these English "schweinhunds" was nice to her one day and maybe wonder why she should hate them like her big brother probably did [like] when ... a Hitler Jugend leader told her that she should.

... After circling Hanover, we left the Autobahn, there was the sign we were looking for: "84 Group (Main) Celle, 60Km." An hour later we entered the town that was to be our new home. Of all the typical German towns that we had passed through thus far, Celle ... surpassed [all] for quaintness and picturesqueness. We followed the signed route through the town, stopping once at the R.A.F. information post to make sure we were on the right track, crossed over the one and only Bailey bridge in town and it was here we saw the sign Belsen, 40 Km. It is very hard to explain the strange feeling that came over me. Now I was in Hitler's Germany good and proper, and with my weapon and my uniform had as much power and authority over that German over there as any Gestapo Agent ever had and here I was of the Jewish faith, a non-Aryan, who not long ago according to that same German standing over there should be in Belsen or in some other concentration camp and be exterminated along with the rest of the six million already murdered.

We continued on to the village of Grosse Hehlen, a suburb of Celle, and five minutes later there we were at the tented city, built, owned and operated by the Canadians of 84 Group and were we glad to see them.

... I took a great interest in the Germans and their attitudes towards the occupation forces. They were still bowing and scraping, doffing their hats and saluting every private just to be sure of not making any mistakes but were definitely amazed and I am sure could not understand why we were not allowed to have anything to do with them. The frauleins took definite advantage of this order and saw only the wonderful opportunity of "getting even." They would go for a stroll where they knew Allied soldiers would be, such as the park, the river, and appear as vivacious and desirable as they possibly could. They knew if a soldier was caught talking or even smiling at them it would mean a heavy fine or imprisonment for the soldier involved. It is said that what you can't have you want most and in this case it sure was true. However plenty of fellows were foolish enough to let their emotions get the better of their judgment and conscience and ended up in trouble. Our own troops were smart since they never seemed to be caught. The two theatres in town were originally put into operation and opened up for the troops. George MacMurray and I went down and while standing in the inevitable queue, I saw just what kind of a perverted sense of humour some English soldiers have, to say nothing of our own airmen. We were lined up on one side of the street and on the other side were dozens of displaced persons, mostly Jews evacuated from Belsen because of the typhus epidemic, waiting and watching for a soldier to throw a cigarette butt away and then dash after it. If a cigarette has that hold on a person – O.K. – but I cannot see any civilized person getting such satisfaction and enjoyment out of purposely tossing a butt into a dirty gutter or down a shallow drain so that the poor displaced persons must fish for it. I couldn't see myself even giving a butt to them so I just didn't smoke when they were around. However, after a couple of weeks I got used to having about three men or children scramble after my cigarette butt. After the show that night we went for a stroll in the park and were approached by two men who asked for a cigarette. They both looked definitely Jewish but according to the regulations I asked them for their identity cards and they both turned out to be Polish refugees. We gave them each a couple of cigarettes and then one who spoke a little English mentioned that he had been in Belsen, and that it was "nicht gut" [not good]. We walked on and I remember George saying; "You know, that the trouble with these guys, they immediately tell you that they've been in Belsen and they expect you to empty your pockets." I was coming to the conclusion that George had a mean tongue, but this statement was the payoff and I told him so on no uncertain terms. This was the first time we had ever had an argument, but certainly our friendship was not quite the same from that point onwards. George meant no harm by the remark I am sure, but he simply was a man who had contempt for anyone who capitalized on his misery, whether past or present. I thought it was a pretty narrow-minded point of view in the case of these people and I told him so.

The black market on cigarettes is really booming. Most of the deals are being made with the Yugoslavian displaced persons who are camped down the road. Our boys are acquiring articles worth hundreds and hundreds of dollars for practically nothing. Not being much of a businessman, plus the fact that I have been smoking most the cigarettes I get, is putting me in the position of an onlooker. Here are the latest black market quotations:

Camera: (Zeiss, Leica or Agfa) from 500 to 1500 cigarettes

Watches: 500 to 800 cigarettes

Binoculars: 300 to 500 cigarettes

Silk: 10 cigarettes per metre

Jewellery and precious stones: 100 to 500 cigarettes

Of course, in addition to the above, you can get all kinds of Nazi souvenirs such as swords, swastikas, flags, etc., etc., etc. Where the Yugoslavians get their stock, no one knows, but there have been many cases of German homes being raided so that is the answer I guess.

The weather is still perfect and I am feeling 100%. This living outdoors is always good for the constitution, particularly now that our food is substantial.

Squadron leader Aplin went to Belsen Sunday and it certainly made an impression on him. I am beginning now to realize just what an outstanding person he is. We had a long talk that morning about the "Jewish question" and if every gentile person felt as he did, it would be a much happier world for everyone. We decided that as no one else was thinking about the welfare of the children at Belsen, other than feeding them 3 meagre meals a day, we would try and help them ourselves. I spoke to all the fellows in Mess today and asked them if they would contribute a chocolate bar from their rations once a week for the children at Belsen and they agreed. The following Sunday we had our first of many picnics. One hundred and fifty chocolate bars, sandwiches, milk and three trucks to convey them into the country for the afternoon. They had a magnificent time and we were sure that if we had gone there without the chocolate bars, etc. but just piled them into the trucks and dumped them into the nearest meadow, they would have enjoyed themselves every bit as much. They all showed the signs of just being liberated, i.e. pale, pinched faces, frail little bodies, all of them with their hair just growing back in. The older ones who had been at Auschwitz had the inevitable numbers tattooed on their wrists. What memories these people must have.

A couple of weeks before we had gone down to Celle prison to see the Beasts of Belsen "on parade." They exercised for twenty minutes in the morning and afternoon, at which time a certain number of troops are allowed to "view" them. The matron in charge gave a running commentary regarding the crimes of each of them. They were all there except [Josef] Kramer who was not allowed to exercise with the rest of them. They all looked like fiends and murderers, that is all except Irma Grese. The matron in charge wasn't around at the moment so I asked the chap next to me who said he had been down here before, what the charge was against that good-looking blond with the checkered skirt, "Oh her" he says, "she actually shouldn't be here, she was a switchboard operator, but because she was employed by the S.S., she is being held along with the rest of them. That is her only crime." I was really amazed at the British authorities for keeping an innocent girl locked up with a bunch of murderers just because of having a job working switchboard at Belsen. However, when I picked up a paper three days later, I saw the same girl's picture and underneath was written: "Leader of the Women's S.S. at Belsen." It turns out that she got more charges against her than any of the others, outside of Dr. [Fritz] Klein.[7] Appearances certainly are deceiving.

Source: Stanley H. Winfield, "Memoir: 1945," The Canadian Letters and Images Project, Department of History Vancouver Island University, https://www.canadianletters.ca/content/document-5551.

Letter

Celle, Germany,
July 17th, 1945

Dear Padre![8]
I realize that I have not written to you since arriving on the continent and I certainly hope that you will accept my apology even though I haven't a good excuse to offer. Until recently I have been kept pretty busy, but I must [say] that things have eased up considerably in the past few weeks. Being at Overseas Headquarters I am sure that you

know what our work is over here, so I will skip all those details. However, I can assure you that [it is] far more interesting than No. 3 D.H.Q.

At any rate Padre, I have something on my mind which I consider is very important. And I am passing it on to you as I feel positive that you will do all you can to help – if it can be done.

Since being with the Disarmament Staff I have had the pleasure, and believe me, it is a pleasure, to be working with an old acquaintance of yours, namely S/L Ted Aplin. To refresh your memory, in case you have forgotten him, he says to associate him with Jack King.

We are located at Celle, which is very close to Belsen concentration camp. About five weeks ago S/L Aplin visited the camp, and since that time he has devoted almost all his free time to the inmates, and believe me, he certainly has made their lot a much happier one, especially the youngsters, of which there are approximately four hundred. One hundred and sixty-five of them are in hospital suffering from either T.B. or typhus. For many of the extremely young ones it was the first display of real attention and kindness they had ever received, and for the others I am quite sure they had forgotten the day when they were treated as human beings. Yesterday we took seventy-five of them to the country for a picnic, and it was an experience I will never forget. I'm sure the kids will never forget it either. I could tell you stories of that afternoon that would raise a lump in your throat just as it did ours, but I don't think that is necessary.

However, more has been done than just entertaining them, and that is where I feel your advice and help is needed. S/L Aplin, and to a certain extent myself, have been doing a little research regarding the final disposition of these people, especially the children. That is to say, just what is being done for their future. As you know, out of an approximate figure of eight millions, only a bare half million Jews are left in Europe. The majority of this remainder are adults, and as far as we can ascertain, a very large percentage of the children that are left are at present in Belsen. To me that sounds fantastic and unbelievable, but I think it is the truth. In approximately ten days the majority of the children are going to Sweden as charges of the Swedish Government, and will be cared for until they have recovered sufficiently.[9] I understand that England is prepared to accept one thousand, but naturally she will not take all the children. The question is, what is to become of the remaining ones. They have neither homes nor families – they have nothing! We talked this over and are both of the opinion that some organization, either Jewish or Gentile, has undertaken to do something towards having these children brought to Canada, which, I think is a darn good country for them to

Figure 45. Negative depicts a mural on the wall of the Royal Canadian
Air Force mess hall in the Trenchard Barracks, Celle, Germany. According
to Stanley Winfield, Ted Aplin arranged for an artist to paint this mural.
Photographer unknown. Vancouver Holocaust Education Centre, Stanley
Winfield fonds, 93.08.0231.

grow up in after what they have been through. However, inasmuch
as we have faith in someone else making the first move, I am afraid
that all concerned might be of the very same opinion, and the result
will [be] that nothing will be done.

That's what we want to know – is anything being done in Canada
for these people who have suffered so much? S/L Aplin has also written to friends in Toronto asking that same question. Due to my lack of
self-expression, I cannot tell you how I feel about these children, but
right now it means more to me than anything else, and I intend to do
everything that I can possibly do to help them. I feel that it should be
the Jews at home that must make themselves responsible – don't you
agree? I think I had better add to this point that that last sentence is
my own personal opinion ...

I have kept sordid, gruesome details out of this letter, but have
decided to send you copies of a letter written by S/L Aplin to a friend
in Canada, and a copy of a report obtained from No. 14 Amplifier
Unit. I think you will find that they give you a truer picture of the conditions at Belsen than what one reads in the newspaper. After reading
them I am sure you will understand how I feel. They certainly deserve
all we can do for them, and more!

I am sending a copy of this letter to my Uncle Harry in Montreal whom I am sure will be interested, and also to Mother and Dad.

Please drop me a line very soon, Padre, as I will be anxiously awaiting your reply, and incidentally, you should be paying this country another visit pretty soon shouldn't you?

Sincerely,

Source: Vancouver Holocaust Education Centre: 96.024.010: The Stanley Winfield Collection. Letter written to Rabbi Jack Eisen.

~

TED APLIN

Royal Canadian Air Force, 8402 Disarmament Wing

The son of a Great War veteran, Edwin Miller (Ted) Aplin was born on 1 April 1909 at Teignmouth, Devon, England.[10] He came from a modest, working-class family. His father was a farm labourer and nurseryman, while his mother was a cook and domestic servant. In 1926 Aplin moved to London, where he was employed as a clerk at both Barclays and Anglo-South American Bank. He later became a clerical officer at Scotland Yard.

Aplin immigrated to Canada in 1930 at the age of twenty-one. He found employment in Toronto at the Imperial Bank of Canada. That same year he met Elinor Grace Leef, an American from Illinois. The couple married the following year and settled in east Toronto. Aplin soon found work with the London Life Insurance Company.

The 1930s were a busy time for Aplin: he changed jobs several times and Elinor gave birth to three sons (a daughter was born in 1945). Aplin worked for the stockbrokerage Gardiner and Wardrop and Company; he sold kraft paper for Pacific Mills Limited; and he sold business forms for Autographic Register Systems. In addition to his work life, the 1930s saw Aplin become increasingly active both socially and politically. He became involved in the League for Social Reconstruction, the Canadian Civil Liberties Union, and the Committee to Aid Spanish Democracy. He also became a member of the Co-operative Commonwealth Federation (CCF). In 1941, the Aplin family moved to Scarborough, Ontario.

In May 1942, Aplin enlisted in the Royal Canadian Air Force. As a pilot officer, he was stationed in Canada for the next two and a half years, instructing new recruits on air force law. In December 1944 Aplin was sent to England, where he became part of 8402 Disarmament Wing and was given the rank of squadron leader. This newly formed group's assigned task was to disarm the Luftwaffe in northwest Germany. The headquarters for 84 Group was located at Scheuen near Celle. However, the work for which they had been trained was limited. As a report written at the end of the war indicated, "it became quite apparent that no major Luftwaffe Headquarters organization existed in the 84 Group Area."[11] Indeed, by the spring of 1945 there was no substantial German air force to disarm. Consequently, a few individuals, like Aplin, became restless and searched for ways to occupy their time.

In early June 1945 Squadron Leader Aplin made his first visit to nearby Bergen-Belsen. Expecting to find the camp empty, instead he found several thousand survivors still living in nearby army barracks. Nearly two full months after the camp's surrender, tens of thousands of survivors were crammed into tight quarters, some still quite ill, faced with inadequate diets as well as lacking in medicine, clothing, and other supplies. Aplin was later shocked to find that Poles, both Jews and Gentiles, were being forced to live in the same part of the camp in cramped quarters. He returned to his tent shaken and aghast.

Aplin spent much of the summer and autumn of 1945 assisting the survivors of Bergen-Belsen. Among other acts, Aplin helped initiate a system using the armed forces postal service to aid survivors in contacting family and friends outside of Germany. In addition, he helped to organize distribution within the camp of goods collected from Canadian families. He is also well known for arranging picnics in the countryside for the children of Bergen-Belsen, many of whom were orphans, with the Canadian airmen stationed nearby.[12] Aplin frequently used air force vehicles for these activities, often without permission, and consequently was threatened with a formal reprimand by his superiors,[13] but was ultimately able to escape formal punishment for his actions.

While in Germany, Aplin was offered a position with the United Nations Relief and Rehabilitation Administration. He declined due to his wife's poor health, and in 1946 he returned to Canada. He resumed work as a salesman, and later he operated his own businesses, Ted Aplin and Company and then Ashton Rhodes Limited. He passed away of cancer on 2 June 1973 at the age of sixty-four.

The life of Ted Aplin has been remembered in myriad ways since his passing. In 1989 journalist Robert Collins did a feature on Aplin for Reader's Digest, titled "Angel of Belsen." In 2007, an award-winning play based on his letters premiered, entitled ... and Stockings for the Ladies. The play recounts the experiences of two Canadian airmen who assisted the survivors at Bergen-Belsen, and was written by Attila Clemann, Aplin's step-grandson; directed by Zach Fraser; and featured Brendan McMurtry-Howlett in the one-man show. Since 2007, the play has had numerous runs across North America.

Letter

Celle, Germany,
June 17th, 1945

Dear Lil,[14]

I have just seen Belsen and am ashamed. Ashamed that Gentiles all over the world have not risen in one vast crusade to erase forever this evil mark on their record. For responsibility for such deeds as were perpetrated here cannot belong alone to the masters of the Nazi creed. This is anti-Semitism carried to its final extreme.

The camp itself is situated in a beautiful part of the country, extraordinary in its resemblance to parts of Ontario around Barrie and Camp Borden. It is concealed from view by thick pine woods, and all roads around it were "Verboten." Adjacent to it is a permanent Panzer Grenadier Division location, with magnificent buildings, barracks, hospital, roads, grounds and lake. Into these quarters have now been moved the remaining survivors, totaling several thousand. The majority of these appear to be females, mainly under thirty, mostly Jewish, of all European nationalities.

Admission to this original site of horror has been prohibited as from midnight last night, due I believe, to unfortunate incidents of an intimate nature between visiting soldiers and some of the girls. Permission has now to be obtained (i.e. to enter the camp) from high Army authority ...

The patients are mostly convalescent, and are living quite freely in the former Army barracks, and roam about the camp at will. They bear the marks of their experiences with them, on their faces and their gestures, in their furtiveness and their physical condition. At first glance all the woman and girls appear to be about six months pregnant, but it soon becomes obvious that such a universal condition would be extremely unlikely. Investigation reveals that during their incarceration, almost all their nourishment was obtained by drinking a very weak soup ... [This] has resulted in dilated stomachs, and a change in position which will possibly remain with them forever. The men are this way also, but the condition is not so apparent to the eye. Having survived at all however, would indicate generally a relatively short term of suffering, although I gathered that some had survived as long as four years. The hospital is filled, but I did not venture in. Typhus still is present in the camp, and danger signs abound. The death rate has fallen off considerably due no doubt to medical control as well as to the vastly reduced numbers of patients as a result of its former intensity.

Today was moving day. Patients or inmates are being segregated into barrack blocks according to nationality. It seems that actual fighting has taken place between certain groups recently. What a tragic sequel to such an experience as theirs!

The horror camp itself of course has been burned down and presents a picture of complete desolation. Bulldozers have been to work, scraped out the remaining embers of the vile wooden brick buildings. But all the essential features are there – the thick barbed wire fences dotted with guard towers, the incinerator, the mass graves, the piles of burned and broken shoes and bits of clothing, the bones, identification tags, and so on ...

The existence and real history of places like Belsen to my knowledge have not been identified in the public's mind with the true nature of Fascism. Allied propaganda has painted them as a product of the German character.

I am convinced that this is dangerous. Bombard the German people with this story. Utilize whatever Anti-Nazi forces remain for the purpose. Insist on them seeing movies of the scenes there. Make them accept their share of responsibility for their leaders' degeneration. But let us not fail to identify all this with Fascism itself. Our own people must also learn that Anti-Semitism leads to Belsen! Let us put truth in our own laws, and stamp out the Anti-Semite who, even if unwittingly, is condoning Belsen.

The suffering of the German people has been, is and will be great. The stupidity which was responsible for giving the green light to Belsen was also responsible for their own condition today. The two are inexorably linked. The rest of the world must be forced to see this relationship, and then maybe it will decide it cannot afford the risk.

In London recently, a Communist told me he felt so strongly on the Jewish question that he had often wished he could become converted or naturalised into a Jew if that were possible, so as to share the burden. I feel that way today.

There have been spearheads in every battle. In this war against Fascism, the Jews have paid in blood the biggest price of all. This the Gentile people can never repay. We can however, pledge ourselves to eradicate vigorously from our midst every sign of ingratitude to, or lack of solidarity with our Jewish brothers in our common fight against Fascism.

Fascism will not be defeated until the inter-relationship of its fundamental, social and economic concepts, and the war, are recognized by everybody. "Matters should not be restricted to the military defeat of the Fascist forces. It is necessary to complete the moral and political defeat of Fascism as well."[15]

The responsibility for ensuring this as far as Canada is concerned rests on you people back at home. If you do your job I don't mind staying here and doing mine. But let's not have our boys crushing Germany here, while even a single remnant of Fascism flourishes in Canada.

Think it over!

Sincerely,
Ted

Source: Clara Thomas Archives, York University: F0151, Aplin Family Fonds. Permission courtesy of Nick Aplin.

Letter

84 Group Disarmament Staff
RCAF Overseas
17 July 1945

Darling,

I have been feeling a bit low today and so will take solace in writing you the story of the picnic on Sunday. It was quite a success and I am hoping to repeat it weekly as long as possible. There are now something like 150 or so children in the children's house and the children's hospital and possibly twice that number in the camp in addition. The latter, however, are living with a parent or parents or relatives. The majority are Jewish but of practically every European nationality.

It is fantastic and almost impossible to believe, but there is good reason for the opinion which has been expressed that this handful of children represents a large percentage of the total Jewish children population surviving in Europe today. Their survival is inexplicable and a reflection of a breakdown in the reputed efficiency of the Nazi machine. A fair number are alive today because of the personal courage and initiative of a Russian woman Luba [Tryszynska][16] whom I have met and who accompanied us on the picnic. When Belsen was taken she was discovered in a small room, a hovel, with 50–60 of these children. They were free from Typhus which was rampant in the camp and by one means or another she had managed to keep them "relatively" clean and fed. How she did it is not known. The other inmates did not know they were there, but she must have squared the SS guards in some way. As mothers, parents or relatives of the children died, she would take them in and hide them, and of course was able to furnish information about their ages, names and the fate of the others. Her husband was killed in Auschwitz for either refusing to work on, or sabotaging the incinerators in the crematoriums (if such a place can be dignified by such a name!). Her own child was deliberately killed before her own eyes. Today she is a stoutish blonde woman with a plump rosy face and twinkling blue eyes. She is bursting with energy and is working in the children's home. Her flock is always around her.

We drove up on Sunday right after lunch with three 3-ton trucks and a couple of staff cars and a jeep. We took boxes of sandwiches, 100 freshly made doughnuts, 200 chocolate bars, 4 gallons of milk, a piano, two violins, two banjos, an accordion, etc. We had four officers (including [Ed] Jamieson whom I wrote you about) the Medical officer, some sergeants and airmen. I had great difficulties in keeping the number of the party down, so that there would be sufficient room for the children. On pulling up to the buildings which are used for the "Kinderheim" [children's home] we were greeted with all the bois-terously gay reception which only children seem to be able to muster up. They were all spic and span with freshly ironed shirts and frocks. The supervisor said they had been washing out their clothes every day since Wednesday when she first told them we were coming. There was some difficulty in sorting out the kids. Some had arrived who did not belong in the home but had heard there was a picnic. Others who were too sick to go had also sneaked out of the hospital in the hope of getting themselves caught up in the crowd. Actually a few managed to do this we discovered after we got out in the woods. It was a bit heartbreaking to see the tears of the little ones on the sidewalk whom we had to leave behind. Especially pitiful were the little kids in bed in the open marquees in front of the hospital (TB cases getting "open air" treatment). They have got to know us and stand up and wave and talk in many different languages whenever we are in earshot.

We took along Miss [Enid] Fernandes, an English Red Cross nurse in charge and some of the teachers, together with some of the chaps from the "Psychological Warfare" branch (who were the first to enter the old camp, and who are still among the most zealous workers there).

All we had to do was start driving and as far as the kids were concerned the picnic was on. The band played on one of the trucks, and everybody was happy including the rest of the population of the camp who waved as we went by. They got such a thrill out of seeing the children laughing and singing again!

The country is rather flat around Belsen but is pleasantly wooded. About 9–10 miles away we discovered a pretty spot with trees and good grass and just stopped and disembarked. We had deliberately refused to organize games, etc. and that was quite unnecessary anyway. The biggest thrill the kids got was in being photographed. There must have been several hundred snaps taken which are being developed now and out of them we should get some good ones. We also took some Ciné-Kodak shots and I believe F/L Sparrow who owns the camera is getting his wife to have the National Film Board look at them. (I took a full roll including most of the little girls who have become my own particular friends, but unfortunately they were all spoiled. The German film I used was a bit large for my camera so that it was necessary to tear it out with pliers).

The youngsters are most anxious to see the pictures so we are hoping to get a stack of additional prints and distribute them as fairly as possible. One reason for this is that they believe if a lot of people have pictures of them, maybe some relative or parent may still be alive somewhere and see one.

Anyway the kids played and talked with the grown-ups, posed for pictures, ate sandwiches and drank milk, and brought tears to our eyes and lumps to our throat, as the case may be. Some of them are very beautiful and look alright, but most of them require a great deal of love and care to enable them to grow into healthy normal adults.

Four little girls were specially dressed in "sailor" frocks and berets and did a Polish sailors' dance and song for us. Another girl of about 14 with shaven head asked me if she could borrow a violin after which she played some excellent numbers beautifully.

Eventually the time came to go, so we sounded the horns of the cars and passed word around that each child would be given a chocolate bar on getting into the truck. Consequently our embarkation problem was solved in a few minutes. The remainder of the bars and candy we presented to sick kids at the hospital.

The whole thing made a deep impression on the airmen and officers present and I anticipate no great personnel difficulty in keeping up this sort of thing as long as necessary. Transportation is the toughest problem. We are already planning for next Sunday when we will probably take out some of the smaller children who are not living in the home. They do not need friendship quite as much, but do feel hurt if they are always left out. There is much work to be done in rehabilitating the people in Belsen including the adults. There is some splendid work underway (but by all too few) in the way of occupational therapy, etc. A young English artist ex-soldier is running an art school, but is short of supplies. In our job here we have access to plenty of various materials of some kinds, and I am hoping to do something about these things too. If possible I want the whole of the RAF 84 Group (and especially the RCAF Section) to take the camp under its wing. But this is rather an ambitious thought and will take some tactful and careful selling.

Canada could do much for these people who have suffered so much more than their share for us ... I could help as a contact with the camp itself at this stage and would endeavour to dig up any further information required or to deliver any material which might be sent ...

Ultimately what is required is an international organization "To succor victims of Nazi Concentration camps" to coordinate and plan the treatment, training, rehabilitation and re-establishment of all of these people. Canada could and should undertake responsibility for a good proportion.

Another step which should be considered seriously by the appropriate organizations in Canada is the adoption of the children. Do you remember the plans we were making to adopt the orphans of the Spanish War? Sweden is undertaking to take a large number of children and adults for medical care and treatment. England has offered (I believe) to take 1,000, but this figure may not include the sick.

(How would you like a little Hungarian girl of 12?) Anyway do what you can and if you can't find time, mail this letter on to somebody.

Last night I went to a show put on by the Hungarian section. There is a magnificent theatre in the camp (formerly for the entertainment of the Wehrmacht) and it was absolutely packed. We had to sit on the floor in front. The entertainment was actually poor, although of course my lack of knowledge of the language did not help. But it did not compare with the Polish show we had. This was a big affair and most of the camp administrative staff was there, and the producers took the opportunity of getting in some digs at the way things are run. Included in the numbers was the reading of a four-page political dissertation by two women which lasted about 20 minutes. There are strange currents of political thought in Belsen, particularly with reference to the Hungarians. There was a Hungarian regiment working with the SS in the old camp and they are reputed to have been worse than the Nazis. They are now walking about freely and there is much ill-feeling in the camp, especially among the other ethnic groups, as a result.

I suppose [this letter] will have taken you a half day to read so far, particularly with my writing deteriorating as it does. I hope you don't mind me devoting so much of this letter to Belsen. If you were here you would be just as keen as I am. Even people who don't usually know about these things or think politically at all are impressed.

One chap, after talking to a girl about her experiences noted her Typhus marks, dagger scars, etc. and having heard her say she never went along one particular road because that was the way they were marched in from the Station (it was lined with dead and dying at the time), was very silent for a long time and then remarked: "I wonder how many of the Germans realize what they have done."

You will have heard that the policy of non-fraternization has now been relaxed – to everybody's relief. Now some of us should be able to tell a few people about Belsen. I am hoping the men will not now rush into the arms of the Germans, but will refrain from doing so for definite and conscious reasons of their own. One other thing I intended to mention above – the Art School in Belsen has uncovered a surprising amount of talent and is shortly planning an exhibition of the work done. Most of it portrays from memory the experiences of the artist in the camp. Some have been done by children. I believe they may later be exhibited in London. Would anybody be interested in getting it for Canada and maybe the States?

I hope you managed to get a good rest while the two big boys were away at camp. Look after yourself now and don't let anything prevent you from preserving your youth. I have been swimming a few times lately and am starting to accumulate a fair suntan. There does not appear to be much chance of leave in England for a long time yet, but arrangements are being made for leave in places like Amsterdam, Brussels, Paris, Biarritz, so I may take a trip one of these days. My German is not progressing as rapidly as I had hoped but I am catching on a bit. Write soon and let me know what you have accomplished. I am looking forward to the pictures of Jackie.

All my love and kisses – Teddie

Source: Clara Thomas Archives, York University: F0151, Aplin Family Fonds. Permission courtesy of Nick Aplin.

Account

This is Bella.[17] She is much like all other little blonde seven year old girls you have seen before – cute and friendly, but just a little shy. There is a roguish gleam in the big blue eyes when she catches your gaze, especially if she is going to ask for something … this time she wants to know if she could ride back from the picnic in an "autocar." Many times she has come out on the weekly outings with the other children from Belsen on the big Air Force 3-tonners. The first was really exciting. All the kids were singing, and some of the airmen mixed in with them, did their best with fiddles, cornets and mouth-organs. And the green fields

Figure 46. Outing with Belsen kids, 1945. Bernard Louis Yale collection.
Ontario Jewish Archives, Blankenstein Family Heritage Centre, accession
2010-5-15, item 28.

and the pine trees, and the sheep and cows and horses! – Was it really
true? It couldn't be a dream of story books because she had never had
any story books. Chocolate tasted so nice in the open air on the grass,
but it would be a good idea to take half back to Mummy.

These weekly picnics were something to look forward to, but
there was no reason for getting in a rut. She would ask her friend the
Canadian Squadron Leader for a ride in a real "autocar" with proper
seats. That settled it, and here she was sitting on his lap riding back to
the Camp. With a sweet little voice she sings an old Yiddish song. With
complete composure and not losing any of its plaintive anguish she
sings it through to the end. Do we know this Polish tune? It's much
gayer than the others. Or this Hungarian ... or maybe we will join in
singing "Tipperary." No, she hasn't been in the Belsen Concentration
Camp, thank God, she said, only in Diepholz which was a labour camp,
and much better. That girl over there must have been in Auschwitz
because she has numbers tattooed on her arm. Auschwitz was the
worst camp because most people were put in the fires there. We were
lucky to be only in Diepholz. Daddy and Mummy had to work hard,

Figure 47. Game of "Ring around the Rosie" with Belsen kids, 1945. Bernard
Louis Yale collection. Ontario Jewish Archives, Blankenstein Family Heritage
Centre, accession 2010-5-15, item 32.

but they weren't killed. Are they still with me? Oh yes, thank God! How
do I like Belsen? O.K. only the English are too soft with the Germans,
they don't know what we had to go through.

Her English was fair and her German good, Polish her mother tongue.
With Yiddish and Hungarian that makes five languages – did you pick
them all up in the camp? Oh yes, but why only five, "Parlez-vous français?"
That is Bella, only seven.[18]

Source: Vancouver Holocaust Education Centre, 96.024.010: Aplin, Ted.
"Bella." Stanley Winfield Collection. Permission courtesy of Nick Aplin.

Article

On return from Europe to Canada, to discover the extent to which so
many of our people have already forgotten or turned their heads from
our continuing responsibilities in world affairs is a severe shock to those

of us who thought we had been fighting for a better world. Recently returned servicemen with whom I have discussed this matter agree that there appears to be too little thought about the war, its causes and effects. And unfortunately the press and those instruments whose public duty it should be to mould a responsible and well-informed public opinion, seem rather to enjoy sensationalism and the destruction of that international confidence among the Allied peoples which enabled the war to be brought to a successful conclusion.

For the past nine months I have been stationed in Germany, just a few miles from the site of the notorious Belsen concentration camp. At the time of its liberation by the British Army in April [1945], floods of publicity were released, the gruesome story in word and picture cried forth from every journal, radio, pulpit and screen. Deputations of members of Parliament, the U.S. Congress, high-ranking military leaders, etc., visited such places as Buchenwald, Dachau, Mordhausen, and so on. You will recall the grim vengeance which was demanded and the soft words of pity which were lavished on the indomitable survivors – those broken, starving skeletons whom we so proudly rescued, and whose rescue we blazoned to the world.

Yet today, if one mentions, for example, that in Belsen alone there remain 16,000 of these unfortunate victims of our erstwhile enemy, the response is either surprise or indifference. Did our interest in these people end with the clicking of the newsreels or the recording of those speeches which sound like hypocrisy today?

Although I was not working in Belsen in any official capacity, it was my very great privilege to learn to know the people in the camp and to have an opportunity of assisting in many of the projects and activities which were going on. Together with other Canadian officers and airmen I eventually came to feel a part of the camp and to know intimately the life, problems, tragedies, hopes and aspirations of the people there. We, as ordinary Canadian citizens, now back home, cannot conceive that our fellow countrymen can be content to sit idly by while conditions in the camps continue to exist as they are.

In the early days following the liberation, Belsen was a very happy place. In spite of all the brutality and suffering which they had endured, the realization of deliverance brought life and laughter to the survivors. The weather was good, the sun shone and the birds sang. Clothes, requisitions from the local German population, were issued, food was plentiful and friendly soldiers, Red Cross workers, Quakers, etc., were doing all they could to help. Talent of extremely high calibre was available among the people in extraordinary profusion: musicians, dancers, writers, artists, architects, teachers, and so on, organized concerts, shows, schools, and art schools. The results were of a remarkably high order, and the impression made upon the British troops certainly will not easily be forgotten. Touring Canadian shows which we took to the camp were frequently astonished to be entertained in return by artists whose performance often made the visitors look like amateurs.

All in all, life was vibrant and with good reason; there was a new hope in the air. Soon would come reunion of wife or husband or child, contact with relatives abroad, and the beginning of a new life.

But that was last summer. One by one all of these hopes have been mocked. As the months went by there came the realization that the close relatives are probably all dead – tortured, starved and killed or worked to death in other camps. Cuts in rations came next: no replacement of worn-out clothes, no shoes, no overcoats, no underwear; none of the essential needs of civilized human beings have been provided. To this day there is no proper source of supply for such elementary things as soap, tooth paste, razor blades, etc. Babies are born into the world with no clothes to wear. I have seen children wearing old dresses and curtains for napkins. In 1946 no adequate mail services have been provided to enable these people to communicate with their desperately anxious relatives [abroad], such as those in the U.S. and Canada. In fact, until recently, it was illegal for them to write at all!

The cold weather had already arrived before more than half the rooms had been provided with stoves and those largely by the initiative of the people themselves. Even now there is no fuel distribution and wood is obtained from the countryside by the strong and sold to those less fortunate. Hardly an efficient method of servicing the needs of 16,000 people!

Food is prepared in central kitchens and served at the rate of 2 meals a day, based on 2,170 calories per day.

In the British zone the military authorities are responsible for the food, clothing and shelter of "displaced persons." They have carried out this responsibility literally and have provided sufficient in each case so that the people will probably not die. But not only have they gone beyond this commitment, they have made it practically impossible for other agencies to fulfill the needs for the social, psychological and physical rehabilitation of their charges.

I can quote cases where for example groups of D.P.'s have been denied the right to purchase essential materials such as shoe nails for the repair of their own shoes, when German cobblers have access to these through military government authority.

While I can only speak with personal knowledge of our camp, namely Belsen, many people in this country may be interested to know that up until the time I left, no one shipment of supplies of any kind had been received from North America from any of the relief agencies. Also, in spite of the abundance of food and clothing here and in spite of the great desire of some people here to assist their known surviving relatives in the D.P. camps, no legal method has yet been provided for them to dispatch parcels with any confidence that they will arrive at their destination.

There may be good reasons for all of these things but they have not been published. In view of the attitudes, however, towards the Germans and towards our Allies, which so many of us have seen developing among representatives of the occupying forces, we are not surprised. At any rate, it would be difficult to convince those staunch allies of ours who saw fascism in action from the vantage point of a concentration camp, that such treatment is necessary.

So much for the question of material and physical welfare. While this is the most obvious place in which our record is revealed as either bad or incompetent, there is an even more important side to the picture.

After almost a year of aimless wandering within the confines of a camp, it is natural that the inmates are worried about how much longer they will have to stay. It is fantastic to imagine that after all this time no one can answer their question: "Where can we go, when can we start to live a normal life again?"

It must be borne in mind that the British authorities have themselves refused to recognize any of the differences which naturally exist between the various groups of displaced persons. While my remarks may well apply to most of the "D.P.'s" in the British zone, I have had in mind particularly the problems of those formerly in concentration camps. It is to these that we bear a definite and obvious responsibility. Many have already returned to their homes in the rest of Europe, especially in the west. These have now begun to rebuild their lives. The remainder come mainly from Eastern Europe. It must not be forgotten that the population of the concentration camps in general consisted of the Nazis' political opposition, together with people of Jewish origin. The political prisoners and the Jews from the western and Soviet European countries have largely returned home, consequently the remainder are mostly Jews from Poland.

In Belsen today there are approximately 8,000 Polish Jews. It is correct to say that practically each one of these is the sole survivor of his or her family. Poland represents the graveyard of their loved ones and without any political attitude, many do not want to return there.

From close personal association I know of no citizens to whom we could offer a more honest and cordial welcome. I know of no more resolute guardians of our principles of democracy. In the difficult years which lie ahead our complicated world could well use those who can recognize the seeds of fascism whenever or wherever they may appear. Apart from all this, they are useful citizens, representing all types of trades and skills and learning.

But even if they could contribute nothing to our way of life or to the future of our country, we still owe them a great debt which they have paid for in blood and suffering. Many of them were languishing in concentration camps or resisting Hitler in the days when we were patting him on the back and waving umbrellas and pieces of paper in the air.

I am sure that the people of Canada and the other United Nations would demand rapid action if the facts, some of which I have briefly outlined above, were brought to their attention. Canada has a voice in the councils of the nations. Let us proudly set an example by using that voice in demanding a drastic improvement in the conditions in the remaining camps and by opening the doors of our great undeveloped country. Our national conscience cannot rest easy until this is done.

There are many fronts on which the moral defeat of fascism have not yet been accomplished. In Germany the furtive Nazis who still skulk or strut about must chortle with unholy glee at the spectacle of the plight of their former victims.

It is time this nonsense was ended. Let us raise our voices and call for the opening of the doors of Palestine and all the United Nations to these deserving and unhappy people. Their numbers are few, so let us not dally any longer about quotas, physical or financial standards.

We are shamed by delay and our consciences cannot wait.

Source: Aplin, "I Saw Belsen ... My Conscience Cannot Wait."

BERNARD YALE

Royal Canadian Air Force, 8402 Disarmament Wing

Bernard Louis Yale was born on 3 May 1922 in Toronto, Ontario. His parents, Morris and Ann (née Krasnanski) Yalofsky, were both born in the Ukraine and lived in Romania prior to their immigration in 1922 to Canada.[19] Yale attended shul and learned Yiddish as a child. His father was an upholsterer who passed away, unexpectedly, at the age of thirty-five.[20]

Yale attended Central Commerce High School in Toronto. Upon graduation, he registered for a course in chartered accounting. In 1943, Yale enlisted in the Royal Canadian Air Force, a decision his mother supported, and was trained as a photographer. He was initially assigned to 39 Wing and later transferred to 443 Squadron, which was part of 144 Wing.

Yale saw action in France, Belgium, the Netherlands, and Germany. Towards the end of the war, he was transferred to 84 Group as part of a disarmament wing. His unit was responsible for disarming and dismantling the German air force. At this time, Yale processed photographs of the Bergen-Belsen concentration camp. Along with Ted Aplin, Stanley Winfield, and others, Yale later assisted the survivors of Bergen-Belsen. During the summer of 1945, he helped organize picnics for the children of the camp.

After the war Yale returned to Toronto and continued to work as a chartered accountant. In 1950 he married Esther Wineberg and they had three children together. In 1953, Yale and Frederick Friedlander founded Yale & Partners LLP, a small public accounting firm that specialized in serving the needs of small, owner-managed businesses.[21] Bernard Yale passed away on 16 September 2001. He was seventy-nine years old.[22]

Interview

[My unit] moved to a field not too far from Hamburg, and this was about the time Belsen was liberated. And we were visited by a British major, [an] Army major who had been in charge of the British troops that liberated Belsen.

He told us some of the details of what they found at Belsen, the condition of the people, he described the terrible state of people who looked like living skeletons, people who were so weak that they felt it would be dangerous to even sound the horn of their vehicles fearing that the shock of sound might be fatal to some people, they were so weak. And he told us that they needed food for the people, for the survivors. And it was against regulations for them to use the stores that were used for the troops, so what he was asking us to do was to provide him with food that we received, parcels from home and after hearing what he found, the boys of the unit filled up a small truck with food with all, everything we had, consisting of parcels we received from home and that was used for the people.

We felt that [the inmates] were Jewish; it didn't enter our minds that many there ... were not Jewish. Subsequently, it turns out that there were a reasonable number who were not Jewish, but most of the inmates and survivors were Jewish.

[Initially] I saw photographs that we processed of bodies, of the quarters that the inmates had been living in being destroyed by the Red Cross because the people were being moved into better quarters, previously occupied by the German guards, German service personnel. And we processed pictures of the ovens, and pictures of the guards who were captured. I have some of those photographs …

[I felt] horror and almost unbelief at what was staring at us in black and white in the photographs, I mean hard to accept that human being would do this to other human beings.

One of my closest friends [Otto Polask, also known as "Paul"] at the time was a young fellow, he was a corporal in the postal section, his either parents or grand-parents came from an area of Poland that was populated by mostly German people, referred to as Volksduetche, and this fellow, he was shocked and horrified and became quite active in activities related to helping survivors subsequently.

My friend Paul was helping Ted Aplin who was our squadron leader who became extremely active in helping the survivors to locate relatives and to correspond with relatives and to help in any way possible. And my friend Paul became aware of what Squadron Leader Ted Aplin was doing and he told me about it and I became involved as well in the activities. As a result of that we started to visit Belsen and take part in arranging picnics for the children who had survived Belsen. And at that time, I saw Belsen but by then the horrible aspects of it were not the things that we were dealing with. We had photographs of them, but we were involved in doing things for the children. This would have been August and September of 45.

We would arrange for picnics, we would pick up the children in trucks and take them out in the country-side, provide them with treats, chocolates, things of that nature, other foods, and play games with them. I took photographs of those activities and the kids really enjoyed that and so did we.

I didn't take the names of any of the children, I took their photographs. I didn't look ahead to a time when I might want to recall their identities or anything like that. It's kind of hard for me to recall any discussions or conversations that we had with the kids really, that I had at any case.

Well the kids, when we took them out, they were having a good time, they were playing games, ring-around-the-rosy, and so on. We have pictures of them doing that.

They were living in Belsen. In the quarters that either the guards or German personnel had lived in. [These children were mostly orphans].

Figure 48. Belsen children en route to outing organized by Ted Aplin on
RCAF vehicle, 1945. Bernard Louis Yale collection. Ontario Jewish Archives,
Blankenstein Family Heritage Centre, accession 2010-5-15, item 33.

Aplin was helping the people utilize our postal service which was against regulations actually. He probably could have gotten into trouble if someone in authority had became aware of this, and my friend Paul who was a postal clerk was helping him to do this. They were using our postal service as to attempt to communicate with relatives and so on. And to intercept mail that would come in. I think some of the officers were also helping Ted Aplin by permitting mail that was ultimately meant to be received by the survivors to come addressed to them, because ... this was Germany after the war had ended and facilities such as postal services and so on, were non-existent for a period of time.

Aplin was ... Anglo-Saxon ... which was that he was a true Royal Canadian Air Force officer, but with a soft heart that became evident as a person got to know Ted and observed some of the things that he was doing. I mean he looked like a regular officer. The relations between the enlisted men and the officers in the Canadian forces was quite good. They didn't have the same rigidity that existed in some other forces I believe. But Ted was an exceptional person. Some of the things I found out about him after I was discharged from the Air Force reinforced my feelings of admiration.

[At the time] I didn't know that he organized officers to help with the receipt of mail and so on. But I recall one incident, it was close to Christmas I think, of [19]45, and some of the fellows in the unit thought it would be nice to invite some of the German children of Celle to a party. To a Christmas party. And Ted was present when this was being discussed and I recall him saying, "You know if you want to have a party for children, the children that you should invite to this party are the children who survived Belsen." So that was another –

I think some of the fellas had gotten to know some of the [children]... although there was a policy of non-fraternization that had been in-voked. We weren't supposed to become friendly with the German pop-ulace at that time. But still, I suppose some of the fellas had gotten to know some of the children of the town and so on, I guess they wanted to do something nice for them.

They referred to [Aplin] as the Angel of Belsen. There was an article in the *Reader's Digest* providing details of some of his activities and it was headed "The Angel of Belsen."[23] And his obituary that appeared in the *Toronto Star* that I have a copy of is headed "Angel of Belsen."

I was in Celle for about seven, eight months, from May to about December. There were Displaced Persons' Camps in the vicinity, people who had been forced laborers from places such as Yugoslavia, Ukraine and so on. And I had discussions with some of these people, who described their experiences and so on. And then periodically truckloads

Figure 49. Bernard Yale with two Bergen-Belsen child survivors playing with his camera, 1945. Bernard Louis Yale collection. Ontario Jewish Archives, Blankenstein Family Heritage Centre, accession 2010-5-15, item 24.

of these people would be on their way back home. I can recall in one case that, well in several cases, they would decorate the trucks with branches from trees, just greenery, it wasn't flowers, but I guess it sort of spruced-up the appearance and gave them a feeling, a good feeling.

One incident that I can recall, we were visited one evening, my unit at Celle by a man who was a survivor of Belsen who originally, according to my recollection, had taught in university in Vienna, and he was describing some of the experiences at Belsen and at one point he was trying to explain the reason that the Germans had done something relating to the inmates and he started to explain, he said, "The reason that they did was ..." and he paused. And said, "I can't think what the reason was." I remember this being sort of poignant sort of incident. And another incident or occurrence that I recall was we had a concert and there was a woman who had been a singer, a professional singer who survived Belsen and she sang some songs at this concert we had.

I knew in advance that Jews had been treated very harshly but after seeing what had occurred at Belsen, then I knew in detail what had taken place, and the memory will never go. And the conviction that the knowledge of what took place should be available to people is very strong in me, and anything that I can do to establish that these things actually did occur I am prepared to do. And to this day, people like Zündel[24] who denies that the Holocaust took place, and others like him, I can't understand the mentality of these people, but then think about the mentality of the perpetrators of what took place. I guess people like Zündel, the mentality of people like Zündel becomes not too difficult to [understand] ...

Well, it was a momentous time, and I was part of it, I was involved in the fight against the Fascists, the Nazis, involved in the liberation of Europe from the Germans, from the Nazis, and I feel proud of having been part of that. As I may have mentioned, I came to the conclusion at an early point that war was insanity and that the concentration camps were the ultimate of the insanity. I think I learned some things, I experienced relationships with a lot of different people and it was a learning experience.

I felt closer to what we discovered had taken place at the concentration camp and felt closer to, I could identify with the experiences of the people who had been hidden by righteous Gentiles during the occupation in Europe by the Germans. I could feel closer to that, I could really relate to that, I don't think there is any question about that.

I don't feel guilt or anything like that and I don't know what I could have done other than what I did. I feel very strongly about Israel. I feel that the establishment of the state of Israel was an extremely important thing for the Jewish people.

It's hard to sort of analyze how events have actually changed you, you know? I think that every experience you have has an effect on you, and of course my experiences during the war and my experiences at Belsen would be ... would have a greater influence. How exactly it has affected me I can't really say right at the moment.

I've always been very cautious about telling people, probably it is a fault in me, I've always been leery of telling people how to live, although I think parents and teachers do have a responsibility to whomever they are involved with, parents to their children, teachers their students. The basic Golden Rule, you know?[25] Which I think is the most important part of all the religions and I think this was expressed by a rabbi at one time, when somebody said, "Tell me what's the most important aspect of religion to you and tell me this when I'm standing on one foot," and the Rabbi said, "The Golden Rule. Everything else is commentary." And that sort of stuck in my mind. It may be a well-known story, I don't know. So, I think that everything that's happened has a bearing. I don't know, try to be a decent person, try to guide my children, my grandchildren, if I see that there is something that needs to be said, I say it.

[I am sharing my story] for several reasons. One – to contribute towards the memory of what actually did occur and to counter-act anyone who tries to deny that it happened and equally important I think to deal with the memory I have of Ted Aplin and the things that he did, and others like him. There were others like him as well, but Ted Aplin is really in my memory because I was involved with him. I think those were the main reasons.

As a child growing up in an Observant Jewish home, I think I've always had faith. But not in some of the details that some people sort of dwell on. The Golden rule really is the most important of religion to me. As long as I remember I've always accepted that, I don't think anything has changed, it's not a situation where I believed in God, then when I saw these things I said "Well there can't be a God if things like this happen," or alternatively where some religious people say "well there must be a reason." I don't get involved in debates like that with myself.

Source: USC Shoah Foundation (Interview code: 40440). Interviewed by Rona Arato. Interview date: 14 April 1998.

~

EDGAR JAMIESON

Royal Canadian Air Force, 8402 Disarmament Wing

Edgar "Ed" Lloyd Jamieson was born on 19 October 1917 in Almonte, a former mill town located in Lanark County in south-eastern Ontario.[26] He grew up in nearby Ottawa, where he attended the High School of Commerce from September 1930 until June 1934. He was enrolled in general business courses and received first class honours each year. He was the winner of the John Bingham Memorial Prize, which is awarded to the student with the highest standing in the fourth year. He also received the Board of Trade Gold Medal, which was given to the student who graduated with the first-place ranking in the general business course.

On 10 December 1934, Jamieson began his career with Canadian Oil as a clerk in Ottawa. In October 1939 he joined the head office accounting department. The Second World War interrupted his career; in June 1941 he enlisted in the Royal Canadian Air Force. A year later he married Noreen (née Moore) on 26 June 1942. The couple would go on to have two daughters, Judith and Michelle.

During the war Jamieson was eventually stationed with the RCAF's 8402 Disarmament Wing in Celle, Germany. Along with his colleagues Ted Aplin and others, he became involved with the displaced persons at Bergen-Belsen. He finished his military career, with distinction, as a flying officer.

After the war, in July 1946, Jamieson rejoined the head office accounting department at Canadian Oil. In 1947, he entered the legal department of the company. Later in his career, Jamieson found work with the British Petroleum Company. A few years after joining the company, he earned his certified general accountant designation at the University of Montreal. In 1982, he retired from BP Canada in Toronto as assistant comptroller.

Jamieson was an active member of and volunteer for the Canadian Cancer Society. In November 1986 he received the Canadian Cancer Society National Recognition Award for his fundraising work. He was also an elder in the United Church. Edgar Jamieson passed away on 4 May 1991 in Calgary, Alberta, at Foothills Hospital. He was seventy-three years old at the time of his death.

Letter

My Darling,
I am going to sit down and write you another long letter somewhat like the previous one I wrote about Belsen. Incidentally it has been

very interesting to me to read the papers and find evidence coming
out in the trials of [Josef] Kramer and the other Belsen guards of the
very things which we heard and reported on in that letter. I can't help
the feeling that the trial of these people is unnecessary and a great
waste of brilliant men whose skill could be put to much better uses
than in the endeavor to be fair and even to defend criminals convicted
already in the eyes of all the world. However, that's another story ...

Now I would like to tell you about the events of last night, beginning in the afternoon. I went up to Belsen after lunch to contact in
particular an artist in the camp whom [Ted Aplin] wants to bring
down to the station to paint some murals on the walls of the YMCA
canteen. So, we spent the afternoon looking him up, and telling him
through an interpreter what was required. We went back to have tea
with the people of the Jewish Relief Team, who arrived not very long
ago, and are working day and night to help the inmates. Two of them
were away picking up another member of team expected back from
leave, so it was with three girls of the team that we had tea. They are
primarily English, but they are more informal and straight-from-the-
shoulder than is usually the case with English girls. Extremely intelligent and working themselves to death to do what they can for the
people in the camp, the vast majority of whom are Jewish. They are
very much alive to current events and their meaning, and in particular
the background of the concentration camps, Nazi-ism, etc. It has taken
on fresh meaning since we've arrived here, particularly in the realization of what it has meant to have been persecuted simply because one
is a Jew – but a lot of it they were fully aware before their arrival here.
A very different and interesting collection of people ...

One of them was acting as master of ceremonies at a show being put
on in the camp that night. We heard about this show before. It is a different one to the original one which played here so long ago and was
supposed to be so very good that I hoped I might get a chance to see
it. So, at their very pressing invitation we stayed on for dinner as well,
arranged to take Ruth [a colleague] over to the theatre, get in ourselves, and later drop over to the officer's country club not far away
for perhaps one dance before it stopped at eleven.

I want to tell you briefly about the first skit which was presented
during the show. It was written by a chap in the camp and is simply
titled the Messiah. Even though it was given in German, which is
the only language common denominator all the various nationalities
have, it was not difficult in the least to gather the sense and dramatic
import of nearly every word.

The scene opens with a thoroughly beaten group of the dregs of
humanity slumped in the centre of the stage. The suspense is built up by

a mournful music off stage by the small orchestra for a couple of minutes before the curtain is drawn. Then they all sing a long dirge about all their troubles and miseries. It is original music for the show, and through it all, even through the gayest, there runs that minor chord of tragedy which is so noticeable in all typically Jewish music. It gets you.

In the midst of this a stranger appears on stage, and tells them he is the new Messiah, come to bring deliverance to the world. The people go and consult an old man, one of their sages, and this patriarch comes up and questions closely the Messiah. At the end he tells them not to believe him, because he is a fake and can only make fools of them. For a minute they take the old man's advice, but then the stranger returns to the attack and argues so persuasively that they are convinced he can lead them out of the valley of the shadow. So, they start to sing and dance happily around him in the center of the stage ...

In the middle of their revelry, three young people burst in upon the scene – two men and a girl grasping rifles and bandaged looking really authentically wounded and breathless. They shout at the revelers "Fools! You dance and sing while outside the city, and even the whole world is burning." At this point the whole stage is illuminated from the wing from which they entered by horrible orange and red flickering light, and even genuine smoke commences to drift across the stage. Their lighting effects throughout were so startlingly good as to be spectacular, and this one was tops completely. So, the young people heard what the celebration was about, and replied that they were wasting time. If they wished to save the city, and relieve their misery, they must do it themselves – to come on and join them in their fight against the flames and the forces of tyranny. Curtain.

Of all the cast, only one girl, I found out, had even ever studied dramatics, and she had never been on a stage in front of an audience. So, they were not even amateurs, and certainly they could not be called actors. Furthermore, they did not act even in the smallest part of the play. They lived every second of it. All the other numbers were the same. I have never been so stirred by such simple presentations, and this mind you when I cannot understand the language. In some of the items which followed, nearly all of which depicted some detail of their lives in various camps, whether gay moments or their feelings to the Germans – whole sections of the audience were crying. They were living it too. It was their own lives they were witnessing, and it was as real as though they were doing it themselves.

The final act was very well done, and one which I thought was very suitable. It portrayed the concert party – one of the things which kept their spirits alive and helped them to keep going through the months in the camps. The stage is revealed in total darkness. (This wasn't fooling because at the end of the Messiah the lights had failed in the theatre, and they had been carrying on with lamps and flashlights, believe it or not!) Anyway, someone is playing a violin, and they are singing softly. Someone comes in from the next barracks, and says he has a stub of a candle. Lights in the barracks had been forbidden by their benevolent masters. They light the candle, and with its dim glow continue to sing – one or two people do solo song and acts, and they finish up in a grand finale by singing the song which had become the theme song of the camps. They all came to the edge of the stage and sang for all they were worth. We found ourselves coming to our feet with the rest of the audience, who were joining in with the people on stage and singing with equal passion. Honestly, I have never seen anything like it. I was wringing wet from perspiration when it was over.

Ruth was telling us afterwards that it had been suggested at one time that the show should be taken to London and put on there. But I agreed that it would never have gone over, because to an ordinary civilian audience who did not know the people in the camps, had no idea of their sufferings, the whole meaning and force of the presentation would be lost. It could only be impressive in the setting where we saw it last night.

The failure of the lights had so delayed proceedings, that by the time we got away from there, and drove out to the country club, we arrived in time to hear the orchestra playing God Save the King. So we'd had that, but the club itself is worthy of a return visit. It is one of the most palatial clubs I've ever been in. So we have decided that we must return another evening in time to do some dancing.

One of the girls was with a British captain from the Military Government responsible for the administration of Belsen, and he invited us around to his mess. We accepted, and there met the major under whom he works, Major Jones. This bird turns out to be one of the biggest clots it has ever been my misfortune to meet. He is the essence of the most offensive type of Englishmen you could imagine, product of some exclusive private school, and Cambridge as he himself boasted and a credit to neither.

There was a food strike in the camp last Sunday, and there was another one threatened for next Monday. He wanted to know what the Jewish Relief Team knew about it, and he went on to infer that they were at least passively on the side of the strikers. The whole gist of his argument was that he, Major Jones, as representative of His Majesty's government and in sole charge (!) of maintaining discipline and order

would brook no such rebellion, that he and he alone was fitted to
know what was best for them, and if they didn't like it he would make
their life pretty miserable. I had never heard such high-handed tactics
spoken of by any British officer, nor such colossal egotism.

The girls kept their tempers admirably and argued that if people
were now recovering from their terrible sufferings sufficiently to make
a demonstration of their free expression of opinion – surely that was
a good thing and a credit to the good work that had been done for
them. It didn't do any good. That anyone should question his work
was unthinkable to him, and he went on to threaten the Jewish team
that if they did not indicate they were on his side by having some of
the agitators removed or kept quiet, that he would ask the team to be
withdrawn. They again tried to convince him that their job was not to
arbitrate disputes, but to do their best to look after the peoples' welfare,
just the same as that was his job, and that came first with them.

Still no soap, and I was becoming as coldly furious with him as
anyone else, so the only answer was to get out as fast as possible.
I managed to be polite in suggesting that we should leave and in
thanking him for his hospitality, and we left. We came back to the
house or hotel, rather, in Bergen where the Jewish Committee are quar-
tered, and they invited us in for coffee. We all went in and sat around
in the huge kitchen of the place – just like you would at home. Believe
it or not, we sat around all over the kitchen, on tables, and chairs, or
stood around arguing and talking until nearly four in the morning.
It began mostly with pulling the man Jones apart, but from that got
around to the Zionist desire to take over Palestine for the Jews, and
from there to the immediate and pressing problems of peace.

It was all in all one of the most different and interesting evenings
I've spent in a long time. And as Ted [Aplin] remarked this morning,
certainly it was more productive than just sitting around in a mess somewhere getting stinko. Certainly, sitting at a ringside table during the
postwar period here in Germany is going to be a thing which I shall long
remember. And I am learning sharply how wrong racial or religious dis-
crimination is, even if I am still unable to completely overcome my prejudice against Germans purely and simply because they are German.

What you can do with this letter, I am sure I do not know. I don't
think it has any particular message, but I do think perhaps a few
people may be interested in reading it. I was wishing a few times
last night that Sid and Muriel could have been present at some of the
discussion. Muriel would be keenly interested in the whole picture,
because of her social worker background, and I am sure Sid would be
too because of his interest in people generally.

Would you like more stuff along this line? Is there anything in particular you would like to hear about? I have kept everything of a personal nature out of this letter hon, because I expect as I write it that you will be passing it around various people, even if nothing else. I'll be writing you later a more usual letter. For now, then,

Yours ever,

Edgar

Source: Courtesy of the Jamieson family. Letter dated 14 October 1945.

Chapter Six

Religious Observation

A significant number of Canadian chaplains of various denominations – including Roman Catholic, Protestant, and Jewish – arrived at Bergen-Belsen during the spring and summer of 1945. While Jews made up the bulk of the inmates, there were also thousands of Catholics, Protestants, and other groups held prisoner in the camp. Canadian chaplains arrived at the camp to offer acts of worship for the living, while others prayed for the dead. In addition, military chaplains assisted in a variety of other ways, such as gathering food, medicine, and supplies, as well as attempting to help inmates locate friends and family members.

During the initial period of the surrender of Bergen-Belsen, military chaplains spent most of their time offering last rites and blessings or reciting the Mourner's Kaddish. Many found that there was not much time to complete additional tasks. In addition, and due to the thousands of corpses around the camp and the lack of an adequate labour force, the anonymous, mass burial of the dead became a serious point of controversy and disgust.

Due to the extreme nature of the conditions in the camp, military chaplains felt overcome by the situation. Padres acknowledged feelings of inadequacy when faced with the growing physical, spiritual, and emotional needs of the inmates around them. According to Reverend Ross Cameron of the RCAF, "Wherever we went, there were unearthly cries from the people thinking that we were there to arrange their removal also. Such hopeless dejection, such complete physical collapse and emaciation are impossible to imagine unless one has seen them."[1] Exhausted, depressed, and shocked, padres began to question themselves, the condition of humankind, and even their respective faiths.

Canadian military chaplains were called upon to offer religious services in front of open graves filled with thousands of dead: men, women, and children who were often left unidentified. As this final chapter demonstrates, padres and other religiously minded personnel also did more than the typical military duties asked of them. Almost always acting on their own initiative, they tended to the sick, gathered food, listened to the stories of the inmates, and encouraged their colleagues to help, all the while maintaining their own respective religious beliefs. Those beliefs were frequently tested by their trying experiences at Bergen-Belsen. In the end, and despite the horrors, the questions, and the doubts, Canadian military personnel maintained their respective faiths.

ROSS KETCHEN CAMERON

Chaplain, Royal Canadian Air Force, 39 Wing

Ross Ketchen Cameron was born in 1904 in Stratford, Ontario, and grew up in nearby Georgetown. In 1929 he received a Bachelor of Arts from University College at the University of Toronto. He subsequently earned a master's degree in philosophy from the same institution, and in 1932 he graduated in theology from Knox College.[2]

From 1933 to 1936 Reverend Cameron was minister at Rogers Memorial Presbyterian Church in Toronto. In 1937 he was called upon to undertake the recently vacated ministerial position at the First Presbyterian Church in Edmonton. Three years later, after accepting a position at the Dovercourt Road Presbyterian Church, Reverend Cameron and his wife, Audrey (née Bradley), returned to Toronto.

As the Second World War commenced, Reverend Cameron left his position at Dovercourt to serve as a chaplain in the Royal Canadian Air Force,[3] with postings in Canada, Great Britain, and north-west Europe. At the end of April 1945, while attached to RCAF's 39 Wing, Reverend Cameron and his colleague, Chaplain Wilfred H. Dunphy, left their station at Soltau and travelled to the recently surrendered Bergen-Belsen concentration camp. Father Dunphy, from Millview, Prince Edward Island, participated in the mass internment and burial services at the camp.

According to the 39 Wing's Operations Record Book, on 3 May 1945 padres Cameron and Dunphy spoke to their men about the situation at Bergen-Belsen in the station theatre. The wing donated several large truckloads of supplies to the camp. Cameron's son Donald remarked

that his visit to Bergen-Belsen was "one of the most moving experiences of his life."⁴ In 1946, Reverend Cameron wrote about his
encounter at the camp in an article for *The Front Line*, a monthly
Presbyterian magazine founded by Norman Allan MacEachern and published in Toronto.⁵

Upon his return to Canada, Reverend Cameron maintained his ties to
the military by serving as chaplain to the 48th Highlanders and Black-
watch Association. He also returned to the Dovercourt Road Presbyterian Church. In 1959, Reverend Cameron was awarded an Honorary
Doctor of Divinity from Knox College, and in 1962 was elected as moderator of the Presbyterian Church of Canada. In 1965 he became minister
at the York Memorial Presbyterian Church in Toronto. He retired in 1975,
and passed away in April 1989 at Toronto General Hospital at the age of
eighty-five. He was predeceased by his wife, Audrey, and was survived by
his son, the Honourable Donald R. Cameron, QC.

Article

In the conquest of Germany during the Winter and Spring of 1945, there
were revelations to the conquering troops which justified almost every
charge that had been made previously against certain Germans. It was
revealed that they had been guilty of hideous and unspeakable atrocities. Conditions and situations were uncovered which German leaders
never expected to have to reveal to the eyes of the world.

We had been told, even before the war began, that concentration
camps were one of the means of punishment which the Nazi party had
devised for its enemies. Such books as those of Phyllis Bottome⁶ and
others revealed something of the fantastic lengths to which the National Socialists were prepared to go to keep the yoke upon the necks
of people whom they had enslaved. But accounts of such things read in
cold print and at a distance of thousands of miles scarcely revealed to
us more than the surface of such conditions.

The British 2nd Army, under the command of Field Marshal Vis-
count Montgomery crossed the Rhine River in March. The area before
it for conquest was generally known as North West Germany, comprising Westphalia, Hanover and Schleswig-Holstein. The advance of the
Army was rapid. The Germans were driven north and took their final
stand north of Hamburg.

The air support of the British 2nd Army was provided by the 2nd
Tactical Air Force, R.A.F., under the command of Air Vice-Marshall Sir
Harry Broadhurst. In the 2nd Tactical Air Force, No. 83 Group, there
were four Canadian Wings. Three were Fighters and one was No. 39

Reconnaissance Wing. All of these gave an exceptionally good account of themselves in covering and supporting the Army's rapid advance. It was my good fortune to be attached to the Reconnaissance Wing. The type of work the Airforce was doing required that it should be at all times, close to the Army. Reconnaissance was a most important feature in the conquest first of Italy and later of Germany. Encamped in the open near Soltau in early April, we met the first Canadian and British prisoners of war released from German prison camps. They were flown from our field to Paris and London. Canadian boys gave generously of comforts, food and clothing, which they seemed to have in tremendous quantities in their parcels from home. These they also gave when an appeal came, at that same time, for the people suffering in the Belsen Concentration Camp about 30 miles distant. Two large truck loads of comforts, medical supplies, clothing and food were given voluntarily, and sent for the thousands of people suffering and dying in Belsen. Five days previously the British troops had uncovered the camp and overcome its S.S. Garrison troops. In company with the Roman Catholic Priest from our Wing, I went through the horrible place.

We Enter Belsen

The camp is situated deep in the woods on a side road. On all the roads, at a distance five miles from the camp, there were large placards forbidding entrance to unauthorised persons, because typhus was rampant. On entering the office at the gate, we were first thoroughly dusted with an antiseptic powder. We were introduced to the Padre and the Chief Medical Officer. The Padre was a minister from Stornoway – Capt. Ross of the Church of Scotland. The Medical Officer was from Aberdeen – Major Forbes.

The camp was a desolate looking place, with many smells emanating from it, but over it all the predominating smell of dead flesh. The people were dying at the rate of 800 a day. Altogether it was estimated that there were 70,000 persons imprisoned there. As we walked into the camp between the rows of barrack blocks we saw people with no animation in their faces and with the most abject hopelessness in their very gait. Some appeared to be in very good health. We were told that they had not been there long. The majority of them were terribly emaciated. Some had been moved out of the barrack blocks and had arranged pieces of canvas or sacking over poles, and were trying to find shelter from the cold wind. Others had burrowed holes in the ground.

We entered a barrack block. It was approximately the size of a barrack block on any of our air stations in which we would have bunks and beds for 60 or 70 airmen. In each of these barrack blocks in Belsen, there were approximately 1,100 people. Conditions in which they were lying and living are indescribable. Many of the dead still lay among the living. Those who were alive had not the strength to remove the bodies of the others. The removal and burial of the dead was being carried on by British troops. The German S.S. men, after they were taken prisoners, refused to work at cleaning up the place, and being prisoners of war, they did not have to. Therefore, our boys had to do that work. They were dressed in their gas equipment with long gloves reaching to their elbows. They took the dead out of each barrack block twice a day, piling them between the buildings, and then returned with trucks and loaded them and drove them to a large unoccupied area where there were great pits in which the dead were thrown. We were told that in one of these pits, 5,000 bodies had been placed. Whenever one died, those who were able, took his clothing. The floor of each barrack block was piled with rags which were indescribably filthy, for a depth of about two feet. They had nothing else on which to lie. We watched a burial procedure. We saw the crematorium, and through an interpreter, we talked with many of the people. The crematorium was much too small to dispose of the bodies we found everywhere in the camp. Only a small section of the camp had been cleared at the time we were there. It required infinite patience, and progress could not be rapid in that horrible work.

The Medical Officer explained to us that they were removing as many persons as possible who could respond to some preliminary treatment, so that their lives might be saved. A hospital had been commandeered not far from the camp, and the people were being taken out as rapidly as possible for that treatment. On the day that we were there the removal of such persons had to stop because they had run short of medical supplies. It was then 3:00 o'clock in the afternoon. They had removed on that day 600 persons. Later we saw those people from Belsen and other concentration camps who were being flown back to their native countries, many of them to die on their native soil. Wherever we went, there were unearthly cries from the people thinking that we were there to arrange their removal also. Such hopeless dejection, such complete physical collapse and emaciation are impossible to imagine unless one has seen them. The Medical Officer said to me: "Never in all my life have I imagined such a mass of dead and dying humanity as is to be found here."

The Treatment of Prisoners

The food which these people were given was totally inadequate to sustain any measure of life for a long period of time. For breakfast, they had a little potato soup, and ersatz coffee and a crust of bread. Bones for soup, and potatoes seemed to be the principal diet. In the centre of the camp were two large concrete reservoirs for the storage of water. Both of these were cracked so that the water could not be contained in them. There was no sanitation of any kind. Water was obtained from two taps which originally supplied the concrete tanks.

We were told of the unspeakable treatment of the prisoners, the pseudo-scientific treatment of both men and women by S.S. men and S.S. women, and we saw for ourselves the horrible results in the wan and broken bodies of those who were unfortunate enough to remain alive during those years of persecution. There seemed to be no designed system of torture as was reported from other camps. As one Polish man said: "To be in Belsen was sufficient torture." About 70 percent of the people in the camp were Jews, and the others were political prisoners. In other words, they were not in any sense criminals. They were people who were unfortunate enough to be born as Jews or had disagreed, politically with the National Socialist Party. For holding such political views, or for having been born Jews, they were subjected, over a period of years, to a treatment which had been patently successful in the vast majority of cases. It was a treatment which was designed to reduce human beings from the dignity of manhood and womanhood to the indignity and squalor of animals. We saw two women fighting over a bone in the gutter. We saw men feeding themselves as apes would do. There was a physical revulsion produced by such sights, which was beyond even the revulsion of the sights of a battlefield. As we came out of the office, having spent about 3½ hours in the camp, Padre Ross showed us a file which had not been opened, containing the papers of a person who might then be alive in the camp. As he opened it the first document in it was a birth certificate. It was of a woman who was an American citizen, born in New York, and who had been caught by the Nazis while on a visit to Austria.

These poor people were taken from their homes, their friends and their families. Wives, husbands, children were torn apart, and their fate was not even the fate of those whom the Nazis had made slaves in their factories and on their farms. They were destined by the evil of National Socialism to be reduced physically, morally and spiritually to the level of animals. This and similar camps were the first products of National Socialism. It is a clear path, step by step from these places to the pagan god whom the Nazis worshipped. In contrast our humanitarianism revolts at such indignities and our Christian ethics teach us to liberate, to help and to heal. The true dignity of human life is to be found in the application of the Gospel of Christ and when men depart from that, there is suffering and death.

Accounts of these atrocities have appeared in words and pictures in books, magazines and movie news reels. They have not been exaggerated. No words or pictures could describe adequately the horrors of concentration camps such as Belsen. The evidence against Kramer, the commandant, and the S.S. men and women under his command, submitted at the trials in Luneburg was sufficient to more than justify his execution and the execution of several men and women under him. It clearly indicates the depths to which humanity can sink when its lower nature is allowed undisciplined expression.

After V-Day the first task was the repatriation of our own prisoners of war. These were flown in thousands from our field. When that had been completed the French, Dutch and Belgian Red Cross Societies set up their marquees and their ambulances began to bring in the sick and dying people of these various nationalities. They were brought from the concentration camps after preliminary medical treatment, and were flown to Paris, Amsterdam and Brussels. They were frightfully emaciated and many of them had been deliberately maimed by their S.S. masters. It was not uncommon to see a man with a foot or hand missing. On one occasion I saw a man with a bandage across his upper lip. Upon enquiry I was told that his S.S. guards had bored holes in his front upper teeth and had put acid into them. His upper jaw was eaten away by the acid.

These accounts are not written simply to bring us to dwell upon evidence of gross brutality. They are written that we may be brought to a clearer realization of the evil which threatened the destruction of our own way of life, and to enable us to remember always that our own men fought and died to destroy these evil things. The liberty and happiness of mankind demand, as one the first requirements, racial tolerance. The brotherhood of man was one of the two cardinal principles of Jesus' faith and teaching.

The treatment of their fellow men by the Germans in these places clearly indicates that following their conquest by our military power there must be a conquest by spiritual power. Morality in very large sections of humanity has broken down. Nor can education alone achieve the liberation of the conquered and suffering people. With it there must be a spiritual awakening. Christian missionaries are needed to carry the gospel in its truth and power to complete the liberation of men who, without it, will continue in spiritual darkness. Whatever God, in His grace, may have given to us in this spacious, plentiful land and in our tradition of freedom and peace, and Christian faith and practice, must be shared with those who have gone so terribly wrong. This God requires of us who have been given so much.

Source: Cameron, "Belsen Concentration Camp: An Eye-Witness Account."

~

SHALOME MICHAEL GELBER

Flying Officer, Royal Canadian Air Force (1941–1945) Senior Field Representative, UNRRA, Joint Distribution Committee, Bergen-Belsen Camp (1945–1946)

Born to parents who were among Canada's leading supporters of Jewish nationalism, Shalome Michael Gelber led a distinguished life. In 1896 his father, Louis Gelber, and Louis's brother, Moses, immigrated to Toronto from the town of Berezhany in Austrian Galicia. The brothers operated Gelber Bros. Limited Wholesale Woollens, which became one of the largest of its kind in Canada. Louis married Sara L. Morris (d. 1954), and together they had five children: aside from Shalome Michael, there was Lionel (1907–89), the eldest, a historian and the author of several books on international affairs who also served in Ottawa as special assistant to Canadian prime minister John Diefenbaker; Marvin (1912–90) was a Toronto Member of Parliament and was later a part of the Canadian delegation, United Nations General Assembly; Arthur (1915–98) was chair of the Board of Trustees of the National Arts Centre and a founder of the Canada-Israel Cultural Foundation; Sylva (1910–2003), the only daughter of Louis and Sara, was director of the Women's Bureau of the Department of Labour and Canadian representative on the United Nations Commission for the Status of Women.

Shalome Michael was educated at Upper Canada College in Toronto and Columbia University in New York. He enlisted in the Royal Canadian Air Force (RCAF) in 1941, eventually becoming an education officer. He first encountered Bergen-Belsen during the spring of 1945 while with the air force.

According to Gelber, deeply moved by this encounter at Bergen-Belsen, and following his discharge from the air force during the summer of 1945, he became a field representative to the United Nations Relief and Rehabilitation Administration and worked with the Joint Distribution

Committee (JDC).[7] It was with the JDC that Gelber assisted at Bergen-Belsen.[8] He worked alongside fellow Canadian David Wodlinger, the JDC's director in the British Zone of Germany.[9] Gelber mainly worked in an administrative capacity in Bergen-Belsen, assisting in the relief activities. Frustrated by British policy in the camp, in 1946 he wrote a scathing, anonymous critique, titled "Are We Breaking Faith?," which appeared in the *New Stateman and Nation*.[10] The piece caused quite a stir, and Gelber claims it was mentioned in debates in the UK House of Commons.[11]

After the war, Gelber accepted a position as manager of Capital Expansion Department for the Palestine Economic Corp. This was followed by a four-year stint as a broker at Bear Stearns. He continued his education with degrees at New York University (NYU), earning his PhD in 1967 in english literature and religion. In 1979 he also earned a PhD in psychology from the Union Graduate School in Ohio. An ordained rabbi, Gelber became dean of the Academy for Jewish Religion and an instructor of Judaism at NYU.[12] In addition, he was a playwright and also practiced as a psychotherapist. He is the author of several books, including *The Failure of the American Rabbi*. He passed away in New York in 2001, leaving behind his widow, Marianne Wientzen Gelber.

Report

… More than [half] of the Jews in the British Zone are settled in Bergen Belsen which is now called for official purposes Hohne Camp, since the former name carries with it a renowned stigma. The old concentration camp has been destroyed. The mass graves, [one] crematorium and several monuments are all that remain. The Displaced Persons live in a well-built military barracks that was used at one time for a Panzer Division. This station was at no time identified with the old concentration camp, and it was felt by the military authorities that it would therefore be the most logical place for the D.Ps to take over.

In actuality it is most depressing and inadequate. There are a series of factors that made it objectionable to the Jews. Like most barracks it is cold, impersonal and dreary. The people are overcrowded, a fact which imposes continued difficulties for people who have enjoyed no privacy for years. Belsen is inaccessible to larger centers of population, the closest town being Celle. The camp itself is rambling and the inhabitants must walk long distances to visit the offices of UNRRA, the military or the voluntary agencies.

In addition to the physical and the psychological problems that the geography of the camp presents, there are other elements that make

life trying for the Jewish D.Ps. For more than a year the Jews have been
obliged to live side by side and in the midst of the non-Jewish Poles. It
is well known that the Poles are by and large anti-Semitic. And even
though this anti-Semitism has often taken violent forms at Belsen it is
only recently that action is being effected to separate the two groups ...

Quite obviously the Jews of the British zone are seriously demoral-
ized. They feel the injustice of their situation deeply and when they
couple the fact that they have as yet been granted no outlet to a free
home with the scandalous observation that they are still languishing in D.P. assembly centers while multitudes of German Nazis are
back on their farms living well in comfortable villages, they feel frustrated and depressed. The overwhelming majority want to emigrate
to Palestine.

... In a confidential memorandum such as this, it might be pointed
out that our relationship with UNRRA and the Military have caused
us much heartache and disappointment. To say that these two bodies willfully misunderstand the problem of the Jewish D.P. would
be an overstatement; at the same time it would be fair to point out
that both UNRRA and the Military officials are so lacking in intellec-
tual appreciation of the problem, that many are so fascinated by the
bureaucratic limitations of their respective large scale organizations
and that others are so profoundly influenced by the prejudices of
anti-semites that JDC [Join Distribution Committee] often finds its
work frustrated.

... When a number of months ago UNRRA presented the Jews with
an ultimatum that they must abandon the brick barracks of Camp 3
and move into the Nissen Huts before a certain hour, I felt that it was
my duty to discuss the matter with the UNRRA director. The director, Mr. [W.R.] Wheatman, was cold and unfriendly to my suggestion
that the ultimatum was unjust and that it should be re-examined. He
said that there were many people in England who would love to live
in Nissen Huts and that he himself had done so during the war. He
could, therefore, see no reason why the Jews objected. I pointed out to
him, that I myself [have] lived in Nissen Huts throughout the war and
I would have no objections if he had ordered me to a Nissen Hut, but I
felt that it was unfair to relegate Jewish D.Ps to such conditions after so
many years in concentration camps. He advised me that the concentration camp reason had been used too often, and I explained to him that
it had to be used often only because there still remain those who are
mindful of its existence. He said he intended to use force and I advised
him that if that were done there would indubitably be an incident. I
pointed out that Belsen is always good newspaper material, and that I

Figure 50. Michael Gelber of Toronto, Ontario, head of vocational training
program at the DP camp in Bergen-Belsen, is shown the work of students in
the dressmaking course by the workshop leader. Courtesy of the American
Jewish Joint Distribution Committee.

would have no hesitation in advising the newspapers that he himself
had created the difficulty, for certainly one year after the war there was
no crisis in Belsen big enough to justify the wholesale evacuation of
people so that soldiers could move in. Eventually, place was found for
the Jews in brick buildings.

   … A number of weeks later I was advised by telephone that as of
that moment Belsen was under a curfew and that no D.P. may enter
or leave the camp without the permission of the UNRRA director
and that such permission would be granted only for very particular
circumstances. The cause of this sudden transformation of the assembly center into a prison was still unknown to any of us. We were
later advised that crimes had been committed in the camp and that
since the criminals had not been found the Military believed that
law breakers were being sheltered by the ordinary camp residents
and that only collective punishment would bring the true criminals

to light of day. What these crimes were, we were still not told and for nearly 20 hours the camp remained closed without any advice being published as to the exact purpose of this action. When eventually the crimes were publicized it became evident that all the large crimes of violence had been committed entirely by the Polish non-Jews and that the punishment of the Jews for the sins of their most hated enemies was nothing more than ridiculous. After well ordered, dignified and intelligent protests filed by Dr. Herman Helgott, the acting President of the Central Jewish Committee, the Jews demonstrated in protest.

The British soldiers used fire hoses on the Jews and the Polish guard threw stones. Despite these obstacles the Jewish crowd broke through the gates, bared their breasts before the drawn arms of the Poles and the Britons, taunting them with the cry, "Shoot if you dare." The soldiers lowered their guns, the Jews returned to the camp and the order was rescinded supposedly as of before the demonstration took place. This is an example of the lack of understanding to such an appalling degree that one wonders just what benefits the Military occupation is bringing, for outside the camp Germans freely cheered the Poles while they threw stones at the Jewish D.Ps.

If one were asked to explain what hope, what desire, what intention keeps the Jews of the British occupied Zone in fairly good spirits and engaged in productive endeavor, the answer would of course be Palestine. For the overwhelming majority feel that their emigration to Palestine is the only solutions to their problem, and anything other than Palestine, they say, after so much hardship, would be to them nothing more than a consolation prize.

Source: YIVO LWSP Folder 497: "Report on Bergen Belsen" by Shalome Michael Gelber, Director, J.D.C. Activities in Paris (28 June 1946), 1–6.

Letter

You start to wonder after you have spent a number of months working in the British Zone of Germany. Then you start to doubt. And many of us who served in His Majesty's Forces ask even ourselves: "Are we breaking faith with those who died?"

One day I was advised by a Lieut.-Col. in charge of a Military Government detachment in Germany that twenty-four Displaced Persons, who had been residing in a modest home, were now to be ordered to an official D.P. Assembly Centre. The home was to be given back to its original German owner. And the twenty-four anti-Nazi D.P.s, many of whom were concentration camp victims, were being sent to something very much worse than the poorhouse. For D.P. Assembly Centres are unhappy places like Belsen. If, therefore, you have any feeling for D.P.s, most of whom are our bravest and longest-suffering allies, you will at least make enquiries about such an order. On making such enquiries I found that the original owner of the house, for whose comfort the D.P.s were being turned out, was a Nazi official, an S.S. man, if you please, and of long standing. This S.S. man of even pre-war vintage had forgotten some of his papers. On finding them, I immediately submitted the papers, which were evidence of his S.S. membership, to the Lieut.-Col. He read them, but to my consternation advised me that since the S.S. man held but a low rank in that most bloodthirsty of Nazi organisations, his home was to be returned to him, notwithstanding his anti-British, anti-human associations. The D.P.s must go. The low-ranked S.S. man may move in.

The de-Nazification programme may be very intense in certain of its activities such as policing. On the whole, however, it seems to many of us to be conspicuous by its absence. The tracking down and punishment of war criminals is one thing. The de-Nazification of a whole culture is another. To achieve the subservience of Germans is not to change their minds. Mr. Churchill once said that a German is either at your throat or at your feet. To-day we have brought the Nazi to our feet. He is, nevertheless, still a Nazi, secretly hoping to be at our throat to-morrow. Nazi arrogance and German servility are only opposite manifestations of the same sadistic psychology. And those British officers who think that they have done a job because they are hunting criminals or keeping the masses in line have missed the historic purpose of occupation. One reason is that they simply do not understand the first thing about the German problem. In the Air Force, a pilot had to devote himself to a year's intensive study before he was considered fit to do the job of destruction. For the task of reconstruction, for the job of building the peace, for securing Europe against a third world war and a resurgent Nazism we are giving the most superficial training – if indeed any training at all.

A number of months ago, for instance, I visited many of the schools in Oldenburg with the Chief School Inspector, a German. It was a depressing experience. For the Inspector spent the largest part of his time apologising to me for his teachers, because they had mostly been members of the National Socialist Party. They were, he said, forced to join. That may be so. But the point is, what were they doing now to undo the damage of Nazism? Were they making provision to teach the children that race theories and militarism and dictatorial government were the invention of the devil? Were they constructing a moral foundation in the souls of their young charges?

Not at all. They apologised for their National Socialist connection only to me – not to the class. The curriculum was what might be called a neutral one. Physics, Chemistry, Mathematics, technical subjects and the like were all in the limelight as though this were 1931 or 1932. Nothing was offered in the school programme to dispel the prejudices acquired before and during Hitler or to eradicate the Nazi influence the children were still acquiring from their families.

And one old Social-Democratic teacher who had been put out of commission during Hitler's time, but is back to work again, exposed our educational programme bitterly to one of my colleagues. He said the children are about 90 per cent Nazis and that our neutral curriculum is encouraging rather than discouraging them to harbour and cherish their evil beliefs. For it shows that we ourselves have no faith in Democracy. It is therefore not enough to cover the wound by starting schools. We must first drain out the poison. There is very little evidence of poison-draining in the schools of Oldenburg. And if you talk to German children as I have done in Hamburg, Braunschweig, Celle and scores of other places, you will be struck by the fact that their minds are ill and that very little cure is being offered them in the schools.

What are the results of our ill-trained occupation force? It is no secret that since large numbers of soldiers have little sense of purpose and significance in Germany, they are setting a foul example. Liquor is cheap and plentiful. And it is as though the appetite for drink "has grown by what it is fed on." Drunkenness and rowdiness amongst officers and men, both, is too general for its complacent acceptance as though it were a "necessary evil of any occupation force." The embarrassment I felt when a German told me one day that the British in his town have a reputation of being a nation of drunkards, was too much to bear. A century ago, according to Napoleon, they were a nation of shopkeepers. Have the mighty fallen?

Then there is the black market. I have no figures or statistics to prove that it is high amongst our men. Neither have the Germans who justify their own illegal activities by pointing out that Tommies they know do the same thing. I was in a military court in Soltau one morning when every case tried, except one, was for black marketeering. To my shame and disappointment the sergeant told me that all the goods exhibited on the court table were from military stores.

This experience would be of little significance if it were out of the ordinary. It could be excused if it were an exception. The sad truth, however, is that black marketeering is not only a general vice amongst the men, but it is actually regarded by many as a virtue. In messes, in clubs and on roads, officers and men will boast of their shrewd operations in illegal traffic, they will show you their prizes of cameras, binoculars and other goods, they will even compare their gains and pride themselves on "outsmarting Jerries," and evading the law. Lack of conscience has made bad examples, not of us all, but of too many.

I believe the problem is one of attitude. If soldiers come to a conquered land with a sense of futility and frustration, they will be corrupted, no matter what their nationality. If, however, they are sent with training, with a high sense of purpose and devotion to the cause of re-education, they will not be completely devoid of corruption, but they will be less susceptible to bad influences and more interested in their responsibilities.

The Frauleins, it is often said, are carrying on where Hitler left off. There is strong evidence to support this case. Some of us were astounded to find that German Frauleins are invited as guests to the officers' rest hotel run by the Army at Bad Harzburg. The invited Frauleins are "vetted" to see if they have been Nazis. And if it is found that they have not been officially Nazis, even though their associations may have been Nazi, then they are passed. Then they may smoke untold numbers of British cigarettes and drink a legion of champagne and dance gaily with our officers at Bad Harzburg. They are experiencing much better treatment from the military than I have ever seen the other ranks of the Wrens or Waafs or A.T.S. enjoy, either during or after the war. Officers, by social contacts with German girls (vetted or not) encourage the men to do likewise with the non-vetted Frauleins. Thus Goebbels' propaganda dances merrily along.

What are we doing in Germany anyway? What is the purpose of our long sojourn in a strange land? Is it not to root out the evil of Nazism and to try to replace it with peace, decency, and good will? Is it not to establish a set of conditions and attitudes in Germany that will secure our children against a revived militarism? If that be our purpose, we are failing in its achievement. We are not befriending our allies like the D.P.s. We are not rallying a significant democratic nucleus in Germany. We are breaking faith, many believe, with those who died and we are endangering the lives of our children.

CANADIAN OFFICER

Source: "Are We Breaking Faith?" *The New Statesman and Nation* (3 August 1946), 78–9.

Article

From Bergen-Belsen, Germany
(British Zone)

This is not the first time that Jewish communities have seen their sun descend behind the wide horizon. Nor is the present black night of persecution – with its nightmares of uprootedness, insecurity and frustration – a new form of disturbance in Jewish experience. Communities have been obliterated many times before. A remnant of survivors has often been sent packing to stumble along new and stony paths. Jews, in fact, have been victims of unbridled wrath, and subsequently displaced persons, for centuries.

Nevertheless, there are features of the current European darkness that are strange and different. For the deep shadow here possesses unique characteristics, and presents bizarre manifestations. It is evident to the observer that the unheard-of horror has brought with it unprecedented results, that the new effects are as dreadful as the new cause was singularly hateful. One learns again from the extraordinary Jewish story at hand that history simply does not repeat itself. For this time not only did "the sun set at noon," as the prophet Amos would have it, but it failed to rise next morning. And since the sun, long after VE-Day, is still stubbornly withholding its light in this morning hour, it is yet not too late to ask, "Watchman, what of the night?" and "Wherein is this night different from all other nights?"

… Here at Bergen-Belsen, where thousands of Jews still languish in indignity and impossible physical conditions, where the term "liberation" has lost its grace and beauty, taking on instead the connotation of a "lesser of two evils" – where Nazi torture has been supplanted, not by freedom and renaissance, but by the frustrating and bureaucratic combination of military government and UNRRA, the latter of which often seems to need more spiritual relief and rehabilitation than the bodies whom it is supposed to succor – at this same Bergen-Belsen one can observe various and sundry shadows of the night which contribute to the overpowering blackness that neither clock nor calendar can jostle into light of day.

The first shadow is status. The Jews are "Displaced Persons." And at Belsen thousands of Jewish D.P.s are relegated to a large camp, the erstwhile home of a Hitlerian Panzer Division. In the barracks of their camp they suffer indignities that can best be described by likening them to those of a cattle-car. The D.P.s are crowded. They are huddled into small rooms, a condition which defies comfort, privacy and modesty. In the eyes of many military officials they "are only D.P.s," a term employed to connote derision and condescension. The fact that many of these D.P.s were Hitler's first enemies and *ipso facto* the best friends of the United Nations is missed in allied military and relief circles.

The D.P. has therefore lost more than his home. His prestige too is displaced, and his status may be said to be a casualty of peace. Of old the Jew cared less about prestige, about the goodwill of princes "in whose nostrils is breath." For was he not, after all, in partnership with God? Tonight he has abandoned God and princes have abandoned him.

... In Belsen and throughout Europe the drama is unfolding. It is a stirring, compelling, new and mighty play. Formal religion has a very small part. God is obscured by more worldly consideration. Traditional morality has a minor role. *However, the theme is noble. It is the story of a shipwrecked crew who are braving the storm to get back to port. It is the romance of a group who, though scarred and wounded in body and spirit, have risen above their ugly situation to fight for an ideal – home. In this sense, then, the drama is religious, godly and moral.*

Those who have worked with the *Hechalutz* movement[13] – with its many collective homes in Belsen where the young victims of the concentration camps live in *camaraderie*, where they work and sing and study Hebrew together – learn what spiritual victory really means. One who has been part of the *Gymnasium*, the Junior school or the technical school, or the Fishing school in Blankensee, or the *Hachsharoth*, which prepare the remnant for rehabilitation in Palestine, may gather that the human spirit can, if it will, triumph over adversity.

Not many kilometres from the feverish Zionist activity of Belsen are mass graves of those who died at the hand of Hitler. Near them a single rusted crematorium still stands as a memorial of the nightmare. It is as though these unhappy souvenirs goad the people on, stimulate them, excite them, warn them. It is as though the very word "Belsen" is continually jostling them to be mindful of their faith that Palestine, if not the best answer, is the only answer.

"Watchman, what of the night?" It is a night full with new qualities and strange conditions. For the Jewish night in Europe is a sign of the times. Dorothy Thompson once wrote that the Jews are the same as anybody else, only more so.[14] There is great wisdom in that remark. The accentuated suffering of the Jew has made him hyper-sensitive. And hyper-sensitiveness has brought extreme reaction to world conditions. But the reaction of the Jew in quality is not too different from that of others.

If the Jews of Europe have grown secular, if many of them are materialists, if some of the old landmarks of Judaism have been destroyed, if devotion to a political creed has been substituted for the Biblical and the Talmudic tradition, if the desire for worldly security is more popular than less tangible values, it is also true that other people have moved in similar directions. Thus the significance of the Jewish story at hand is more than local. It indicates, in a certain sense, the sort of world in which we live. In fact, it has so much universal meaning that it could serve as a good point of departure for a study of the contemporary world.

Source: "Wherein Is This Night Different?"[15] *Menorah Journal* 35, no. 1 (1947): 21–30.

$\sim$

SAMUEL CASS

Military Chaplain, 1st Canadian Army

Samuel Cass was born on 1 May 1908 in Toronto to Chaye Baila and Aaron Cass. In 1929 he received a Bachelor of Arts degree from the City College of New York. He earned a Master of Hebrew Literature in 1933 and Doctor of Hebrew Literature in 1948 at the Jewish Theological Seminary of America. Cass was ordained in 1933 and took a position as rabbi at Vancouver's Congregation Beth Israel (Conservative).[16] He was among the first Canadian-born rabbis to occupy such a position. In 1941 he became rabbi of Herzl Conservative Congregation, Seattle, Washington.

In 1942, he served as senior Jewish chaplain for the Canadian army and navy. In 1944, Cass was shipped overseas, initially serving with the First Canadian Army and later with Canadian Military Headquarters in London. He was with the Canadian Army during the liberation of Belgium and the Netherlands. On 12 April 1945 units from the Canadian 2nd Infantry Division liberated Westerbork transit camp. On 20 April 1945, Cass was at Westerbork where he conducted services and assisted the survivors.[17] He later made his way to Bergen-Belsen and worked to bring supplies to the camp.

In 1946, Cass became director of McGill University's B'nai B'rith Hillel Foundation. He also worked, until 1967, on behalf of Macdonald College and Sir George Williams University. He then enrolled in a master of social work program at McGill and, after graduation, worked for the Miriam Home for the Exceptional.

Cass was active in Canada's Jewish community. He was president of the Board of Jewish Ministers of Greater Montreal and National Chairman of the Academic Awards Committee of the Canadian Friends of the Hebrew University. He was also an honorary chaplain for the Dominion Command of the Royal Canadian Legion.

In the mid-1970s, Cass began research on the Jewish chaplaincy services in the Canadian Armed Forces. Tragically, he never had the opportunity to complete the project. On 8 September 1975, while driving from Montreal to Toronto, Cass and his family were in a car accident.[18] Cass, his wife Annabel, their twenty-six-year-old son Ely, and his wife's aunt, Lottie Weiss, were killed instantly. Samuel Cass was sixty-seven years old at the time of his death.

Diary

Celle, Germany – 6 Dec 1945

This has been a long day of travelling mostly on wet roads in a light drizzle. The first thing I did this morning was to load up the back of my Hup [Hupmobile] with food and comforts of the packages recently received by [chaplains Isaac] Rose and [Hyman] Gevantman, and that operation concluded, started to roll at 10:30 AM. My route was from Apeldoorn to Enschede where I arrived about noon and began to look around for the familiar facilities formally available to use, but on checking in to the Town Major, I was politely told that all our amenities had been closed up. I had food in the car so I went to Synagogue where the Cantor resides (formerly of Apeldoorn) and prepared a lunch for my driver and myself. At one we were ready to go on. The German Border is only a few miles around and we were making for the Autobahn road to Berlin some 20 to 25 miles South-east of Munster. We hit the autobahn at 4:30 PM a super military road. Of course, in spots the road beds and bridges have been damaged in the fighting, so we had to detour even off this highway. I had to endure hours and hours of continuous travel, much of it over slippery and traffic-choked roads. A little beyond Hanover we got off the Autobahn and rode into the Medieval German town of Celle, which in these past years of Nazi tyranny harbored a Concentration Camp.

I took up quarters in the house of the British Jewish Relief Unit. After a snack of supper at 10:00PM, I chatted with the head of the Team, a Mrs. [Rose] Henriques, whose husband runs a Jewish Settlement Club in the East end of London. Her Team here services practically all of the scattered settlements of Jews, both German and D.P., in the

British Zone. She had just returned from Berlin where she gathered together some fifty children who will eventually be brought to England. Temporarily they have been evacuated from Berlin to Belsen and Lunenberg. In Celle there are about 500 Jews, former inhabitants of Belsen, who live in the same town receiving the same rations as the Germans. The Team has opened up a cultural centre, really a Social Club, where they can gather together and get a bit of social life. Right next door to the Club is the Synagogue New, about 200 years old, which was not totally damaged and is now restored. I visited this Synagogue and was informed by my Guide that the Burgonmeister is now building a Mikvah in the rear yard of the Synagogue. Celle is also a transient town for D.P.s on their way to and from Belsen. There is a tremendous amount of going to and fro in search of relatives. Belsen people go off for a four and five weeks trip to Poland. Polish Jews in Poland are using every avenue of escape to get out of that cursed land.

Recently the Team opened up a Transient Camp where these people can stay overnight. They have also opened up two Kosher restaurants where a hot noon day meal is served to all.

Bergen-Belsen, Germany – 8 Dec 45

I arrived here yesterday morning after ten o'clock, driving from Celle, through the town of Bergen, only an hour's ride on a fairly good road lined with heavily wooded forests on both sides. The weather turned cold overnight, and snow had fallen to carpet the earth with a thin blanket of white. Coming up on the road you find no mention of Belsen. All you see is a sign put up by our military authorities reading "HOHNE CAMP" after a farm or house that is in the neighborhood. As you approach the gates of the camp itself, you find that it is called an "ASSEMBLY CENTRE" – a military government creation for the assembly of DPs – but all these attempts at eradicating the foulness of the Nazi extermination camp are of no avail. The living evidence is still there.

The camp which houses the DPs today was formerly the barracks of crack SS and Panzer troops in training. It is a typical barracks, a town in itself, with symmetrical concrete buildings, well-built roads, and parade and sport grounds. In the first hour of my visit I made a tour of the camp in a small civilian auto, driven by a member of the Central Jewish Committee and accompanied by the Senior British Jewish Chaplain, a Rev. Wagner, with whom I had an appointment to meet in Camp.

This Central Jewish Committee includes not only the several camps that make up Belsen, but all the other camps and organized

communities in the British Zone. The Committee is headed by a
Mr. [Josef] Rosensaft, a man of slight build and slight stature, who
is nicknamed "The Atom Bomb."[19] (In all matters, some shattering
force is necessary to move the authorities, and presumably Rosensaft
has explosive energy. So far very few of the set notions of the British
authorities have been blown to bits.) The Committee has one building set aside for all its administrative work, the L5 block, which also
contains a commissary where I unloaded my supplies. Distribution is
made to all the communities in accordance with their requirements.
(Before leaving Celle, I left a supply with the relief team there for the
Berlin kiddies who had been taken to Lunenberg). To come back to
my tour – En route through the various blocks of concrete buildings,
I learned a few of the problems faced by our Jewish DPs. I was taken
to a Canteen which housed a Synagogue – not anything sumptuous –
just a German barrack cupboard in which Sifre Torah was placed, the
usual tables, a few benches and chairs, prayer books, and inscriptions
on the wall. The night before, or rather early that morning, a group of
Poles had broken in through the window, and made a "pogrom" on
the Shuhl – broke everything available, tore prayer books and inscriptions from the Walls, and threw the scrolls on top of debris in wild disorder. The Camp, under British Military rule, is policed by a company
of Polish soldiers because of the preponderance of Poles in the Camp.
There are also some Jewish policemen, chosen from the inmates, but
they are unarmed. A request will no doubt be made that a company of
the Jewish Brigade be stationed there to protect our people. It is well
known that the Poles who vandalize Synagogues, have no scruples
to attack the person of the Jew. On our tour, we saw a young Jewish
girl being taken into custody by a British soldier. Her crime? She had
a bag of white buns in her possession. She said she had bought them
on an official ration card, while she resided in Hanover for a while. We
took her out of the clutches of the soldier by calling over his superior
and asking him where he got the nerve to question the authority of
this girl to have the buns in her possession. It's trivial, but these little
things mount up ... To continue the story of the girl – If we just didn't
happen along, the girl would not only have spent a few uncomforta-
ble hours in the hands of the Polish military, but most important, her
buns would have been taken away. These petty annoyances are really
a form of organized looting.

Who is in Belsen today? The answer is Jews and Poles. The Poles
number about 18,000, the great majority of them voluntary workers
for the Nazis, and many of them needed no lessons from their Nazi
masters in Jew-baiting. They are now DPs who don't wish to return

to Poland, no doubt fearing the reception they will receive as a conse-
quence of their voluntary enlistment in the Nazi labor battalions. Of
the 48,000 Jews who were alive on the day Belsen was liberated, 30,000
have died. Some 10,000 were transferred to Sweden, many of them
permanently invalided, and some 6 to 8,000 live in the camp now. No
[Earl G.] Harrison has come to the British zone to personally report
to [Primer Minister Clement] Attlee how the Military Government is
dealing with the Jews. Only now, after considerable wrangling and
fighting, are Jews getting into their own camps, and are being separated
from the Poles. Camp 5, for example, is an all Jewish camp. Mostly they
are Polish Jews, with a sprinkling of Hungarian, Romanian, Yugo-Slav,
Russian etc. Many of them are alive because they came to Belsen only in
the last weeks from other Concentration Camps. Many of them worked
on V-1 and V-2 manufacture. They live in barracks style, are fed from
central canteens, and wear every conceivable type of garment which
people discarded five and ten years ago. As I told you, the weather has
suddenly turned cold. My own toes and finger tips are freezing, and
I am certain they felt the cold even more, even though while in Concentration Camp they stood up to eleven hours on a roll call in zero
weather, with bare feet and a thin rag over their bodies. Many died
during these roll calls. The hardy ones survived – but whether they
can continue to do so under present conditions, no one can foretell.
Clothing, underwear and shoes are desperately needed. Belsen was liberated in April – VE Day was in May. But neither the JDC nor any other
International Relief Agency have had the ability or perhaps even the
foresight to get stock of adequate shoes and clothing for these people.
Conditions in the American and Russian zones are surely worse in this
regard, for the numbers are greater. Food conditions are not the bright-
est. Officially they get 2,000 calories per day, which amounts to bread
and coffee in the morning, a watery vegetable soup and thin stew for
lunch, and hard tack and coffee in the evening. A loaf of brown bread
must last eight people for more than a day. They get a small square of
margarine, a small quantity of sugar and an occasional extra. Of course
they cannot thrive on such a diet. It is true, it is higher in caloric value
than the official German ration. But for every German there is the black
market, a farm or garden, to supplement the ration. I am certain no one
is starving, a least in this zone. But even to compare the needs of the
Jews to those of the native Germans is downright nonsense.

In the course of my morning rounds, I dropped into the Beth Hechalutz, a cooperative Kibbutz, organized by the young boys and girls to
prepare themselves for Aliyah to Palestine. Palestine is magic not only
to their physical surroundings but to their entire spirit. It offers hope,

pride, labor, and creativity, a future, even in the depressing and dismal atmosphere of life in a military barracks. The greetings of every young person is – "May we meet in Eretz Israel."

I moved on to Celle, the first stage of the return journey, where I am now comfortably settled for the night in the quarters of the Jewish Relief Team.

Continuing the story of Belsen – After lunch at Bergen where I was put up in the Relief Team Mess, I was shown around the old Bergen-Belsen Camp. Officially, it is known as Camp No. 1. Those who have been in it call it the "Todt" Camp. From the former SS Barrack town, the original Camp was situated about a mile or so away, its approaches hidden by rough road and forest. For miles around, one can still see high watch-towers and barbed wire which guarded against escape. At the entrance is a signpost put up by Mil Gov stating very briefly the facts of the Horror Camp in English and German. Passing beyond the wooden barracks huts which housed the guards and other details, one comes into the camp compound proper, now a vast space strewn with rubble of the verminous, typhus ridden, stench filled building where tens of thousands men, women and children met cruelty, torture and death. What I saw was only one compound – the women's compound and other sections were barred from view by thick woods and heavily reinforced barbed wire fences. Some German labor was working among the rubble heaps, attempting to clean it up, and remove the evidence which nature in her own way will cover with green and vegetation once more. With every step you felt you were walking on graves and blood. Beyond this compound, again through barbed wire (where we got out of the car), we came to the crematorium, filled still today with the ashes of human flesh. My guide, himself rescued from death by a miracle, pointed out that in size this incinerator doesn't begin to compare with Auschwitz. Nearby was an open pyre of charred logs where the hideous job was finished. Walking across the open field, I passed what was at first mounds of rotting shoes and clothing and hair of victims. Snow covered the field and also the remnants of these mounds, among which I saw human bones still lying about hard frozen to the ground. A worker with a team of horses was ploughing up this field. It will no doubt be fertile. Further on were the mass graves. Ten of them, each containing 5,000 bodies, one or two smaller ones among them. A Mogen David and a Cross signify their resting places, also a Yizkor tablet erected by the Jewish Committee in September when a Conference was held in Belsen Camp. Beyond again was barbed wire – in the back of which [was] ... the shooting gallery. That is the picture of Camp No 1. It requires little imagination to picture what this meant – and the Germans have not yet said "*Chatanu!*"

I had a few interviews in the L5 Block. The sun was getting low in the horizon. Shabbos would soon be here. So, I rushed back to L5. My main interview was Yeshua Zanger, a son of the Krakower Rebbe, who is now in Montreal. Some time ago I received a letter from an uncle of his in Toronto asking if I could not facilitate the entry of the young man into Canada. It was Shabbos already when I left the office, and I went directly to the children's House, to whom I brought a box of B-Bats (lollipops) a gift from our friends in Ottawa. They were to have a bite of supper and a sing song at 6:30 – so I took advantage of the hour or so to pay a visit to Dr. Aida Bimko,[20] who, as you recall, gave evidence in the trial of [Josef] Kramer, [Irma] Grese and their gang. Here I met Rosensaft, all the leaders of the JDC and British Relief Teams and others. An important meeting was going on. The UJA is to have a conference in Atlantic City this week-end and Rosensaft was asked by JDC to be present. The meeting decided that he should go, but whether he got away I don't know. It is doubtful whether the British authorities would allow it.

I cannot omit telling you about my visit with the children – an unforgettable experience, and a thrilling moment. The children live in the same type of Barrack Block as everyone else, but from the moment you enter, you are impressed with the tender devotion shown to these orphans who represent our hope for the future. First of all I inspected their quarters, neat and clean. I had a long chat with their teachers, among whom were two professional teachers from Eretz Israel, members of the Jewish Brigade, whose presence in the Camp is entirely unofficial. In the past six months, they have taught the children to speak Hebrew with a fair fluency. Such unofficial committees of the Brigade have been at work in all the Camps, imbuing the children with a sense of pride and feeling of friendship and hope. At 6:30PM the children gathered in the dining hall. I sat on a bench among them. They started off with songs, all in Hebrew, singing with evident joy and gusto. One of the girls told the story of Chanukah in Hebrew. I led them in a song. The children were of all ages, from tiny tots of three to girls and boys of fifteen. (Among the 6,000 Jews in the Camp, there are 241 children – that figure speaks for itself.) They came from everywhere. Many had come to Belsen in the last months before liberation. Some had been hidden by their parents and discovered. The girl on my left told me she refused to admit her identity right from the time she was betrayed and caught up to her arrival in Belsen, where, in full knowledge of the possible consequences, she identified herself as Jewish. These youngsters had "Certificates" from all the Concentration Camps and Ghettos and had known the torture of slave labor. Opposite me were two girls, sisters, who had been hiding in Poland, and after liberation came to Belsen where they found their mother and rejoined her. Now the mother has gone back to seek a possible trace of the whereabouts or fate of the father. So it goes. Each has his or her story of the miracle of how they survived. (One of the girls I met in the Beth Hechalutz on hearing I was a Chaplain, said she is alive only because the British Chaplain who had been in the Camp the first days, pulled her out from among the dead, and rushed her to the hospital. Otherwise she would have been shoveled up with the rest of the dead bodies among whom she was lying, too weak to respond in any way by her own effort to all that was going on around her.) Well, sitting among these children was a moving experience. Singing was interrupted by sandwiches and tea (their supper) and sucking on the B-Bats. After more singing, we went into the recreation room where we danced the Ulaika, a Russian dance, to Hebrew tunes. Everyone gathers in a circle two deep, preferably a boy and a girl each behind the other. The starter enters the circle, dances around it, chooses a partner, who dance across the circle once with arms linked, the person in second row following behind to continue to dance. After everyone in circle has had several dances, it ends with a snake dance, partners separating and meeting again, changing partners, etc. Really a jolly dance and most sociable. It was lots of fun, and I was a popular partner.

After supper I went to Beth Hechalutz to be with the older boys and girls for their "M'Sevas Shabbos," which included songs, a lecture on the Jewish Brigade, and a more sophisticated Ulaika, longer and more intricate, ending with a few vigorous Horas and spinning wheels. The night was icy cold under the clear starry sky with snow [underfoot] as I went back to Bergen to join the team at a party they were giving to an officer of the camp staff who was returning to England for demobilization. My mind though, was not with them. Perhaps even they detected it. For I was thinking of these youngsters, of their remarkable spirit, of the tremendous creative potentialities which are still in them.

There are a number of Synagogues in the Belsen Camp, as to be expected among so large a community. But there is no Synagogue building as such. One of the larger rooms in the block is set aside as a Synagogue. I decided to attend the Yeshivah Synagogue. There are several hundred students in a Yeshivah who study day and night. Thus their act of swaying during prayer is perfected to the highest degree. The Baal Tefilah who rendered the Shachris was formerly a great Cantor in Cracow. The Mussef was in the Chassidic tradition. It was absorbing to study their faces. Most of the young men with long Payoth, the older ones with respectable beards. Their clothing represented every conceivable style obtainable in the East European countries, including Kappototh. The ensemble that intrigued me was a Jerry camouflage cover-all, high Russian felt boots, soft felt slouch hat, shirt of non-descript colour, and tzitzis protruding from the front middle. Their spirit is remarkable, considering the trials they've been through. Many of them worked on V-1 and V-2 rockets. After Shuhl, there was a Kiddush with home-made Schnapps, a thick mixture that passed for cake and another for Kugel.

In the afternoon, I made some more visits, just dropping in to chat with people. Again I visited Dr. Bimko [Hadassah Rosensaft], and also inspected the Hospital, run by UNRRA. Every relief organization is represented in the Camp.

I came back to Celle starting the return journey soon after Shabbos was out. There is a transient Camp here where people stay overnight, going to and from Belsen. The quarters themselves are abominably inadequate. Here I met men and women who are fast becoming a gypsy folk, Jews from Russia, who fought as partisans and guerilla[s], Jews who are escaping Poland, Jews from every other Camp in Europe on the search for relatives or in hopes of finding a friend.

The one question on their lips is "When do we get to Palestine?" It is the only place which can help them recapture their dignity and make them normal again. The head of the British Jewish Relief Team spoke to me of Polish Jews as "ignorant Polish Jew," as compared with "the cultured German Jew." Yes, there are still people who think that way, who cannot understand the urge of these survivors to live once more as free people, creative. I explained to her that that their will to live [is] not a blind, ignorant striving, but is refined in the crucible of fire through which they have been through. I don't know whether I convinced her, or changed her mind. But the facts are there, as clear as bright sunshine, for all to see.

These several letters are just fleeting impressions of these past few days in Belsen area. Some day they may make sense – right now the problem of these people is one great muddle.

Source: Library and Archives Canada: Samuel Cass Fonds, MG 30, D225, vol. 9, "A Record of a Chaplain's Experience – World War II (1942–1946)" by Samuel Cass.

ABRAHAM BRENNER

Royal Canadian Corps of Signals

Abraham (Abe) Brenner was born in Montreal, Quebec, on 28 February 1912. Little is known about his life before and after the war. In 1942, he enlisted in the Royal Canadian Corps of Signals. For his service as a signalman he was awarded the 1939–1945 Star, Defense Medal, and Canadian Volunteer Service Medal.

During the spring of 1945 Brenner was stationed in Hannover, Germany. He and some of his fellow Jewish soldiers learned that in the nearby town of Celle, the closest town to Bergen-Belsen, was a small Jewish community of survivors. Accordingly, Brenner and some of his colleagues travelled to Celle, and then on to Bergen-Belsen to attend a Yom Kippur service in one of the few Jewish communities remaining after the Holocaust. He wrote about the experience in a letter home to his friend Bill Berger, editor of the Y Beacon newspaper in Montreal.[21]

Upon the completion of his tour of duty he was discharged on 18 December 1945. He was thirty-three years old when he was relieved of duty. After the war, he married and worked as a butcher.

Letter

Yom Kippur Night in Belsen

There we were: ten Jewish Canadian soldiers. While attending our New Year Services at a camp in Hannover, we had heard that there was a Jewish Settlement in Celle, Germany, and decided to visit it during the Yom Kippur Holidays. When the time came, being granted leave from our various units, we met together, and arrived in Celle a day before Yom Kippur.

Our first greeting was the Jewish flag unfurled in front of the synagogue. Being informed that there were many fellow Jews in nearby Belsen, we unanimously agreed to go over there. After travelling about 30 kilometers, we reached the notorious camp that the world will never forget.

Making our way in, we eventually discovered the Jewish part of the camp. Its people gazed at us in astonishment. This was the first time they had ever seen Canadian soldiers, and it took endless explanations before they finally began to understand that we were those fortunates – Jews from America.

The poor souls encircled us, bombarding us with hundreds of questions. Many were the queries about relatives and friends who had come to Canada during the past few decades. What a pleasure it was to bring news of their distant kinsmen, in those rare cases in which we recognized the names.

The day passed and the time came for Kol Nidre and the ushering in of Yom Kippur.[22] In front of the Altar, a Hungarian Rabbi officiated. He prayed to the Lord in Yiddish to forgive these people their sins. He was saying these prayers before the same people who had seen their own kin murdered, killed and gassed, for the last six years. These pitiful outcasts were overcome with emotion. The sight was a tragedy – men and women wailing in utter desolation, the men beating their breasts and knocking their heads against walls of the synagogue. Amongst the ten of us, there was not a dry eye nor unbleeding heart, as we realized … how fortunate we were to have our families living in Canada and not in Europe. They, at least, had not been condemned, as so many of these people had been, for being Jews.

Kol Nidre was then sung, but not in the manner that we used to hear it back home. It was heart rending. The Rabbi chanted with such broken emotion and tears in his voice, that we shall never forget the scene that we witnessed. The responses of the congregation rang out loudly, that at times it almost sounded as if they were being shouted for the whole world of Jewry to hear. When the time came for Kaddish to be said, there was not a member in the congregation who did not recite it for a mother, father, wife, husband or child. It was as if the whole were in mourning.

The day services were similar. Fasting meant nothing to these people, for they had fasted not only on Yom Kippur but many a time whilst they were in various stalags.

The tragic part of the services for me was that when I recalled former Yom Kippurs, I could remember seeing children there and venerable old Jews. But here, all whom I saw were between the ages of fourteen and forty. The children and the old people had perished completely.

On forthcoming Yom Kippurs that we hope to celebrate some day in Canada, these scenes that we were able to see, of what has been done to a people, just because they were Jews, will always live in our memories.

One of the Ten
Sgmn Abraham Brenner

Source: Montreal Holocaust Memorial Centre Archives, Montreal, 2000.64.01, Abraham Brenner Collection. Gift from Rudi Brenner. Letter dated October 1945.

Notes

Preface

1 Mark Celinscak, "At War's End: Allied Forces at Bergen-Belsen" (PhD diss, York University, 2012).

2 Joanne Reilly, *Belsen: The Liberation of a Concentration Camp* (London: Routledge, 1998), 1.

3 For example, see Reilly, *Belsen*, and Ben Shephard, *After Daybreak: The Liberation of Belsen, 1945* (London: Jonathan Cape, 2005).

4 The word "encounter" is used throughout this volume. For the purposes of this work, it simply means to come across an extraordinary and unexpected situation. It is also broad enough to encompass the experience of those who assisted at Bergen-Belsen as well as those who were witnesses but did not work at the camp in any formal sense.

5 "The 11th Armoured Division (Great Britain)," The United States Holocaust Memorial Museum (online), https://www.ushmm.org/wlc/en/article.php?ModuleId=10006188.

6 Reilly, *Belsen*, 23.

7 Paul Kemp, "The British Army and the Liberation of Bergen-Belsen, April 1945," in *Belsen in History and Memory*, ed. Jo Reilly, David Cesarani, Tony Kushner, and Colin Richmond (London: Frank Cass, 1997), 135.

8 Ben Flanagan and Donald Bloxham, eds., *Remembering Belsen: Eyewitnesses Record the Liberation* (London: Vallentine Mitchell, 2005), 6.

9 Paul Kemp, "The Relief of Belsen, April 1945: Eyewitness Accounts," compiled by Paul Kemp (London: Imperial War Museum, 1991), 6.

10 Clara Thomas Archives: F0151: Aplin Family Fonds.

11 Irving Abella and Harold Troper, *None Is Too Many: Canada and the Jews of Europe, 1933–1948* (Toronto: University of Toronto Press, 1982).

Introduction

1 For further discussion see Mark Celinscak, "The Holocaust and the Canadian War Museum Controversy," *Canadian Jewish Studies* 26, no. 1 (2018): 11–30; Senate of Canada, "Proceedings of the Subcommittee on Veterans Affairs," issue 4 – Evidence for 3 February 1998.

2 For other recent studies regarding Canadian responses to the Holocaust see Norman Erwin, "The Holocaust, Canadian Jews, and Canada's 'Good War' against Nazism," *Canadian Jewish Studies* 24 (2016): 103–23; Ulrich Frisse, "The 'Bystanders' Perspective': *The Toronto Daily Star* and Its Coverage of the Persecution of the Jews and the Holocaust in Canada, 1933–1945," *Yad Vashem Studies* 39, no. 1 (2011): 213–43; and Magdalena Kubow, "Kanada? *The Canadian Jewish News* and the Memory of the Holocaust in Canada," *Holocaust Studies: A Journal of Culture and History* 19, no. 3 (2013): 131–60.

3 See Lauran Brandon, "Genesis of a Painting: Alex Colville's War Drawings," *Canadian Military History* 4, no. 1 (Spring 1995): 100–4 and "Reflections on the Holocaust: The Holocaust Art of Aba Bayefsky," *Canadian Military History* 6, no. 2 (Autumn 1997): 62–72.

4 For example, see Robert H. Abzug, *Inside the Vicious Heart: Americans and the Liberation of Nazi Concentration Camps* (New York: Oxford University Press, 1985); Michael Hirsh, *The Liberators: America's Witnesses to the Holocaust* (New York: Bantam Books, 2010); Dan Stone, *The Liberation of the Camps: The End of the Holocaust and Its Aftermath* (New Haven: Yale University Press, 2015); John J. Michalczyk, *Filming the End of the Holocaust: Allied Documentaries, Nuremberg and the Liberation of the Concentration Camps* (New York: Bloomsbury Academic, 2014).

5 Paul R. Bartrop, "Vught," in *The Holocaust: An Encyclopedia and Document Collection*, ed. Michael Dickerman and Paul R. Bartrop (Santa Barbara: ABC-CLIO, 2017), 682.

6 Ibid., 683.

7 Paul R. Bartrop, "Westerbork," in *The Holocaust: An Encyclopedia and Document Collection*, ed. Michael Dickerman and Paul R. Bartrop (Santa Barbara: ABC-CLIO, 2017), 708.

8 Ibid.

9 Richard Menkis, "'But You Can't See the Fear that People Lived Through': Canadian Jewish Chaplains and Canadian Encounters with Dutch Survivors," *American Jewish Archives Journal* 60, no. 1–2 (2008): 32–3.

10 "Papers," Kamp Amersfoort, 1 September 2016, https://www.kamparchieven.nl/en/camps-in-the-netherlands/camp-amersfoort.

11 Paul Kemp, "The Liberation of Bergen-Belsen Concentration Camp in April 1945: The Testimony of Those Involved," *Imperial War Museum Review*, no. 5 (1991): 30–1.

12 Paul Kemp, "The British Army and the Liberation of Bergen-Belsen, April 1945," in *Belsen in History and Memory*, ed. Jo Reilly, David Cesarani, Tony Kushner, and Colin Richmond (London: Frank Cass, 1997), 134.

13 Ben Shephard, *After Daybreak: The Liberation of Bergen-Belsen, 1945* (New York: Schocken, 2005), 32. For additional information on the Hungarians who worked at Bergen-Belsen, see Cecil D. Eby, *Hungary at War: Civilians and Soldiers in World War II* (University Park: Pennsylvania State University Press, 1998).

14 P. Kemp, "The British Army," 135.

15 "Introducing the 'Cookie Pusher' of the Montreal St. Andrew Society," *Journal of the St. Andrew's Society of Montreal* (Fall 1993).

16 For MacLellan's recognition in Washington at the 1981 International Liberators Conference, see Brewster Chamberlin, Marcia Feldman, and Robert Abzug, eds., *The Liberation of the Nazi Concentration Camps 1945: Eyewitness Accounts of the Liberators* (Washington: United States Holocaust Memorial Council, 1987); for his acknowledgement by the Canadian Jewish Congress, see "Keith MacLellan Honored for Wartime Services," *The Suburban*, 2 November 1988, A26. It is possible that Alan Rose, executive vice-president of the Canadian Jewish Congress, who entered Bergen-Belsen shortly after MacLellan with the 7th Armoured Division, made sure that MacLellan was recognized for his wartime contributions. A special thank you to Dr. Keith MacLellan as well as to Anne-Marie and Andrew MacLellan for additional details.

17 National Archives (UK): RAMC 1103, *An Account of the Operations of Second Army in Europe, 1944–1945*, compiled by Headquarters Second Army (vol. 2), 376.

18 Derrick Sington, *Belsen Uncovered* (London: Duckworth, 1946), 7–11.

19 For general descriptions see Daniel R. Hartigan, *A Rising Courage* (Calgary: Drop Zone, 2000), 1, and the DVD *Victory from Above: The 1st Canadian Parachute Battalion* (Koch International, 2002), 88 minutes, DVD.

20 WO 177/360, War Diary, A.D.M.S. 6 Airborne Division (also see Appendices A and D). In addition, the 224 Field Ambulance was later instructed to send a surgeon, Major H. Daintree-Johnson, to Bergen-Belsen. See Howard N. Cole, *On Wings of Healing: The Story of the Airborne Medical Services, 1940–1960* (Edinburgh: William Blackwood and Sons, 1963), 177. My thanks to David Johnson for additional details about H. Daintree-Johnson.

21 "Paratrooper Remembered on Banff Avenue," *Banff Crag and Canyon*, 10 November 2009, 7.

22 For a description of Richer and Lattion's encounter at the camp, see Charles H. Richer, "Sgt. Mike Lattion (obituary)," in *1st Canadian Parachute Battalion Association Newsletter* 6, no. 20 (April 1997): 41–3. Richer notes

that Lattion produced films of Bergen-Belsen that were later shown in newsreels around the world. However, upon leaving the camp, the two men were ordered to turn over their material to an officer in the War Crimes Committee. My thanks to Patrick Rossiter for providing me with a copy of the newsletter. Mr Rossiter's father, John A. Rossiter, was an intelligence officer in the 1st Canadian Parachute Battalion. It is likely that Rossiter also entered the camp alongside the battalion's commanding officer, Fraser Eadie.

23 Joanne Reilly, *Belsen: The Liberation of a Concentration Camp* (London: Routledge, 1998), 27.

24 Laidlaw sent photos of Bergen-Belsen home to his parents. These photos were later displayed in the office window of the local newspaper; see "Gruesome Pictures of Concentration Camp," *St. Marys Journal Argus*, 17 May 1945, 12J. My thanks to Amy Cubberley, museum curator and archives assistant at the St. Marys Museum, for calling my attention to this detail.

25 WO 171/7950, War Diary, 224 Military Government Detachment. *Note*: By April 1945 there were two main camps at Bergen-Belsen, the "residence camp" (*Aufenthaltslager*) and the "prisoners' camp" (*Häftlingslager*).

26 WO 219/3944A, Report on visit to Belsen Concentration Camp, 12A. I have discussed Proskie's involvement at Bergen-Belsen in greater detail in an interview with CBC Radio. See Mark Celinscak, "John Proskie's Story," interview with Kim Trynacity, "Radio Active," CBC Edmonton (26 October 2011). My thanks to the University of Alberta's Donna McKinnon and the CBC's Kevin Wilson for arranging the interview.

27 WO 171/8095, War Diary, 904 Military Government Detachment.

28 WO 171/8035, War Diary, 618 Military Government Detachment.

29 Operations Record Book, No. 5 Mobile Field Photographic Section, RCAF, 3–4 May 1945.

30 The three official war artists from Canada were Alex Colville, Donald Anderson, and Aba Bayefsky. Of the three, only Colville was given official permission to enter the camp. Bayefsky and Anderson went along with groups of RCAF airmen who assisted at the camp.

31 Library and Archives Canada, R2111–0-5-E, MG 30, D292, Progress Report by LT D.A. Colville.

32 Laura Brandon, "Reflections on the Holocaust: The Holocaust Art of Aba Bayefsky," *Canadian Military History* 6, no. 2 (Autumn 1997), 67.

33 Additional artists also entered the camp, such as H.S. Abramson from the 39 Reconnaissance Wing, RCAF. In addition, Canada's first female official war artist and the only one to be sent overseas, Molly Lamb (later Bobak), visited Bergen-Belsen in the months after the camp's surrender but did not depict it.

34 Shephard, *After Daybreak*, 87.

35 WO 222/201, Account given to the Royal Society of Medicine by Lieut-Colonel J.A.D. Johnston, R.A.M.C.

36 RAMC 1103, *An Account of the Operations of Second Army in Europe, 1944–1945*, 421.

37 WO 177/1257, War Diary, 29 (Br.) General Hospital.

38 J.A.D. Johnston, "The Relief of Belsen Concentration Camp. Recollections and Reflections of a British Army Doctor," Rosenstaft Papers, United States Holocaust Memorial Museum, 12.

39 As noted in Shephard, *After Daybreak*, 115.

40 Susan Armstrong-Reid and David Murray, *Armies of Peace: Canada and the UNRRA Years* (Toronto: University of Toronto Press, 2008), 275.

41 Ibid., 278.

42 Paul Weindling, *John W. Thompson: Psychiatrist in the Shadow of the Holocaust* (Rochester: University of Rochester Press, 2010), 93.

43 Operations Record Book, 437 Squadron, RCAF, April 1945.

44 W.R. Feasby, ed., *Official History of the Canadian Medical Services, 1939–1945: Organization and Campaigns* (Ottawa: Queen's Printer, 1956), 1:293.

45 "Report of Activities of R.C.A.F. Nutrition Group Detached to S.H.A.E.F.," 25 June 1945, John McCreary fonds, University of British Columbia, 2.

46 Ibid.

47 Leslie Hardman and Cecily Goodman, *The Survivors: The Story of the Belsen Remnant* (London: Valentine Mitchell, 2009 [1958]), 46–7.

48 Operations Record Book, no. 126 Wing, RCAF, April–May 1945.

49 Leo Velleman, "Belsen," in *Flap: 39 Reconnaissance Wing* (Hamburg: Vollmer and Bentlin KG, 1945), n.p.

50 Operations Record Book, no. 440 Squadron, May 1945.

51 WO 171/5290, War Diary, 4th Battalion, Wiltshire Regiment, June 1945.

52 *The Maroon Square: A History of the 4th Battalion, The Wiltshire Regiment*, comp. A.D. Parsons, D.I.M. Robbins, and D.C. Gilson (London: Franley, 1955), 198.

53 W.I. Smith, *Experiences of a CANLOAN Officer, 1944–1945* (Ottawa: Public Archives, 1977), 6. Born in Port La Tour, Nova Scotia in 1919, Smith obtained a PhD (history) from the University of Minnesota after the war. From 1970 to 1984 he was Dominion archivist at the Public Archives of Canada (now Library and Archives Canada). He is also the author of *Code Word CANLOAN* (Toronto: Dundurn, 1992), a history of Canadian officers who served in the British Army during the Second World War. Regarding Bergen-Belsen, Smith quotes from some of his own wartime letters to his parents. However, the letters are not accurately quoted in the book; a number of revisions and omissions are evident. In particular, see the letter dated 29 July 1945, Library and Archives Canada, MG 31, E 96, Wilfred I. Smith Fonds, vol. 24.

54 Air Ministry (AIR) 55/169, Historical Record of Disarmament 84 Group, 8.
55 8402 (RCAF) Disarmament Wing was part of 84 Group (RAF).

Reading Testimony

1 This chapter has been adapted from "Experience, Narrative and Meaning," in my *Distance from the Belsen Heap: Allied Forces and the Liberation of a Nazi Concentration Camp* (Toronto: University of Toronto Press, 2015), 3–22.
2 I expand on the subject in "Unlikely Documents, Unexpected Places: Challenging the Limits of Archive," *Auto/Biography Studies*: a/b 33, no. 3, "Lives Outside the Lines: Gender and Genre" (December 2018): 587–97.
3 Jean Bruce, *Back the Attack! Canadian Women during the Second World War, at Home and Abroad* (Toronto: Macmillan Canada, 1985).
4 There was overlap between the St. John Ambulance and the British Red Cross during the war.
5 "Obituary: Elsie May Deeks," *Winnipeg Free Press*, 20 June 2005.
6 United States Holocaust Memorial Museum, 2012.367.1: Elsie Deeks collection.
7 UNRRA, founded in 1943, was an international agency that administrated relief measures for victims of war. The JDC, founded in 1914, is a Jewish relief organization based in New York City.
8 Museum of Jewish Heritage, ID no. 1987.T.37: Testimony of Michael Gelber, 3 March 1987.
9 For example, see Christopher Browning, *Ordinary Men: Reserve Police Battalion 101 and the Final Solution in Poland* (New York: HarperCollins, 1992), and Browning, *Remembering Survival: Inside a Nazi Slave-Labor Camp* (New York: Norton, 2010). For a primarily theoretical discussion, see Browning, "German Memory, Judicial Interrogation, and Historical Reconstruction: Writing Perpetrator History from Postwar Testimony," in *Probing the Limits of Representation*, ed. Saul Friedländer (Cambridge: Harvard University Press, 1992), 22–36.
10 Browning, *Remembering Survival*, 9.
11 Christopher Browning, *Collected Memories: Holocaust History and Postwar Testimony* (Madison: University of Wisconsin Press, 2003), 39.
12 Yehuda Bauer, "On Oral and Video Testimony," *Past Forward* (Autumn 2010): 22.
13 Paul Ricoeur, *Temps et récit* (Paris: Seuil, 1985), 3:204: "what was and is no more." Translations mine unless otherwise noted.
14 Walter Laqueur, *Thursday's Child Has Far to Go: A Memoir of the Journeying Years* (Toronto: Maxwell Macmillian, 1992), 401.
15 Hayden White, *Content of the Form* (Baltimore: Johns Hopkins University Press, 1987), 1.
16 Maurice Halbwachs, *On Collective Memory*, ed. and trans. Lewis A. Coser (Chicago: University of Chicago Press, 1992), 38.

17 Marianne Hirsch, "Editor's Column: What's Wrong with These Terms? A Conversation with Barbara Kirshenblatt-Gimblett and Diana Taylor," *PMLA* 120, no. 4 (October 2005): 1500.

18 Joan. W. Scott, "The Evidence of Experience," *Critical Inquiry* 17, no. 4 (Summer 1991): 779.

19 Edward Sapir, *Culture, Language and Personality* (Berkeley: University of California Press, 1962), 69.

20 Sidonie Smith and Julia Watson, *Reading Autobiography: A Guide for Interpreting Life Narratives* (Minnesota: University of Minnesota Press, 2001), 25–6.

21 White, *Content of the Form*, 48.

22 Hayden White, *Tropics of Discourse* (Baltimore: Johns Hopkins University Press, 1978), 82.

23 Ibid., 24.

24 Saul Friedländer, "Introduction," in *Probing the Limits of Representation: Nazism and the "Final Solution,"* ed. Friedländer (Cambridge, MA: Harvard University Press, 1992), 9.

25 Hayden White, "Historical Emplotment and the Problem of Truth," in *Probing the Limits of Representation*, 38.

26 Ibid.

27 David Carr, *Time, Narrative, and History* (Bloomington: Indiana University Press, 1986), 16.

28 David Carr, "The Reality of History," in *Meaning and Representation in History*, ed. Jörn Rüsen (New York: Berghahn, 2006), 126.

29 Carr, *Time, Narrative, History*, 16.

30 Ibid., 61.

31 Paul Ricoeur, David Carr, and Charles Taylor, "Discussion: Ricoeur on Narrative," in *On Paul Ricoeur: Narrative and Interpretation*, ed. D. Wood (New York: Routledge, 1991), 186.

32 Paul Ricoeur, *Time and Narrative*, trans. K. McLaughlin and D. Pellauer (Chicago: University of Chicago Press, 1984), 1:3.

33 Richard Kearney, "Parsing Narrative – Story, History, Life," *Human Studies Journal* 29, no. 4 (December 2006): 485–6.

34 Ibid., 486.

35 Ibid., 487.

36 Ibid.

37 Ibid., 488.

38 Sara R. Horowitz, *Voicing the Void: Muteness and Memory in Holocaust Fiction* (Albany: State University of New York Press, 1997), 44.

39 Marlene Kadar, *Essays on Life Writing: From Genre to Critical Practice* (Toronto: University of Toronto Press, 1992), 10.

40 Wilhelm Dilthey, *Selected Writings*, ed. and trans. H.P. Rickman (Cambridge: Cambridge University Press, 1976), 213.

41 Ibid., 215.

42 Ibid., 218.

43 James Olney, *Metaphors of Self: The Meaning of Autobiography* (Princeton: Princeton University Press, 1972), xi.

44 Ibid., 37.

45 David McCooey, *Artful Histories: Modern Australian Autobiography* (Cambridge: Cambridge University Press, 1996), 164.

46 Ibid., 189.

47 Jeremy D. Popkin, *History, Historians, and Autobiography* (Chicago: University of Chicago Press, 2005), 279.

48 Ibid.

49 Smith and Watson, *Reading Autobiography*, 4.

50 Ibid., 14.

51 Ibid., 193.

52 Sandrine Arons, "Self-Therapy through Personal Writing: A Study of Holocaust Victims' Diaries and Memoirs," in *The Psychological Impact of War Trauma on Civilians*, ed. S. Krippner (Westport: Praeger, 2003), 124.

53 Karl J. Weintraub, "Autobiography and Historical Consciousness," *Critical Inquiry* 1, no. 4 (June 1975): 827.

54 James Young, *Writing and Rewriting the Holocaust* (Bloomington: Indiana University Press, 1988), 29.

55 Robert McGill, "The Life You Write May Be Your Own," *Southern Literary Journal* 36, no. 2 (Spring 2004): 38.

56 Janet Malcolm, *The Silent Woman: Sylvia Plath and Ted Hughes* (London: Picador, 1994), 110.

57 McGill, "The Life You Write," 38.

58 Mary Jean Corbett, "Literary Domesticity and Women Writers' Subjectivities," in *Women, Autobiography, Theory: A Reader*, ed. Sidonie Smith and Julia Watson (Madison: University of Wisconsin Press, 1998), 262.

59 Weintraub, "Autobiography and Historical Consciousness," 826.

60 Browning, *Collected Memories*, 40.

61 Ibid., 84.

62 Henry Greenspan, "Survivors' Accounts," in *The Oxford Handbook of Holocaust Studies*, ed. Peter Hayes and John K. Roth (Oxford: Oxford University Press, 2011), 415.

63 Julia Creet, "On the Sidewalk: Testimony and the Gesture," in *Memory, Haunting, Discourse*, ed. Maria Holmgren Troy and Elisabeth Wennö (Karlstad: Karlstad University Press, 2005),

64 Bauer, "On Oral and Video Testimony," 20. For further discussion of Eichmann's revelations concerning the Wannsee Protocol, see David Cesarani, *Eichmann: His Life and Crimes* (London: W. Heinemann, 2004), 112–16.

65 Sissela Bok, "Autobiography as Moral Battleground," in *Memory, Brain and Belief*, ed. Daniel L. Schacter and Elaine Scarry (Cambridge: Cambridge University Press, 2000), 308.

66 Wilhelm Dilthey, *The Formation of the Historical World in the Human Sciences*, ed. Makkreel and Rodi (Princeton: Princeton University Press, 2002), 222.

67 Ibid., 253.

68 Paul Ricoeur, *Oneself as Another*, trans. Kathleen Blamey (Chicago: University of Chicago Press, 1992), 140.

69 Popkin, *History, Historians, and Autobiography*, 43.

70 Avishai Margalit, *The Ethics of Memory* (Cambridge: Harvard University Press, 2002), 79.

71 Carr, *Time, Narrative, and History*, 155.

72 Cass also refers to the Jewish survivors as "these people," thus recognizing the divide.

73 Alasdair MacIntyre, *After Virtue: A Study in Moral Theory* (London: Duckworth, 1981), 199.

74 Suzanne Langlois, "Making Ideal Histories," in *Secret Spaces, Forbidden Places*, ed. F. Lloyd and C. O'Brien (New York: Berghahn, 2000), 117.

75 White, *Content of the Form*, 24.

76 McCooey, *Artful Histories*, 190.

1. Canadians Arrive at Bergen-Belsen

1 Harry Gutkin, *The Worst of Times, The Best of Times* (Markham: Fitzhenry and Whiteside, 1987), 75–6.

2 Alex Dworkin Canadian Jewish Archives, HDPSV257-SV259: Transcript of Alan Rose Holocaust Documentation Project Interview, 17 March 1982, Canadian Jewish Congress Records.

3 "Obituary: Ronald Ford 'Andy' Anderson," *Globe and Mail*, 20 November 2015.

4 Bernd Horn and Michel Wyczynski, *Paras Versus the Reich: Canada's Paratroopers at War, 1942–1945* (Toronto: Dundurn, 2003).

5 Rick Kardonne, "Special Commemoration Marks Liberation and End of War," *Jewish Tribune* (Canada), 12 May 2005.

6 "Obituary: Ronald Ford 'Andy' Anderson."

7 Mark Bonokoski, "Nordic's Last Hero Remembers." *Toronto Sun*, 16 September 2009.

8 *Note*: Many of the first-hand accounts presented in this volume have been condensed for reasons of space and to avoid repetition. An ellipsis indicates when material has been omitted.

9 "Lieutenant-Colonel Mervin Mirsky, O.B.E. and Mention," in *Canadian Jews in World War II*, vol. 1, ed. David Rome (Montreal: Canadian Jewish Congress, 1947), 5.

10 Mervin Mirsky, "Sister Pop: A Very Special WWII Remembrance," *Ottawa Jewish Bulletin and Review*, 6 April 1990, 8.

11 Cynthia Nyman Engel, "Former Vaad President Mervin Mirsky Passes Away at 96," *Ottawa Jewish Bulletin*, 19 July 2010, 5.

12 Mervin Mirsky, "I Saw Holocaust Horrors in Person," *Ottawa Citizen*, 18 February 1998, A18

13 Kelly Egan, "Pure Spring was in Every Fridge," *Ottawa Citizen*, 2 July 2010.

14 Engel, "Mervin Mirsky Passes Away," *Jewish Telegraphic Agency*, 19 July 1995.

15 Bram D. Eisenthal, "Alan Rose Dies at 74; Was Leader of Canadian Jewry," *Jewish Telegraphic Agency*, 19 July 1995.

16 Alex Dworkin Canadian Jewish Archives, HDPSV257-SV259: Transcript of Alan Rose Holocaust Documentation Project Interview, 17 March 1982, Canadian Jewish Congress Records.

17 Irwin Block, "Decorated Soldier Was Leading CJC Official for Almost 25 Years; Alan Rose Served in Europe, Africa, Israel," *Montreal Gazette*, 19 July 1995.

18 Eisenthal, "Alan Rose Dies at 74."

19 Members of the British Union of Fascists were known as "Blackshirts." That party, founded in 1932 by politician Oswald Mosley, was the predecessor of the Union Movement, a British far-right political party founded in 1948, also by Oswald Mosley.

20 Wolfgang Saxon, "Maurice Victor, 81, a Neurologist and Teacher," *New York Times*, 29 June 2001, B8.

21 Franklin Bialystok, *Delayed Impact: The Holocaust and the Canadian Jewish Community* (Montreal: McGill-Queen's University Press, 2000), 14.

22 According to his personnel records, Victor was attached to the 1st Headquarters Army Group, Corps of Royal Canadian Engineers on 8 April 1945. My thanks to analyst Le Phung of Library and Archives Canada for additional details. Also see Gutkin, *The Worst of Times*, 71–2.

23 Saxon, "Maurice Victor."

24 My thanks to Dr. Benjamin Victor, Université de Montréal, for additional information.

25 The CANLOAN program enabled hundreds of Canadian Army officers to volunteer to join regiments of the British Army.

26 "Captain Leo Jack Heaps, M.C.," in *Canadian Jews in World War II*, vol. 1, ed. David Rome (Montreal: Canadian Jewish Congress, 1947), 21.

27 Bernie Farber, "A Two-Man Band of Brothers," *National Post*, 10 November 2010.

28 W.I. Smith, *Code Word CANLOAN* (Toronto: Dundurn, 1992), 214.

2. Documenting the Horror Camp

1　Abramson Family, Private Collection, Montreal; Henry S. Abramson Collection, Letter dated 4 May 1945.
2　The quote is from the film *Portraits of War*, produced by Paul Kemp (Stornoway Productions, 2007), DVD, 48 minutes.
3　A.J. Ezickson, "Press," *Popular Photography*, November 1948, 164.
4　"Obituary: Ron Laidlaw," *Globe and Mail*, 16 August 2008.
5　Greg van Moorsel, "Hitler's Visit Still Haunting," *London Free Press*, 5 April 2007.
6　Irma Grese held the positions of *Arbeitsdienstführerin* (labour duty leader) and *Rapportführerin* (report leader) in Bergen-Belsen. She worked in the women's section of the camp. Grese, who was from Wrechen, Mecklenburg-Strelitz, Germany, was dubbed in the British press the "Blonde Angel of Hell" or the "Beastess of Belsen."
7　My thanks to Greg Sennema, librarian at Wilfrid Laurier University, for providing biographical details.
8　My thanks to Major Mathias Joost, Operational Records Team, Directorate of History and Heritage, for additional details regarding the service record of Fred Hopkinson.
9　Library and Archives Canada, R5642-0-2-E, interview with Al Calder by Dan Conlin, 23 September 1986, Dan Conlin Fonds.
10　"Fighting the Second World War with Their Cameras," CBC News Saskatchewan, 11 November 2015.
11　Graham Metson, "A Personal Realist," in *Alex Colville: Diary of a War Artist*, comp. Graham Metson and Cheryl Lean (Halifax: Nimbus, 1981), 16.
12　Alex Colville, "There Were at Least 30,000 Bodies," *Maclean's*, 1 January 2000, 164.
13　William Yardley, "Alex Colville Dies at 92; Leading Canadian Painter," *New York Times*, 22 July 2013, B7.
14　Hugh Halliday, "Donald Kenneth Anderson: Official War Artist (1920–2009)," *Canadian Military History* 19, no. 4 (Autumn 2010), 50.
15　Joan Murray, *Canadian Artists of the Second World War* (Oshawa: Robert McLaughlin Gallery, 1981), 26.
16　Robert McLaughlin Gallery, Oshawa; Donald Anderson interview with Joan Murray, 23 June 1981. Donald Anderson, artist file. Joan Murray artists' files.
17　DDT is dichlorodiphenyltrichloroethane and was used to control typhus among civilians and troops.
18　Library and Archives Canada, R3940: C.M. Donald interviews Aba Bayefsky (1995–96).

19 Ibid.
20 "Acclaimed Artist Dies at Age 78," *Canadian Jewish News*, 17 May 2001, 32.
21 Laura Brandon, "Reflections on the Holocaust: The Holocaust Art of Aba Bayefsky," *Canadian Military History* 6, no. 2 (Autumn 1997), 67.
22 Murray, *Canadian Artists*, 30.
23 Christopher Varley, *Aba Bayefsky Revisited: A Retrospective Exhibition* (Toronto: Koffler Gallery, 1989), 13.
24 The RAF Second Tactical Air Force was one of three tactical air forces within the Royal Air Force during the Second World War.
25 Ted Aplin was a squadron leader with the 8402 Disarmament Wing. He assisted the survivors at Bergen-Belsen. See his accounts in the ensuing pages.
26 My thanks to Ronney Abramson for additional biographical details.
27 Leo Velleman, "Belsen." *Flap: 39 Reconnaissance Wing* (Hamburg: Vollmer & Bentlin KG, 1945), n.p.
28 "H.S. Abramson Awarded French Art Scholarship," *Montreal Standard*, 16 March 1946.
29 Ronney Abramson became an accomplished singer-songwriter and was signed to Capitol Records. She released several acclaimed albums in the 1970s. Later, along with Ron Garant and Fred Mollin, she created the Rugrats (not to be confused with the later American animated children's television series), a children's musical group. The group won the Best Children's Album category at the 1984 Juno Awards.
30 Roy Shields, "Gallery 'With a Purpose' Opened by Artist Couple," *Monitor*, 26 February 1953.
31 John Davidson, "Portrait Photography with a New Twist: Henry Abramson Has Invented a Camera That Gives His Subjects the Bends," *Globe and Mail*, 4 July 1989, A22
32 The Allied Expeditionary Forces (AEF) Programme was operated by the BBC on behalf of the Allied forces in Europe.

3. Relief Measures

1 National Archives, WO 219/3944A: Belsen Concentration Camp by J. Proskie, 22 April 1945.
2 Special Collections, Woodruff Library, Emory University, interview by Ruth Scheinberg, 7 August 1980.
3 My thanks to Donna McKinnon and Ken Crocker at the University of Alberta for this information.
4 "23,000 Hungry at Belsen Fed by Canadian Expert," *Toronto Daily Star*, 18 July 1945, 24.
5 "City Man Fed Starving of Nazi Death Camps," *Edmonton Journal*, 9 September 1993, B2.

6 "Generous Move by RAF Men to Help Belsen Survivors," *Army News*, Northern Territory Printing and Press Unit, Darwin, 25 June 1945, 3.

7 "Obituary: Rosalie Rector," *Edmonton Journal*, 10 February 2007.

8 University of South California's Shoah Foundation Institute, interview (28524) with Matthew Nesbitt, 15 April 1997.

9 Emory University, Special Collections, Woodruff Library: Fred Roberts Crawford Witness to the Holocaust Project: Matthew Nesbitt interview, 7 August 1980.

10 "Concurrent Resolution," Journal of the House of Representatives, South Carolina General Assembly, 12 April 1988.

11 Celia Sibley, "Bearing a Painful Witness: Death Camp Liberator Shares Memories of the Horrors," *Atlanta Journal and Constitution*, 20 May 1995, 1J.

12 My thanks to those individuals who shared with me their memories of Mr. Nesbitt, including Dr. David Blumenthal, Ms. Terry Anderson, Mrs.Jackie Metzal, Mr. John Kovac, and Mr. and Mrs. Doug and Mary Wilmer.

13 My thanks to Rea Flamer for additional details about the life of Saul Stein.

14 "Chilling Tales Told at Holocaust Remembrance Ceremony," *CTV Montreal*, 27 January 2011.

15 Maurice de Hirsch (1831–96) was a German Jewish philanthropist who set up charitable foundations to assist oppressed European Jewry.

16 The first major Nazi camp to be liberated by the Allies was Majdanek. Located in Lublin, Poland, it was liberated in the summer of 1944 by the Red Army.

17 Sandra Martin, "Lyle Creelman, Nurse and Administrator, 1908–2007," *Globe and Mail*, 10 March 2007, S9.

18 Susan Armstrong-Reid, *Lyle Creelman: The Frontiers of Global Nursing* (Toronto: University of Toronto Press, 2014), 75.

19 Ibid., 92.

20 Susan Armstrong-Reid and David Murray, *Armies of Peace: Canada and the UNRRA Years* (Toronto: University of Toronto Press, 2008), 354.

21 Martin, "Lyle Creelman, 1908–2007."

22 Dr. T.B. Layton was in charge of the UNRRA hospital at Bergen-Belsen.

23 Australian nurse Muriel Knox Doherty was principal matron at Belsen hospital.

24 Creelman is referring to Gisella Perl, who was a Romanian Jewish gynecologist. Perl was deported to Auschwitz in 1944, where she helped pregnant women avoid being experimented on in the camp by aborting their pregnancies. She was later transferred to Bergen-Belsen. See Perl, *I Was a Doctor in Auschwitz* (New York: Arno, 1979 [1948]).

25 Paul Weindling, *John W. Thompson: Psychiatrist in the Shadow of the Holocaust* (Rochester: University of Rochester Press, 2010), 14.

26 Ibid., 4.

27 Thompson is quoting Elie Wiesel, "In the Face of Barbarians a Victory of Spirit," *New York Times*, 27 October 1963, 266.

28 "Obituary: Elsie Deeks," *Winnipeg Free Press*, 20 June 2005.

29 The St. John Ambulance was established in 1833 in Canada. Voluntary Aid Detachment (VAD) workers consisted of civilians who volunteered to provide nursing care for military personnel in the British Empire.

30 Jean Bruce, *Back the Attack! Canadian Women during the Second World War, at Home and Abroad* (Toronto: Macmillan, 1985), 155.

31 "Obituary: Elsie Deeks."

32 My sincerest thanks to Miss Elizabeth Thomson and Judy Thomson Saxerud for their assistance in learning more about Elsie Deeks.

33 "John Ferguson McCreary: A Man for All Seasons," *Canadian Medical Association Journal* 122 (12 January 1980): 123.

34 Robert Hill, *Jack McCreary: Paediatrician, Pedagogue, Pragmatist, Prophet* (Vancouver: Tantalus Research, 2006), 8.

35 Robert Krell, "Children Who Survived the Holocaust: Reflections of a Child Survivor/Psychiatrist," *Echoes of the Holocaust*, no. 4 (June 1995).

36 "John Ferguson McCreary," 124.

37 Sir Jack Drummond was the scientific advisor to the Ministry of Food and later a nutrition consultant to the Supreme Headquarters Allied Expeditionary Force (SHAEF) and the Allied Control Commissions (ACC).

38 "Obituary: Thompson, James Ernest," *Red Deer Advocate*, 3 March 2005.

39 Library and Archives Canada: RG24-G-3-1-a, R112, RCAF [Royal Canadian Air Force] file – No. 437 Squadron (RCAF) – Operations record book – Sep 1944 to Mar 1946.

40 "Obituary: Thompson, James Ernest."

4. Eyewitness Testimony

1 Sarah and Chaim Neuberger Holocaust Education Centre: Allan Ironside Collection.

2 University of South California's Shoah Foundation Institute: Interview (48192) with Larry D. Mann, 10 November 1998.

3 Ed Gould, *Entertaining Canadians: Canada's International Stars, 1900–1988*. Victoria: Cappis, 1988), 178.

4 Clara Thomas Archives: F0520, series S00483: Larry Mann interview, 7 September 1995, Knowlton Nash Fonds.

5 "Larry D. Mann, Veteran Actor, Dies at 91," CBC News, 6 January 2014.

6 My thanks to Susan Towers, Kathy Redford, Jamie Ashby, and David Smith for additional details about the life of Leo Velleman.

7 Ken McKay, *Figuratively Speaking: Puppetry in Ontario* (North York: The Puppet Centre, 1990).

8 "Obituary: Leo Velleman," *Comox Valley Record*, 10 March 2009.

9 *The Story Behind the Allan Ironside History Scholarship*, Orillia Historical Society, n.d.

10 Ibid.

11 My special thanks to Dr. Nancy Ironside for calling my attention to her father's letters and photographs.

12 "King Whyte: Telecaster, Writer on Outdoor Subjects," *Globe and Mail*, 28 June 1962, 11.

13 The psychological warfare group of SHAEF was a joint Anglo-American organization.

14 "Love Letters from a Witness to War," *Maclean's*, 9 May 1988, 52–6.

15 Paul Rutherford, *When Television Was Young: Primetime Canada 1952–1967* (Toronto: University of Toronto Press, 1990), 154.

16 "King Whyte: Telecaster, Writer," 11.

17 Ibid.

18 Whyte is likely referring to Major William A. Davis of the United States of America Typhus Commission, who was sent to Bergen-Belsen to control the typhus outbreak. See Davis, "Typhus at Belsen: Control of the Typhus Epidemic," *American Journal of Epidemiology* 46, no. 1 (July 1947): 66–83.

19 "Community Chests and Councils Division of the Canadian Welfare Council," *Canadian Welfare* 25–26 (Ottawa: Canadian Welfare Council, 1950), 11.

20 Ibid.

21 Monty Berger and Brian Jeffrey Street, *Invasions without Tears: The Story of Canada's Top Scoring Spitfire Wing in Europe during the Second World War* (Toronto: Random House, 1994), 207.

22 Department of National Defence, Directorate of History and Heritage, 87/241: "War Diary of Flight Lieutenant Carl Reinke, RCAF."

23 Department of National Defence, Directorate of History and Heritage, 72/381: "Fighter Wings on the Continent" by Carl Reinke, Royal Canadian Air Force.

24 Reinke is referring to the United Nations Conference on International Organization (UNCIO), which took place from 25 April to 26 June 1945 in San Francisco. Delegates from fifty Allied nations met and helped create the the United Nations Charter.

25 Karl Dönitz was briefly the German head of state in 1945 after the death of Adolf Hitler.

26 Folke Bernadotte (1895–1948), count of Wisborg, was a Swedish diplomat.

27 Tom Hawthorn, "B.C. Politico Kept His Pencil Sharp," *Globe and Mail*, 23 October 2003, R11.

28 Frank Snowsell, "Letter Tells the Tale of Why Our Side Fought War," *Vancouver Sun*, 10 November 1993, A3.

29 Hawthorn, "B.C. Politico."

30 Ibid.

31 "Obituary: Frank Snowsell," *The Times Colonist*, 4 September 2003.

32 Archives of Ontario, B268404: Application for Duties with Military Government by F/L G.R.B. Panchuk

33 Bohdan Panchuk, *Heroes of Their Day: The Reminiscences of Bohdan Panchuk*, ed. Lubomyr Y. Luciuk (Toronto: Multicultural History Society, Ontario Heritage Foundation, 1983), 87.

34 John Kolasky, *The Shattered Illusion: The History of Ukrainian Pro-Communist Organizations in Canada* (Toronto: PMA Books, 1979), 93.

35 Wentorf Displaced Persons Camp housed Eastern European refugees after the war. It was situated in Wentorf bei Hamburg in Schleswig-Holstein, Germany.

36 Unterlüß is a village in the district of Celle in Lower Saxony, Germany.

37 There were Ukrainians held at the Heidenau DP Camp in the British Zone.

38 The 14th Waffen Grenadier Division of the SS (1st Galician). Former soldiers of the division immigrated to Canada and the United Kingdom after the war. A monument to the division stands at St. Volodymyr Ukrainian Cemetery in Oakville, Ontario. The monument, along with the division itself, is the subject of debate and controversy. See Bernie Farber, "Canada's Monument to Nazi Soldiers," *National Post*, 22 July 2020.

39 The city of Rimini in northern Italy was the location of prisoner-of-war camps. Thousands of soldiers of the 14th Waffen SS Division Galicia were interned at Rimini after the war.

5. Displaced Persons Camp

1 Vancouver Holocaust Education Centre, 96.024.010: The Stanley Winfield Collection, letter dated 17 July 1945.

2 Stanley H. Winfield, "Journey to Galicia – A Glimpse of the Past," *The Scribe* 11, no. 2 (Fall 1989): 15.

3 Robert Matas, "No One Would Listen to Soldier's Account of Nazi Death Camps," *Globe and Mail*, 24 January 2005, A1

4 Paul D.K. Fraser, "Stanley Winfield," *The Advocate* 70, part 1 (January 2012): 115.

5 "Obituary: Winfield, Stanley Harold," *Vancouver Sun*, 20 August 2011.

6 Ibid.

7 Fritz Klein (1888–1945) was a German doctor and war criminal. He worked at Auschwitz-Birkenau, Neuengamme, and the Bergen-Belsen concentration camp. He was prosecuted at the Belsen trial by a British military court at Lüneburg and was later hanged.

8 Jacob (Jack) Eisen was the first rabbi appointed as chaplain with the RCAF. He served as principal Jewish chaplain with the RCAF in Canada and overseas.

9 Thousands of survivors from Bergen-Belsen were sent to Sweden for recuperation after the war.

10 My sincerest thanks to Nick Aplin and Attila Clemann for their insight and support regarding the life and war experiences of Ted Aplin.

11 National Archives, AIR 55/169: Historical Record of Disarmament 84 Group (Part A), 9.

12 Derrick Sington, *Belsen Uncovered* (London: Duckworth, 1946), 174.

13 Stanley Winfield, "Ted Aplin – 'The Angel of Belsen,'" *Zachor* (newsletter, Vancouver Holocaust Education Centre), May 1994, 5.

14 Lillian Sandler was a friend of the Aplin family and a lawyer who fought to establish a successful practice in Toronto in what was at the time a most difficult profession for both women and Jews.

15 Aplin is quoting Soviet politician and diplomat Vyacheslav Molotov. See Molotov, *On the Transformation of the People's Commissariat of Defence and of the People's Commissariat of Foreign Affairs form All-Union People's Commissariats in to Union-Republican People'e Commissiariats: Report in the Supreme Soviet of the U.S.S.R. on February 1, 1944* (Soviet War News, 1944).

16 Luba Tryszynska was born 5 June 1918 in a small village in Zastawie near Brest-Litovsk, Belarus. In January 1943, she was deported to the Auschwitz II-Birkenau concentration camp and in December 1944 to Bergen-Belsen. She helped shelter more than fifty children left for dead at the camp. In 1947, she immigrated to the United States.

17 Bella Zajdner (sometimes spelled Bela Seidner) was born in either 1937 or 1938 in Lodz, Poland. Aside from her mother, Chaja, and father, Jakob, she had a sister named Pola. See ITS Digitized Collections, USHMM, 0.1, "Central Names Index," Bella Zajdner, 64720044–64720057. My thanks to Ms. Jo-Ellyn Decker of the United States Holocaust Memorial Museum for her assistance in locating the identity of Aplin's "Bella." In addition, Pola gave an interview in 1946 while living in the displaced persons' camp at Bergen-Belsen. See Ghetto Fighters' House Archives, Western Galilee, catalog no. 5595: Pola Zajdner: testimony in the Bergen-Belsen DP camp.

18 After the war, in 1948, the Zajdner family made their way to Israel. Bella would later serve in the Israeli Defense Forces. After being discharged, she married, had two children, and lived for several years in both Ethiopia and Brazil before returning to Israel. At the time of her passing in 2005 Bella Zajdner had already welcomed three grandchildren into the world; two more have since been born. A special thank you to Mr. Amos Gonen and Ms. Pnina Lifshitz-Aviram for further details.

19 Ontario Jewish Archives, 2010–5/15: Bernard Yale Fonds.

20 University of South California's Shoah Foundation Institute: Interview (40440) with Bernard Yale, 14 April 1998.

21 My thanks to Sharon Yale for additional biographical details.

22 "Obituary: Yale, Bernard Louis," *Globe and Mail,* 18 September 2001.

23 Robert Collins, "Angel of Belsen," Reader's Digest, November 1990, 69–73.

24 Ernst Zündel (1939–2017) was a German neo-Nazi publisher and Holocaust denier. He lived in Canada from 1958 to 2000 and was jailed several times for inciting racial hatred and other charges.

25 The Golden Rule is the principle of treating others as one wants to be treated.

26 My thanks to Judy Jamieson for providing biographical details.

6. Religious Observation

1 R.K. Cameron, "Belsen Concentration Camp: An Eye-Witness Account of an R.C.A.F. Padre," *Front Line* 7, no. 11 (November 1946): 4.

2 Kenneth Munro, *First Presbyterian Church, Edmonton: A History* (Victoria: Trafford, 2004), 177.

3 "Rev. Ross Ketchen Cameron, Former Presbyterian Moderator," *Toronto Star,* 28 April 1989,

4 Ibid.

5 Cameron, "Belsen Concentration Camp."

6 Phyllis Bottome was a British novelist and author of *The Mortal Storm* (1937), an acclaimed anti-fascist book set in Vienna that warns against the dangers of antisemitism in Nazi Germany.

7 Canadian Jewish Congress Charities Committee National Archives, "GELBER, Michael (Dr.) – Interview – Rescue & Relief Work UNRAA 1944–45; Post-Holocaust Situation in Bergen-Belsen D.P. Camp."

8 Sylva M. Gelber, *No Balm in Gilead: A Personal Retrospective of Mandate Days in Palestine* (Ottawa: Carleton University Press, 1989), 206.

9 During the time he spent working in Bergen-Belsen, Gelber had not yet been ordained a rabbi and did not work in the military's chaplaincy services. I have included him in this chapter because so much of his writing explores a religious point of view. Gelber considered himself a Reform Jew and spent his life practising and studying Judaism.

10 Shalome Michael Gelber, "Are We Breaking Faith?" *New Statesman and Nation,* 3 August 1946, 78–9. The article is signed "Canadian Officer," but Gelber is the author.

11 ID no. 1987.T.37: Testimony of Michael Gelber (3 March 1987). Museum of Jewish Heritage, New York.

12 "Paid Notice: Deaths – Gelber, Rabbi Shalome Michael, PhD." *New York Times,* 9 December 2001.

13 A Jewish youth movement begun in Eastern Europe to promote agricultural settlement in Israel.

14 Dorothy Thompson (1893–1961) was an American journalist and radio broadcaster. She urged her American listeners to recognize the danger that Nazi Germany posed to democracy and to Europe's Jews.

15 For his title Gelber evokes Isaiah 21:11, which asks, "Watchman, what of the night?" Awaiting a message of hope, the Israelites are initially confused by the ensuing response: "Morning is coming, but also the night." It soon becomes clear that Israel is responsible for its own situation. Gelber thus stresses that the future for the remaining Jews of Europe must be in Palestine.

16 Richard Menkis, "'But You Can't See the Fear That People Lived Through': Canadian Jewish Chaplains and Canadian Encounters with Dutch Survivors, 1944–945," *American Jewish Archives Journal* 60 (2008): 26.

17 Gerd Korman, *Nightmare's Fairy Tale: A Young Refugee's Home Fronts, 1938–1948* (Madison: University of Wisconsin Press, 2005), 105.

18 Richard Menkis, "Cass, Samuel (1908–1975)," *Encyclopaedia Judaica*, 2nd ed., vol. 4, ed. Fred Skolnik and Michael Berenbaum (Detroit: Macmillan, 2007), 507.

19 Josef Rosensaft (1911–75) was a Holocaust survivor who helped establish the Central Committee of Liberated Jews that first assisted the refugees in Bergen-Belsen Displaced Persons camp, and later, those in DP camps throughout the entire British sector.

20 Cass is referring to Hadassa Bimko (later Rosensaft), a survivor of both Auschwitz and Bergen-Belsen, who was asked to organize and lead a group of doctors and nurses to care for the camp's ill inmates.

21 The Montreal Holocaust Center received the letter from the family of Bill Berger. Staff at the centre have attempted to locate Brenner and his family.

22 Kol Nidre is recited in the synagogue before the beginning of the evening service on every Yom Kippur.

Bibliography

Archival Sources

Abramson Family, Private Collection, Montreal
Henry S. Abramson Collection
Aliyah Bet and Machal Archives, University of Florida Libraries, Gainesville
C.D. Wilson interview conducted by David J. Bercuson (10 May 1979)
American Jewish Historical Society, Center for Jewish History, New York
Machal and Aliyah Bet Records, box 18, file 6: Heaps, Leo
Machal and Aliyah Bet Records, box 18, file 21: Levine, Abraham (Abe)
Machal and Aliyah Bet Records, box 19, folder 29: Wilson, Clifford Denny
Machal and Aliyah Bet Records, box 30, file 1: Manuscript – Heaps, Leo
  – *Israel, Shalom*
Machal and Aliyah Bet Records, box 32: Jim McGunigal interviewing Dennis
  Wilson, Harvey Serulnikov (Serlin), and Harold Katz
Archives and Special Collections, University of New Brunswick, Fredericton
UA RG 340: Joe Stone photographs
Archive of the Faculty of Health Sciences, McMaster University, Hamilton
Dr Charles Roland Oral History Collection, 1994.44.11 (box 22): interview with
  Dr A. Riley Armstrong, HCM 18-81 (25 November 1981), Early Canadian
  Medicine Series
Archives of Ontario, Toronto
F 1417: Bohdan Panchuk Fonds
B268404: Application for Duties with Military Government by F/L G.R.B.
  Panchuk
Brian Musson Collection, Paris
Peter Holborne, RCAF, photographs
Canadian Jewish Congress Charities Committee National Archives, Montreal
Dr Michael Gelber: Rescue & Relief Work UNRAA 1944–45 and Post-
  Holocaust Situation in Bergen-Belsen D.P. Camp – interview (1964)

HDP SV257-SV259: Transcript of Alan Rose Holocaust Documentation Project Interview (17 March 1982), Canadian Jewish Congress Records

P02/04/6: Gordon George Earle photographs

P0015: Monty Berger Fonds

P0127: Alan Rose Fonds

Canadian Parachute Battalion Association Archives, Ottawa

RF Anderson file 11-2: "From the Rhine to the Baltic" by Ronald Ford Anderson

Canadian War Museum, Ottawa

Artist file, Alex Colville

Artist file, Donald K. Anderson: "Donald Kenneth Anderson (draft)" by Hugh Halliday

19710261-1309: "Belsen" by Donald K. Anderson, Beaverbrook Collection of War Art

19710261-1393: "Belsen Concentration Camp, Malnutrition Wards" by Aba Bayefsky, Beaverbrook Collection of War Art

19710261-2033: "Bodies in a Grave, Belsen" by Alex Colville, Beaverbrook Collection of War Art

19970112-001: "Remembering the Holocaust" by Aba Bayefsky, Beaverbrook Collection of War Art

Textual Records: 58A 1 279.9: Authorization for Dr Christie to enter Belsen concentration camp

Photo Archives 52C 4 82.1: Corporal Roy Fergus photograph album [graphic material]

Photo Archives 52C 4 96.1: Photo album of Squadron Leader Dr.

Photo Archives, S 2.6: Bergen-Belsen concentration camp after liberation [graphic material], photos by L. Bloom and L. Thompson, RCAF

Sound Recordings 31 D 5 Colville: interview with Alex Colville, CWM Oral History Project (September 1980)

Sound Recordings 31D 6 Smith: interview with Theodor (Ted) R. Smith, CWM Oral History Project (24 October 2005)

58A 1 75.22: 84 Group memo regarding closing the medical post at Headquarters by W.A. Nield (26 June 1945)

58A 1 219.1: War Diary of the 3rd Battalion, North Nova Scotia Highlanders

58A 1 238.4: Letters written to F/Sgt. J.D. Stennett

City of Victoria Archives, Victoria

CA CVIC PR 77: Blenkinsop Family Fonds

Clara Lander Library, Winnipeg Art Gallery, Winnipeg

Henry S. Abramson file

Clara Thomas Archives, York University, Toronto

F0151: Aplin Family Fonds

F0520, series S00483: Larry Mann interview (7 September 1995), Knowlton Nash Fonds

Clifford Family, Private Collection, St Catharines
Reflections on November 11th by William (Bill) Clifford
College of Registered Nurses of British Columbia Archives, Vancouver
Biographical files: Lyle Creelman
CTV Television Network Archive, Toronto
Clifford Robb interview (25 March 1985)
Delta Museum and Archive, Delta
MSS DE 983-165(T): Interview with Norman Jack and Jean Crees
Department of National Defence, Directorate of History and Heritage, Ottawa
72/381: "Fighter Wings on the Continent" by Carl Reinke, Royal Canadian Air
    Force
87/241: "War Diary of Flight Lieutenant Carl Reinke, RCAF"
Army Headquarters Report No. 17: "The 1st Canadian Parachute Battalion in
    the Low Countries and in Germany Final Operations" by R.B. Oglesby
Army Headquarters Report No. 19: "Operation 'Plunder': The Canadian
    Participation in the Assault across the Rhine and the Expansion of the
    Bridgehead" by 2 Canadian Corps by Paul Augustus Mayer
Army Headquarters Report No. 152: "The Concluding Phase: The Advance
    into North-West Germany and the Final Liberation of the Netherlands" by
    W.E.C. Harrison
Canadian Military Headquarters Report No. 99: "Progress of War Artist
    Programme, Canadian Army Overseas" by C.P. Stacey
Canadian Military Headquarters Report No. 174: "The Canadian Army
    Occupations Forces in Germany" by C.E. Brissette
Photo Archive, PL-43508, PL-43510, PL-43511, PL-43512, PL-43514, PL-43515,
    PL-43516: Official photographs of Bergen-Belsen, RCAF
Duquesne University, Simon Silverman Phenomenology Center, Pittsburgh
Karl Stern Papers: John W. Thompson letter to Karl Stern, n.d. [1945]
Emory University, Special Collections, Woodruff Library, Atlanta
Box 25, reel 13: William Ned Cartledge and Matthew Nesbitt. Series
    VII – "Witness to the Holocaust" television series (4/21/81)
Fred Roberts Crawford Witness to the Holocaust Project: Matthew Nesbitt
    interview (7 August 1980)
The Empire Club of Canada, Toronto
"The Conditions of Civilians in Western Europe at the Conclusion of the German
    Occupations" by Wing Commander John F. McCreary (27 February 1947)
E.P. Taylor Research Library & Archives, Art Gallery of Ontario, Toronto
Info D: Henry Abramson file
Ghetto Fighters' House Archives, Western Galilee
Catalog no. 5595: Pola Zajdner: testimony in the Bergen-Belsen DP camp
Photo Archive, 25614: The teaching staff of the school in the Bergen-Belsen DP
    camp in 1946

Historica Dominion Institute, Toronto
Ronald Andy Anderson interview (1 November 2011)
Marcel Auger interview (3 June 2010)
Alex Colville interview (29 April 2010)
Patricia Collins (née Holden) interview (25 October 2010)
Hopkinson Family, Private Collection, Mount Hope
Fred Hopkinson Collection, RCAF, Public Relations
Institute of International Studies, University of California Berkeley, Berkeley
Conversations with History: Sir Brian Urquhart interview. Conducted by
     Harry Kreisler (19 March 1996)
Jamieson Family, Private Collection, Toronto
Edgar Jamieson Collection, 84 Group, RCAF
Jewish Public Library Archives, Montreal
ML Archives Bergen-Belsen Survivors: Bergen-Belsen Survivors Association of
     Montreal JewCan Literature Heaps: Leo Heaps Collection
Joint Distribution Committee Archives, New York
NY AR194554/4/3/6/325: "Report on Bergen-Belsen" by Shalome Michael
     Gelber (28 June 1946)
NY AR4564/390: "Report on the Activities of the AJDC in the British Zone,
     Germany, December 8, 1945 to September 20, 1946," by David Wodlinger
     (20 September 1946)
NY AR194554/4/32/6: Displaced Persons
NY AR194554/4/32/11: Religious, Cultural, and Educational
NY AR194554/4/32/10: Relief Supplies
Laidlaw Family, Private Collection, Toronto
Memoir of Ron Laidlaw, RCAF, Public Relations
Laurier Military History Archive, Wilfrid Laurier University, Waterloo
No Price Too High Collection, Record Group 2: King Whyte Letters and
     Photographs
Laurier Military History Archive MG-0003-1-10-8a. Whyte, Maureen (2 of 2)
Library and Archives Canada, Ottawa
MG 30, D 225: Samuel Cass Fonds
MG30, D 292, R2111-0-5-E: Progress Report by Lt D.A. Colville (1 April –
     7 May 1945)
MG 30 E 283: Gordon Roy McGregor Fonds
MG 31, E 96: Wilfred I. Smith Fonds
MG31-K9: Frank and Libbie Park Fonds, Reports, Correspondence, L.C.
     Rutherford (Libbie Park), box 20, files 301–2
Operations Record Book, No. 5 Mobile Field Photographic Section, RCAF
     (May 1945)
Operations Record Book, No. 126 Wing, RCAF (April–May 1945)
Operations Record Book, 437 Squadron, RCAF (April 1945)

Operations Record Book, No. 440 Squadron (May 1945)
R10120–0-7-E: Matthew Halton Fonds
R1190–0-3-E: Canadian Broadcasting Corporation Radio War Recordings
R3940: C.M. Donald interviews Aba Bayefsky (1995–6)
R5642–0-2-E: Interview with Al Calder by Dan Conlin (23 September 1986)
R13884–0-9-E: Keith W. MacLellan Fonds
81946: Salsberg, J.B. – Recollections (1970/1979), Paul Kligman Fonds
86195: *L'Envers de la Swastika - Atrocités nazies = Behind the Swastika - Nazi Atrocities* (1945), National Film Board of Canada
110624: Proceedings of the CFPU (1986-09-19/21), Dan Conlin Fonds
184951: Halton, Matthew – Report (1945-10-28), CBC Radio
222728: Whyte, King – Report (1945-11-17), CBC Radio
250249: [World War II Comment and Report] (1945-05-09), CBC Radio
250255: [Galloway, Stome] and Warren Wilkes – Comment (1945-05-10), CBC
250589/250591/250595/250597/250642/250649/250651/250668: Fairbairn, Donald B. – Reports (1945-09-19/1945-10-11), CBC Radio
250670/250698: Fairbairn, Donald B. and Benoit Lafleur – Reports (1945-10-12 /1945-10-19), CBC Radio
283728: *Alex Colville: The Splendour of Order*: [background interviews] (1983-07-14), Cygnus Communications
325790: Bayefsky, Aba – Interview (1995-12-07), Aba Bayefsky Fonds
435783: [Proceedings of the Convocation Ceremony of St. Andrew's College, University of Saskatchewan] (1972-05-03), Emil Fackenheim Fonds
473013: Ouimet, Marcel – Entrevue (1976-11-18), Archives publiques du Canada
Local History and Archives, Hamilton Public Library, Hamilton
R770.92 BLOOM CESH: Lloyd Harold Bloom Collection
McGill University, Department of Rare Books and Special Collections, Montreal
Lighthall Family Collection
McLaughlin Archives, University of Guelph, Guelph
RE1 OAC A0774: General file on Professor Hugh D. Branion, RCAF Nutrition Group
Museum of Jewish Heritage, New York
ID no. 1987.T.37: Testimony of Michael Gelber (3 March 1987)
ID no. 1974.T.5: Testimony of Harry Beckenstein (24 November 1974)
ID no. 1989.T.184: Testimony of Ruth Horak (13 July 1989)
Montreal Holocaust Memorial Centre Archives, Montreal
2000.10.10: Saul Stein letter (30 April 1945)
Abraham Brenner Collection
National Archives, London
AIR 55/108: Operation "Plainfare": A Short History of R.A.F. Celle
AIR 55/169: Historical Record of Disarmament 84 Group

WO 171/4306: War Diary, 3rd Parachute Brigade
WO 171/4697: War Diary, 3/4 County of London Yeomanry
WO 171/4773: Report on Belsen Camp by Lt-Col. R.I.G. Taylor
WO 171/5290: War Diary, 4 Battalion, Wiltshire Regiment
WO 171/7950: War Diary, 224 Military Government Detachment
WO 171/8035, War Diary, 618 Military Government Detachment
WO 171/8095: War Diary, 904 Military Government Detachment
WO 177/360: War Diary, A.D.M.S. 6 Airborne Division
WO 177/1257: War Diary, 29 British General Hospital
WO 219/3944A: 21 Army Group: Report on Relief Measures at Belsen (18–30 April 1945)
WO 219/3944A: Report on Visit to Belsen Camp by ADMG Sups (22 April 1945)
WO 219/3944A: Belsen Concentration Camp by J. Proskie (22 April 1945)
WO 222/201: Account given to the Royal Society of Medicine by Lieut-Colonel J.A.D. Johnston
WO 222/201: Account given to Royal Society of Medicine by Col. Lipscomb (4 June 1945)
WO 222/208: Cases of Starvation in Belsen Camp by Captain P.L. Mollison (1945)
National Archives, UK
RAMC 1103: An Account of the Operations of Second Army in Europe, 1944–1945, compiled by Headquarters Second Army (vol. 2).
National Gallery of Canada Library and Archives, Ottawa
Vertical file: Henry S. Abramson
Ontario Jewish Archives, Toronto
45, H-24: Alex Pancer photographs and letters
2010–5/15: Bernard Yale Fonds
Oral History Division, Hebrew University, Jerusalem
Interview no. (4)46: Josef Rosensaft interview (1964)
Interview no. (4)51: Michael Gelber interview (1964)
Interview no. (119)98: Leslie Hardman interview (1975)
Powell River Historical Museum and Archive, Powell River
Record of Service, 263: Holborne, A.P. (Pete) – Corporal RCAF Overseas
Record of Service, 609: Vandervoot, Harold – LAC RCAF Overseas
Presbyterian Church in Canada Archives and Records Office, Toronto
Reverend Ross Ketchen Cameron papers
Queen's University Archives, Kingston
1989–001p, V054: Lloyd Thompson Fonds
Research and Documentation Centre, Gedenkstätte Bergen-Belsen, Lohheide
David Rosenthal Fonds: *Unzer Sztyme* (12 July 1945)
William E. Roach Fonds

Robert McLaughlin Gallery, Oshawa
Aba Bayefsky interview with Joan Murray (27 April 1979). Aba Bayefsky, artist file. Joan Murray artists' files
Alex Colville interview with Joan Murray (18 December 1978). Alex Colville, artist file. Joan Murray artists' files
Donald Anderson interview with Joan Murray (23 June 1981). Donald Anderson, artist file. Joan Murray artists' files
Campbell Tinning interview with Joan Murray (16 May 1979). Campbell Tinning, artist file. Joan Murray artists' files
Sarah and Chaim Neuberger Holocaust Education Centre, Toronto
Allan Ironside Collection
Clifford Robb Collection
Sound and Moving Image Archive, British Library, London
C459/41/1-5: George Rodger interview (1992)
F3378: Janet Vaughan interview (1991
V3335/2: Bob Daniell interview (1994)
Stubbs Family, Private Collection, Waterloo
Photographic collection of James Arthur Stubbs, RCAF
Thompson Family, Private Collection, Bowden
James Ernest Thompson interview with Nicky Saunders (1999)
J.E. Thompson Flight Logs, 437 Squadron, RCAF (April–May 1945)
Trent Valley Archives, Peterborough
Fonds 40: John A.I. Young
United Church of Canada, BC Conference Archives, Burnaby
Box 1919, file 57: Interview Rev. N.J. Crees (4 February 1977), Heritage Alive Project Fonds
United Nations Archive, New York
S-0408-0043: UNRRA Germany Mission – British zone headquarters' subject files of regional units and teams
S-0408-0043, file 3 (Medical-Miscellaneous): "Report: Nursing Personnel for Belsen-Falling Bostel," by Lyle Creelman (10 October 1945)
S-0408-0042: UNRRA Germany Mission – British zone headquarters' subject files of regional units and teams
S-0422-0002: Subject files of Assembly Centres and Camps of the Central Registry of the British Zone
S-1021-0084-01: UNRRA – Office of the Historian – Monographs, Documents, and Publications
United States Holocaust Memorial Museum, Washington
International Tracing Service (ITS) Digitized Collections, USHMM, 0.1, "Central Names Index," Edward Blenkinsop, 14704159-14704167
ITS Digitized Collections, USHMM, 0.1, "Central Names Index," Violette de Chassaigne, 17090520-17090523

ITS Digitized Collections, USHMM, 2.1.1.1, "Lists of all persons of United Nations and other foreigners, German Jews, and stateless persons; American Zone; Bavaria, Hesse," Robert Jenkinson, 70263290 and 70263696.

ITS Digitized Collections, USHMM, 0.1, "Central Names Index," Bella Zajdner, 64720044-64720057

ITS Digitized Collections, USHMM, 1.1.30, "General Information on Bergen-Belsen Concentration Camp," Report on the Search in Belsen by Lieutenant Francois Poncet (10 June 1946), 8009600, pages 5–62

RG-50.234*0024: Oral history interview with Alan Rose

RG-60.3800: "Eyewitnesses and War Correspondents at Plenary," International Liberators Conference (27 October 1981)

2012.367.1: Elsie Deeks collection

Photo Archive, 00818: Dr and Rabbi Michael Gelber of Toronto, Ontario

Photo Archive, 2004.535: Bergen-Belsen liberation photographs by Stanley Brocklebank

Photo Archive, 2009.378: Gerard LaBossiere collection

Photo Archive, 41271-41276: Dr Charles Sutherland Rennie photographs

Photo Archive, 46347 and 46348: David Wodlinger of Toronto, Ontario, JDC Chief of Operations in the British zone of Germany

University of British Columbia Archives, Vancouver

D805.G3 S66 1945a: Bergen-Belsen by Frank Snowsell (1 May 1945)

4-1: Report of Activities of R.C.A.F. Nutrition Group Detached to S.H.A.E.F. 25 June 1945

John McCreary Fonds. Professional affiliation series.

John McCreary Fonds, box 4: Personal files, R.C.A.F. correspondence

Lyle Creelman Fonds, box 2–2: 1944–1945 Record of Service with UNRAA

University of Manitoba Faculty of Medicine Archives, Winnipeg

CA UMFMA Victor_M: Maurice Victor File

University of South California's Shoah Foundation Institute, Los Angeles

05795: Interview with Leslie Hardman (23 November 1995)

28524: Interview with Matthew Nesbitt (15 April 1997)

39023: Interview with Mervin Mirsky (22 February 1998)

40440: Interview with Bernard Yale (14 April 1998)

47651: Interview with Ralph Millman (25 September 1998)

48192: Interview with Larry D. Mann (10 November 1998)

53556: Interview with Edmund Morris (5 August 1981)

53654: Interview with David Portigal (4 April 1988)

54677: Interview with Marvin Silver (30 January 1995)

54699: Interview with Saul Stein (3 June 1999)

54720: Interview with Bernard Pépin (15 September 2000)

Vancouver Holocaust Education Centre, Vancouver

96.024.010: Stanley Winfield collection

HVT-3095: Stanley H. Winfield interview (14 November 1990)
Peter Gorst Photographs
Veterans Affairs Canada, Government of Canada, Ottawa
"Heroes Remember" Series: Interview with Alex Colville (24 May 1997)
Weiner Library, London
01623: Belsen Concentration Camp Report, Appendix B by Glyn Hughes
15323: Addresses and Speeches, Commemorative Ceremony of the 50th
    Anniversary of the Liberation of Concentration Camps, held in the
    memorial of Bergen-Belsen (27 April 1995)
HA6B-1/20, Jews in Germany Camps: "Bergen Belsen Exhibition, October
    1947–April 1948"
WGST Radio, Atlanta
Matthew Nesbitt interview (18 April 1987)
Wilks Family, Private Collection, Toronto
Photographic collection of Charles H. Wilks, RCAF
World War II Round Table, Atlanta
Matthew Nesbitt Lecture at Atlanta's 57th Fighter Group (15 January 1987)
Yad Vashem Archives, Jerusalem
Photo Archive, 111/4-13: John F. McCreary photos
Photo Archive, 7036/4, 7036/5, 7036/6: Photographs by Aba Bayefsky
Photo Archive, 93359: Canadian Zionist Federation photos

Secondary Sources

Abella, Irving. "Canadian War Museum." *Globe and Mail*, 22 November 1997, D3.
Abella, Irving, and Franklin Bialystok. "Canada." In *The World Reacts to the
    Holocaust*, edited by David S. Wyman, 749–81. Baltimore: Johns Hopkins
    University Press, 1996.
Abella, Irving, and Harold Troper. *None Is Too Many: Canada and the Jews of
    Europe, 1933–1948*. Toronto: Lester and Orpen Dennys, 1982.
Abzug, Robert H. *Inside the Vicious Heart*. New York: Oxford University Press,
    1985, 1987.
– "The Liberation of the Concentration Camps." In *Liberation 1945*, edited by
    Susan D. Bachrach, 23–46. New York: United States Holocaust Memorial
    Council, 1995.
"Acclaimed Artist Dies at Age 78." *Canadian Jewish News*, 17 May 2001, 32.
Aplin, E.M. "I Saw Belsen … My Conscience Cannot Wait." *Today: An Anglo-
    Jewish Monthly* 2, no. 5 (April 1946): 18–19, 38.
Armstrong-Reid, Susan. *Lyle Creelman: The Frontiers of Global Nursing*. Toronto:
    University of Toronto Press, 2014.
Armstrong-Reid, Susan, and David Murray. *Armies of Peace: Canada and the
    UNRRA Years*. Toronto: University of Toronto Press, 2008.

Arons, Sandrine. "Self-Therapy through Personal Writing: A Study of Holocaust Victims' Diaries and Memoirs." In *The Psychological Impact of War Trauma on Civilians*, edited by Stanley Krippner and Teresa M. McIntyre, 123–34. Westport: Praeger, 2003.

Balzar, Timothy. *The Information Front: The Canadian Army and News Management during the Second World War*. Vancouver: UBC Press, 2011.

Bardgett, Suzanne. "The Depiction of the Holocaust at the Imperial War Museum since 1961." *Journal of Israeli History: Politics, Society, Culture* 23, no. 1 (Spring 2004): 146–56. https://doi.org/10.1080/1353104042000241974.

Bardgett, Suzanne, and David Cesarani, eds. *Belsen 1945: New Historical Perspectives*. London: Vallentine Mitchell, 2006.

Bauer, Yehuda. "On Oral and Video Testimony." *Past Forward*, Autumn 2010, 20–2.

Bayefsky, Edra. "Aba Bayefsky: Life and Work." *Outlook Magazine*, July–August 2012, 7–8, 31.

"Belsen Camp Murder of Briton Revealed." *Maple Leaf*, 5 October 1945, 1.

"Belsen Horrors Recalled: Local Girl Sees Little Chance of Normalcy for Inmates." *Winnipeg Tribune*, 6 May 1946, 4.

Benarde, Scott R. "How the Holocaust Rocked Rush Front Man Geddy Lee." *Jweekly*, 25 June 2004.

Benedek, Ann. "Top Official Stands Back to Count Medals." *Canadian Churchman* 105, no. 5 (May 1979): 1, 8.

Bercuson, David J. *The Secret Army*. Toronto: Lester and Orpen Dennys, 1983.

"Bergen-Belsen Death Camp Did Not Have Gas Chambers." *Toronto Star*, 20 September 2007.

Berger, Monty, and Brian Jeffrey Street. *Invasions without Tears: The Story of Canada's Top Scoring Spitfire Wing in Europe during the Second World War*. Toronto: Random House of Canada, 1994.

Bialystok, Franklin. *Delayed Impact: The Holocaust and the Canadian Jewish Community*. Montreal: McGill-Queen's University Press, 2000.

Black, Debra. "Bell Pulls 'Death Camp' Ads." *Toronto Star*, 15 September 2007.

Block, Irwin. "Decorated Soldier Was Leading CJC Official for Almost 25 Years; Alan Rose Served in Europe, Africa, Israel." *Montreal Gazette*, 19 July 1995.

Bogarde, Dirk. *Cleared for Take-Off*. London: Penguin, 1995.

– *For the Time Being: Collected Journalism*. London: Viking, 1998.

– *Snakes and Ladders*. London: Chatto and Windus, 1978.

Bok, Sissela. "Autobiography as Moral Battleground." In *Memory, Brain and Belief*, edited by Daniel L. Schacter and Elaine Scarry, 307–24. Cambridge: Cambridge University Press, 2000.

Bonokoski, Mark. "Nordic's Last Hero Remembers." *Toronto Sun*, 16 September 2009.

Bracken, Robert. *Spitfire: The Canadians*. Erin, ON: Boston Mills, 1995.

Brandon, Laura. *Art and War*. London: I.B. Tauris, 2007.

– *Art or Memorial? The Forgotten History of Canada's War Art*. Calgary: University of Calgary Press, 2006.

– "'Doing Justice to History': Canada's Second World War Official Art Program." Canadian War Museum, 2005, 1–4.

– "Genesis of a Painting: Alex Colville's War Drawings." *Canadian Military History* 4, no. 1 (Spring 1995): 100–4.

– "Reflections on the Holocaust: The Holocaust Art of Aba Bayefsky." *Canadian Military History* 6, no. 2 (Autumn 1997): 62–72.

Brandon, Laura, Peter Stanley, Roger Tolson, and Lola Wilkins. *Shared Experience, Art and War: Australia, Britain and Canada in the Second World War*. Canberra: Australian War Memorial, 2005.

Branion, H.D., Gordon Butler, L. Chute, J.F. McCreary, and R.L. Noble. "Sir Jack Drummond, F.R.S." *Nature*, 27 December 1952, 1139. https://doi.org/10.1038/1701131b0.

Broadfoot, Barry. *Six War Years, 1939–1945: Memories of Canadians at Home and Abroad*. Toronto: Doubleday Canada, 1974.

Brode, Patrick. *Casual Slaughters and Accidental Judgments: Canadian War Crimes Prosecutions, 1944–1948*. Toronto: University of Toronto Press, 1997.

Brooks, Jane. "Nursing Typhus Victims in the Second World War, 1942–1944: A Discussion Paper." *Journal of Advanced Nursing* 70, no. 7 (July 2014): 1510–19. https://doi.org/10.1111/jan.12314.

– "'Uninterested in Anything except Food': The Work of Nurses Feeding the Liberated Inmates of Bergen-Belsen." *Journal of Clinical Nursing* 21, no. 19 (October 2012): 2958–65. https://doi.org/10.1111/j.1365-2702.2012.04149.x.

Brown, George, and Michel Lavigne. *Canadian Wing Commanders of Fighter Command in World War II*. Langley: Battleline, 1984.

Browning, Christopher R. *Collected Memories: Holocaust History and Postwar Testimony*. Madison: University of Wisconsin Press, 2003.

– "German Memory, Judicial Interrogation, and Historical Reconstruction: Writing Perpetrator History from Postwar Testimony." In *Probing the Limits of Representation*, edited by Saul Friedländer, 22–36. Cambridge: Harvard University Press, 1992.

– *Ordinary Men: Reserve Police Battalion 101 and the Final Solution in Poland*. London: Penguin, 1992; 1998.

– *Remembering Survival: Inside a Nazi Slave-Labor Camp*. New York: Norton, 2010.

Bruce, Harry. "Death, Art and Alex Colville." *Saturday Night*, May 1972, 30–5.

Bruce, Jean. *Back the Attack! Canadian Women during the Second World War, at Home and Abroad*. Toronto: Macmillan, 1985.

Caiger-Smith, Martin, ed. *The Face of the Enemy: British Photographers in Germany, 1944–1952*. Berlin: Nishen, 1988.

Cameron, R.K. "Belsen Concentration Camp: An Eye-Witness Account of an R.C.A.F. Padre." *Front Line* 7, no. 11 (November 1946): 1–6.

Canada, House of Commons. Debates: Official Reports. Vol. 5. Ottawa: Queen's Printer, 1944.

"Canadian Labor Groups Oppose Racial Bars in Immigration; Ask Entry of Refugees." Jewish Telegraphic Agency, 26 July 1946.

Capon, Alan. "Reconnaissance Picton Photographer Shot for D-Day." *Whig*, 29 August 1985, 1.

"Captain Leo Jack Heaps, M.C." In *Canadian Jews in World War II*, volume 1, edited by David Rome (Montreal: Canadian Jewish Congress, 1947).

Carlson, Don. *R.C.A.F. Padre with Spitfire Squadrons*. Red Deer: D.G. Carlson, 1980.

Carr, David. "The Reality of History." In *Meaning and Representation in History*, edited by Jörn Rüsen, 123–36. New York: Berghahn, 2006.

– *Time, Narrative, and History*. Bloomington: Indiana University Press, 1986.

Cass, Samuel. "Chaplains Thank Canadian Jewry." *Canadian Jewish Chronicle*, 28 December 1945, 11.

– "Rabbi Cass Asks Every Jewish Family to Help." *Jewish Western Bulletin*, 25 January 1946, 2.

Castonguay, Jacques. *Unsung Mission: History of the Chaplaincy Service of the RCAF*. Translated by Michael Hoare. Montreal: Institut de Pastorale, 1968.

Celinscak, Mark. "At War's End: Allied Forces at Bergen-Belsen." PhD diss., York University, 2012.

– "Bergen-Belsen in Historical Context." In ... *And Stockings for the Ladies*, by Attila Clemann, viii–xii. Self-published. Printed in Victoria by First Choice, 2013.

– "Canadians and the Liberation of Bergen-Belsen." Interview by Steve Guthrie. "Newswatch Late Edition," CHEX Peterborough, 24 February 2014.

– *Distance from the Belsen Heap: Allied Forces and the Liberation of a Nazi Concentration Camp*. Toronto: University of Toronto Press, 2015.

– "The Final Rescue? Liberation and the Holocaust." In *Unlikely Heroes: The Place of Holocaust Rescuers in Research and Teaching*, edited by Ari Kohen and Gerald J. Steinacher, 57–85. Lincoln: University of Nebraska Press, 2019.

– "The Holocaust and the Canadian War Museum Controversy." *Canadian Jewish Studies/Études juives canadiennes* 26, no. 1 (2018): 11–30. https://doi.org /10.25071/1916-0925.40063.

– "John Proskie's Story." Interview by Kim Trynacity. "Radio Active," CBC, 26 October 2011.

– "Unlikely Documents, Unexpected Places: Challenging the Limits of Archive." *Auto/Biography Studies: a/b* 33, issue 3, "Lives Outside the Lines: Gender and Genre" (December 2018): 587–97. https://doi.org/10.1080 /08989575.2018.1503399.

Celis, Peter. *One Who Almost Made It Back: The Remarkable Story of One of World War Two's Unsung Heroes, Sqn Ldr Edward "Teddy" Blenkinsop, DFC, CdeG (Belge), RCAF.* London: Grub Street, 2008.

Cesarani, David. *Eichmann: His Life and Crimes.* London: W. Heinemann, 2004.

Chamberlin, Brewster, Marcia Feldman, and Robert Abzug, eds. *The Liberation of the Nazi Concentration Camps 1945: Eyewitness Accounts of the Liberators.* Washington: United States Holocaust Memorial Council, 1987.

"Chilling Tales Told at Holocaust Remembrance Ceremony." CTV Montreal, 27 January 2011.

"City Man Fed Starving of Nazi Death Camps." *Edmonton Journal,* 9 September 1993, B2.

Clark, Lloyd. *Crossing the Rhine: Breaking into Nazi Germany, 1944 and 1945.* New York: Atlantic Monthly, 2008.

Clemann, Attila. ... *And Stockings for the Ladies.* Self-published. Printed in Victoria by First Choice, 2013.

Cole, Howard N. *On Wings of Healing: The Story of the Airborne Medical Services, 1940–1960.* Edinburgh: William Blackwood and Sons, 1963.

Collins, Arthur S. *Before I Forget.* Raleigh: Lulu, 2007.

Collins, Robert. "Angel of Belsen." *Reader's Digest,* November 1990, 69–73.

– *You Had to Be There: An Intimate Portrait of the Generation that Survived the Depression, Won the War, and Re-invented Canada.* Toronto: McClelland and Stewart, 1997.

Collis, Robert, and Han Hogerzeil. *Straight On.* London: Methuen, 1947.

Colville, Alex. *Alex Colville: Diary of a War Artist.* Compiled by Graham Metson and Cheryl Lean. Halifax: Nimbus, 1981.

– "Beauty and the Beast." In *Between Ethics and Aesthetics: Crossing the Boundaries,* edited by Dorota Glowacka and Stephen Boos, 251–4. New York: State University of New York Press, 2002.

– "There Were at Least 30,000 Bodies." *Maclean's,* 1 January 2000, 164.

"Community Chests and Councils Division of the Canadian Welfare Council." *Canadian Welfare* 25–26 (Ottawa: Canadian Welfare Council, 1950), 11–12.

"Concurrent Resolution." Journal of the House of Representatives, South Carolina General Assembly, 12 April 1988.

Conti, Jean W., ed. *Health and Human Relations in Germany: Report of a Conference on Problems of Health and Human Relations in Germany, Nassau Tavern, Princeton, N.J., June 26–30, 1950.* New York: Josiah Macy Jr Foundation, 1950.

Corbett, Mary Jean. "Literary Domesticity and Women Writers' Subjectivities." In *Women, Autobiography, Theory: A Reader,* edited by Sidonie Smith and Julia Watson, 255–63. Madison: University of Wisconsin Press, 1998.

Creelman, Lyle M. "With the UNRRA in Germany." *Canadian Nurse* 43, no. 7 (January 1947): 532, 552–6. Article continued in volume 43, no. 9 (September 1947): 710–12.

Creet, Julia. "On the Sidewalk: Testimony and the Gesture." In *Memory, Haunting, Discourse*, edited by Maria Holmgren Troy and Elisabeth Wennö, 139–59. Karlstad: Karlstad University Press, 2005.

Crerar, Duff. "In the Day of Battle: Canadian Catholic Chaplains in the Field, 1885–1945." *CCHA Historical Studies* 61 (1995): 53–77.

Crew, F.A.E. *The Army Medical Services: Northwest Europe*. Vol. 4. London: Her Majesty's Stationary Office, 1962.

Csillag, Ron. "Bayefsky Donates 22 Works to Yad Vashem." *Canadian Jewish News*, 6 April 2000, 5.

Davidson, John. "Portrait Photography with a New Twist: Henry Abramson Has Invented a Camera that Gives His Subjects the Bends." *Globe and Mail*, 4 July 1989, A22.

Davis, W.A. "Typhus at Belsen: Control of the Typhus Epidemic." *American Journal of Hygiene* 46 (1947): 66–83. https://doi.org/10.1093/oxfordjournals. aje.a119156.

D-Day to Victory. Directed by Paul Kilback. Impossible Pictures, 2011.

Dickerman, Michael, and Paul R. Bartrop, eds. *The Holocaust: An Encyclopedia and Document Collection*. Santa Barbara: ABC-CLIO, 2017.

Dilthey, Wilhelm. *The Formation of the Historical World in the Human Sciences*. Edited and translated by Rudolf A. Makkreel and Frithjof Rodi. Princeton: Princeton University Press, 2002.

– *Selected Writings*. Edited and translated by H.P. Rickman. Cambridge: Cambridge University Press, 1976.

Dodick, Mark. "Present, Past Meld in Reunion for Mahal Fliers." *Canadian Jewish News*, 21 August 1986, 19.

Doherty, Muriel Knox. *Letters from Belsen 1945: An Australian Nurse's Experiences with the Survivors of War*. Edited by Judith Cornell and R. Lynette Russell. St Leonards: Allen and Unwin, 2000.

Dow, Helen J. *The Art of Alex Colville*. Toronto: McGraw-Hill Ryerson, 1972.

Draper, Paula, and Harold Troper, eds. *Archives of the Holocaust*. Vol. 15. New York: Garland, 1991.

Drea, Edward J. "Recognizing the Liberators: U.S. Army Divisions Enter the Concentration Camps." *Army History* (Fall/Winter 1992–93): 1–5. www.jstor.org/stable/26304162.

"Dr. J.W. Thompson, Who Aided Concentration Camp Victims, Dead at 59." Jewish Telegraphic Agency, 25 August 1965.

Drummond, Jack. "Foreword." In *The Biology of Human Starvation*, by Ancel Keys, Josef Brozek, Austin Henschel, Olaf Mickelsen, and Henry Longstreet Taylor, xiii–xvi. 2 vols. Minneapolis: University of Minnesota Press, 1950.

Eadie, Jim. "Coe Hill Legion Honours Harold and Joan Nash." *Bancroft This Week*, 7 May 2014.

Eby, Cecil D. *Hungary at War: Civilians and Soldiers in World War II.* University
  Park: Pennsylvania State University Press, 1998.

Egan, Kelly. "Pure Spring Was in Every Fridge." *Ottawa Citizen,* 2 July 2010.

"Eight Jews Stabbed, One Shot by Polish Dp's at Bergen-Belsen Camp;
  Situation Tense." Jewish Telegraphic Agency, 19 May 1946.

Eisenthal, Bram D. "Alan Rose Dies at 74; Was a Leader of Canadian Jewry."
  Jewish Telegraphic Agency, 19 July 1995.

Ellis, L.F. *Victory in the West: The Defeat of Germany.* Vol. 2. London: Her
  Majesty's Stationary Office, 1968.

Engel, Cynthia Nyman. "Former Vaad President Mervin Mirsky Passes Away
  at 96." *Ottawa Jewish Bulletin,* 19 July 2010, 5.

Erwin, Norman. "The Holocaust, Canadian Jews, and Canada's 'Good War'
  Against Nazism." *Canadian Jewish Studies/Études juives canadiennes* 24
  (2016): 103–23. https://doi.org/10.25071/1916-0925.39962.

"Even Parachutists Lacking Limbs 'Full of Fight.'" Name of newspaper
  unidentified. From private collection, Costigan family, ca. July 1945.

Ezickson, A.J. "Press." *Popular Photography,* November 1948, 1, 163–8.

Farber, Bernie. "Canada's Monument to Nazi Soldiers." *National Post,* 22 July
  2020.

– "A Two-Man Band of Brothers." *National Post,* 10 November 2010.

Farrell, Jon. "History in the Taking: Some Notes about the Canadian Army Film
  and Photo Unit." *Canadian Geographical Journal* 30, no. 6 (June 1945): 276–87.

Feasby, W.R., ed. *Official History of the Canadian Medical Services, 1939–1945:
  Organization and Campaigns.* Vol. 1. Ottawa: Queen's Printer and Controller
  of Stationary, 1956.

Feinstein, Stephen C., ed. *Absence/Presence: Critical Essays on the Artistic
  Memory of the Holocaust.* Syracuse: Syracuse University Press, 2005.

"Fighting the Second World War with Their Cameras." CBC News
  Saskatchewan, 11 November 2015.

Flanagan, Ben, and Donald Bloxham, eds. *Remembering Belsen: Eyewitnesses
  Record the Liberation.* London: Vallentine Mitchell, 2005.

Forbes, Patrick. *6th Guards Tank Brigade: The Story of Guardsmen in Churchill
  Tanks.* London: S. Low, Marston, 1946.

"Former Wilno Parish Priest Dies in Toronto at 72." *Ottawa Citizen,* 18
  February 1986, D3.

Foss, Brian. "Molly Lamb Bobak: Art and War." In *Molly Lamb Bobak: A
  Retrospective,* edited by Cindy Richmond, n.p. Regina: Mackenzie Art
  Gallery, 1993.

– *War Paint: Art, War, State and Identity in Britain, 1939–1945.* New Haven: Yale
  University Press, 2007.

Fraser, Paul D.K. "Stanley Winfield." *The Advocate* 70, pt. 1 (January 2012):
  114–18.

Freedman, Menachem. "We Can't Let Ottawa's Holocaust Monument Become an Empty Symbol." *Globe and Mail*, 22 May 2014.

Friedländer, Saul, ed. *Probing the Limits of Representation: Nazism and the "Final Solution."* Cambridge, MA: Harvard University Press, 1992.

Frisse, Ulrich. "The 'Bystanders' Perspective': The *Toronto Daily Star* and Its Coverage of the Persecution of the Jews and the Holocaust in Canada, 1933–1945." *Yad Vashem Studies* 39, no. 1 (2011): 213–43.

Geddes, John. "The Monumental Politics behind Ottawa's Newest Memorials." *Maclean's*, 9 January 2015.

Gefen, Pearl Sheffy. "Forty Years Ago as a Frail Israel Fought for Life Our War Heroes Said: 'Lean on Us.'" *Toronto Star*, 2 October 1988, D5.

Gelber, Shalome Michael (signing as "Canadian Officer"). "Are We Breaking Faith?" *New Statesman and Nation*, 3 August 1946, 78–9.

– *The Failure of the American Rabbi: A Program for the Revitalization of the Rabbinate in America.* New York: Twayne, 1961.

– "Wherein Is This Night Different? From Bergen-Belsen, Germany." *Menorah Journal* 35, no. 1 (January–March, 1947): 21–30.

Gelber, Sylva M. *No Balm in Gilead: A Personal Retrospective of Mandate Days in Palestine.* Ottawa: Carleton University Press, 1989.

"Generous Move by RAF Men to Help Belsen Survivors." *Army News.* Darwin: Northern Territory Printing and Press Unit, 25 June 1945, p. 3.

"German Appeals for Germany." *Windsor Daily Star*, 3 February 1943, 2.

"Germans Still 90 P.C. Nazi Hate Allies, Official Says." *Toronto Daily Star*, 23 August 1946.

Gödeck, Monica, ed. *The Topography of the Bergen-Belsen Camp: Six Maps.* Stuttgart: Druck and Design, 2008.

Gödecke, Monika, Rolf Keller, Thomas Rahe, and Wilfried Wiedemann. *Bergen-Belsen: Explanatory Notes on the Exhibition.* Hannover: Niedersächsische Landeszentrale für Politische Bildung, 1991.

Goldberg, Adara. *Holocaust Survivors in Canada: Exclusion, Inclusion, Transformation, 1947–1955* (Winnipeg: University of Manitoba Press, 2015).

Gould, Ed. *Entertaining Canadians: Canada's International Stars, 1900–1988.* Victoria: Cappis, 1988.

Goutor, David. "The Canadian Media and the 'Discovery' of the Holocaust, 1944–1945." *Canadian Jewish Studies/Études Juives Canadiennes* 4–5 (1996–7): 88–119. https://doi.org/10.25071/1916-0925.19813.

Graham, Andrew. *Sharpshooters at War: The 3rd, the 4th and the 3rd/4th County of London Yeomanry, 1939 to 1945.* London: Sharpshooters Regimental Association, 1964.

Granatstein, J.L., and Norman Hillmer, eds. *Battle Lines: Eyewitness Accounts from Canada's Military History.* Toronto: Thomas Allen, 2004.

Grant, Doris. "Campbell Interrogated Bergen-Belsen Inmates; 60th Anniversary of VE- Day." *Barrie Advance*, 4 May 2005, 5.

Greenberg, Reesa. "Constructing the Canadian War Museum/Constructing the Landscape of a Canadian Identity." In *(Re)visualizing National History: Museums and National Identities in Europe in the New Millennium*, edited by Robin Ostow, 183–99. Toronto: University of Toronto Press, 2008.

Greenhous, Brereton, Stephen J. Harris, William C. Johnston, and William G.P. Rawling. *The Crucible of War, 1939–1945: The Official History of the Royal Canadian Air Force*. Vol. 3. Toronto: University of Toronto Press, 1994.

Greenspan, Henry. "Survivors' Accounts." In *The Oxford Handbook of Holocaust Studies*, edited by Peter Hayes and John K. Roth, 414–27. Oxford: Oxford University Press, 2011.

Griffin, Kevin. "Holocaust Horrors Recalled." *Vancouver Sun*, 4 May 1995, B4.

"Gruesome Pictures of Concentration Camp." *St Marys Journal Argus*, 17 May 1945, 12J.

Gutkin, Harry. *The Worst of Times, The Best of Times*. Markham: Fitzhenry and Whiteside, 1987.

Haines, Judy. "Doris Haines." *Globe and Mail*, 26 January 2009, L6.

Halbwachs, Maurice. *On Collective Memory*. Edited and translated by Lewis A. Coser. Chicago: University of Chicago Press, 1992.

Halliday, Hugh. "Donald Kenneth Anderson: Official War Artist (1920-2009)." *Canadian Military History* 19, no. 4 (Autumn 2010): 50–6.

– *Typhoon and Tempest: The Canadian Story*. Toronto: CANAV, 1992.

Hancock, Glen. *Charley Goes to War*. Kentville: Gaspereau, 2004.

Harclerode, Peter. *Fighting Brigadier: The Life and Campaigns of Brigadier James Hill*. Barnsely: Pen and Sword Military, 2010.

– *Go to It! The Illustrated History of the 6th Airborne Division*. London: Bloomsbury, 1990.

Hardman, Leslie. "Rev. Leslie Hardman." In *Belsen in History and Memory*, edited by Jo Reilly, David Cesarani, Tony Kushner, and Colin Richmond, 225–33. London: Frank Cass, 1997.

Hardman, Leslie H., and Cecily Goodman. *The Survivors: The Story of the Belsen Remnant*. London: Vallentine Mitchell, 2009 [1958].

Hartigan, Daniel R. *A Rising Courage: Canada's Paratroops in the Liberation of Normandy*. Calgary: Drop Zone, 2000.

Harvey, J. Douglas. *Boys, Bombs and Brussels Sprouts*. Toronto: McClelland and Stewart, 1981.

Hawthorn, Tom. "B.C. Politico Kept His Pencil Sharp." *Globe and Mail*, 23 October 2003, R11.

Heaps, Leo. *Escape From Arnhem: A Canadian among the Lost Paratroops*. Toronto: Macmillan, 1945.

– *The Grey Goose of Arnhem*. London: Weidenfeld and Nicholson, 1976.

Hill, Robert. *Jack McCreary: Paediatrician, Pedagogue, Pragmatist, Prophet.*
   Vancouver: Tantalus Research, 2006.
Hirsch, Marianne. "Editor's Column: What's Wrong with These Terms?
   A Conversation with Barbara Kirshenblatt-Gimblett and Diana
   Taylor." *PMLA* 120, no. 5 (October 2005): 1497–1508. https://doi.
   org/10.1632/003081205X79104.
Hirsh, Michael. *The Liberators: America's Witnesses to the Holocaust.* New York:
   Bantam Books, 2010.
"Holocaust Song Has Cellular Firm Squirming." *Reuters UK*, 15 September
   2007.
Horn, Bernd, and Michel Wyczynski. *Paras versus the Reich: Canada's
   Paratroopers at War, 1942–45.* Toronto: Dundurn, 2003.
Horowitz, Sara R. *Voicing the Void: Muteness and Memory in Holocaust Fiction.*
   Albany: State University of New York Press, 1997.
"H.S. Abramson Awarded French Art Scholarship." *Montreal Standard*, 16
   March 1946.
"Interview with Allan [sic] Rose." In *Bitburg and Beyond: Encounters in
   American, German and Jewish History*, edited by Ilya Levkov, 680–5. New
   York: Shapolsky, 1987.
"Introducing the 'Cookie Pusher' of the Montreal St. Andrew Society." *Journal
   of the St. Andrew's Society of Montreal*, Fall 1993, 2.
Ironside, Allan. *Anecdotes of Olde Orillia: A Collection of the Works of Allan
   Ironside.* Edited by J.T. Grossmith. Orillia: Orillia Historical Society, 1984.
"JDC Worker Makes Plea for Victims." *Jewish Western Bulletin*, 14 March 1947, 1.
"John Ferguson McCreary: A Man for All Seasons." *Canadian Medical
   Association Journal* 122 (12 January 1980): 123–4.
Kadar, Marlene. *Essays on Life Writing: From Genre to Critical Practice.* Toronto:
   University of Toronto Press, 1992.
"Kadziolka, Rev. Dr. Stanislaus Jan." *Ottawa Citizen*, 17 February 1986, C4.
Kardonne, Rick. "Special Commemoration Marks Liberation and End of War."
   Jewish Tribune (Canada), 12 May 2005.
Kearney, Richard. "Parsing Narrative – Story, History, Life." *Human Studies*
   29, no. 4 (December 2006): 477–90. https://www.jstor.org/stable
   /27642770.
"Keith MacLellan Honored for Wartime Services." *The Suburban*, 2 November
   1988, A26.
Kemp, Anthony. *The SAS at War, 1941–1945.* London: Penguin, 1991.
Kemp, Paul. "The British Army and the Liberation of Bergen-Belsen, April
   1945." In *Belsen in History and Memory*, edited by Jo Reilly, David Cesarani,
   Tony Kushner, and Colin Richmond, 134–48. London: Frank Cass, 1997.
–   "The Liberation of Bergen-Belsen Concentration Camp in April 1945: The
   Testimony of Those Involved." *Imperial War Museum Review* 5 (1991): 28–41.

"King Whyte: Telecaster, Writer on Outdoor Subjects." *Globe and Mail*, 28 June 1962, 11.

Kirshner, Sheldon. "Canadian Pilot Witnessed Horrors of Bergen-Belsen." *Canadian Jewish News*, 20 January 2011, 16.

Klein, L. Ruth, ed. *Nazi Germany, Canadian Responses: Confronting Antisemitism in the Shadow of War*. Montreal: McGill-Queen's University Press, 2012.

Klemme, Marvin. *The Inside Story of UNRRA: An Experience in Internationalism*. New York: Lifetime Editions, 1949.

Knelman, Martin. "Holocaust Monument in Ottawa Corrects 70-Year Mistake." *Toronto Star*, 14 May 2014.

Kohler, Nicholas. "Band of Brothers." *National Post*, 11 November 2004, A1.

Kolasky, John. *The Shattered Illusion: The History of Ukrainian Pro-Communist Organizations in Canada*. Toronto: PMA Books, 1979.

Kolb, Eberhard. *Bergen-Belsen: From "Detention Camp" to Concentration Camp, 1943–1945*. 2nd ed. Göttingen: Vandenhoeck and Ruprecht, 1986.

Korman, Gerd. *Nightmare's Fairy Tale: A Young Refugee's Home Fronts, 1938–1948*. Madison: University of Wisconsin Press, 2005.

Kostenuk, Samual, and John Griffin. *RCAF Squadron Histories and Aircraft, 1924–1968*. Toronto: A.M. Hakkert, 1977.

Krell, Robert. "Children Who Survived the Holocaust: Reflections of a Child Survivor/Psychiatrist." *Echoes of the Holocaust* 4 (June 1995): 14–21.

Kubow, Magdalena. "Kanada? *The Canadian Jewish News* and the Memory of the Holocaust in Canada." *Holocaust Studies: A Journal of Culture and History* 19, no. 3 (2013): 131–60. https://doi.org/10.1080/17504902.2013.11087383

"LAC Blooms on Vegetables." *Maple Leaf*, 22 January 1946, 2.

Langlois, Suzanne. "Making Ideal Histories: The Film Censorship Board in Postwar France." In *Secret Spaces, Forbidden Places: Rethinking Culture*, edited by Fran Lloyd and Catherine O'Brien, 107–20. New York: Berghahn, 2000.

Laqueur, Walter. *Thursday's Child Has Far to Go: A Memoir of the Journeying Years*. Toronto: Maxwell Macmillan, 1992.

"Larry D. Mann, Veteran Actor, Dies at 91." *CBC News*, 6 January 2014.

Lavsky, Hagit. *New Beginnings: Holocaust Survivors in Bergen-Belsen and the British Zone in Germany, 1945–1950*. Detroit: Wayne State University Press, 2002.

Law, Cecil. *Kamp Westerbork, Transit Camp to Eternity: The Liberation Story*. Clementsport: Canadian Peacekeeping Press, 2000.

Lawlor, Allison. "Ted Light, Military Chaplain 1914–2005." *Globe and Mail*, 13 June 2005, S6.

Lee, Geddy, Alex Lifeson, and Neil Peart. "Red Sector A." *Grace Under Pressure*. Track 3. Anthem Records, 1984, compact disc.

Lee, Geddy, and Ben Mink. "Grace to Grace." *My Favourite Headache*. Track 11. Atlantic, 2000, compact disc.

Lejeune, Philippe. *On Autobiography*. Edited by Paul John Eakin. Translated by
    Katherine Leary. Minneapolis: University of Minnesota Press, 1989.
– *On Diary*. Edited by Jeremy D. Popkin and Julie Rak. Translated by
    Katherine Durnin. Manoa: University of Hawaii Press, 2009.
Lerner, Loren, ed. *Afterimage: Evocations of the Holocaust in Contemporary
    Canadian Arts and Literature*. Montreal: Concordia University Institute for
    Canadian Jewish Studies, 2002.
Levi, S. Gershon. *Breaking New Ground: The Struggle for a Jewish Chaplaincy in
    Canada*. Edited by David Golinkin. Montreal: Canadian Jewish Congress, 1994.
Levinson, Lottie. "Lottie Levinson in Europe Scores Zionist Nationalism."
    Jewish Western Bulletin, 4 January 1946, 1, 4.
"The Liberated of Belsen." *OHTWOEE* 3, no. 20, 23 July 1945.
"Lieutenant-Colonel Mervin Mirsky, O.B.E. and Mention." In *Canadian Jews
    in World War II*, vol. 1, edited by David Rome. Montreal: Canadian Jewish
    Congress, 1947.
"Local Men's Work in UNRRA Praised." *Montreal Gazette*, 30 January 1946, 7.
"Love Letters from a Witness to War." *Maclean's*, 9 May 1988, 52–6.
MacIntyre, Alasdair. *After Virtue: A Study in Moral Theory*. London:
    Duckworth, 1981.
Malcolm, Janet. *The Silent Woman: Sylvia Plath and Ted Hughes*. London:
    Picador, 1994.
Mann, Larry. "Beaching on Normandy Easier a Second Time." *Edmonton
    Journal*, 9 September 1979, I1.
Margalit, Avishai. *The Ethics of Memory*. Cambridge, MA: Harvard University
    Press, 2002.
Margolis, Rebecca. "The Canadian Army Newsreels as a Representation of the
    Holocaust." In *Lessons and Legacies XI: Expanding Perspectives on the Holocaust
    in a Changing World*, edited by Hilary Earl and Karl A. Schleunes, 121–43.
    Evanston: Northwestern University Press, 2014.
The Maroon Square: A History of the 4th Battalion, The Wiltshire Regiment.
    Compiled by A.D. Parsons, D.I.M. Robbins, and D.C. Gilson. London:
    Franley, 1955.
Martin, Sandra. "Lyle Creelman, Nurse and Administrator, 1908–2007." *Globe
    and Mail*, 10 March 2007, S9.
Matas, Robert. "No One Would Listen to Soldier's Account of Nazi Death
    Camps." *Globe and Mail*, 24 January 2005, A1.
McCooey, David. *Artful Histories: Modern Australian Autobiography*.
    Cambridge: Cambridge University Press, 1996.
McCreery, Christopher. *The Maple Leaf and the White Cross*. Toronto: Dundurn,
    2008.
McGill, Robert. "The Life You Write May Be Your Own: Epistolary
    Autobiography and the Reluctant Resurrection of Flannery O'Connor."

Southern Literary Journal 36, no. 2 (Spring 2004): 31–46. https://www.jstor
.org/stable/20067788.

McKay, Ken. *Figuratively Speaking: Puppetry in Ontario*. North York: The
Puppet Centre, 1990.

Meisels, Leslie. *Suddenly the Shadow Fell*. Toronto: Azrieli Foundation, 2014.

Menkis, Richard. "'But You Can't See the Fear that People Lived Through':
Canadian Jewish Chaplains and Canadian Encounters with Dutch
Survivors." *American Jewish Archives Journal* 60, nos. 1–2 (2008): 24–50.

– "Cass, Samuel (1908–1975)." In *Encyclopaedia Judaica*, 2nd ed., vol. 4, edited
by Fred Skolnik and Michael Berenbaum. Detroit: Macmillan, 2007.

Menkis, Richard, and Ronnie Tessler. *Canada Responds to the Holocaust, 1944 to
1945*. Vancouver: Vancouver Holocaust Education Centre, 2005.

Metson, Graham. "A Personal Realist." In *Alex Colville: Diary of a War Artist*,
compiled by Graham Metson and Cheryl Lean, 16–19. Halifax: Nimbus,
1981.

Michalczyk, John J. *Filming the End of the Holocaust: Allied Documentaries,
Nuremberg and the Liberation of the Concentration Camps*. New York:
Bloomsbury Academic, 2014.

Milberry, Larry, and Hugh A. Halliday. *The Royal Canadian Air Force at War,
1939–1945*. Toronto: CANAV, 1990.

"Ministry Call First Shunned by Cowboy." *Ladner Optimist*, 18 October 1951, 3.

Mirsky, Mervin. "I Saw Holocaust Horrors in Person." *Ottawa Citizen*, 18
February 1998, A18.

– "Sister Pop: A Very Special WWII Remembrance." *Ottawa Jewish Bulletin and
Review*, 6 April 1990, 8.

Molotov, Vyacheslav. *On the Transformation of the People's Commissariat of
Defence and of the People's Commissariat of Foreign Affairs form All-Union
People's Commissariats in to Union-Republican People'e Commissiariats: Report
in the Supreme Soviet of the U.S.S.R. on February 1, 1944*. London: Soviet War
News, 1944.

Monnon, Ernest, and Mary Ann Monnon. *"Right On, You Got the Elbow Out!":
Wartime Memories of the R.C.A.F.* Toronto: Dundurn, 1990.

Morse, Jennifer. "War Art: Aba Bayefsky." *Legion Magazine*, 1 May 1998.

Mortimer, Gavin. *Stirling's Men: The Inside History of the SAS in World War II*.
London: Cassell, 2004.

Munro, Kenneth. *First Presbyterian Church, Edmonton: A History*. Victoria:
Trafford, 2004.

Murray, Joan. *Canadian Artists of the Second World War*. Oshawa: Robert
McLaughlin Gallery, 1981.

"Nazi Underground Seen Future Evil." *Montreal Gazette*, 18 November 1944, 19.

"Nazi Underground to Be Best of All." *Leader-Post Regina*, 18 November 1944,
16.

Nicholson, G.W.L. *Seventy Years of Service: A History of the Royal Canadian Army Medical Corps*. Ottawa: Borealis, 1977.

Nijboer, Donald. *No 126 Wing RCAF*. Oxford: Osprey, 2010.

Nolan, Brian. *Airborne: The Heroic Story of the 1st Canadian Parachute Battalion in the Second World War*. Toronto: Lester, 1995.

"Obituary: Elsie May Deeks." *Winnipeg Free Press*, 20 June 2005.

"Obituary: Leo Velleman." *Comox Valley Record*, 10 March 2009.

"Obituary: Ronald Ford 'Andy" Anderson." *Globe and Mail*, 20 November 2015.

"Obituary: Ron Laidlaw." *Globe and Mail*, 16 August 2008.

"Obituary: Rosalie Rector." *Edmonton Journal*, 10 February 2007.

"Obituary: Thompson, James Ernest." *Red Deer Advocate*, 3 March 2005.

"Obituary: Winfield, Stanley Harold." *Vancouver Sun*, 20 August 2011.

"Obituary: Yale, Bernard Louis." *Globe and Mail*, 18 September 2001.

O'Hanlon, Betty. *Finding a Familiar Stranger*. Edmonton: Plains, 1988.

Olney, James. *Metaphors of Self: The Meaning of Autobiography*. Princeton: Princeton University Press, 1972.

O'Neill, Patrick B. "The Halifax Concert Party in World War II." *Theatre Research in Canada* 20, no. 2 (Fall 1999): 1–16. https://journals.lib.unb.ca/index.php/TRIC/article/view/7086.

"Paid Notice: Deaths – Gelber, Rabbi Shalome Michael, PhD." *New York Times*, 9 December 2001.Panchuk, Bohdan. *Heroes of Their Day: The Reminiscences of Bohdan Panchuk*. Edited by Lubomyr Y. Luciuk. Toronto: Multicultural History Society, Ontario Heritage Foundation, 1983.

"Paratrooper Remembered on Banff Avenue." *Banff Crag and Canyon*, 10 November 2009, 7.

Perl, Gisella. *I Was a Doctor in Auschwitz*. New York: Arno, 1979 [1948].

Perley, Warren. "TV Records Tearful Memories of Holocaust Horror." *Montreal Gazette*, 13 August 1981, 12.

Perlove, B. "Don't Forget! Fifty Forum Reporter Sees Horrors of Belsen." *Fifty Forum*, 17 August 1945, 1.

Phillips, Raymond, ed. *Trial of Josef Kramer and Forty-Four Others: The Belsen Trial*. London: W. Hodge, 1949.

Piovesana, Roy. *Hope and Charity: Diocese of Thunder Bay*. Thunder Bay: Roman Catholic Bishop of Thunder Bay, 2002.

Popkin, Jeremy D. *History, Historians, and Autobiography*. Chicago: University of Chicago Press, 2005.

– "Holocaust Memories, Historians' Memoirs: First-Person Narrative and the Memory of the Holocaust." *History and Memory* 15, no. 1 (Spring/Summer 2003): 49–84. https://doi.org/10.2979/his.2003.15.1.49.

Portraits of War. Produced by Paul Kemp. Stornoway Productions, 2007. DVD, 48 minutes.

Posner, Michael. "Patricia Holden Collins Was Groundbreaking Wartime Photographer." *Globe and Mail*, 8 December 2011.

Prayer for the Dead: Herzl Kashetsky. Produced and directed by Lisa Lamb. New Brunswick Museum, Saint John Jewish Historical Museum, and Fundy Community Television, 1997.

"Prison Occupants Return to Normal." *Saskatoon Star-Phoenix*, 6 May 1946, 6.

Purden, Carolyn. "The Two Lives of Ted Light." *Canadian Churchman*, July–August 1969, 10, 12.

"Rabbi Finds Belsen Benefactor." *Windsor Star*, 20 December 1962, 1.

"Rabbi Seeks Wartime 'Friends.'" *Montreal Gazette*, 15 December 1962, 3.

Ralph, Wayne. *Aces, Warriors and Wingmen: The Firsthand Accounts of Canada's Fighter Pilots in the Second World War*. Mississauga: John Wiley and Sons, 2005.

Randall, John, and M.J. Trow. *The Last Gentleman of the SAS*. New York: Random House, 2014.

Ravvin, Norman. "A Museum, War Art and Canadian Identity." *Canadian Jewish News*, 31 August 2006, 41.

Rawling, Bill. *Death Their Enemy: Canadian Medical Practitioners and War*. Ottawa: Bill Rawling, 2001.

Reilly, Jo, David Cesarani, Tony Kushner, and Colin Richmond, eds. *Belsen in History and Memory*. London: Frank Cass, 1997.

Reilly, Joanne. *Belsen: The Liberation of a Concentration Camp*. London: Routledge, 1998.

– "'With Waving Flags': Bergen-Belsen and the Myth of Liberation." *Patterns of Prejudice* 29, nos. 2–3 (April–July 1995): 61–74.

Reinisch, Jessica. "Introduction: Relief in the Aftermath of War." *Journal of Contemporary History* 4, no. 3 (2008): 371–404. https://doi.org/10.1177 %2F0022009408091819

The Relief of Belsen, April 1945: Eyewitness Accounts. Compiled by Paul Kemp. London: Imperial War Museum, 1991.

Rennick, Joanne Benham. *Religion in the Ranks: Belief and Religious Experience in the Canadian Forces*. Toronto: University of Toronto Press, 2011.

"Rev. Ross Ketchen Cameron, Former Presbyterian Moderator." *Toronto Star*, 28 April 1989.

Richer, Charles H. "Sgt. Mike Lattion (Obituary)." *1st Canadian Parachute Battalion Association Newsletter* 6, no. 20 (April 1997): 41–3.

Ricoeur, Paul. *Critique and Conviction: Conversations with François Azouvi and Marc de Launay*. Translated by Kathleen Blarney. New York: Columbia University Press, 1998.

– *Oneself as Another*. Translated by Kathleen Blamey. Chicago: University of Chicago Press, 1992.

– *The Symbolism of Evil*. Translated by Emerson Buchanan. Boston: Beacon, 1970.

– *Temps et récit*. 3 vols. Paris: Seuil, 1983.

– *Time and Narrative*. 3 vols. Translated by K. McLaughlin and D. Pellauer. Chicago: University of Chicago Press, 1984.

Ricoeur, Paul, David Carr, and Charles Taylor. "Discussion: Ricoeur on Narrative." In *On Paul Ricoeur: Narrative and Interpretation*, edited by D. Wood, 160–87. New York: Routledge, 1991.

Roberts, Amanda. "The Saltsman Letters." *Muskoka Times* (ca. March 2000).

Rome, David, ed. *Canadian Jews in World War II*. Montreal: Canadian Jewish Congress, 1947.

Rose, Alan. "Testimony at the Liberators of Nazi Concentration Camps Conference." In *Bitburg and Beyond: Encounters in American, German and Jewish History*, edited by Ilya Levkov, 686–7. New York: Shapolsky, 1987.

Rutherford, Paul. *When Television Was Young: Primetime Canada 1952–1967*. Toronto: University of Toronto Press, 1990.

Sapir, Edward. *Culture, Language and Personality*. Berkeley: University of California Press, 1962.

"Saul Laskin Describes Belsen Camp." *Daily Times Journal*, 26 March 1946.

Saunders, Tim. *Operation Varsity: The British and Canadian Airborne Assault*. Barnsley: Pen and Sword, 2008.

Saxon, Wolfgang. "Maurice Victor, 81, a Neurologist and Teacher." *New York Times*, 29 June 2001, B8.

Schulze, Rainer. "'Keeping Very Clear of Any 'Kuh-Handel': The British Foreign Office and the Rescue of Jews from Bergen-Belsen." *Holocaust Genocide Studies* 19, no. 2 (Fall 2005): 226–51. https://doi.org/10.1093/hgs/dci021.

Scott, Joan. W. "The Evidence of Experience." *Critical Inquiry* 17, no. 4 (Summer 1991): 773–97. https://doi.org/10.1086/448612.

Senate of Canada. "Proceedings of the Standing Committee on Immigration and Labour." 29 May 1946.

– "Proceedings of the Subcommittee on Veterans Affairs." Issue 4 – Evidence for 3 February 1998.

Service of Praise and Thanksgiving for the Victories of the Allied Nations. Officiant: The Rev. Dr. Louis M. Sanker, Senior Jewish Chaplain, RAF and Tactical Air Force. London: Office of the Chief Rabbi, 1945.

Shadbolt, Jack. *In Search of Form*. Toronto: McClelland and Stewart, 1968.

Shanahan, Noreen. "Belsen Diarist Hated Medicine and Loved Writing." *Globe and Mail*, 29 March 2013.

Shapiro, Marshall. "Adath Israel Honours Jewish War Vets." *Jewish Tribune*, 10 November 2005.

Shephard, Ben. *After Daybreak: The Liberation of Bergen-Belsen, 1945*. New York: Schocken, 2005.

– "The Medical Relief Effort at Belsen." In *Belsen 1945: New Historical Perspectives*, edited by Suzanne Bardgett and David Cesarani, 31–50. London: Vallentine Mitchell, 2006.

Shields, Roy. "Gallery 'With a Purpose' Opened by Artist Couple." *Monitor*, 26
    February 1953.
Sibley, Celia. "Bearing a Painful Witness: Death Camp Liberator Shares
    Memories of the Horrors." *Atlanta Journal and Constitution*, 20 May 1995, 1J.
Sington, Derrick. *Belsen Uncovered*. London: Duckworth, 1946.
Smart, Tom. *Alex Colville: Return*. Halifax: Douglas and McIntyre, 2004.
– "A Broken Neck, a Shattered Heart." *Telegraph-Journal* (New Brunswick), 5
    May 2012, F3.
Smith, Sidonie, and Julia Watson. *Reading Autobiography: A Guide for
    Interpreting Life Narratives*. Minnesota: University of Minnesota Press, 2001.
Smith, Ted. "Horror beyond Belief." In *Never Forget: More Stories from the
    Conflict Zones*, by Paul Hunter and Jim Rankin, 57–60. Toronto: Star
    Dispatches, 2013.
Smith, Wilfred I. *Code Word CANLOAN*. Toronto: Dundurn, 1992.
– *Experiences of a CANLOAN Officer, 1944–1945*. Ottawa: Public Archives,
    1977.
– "Introduction." In *Relentless Verity: Canadian Military Photographers since
    1885*, by Peter Robertson, 8–33. Toronto: University of Toronto Press, 1973.
Snowsell, Frank. "Letter Tells the Tale of Why Our Side Fought War." *The
    Vancouver Sun*, 10 November 1993, A3.
Sonnenschein, Bronia. *Victory over Nazism: A Holocaust Survivor's Journey*.
    Edited by Dan Sonnenschein. Vancouver: Deskside, 1998.
The Splendour of Order. Directed by Don Hutchison. National Film Board, 1983,
    58 minutes.
Srikanthan, Thulasi. "Tradition of Patriotism: As a Young Woman, Yvonne
    Hamon Served Her Country in WWII." *Toronto Star*, 8 November 2006, A4.
Stacey, C.P. *The Victory Campaign: The Operations in North-West Europe, 1944–
    1945*. Vol. 3. Ottawa: Queen's Printer and Controller of Stationery, 1960.
Stanley, Elmer M. "Death Camp Happy Now Toronto Nurses Aid." *Toronto
    Daily Star*, 19 September 1945, 1.
"Stettler Doctor Returns to Describe Crossing of Rhine with Paratroopers."
    Edmonton Journal, 4 July 1945, 1, 5.
Stone, Dan. *The Liberation of the Camps: The End of the Holocaust and Its
    Aftermath*. New Haven: Yale University Press, 2015.
The Story Behind the Allan Ironside History Scholarship. Orillia Historical Society,
    n.d.
Stubbs, Andrew. *White Light Primitive*. Regina: Hagios, 2009.
Stuchen, Philip. "Mass-Employment for Displaced Persons." *Queen's
    Quarterly: A Canadian Review* 54, no. 3 (Autumn 1947): 360–5.
– "The Problem of Palestine." *Queen's Quarterly: A Canadian Review* 54, no. 4
    (Winter 1947–48): 413–20.
"Study in Evil: The SS Women of Belsen." *Daily Mail*, 23 April 1945, 3.
"The End of Belsen?" *Time*, 11 June 1945, 36.

Thom, Ian M. *Jack Shadbolt: Early Watercolours, July 17 to August 21, 1980.*
    Victoria: Art Gallery of Greater Victoria, 1980.
Thompson, Lloyd E. *At Face Value: Portraits by Lloyd E. Thompson.* Picton:
    Picton Gazette, 1976.
Tibbs, David J. *Parachute Doctor: The Memoirs of Captain David Tibbs.* Edited by
    Neil Barber. Sevenoaks: Sabrestorm, 2012.
Toman, Cynthia. *An Officer and a Lady: Canadian Military Nursing and the Second
    World War.* Vancouver: UBC Press, 2007.
Trepman, Paul. *Among Men and Beasts.* Translated by Shoshana Perla and
    Gertrude Hirschler. New York: Bergen Belsen Memorial Press, 1978.
Turner, Kevin. "Nazi Death Camp Photos Record the Unimaginable." *News
    Leader* (Fernandina Beach, FL), 5 January 2005, 1A, 8A.
"23,000 Hungry at Belsen Fed by Canadian Expert." *Toronto Daily Star*, 18 July
    1945, 24.
"UNRRA Is Praised for Humane Tasks." *Montreal Gazette*, 19 February 1946, 9.
"Vancouver Jewry Subscribe $40,000 to External Welfare." *Jewish Western
    Bulletin*, 3 May 1946, 1.
Van Moorsel, Greg. "Hitler's Visit Still Haunting." *London Free Press*, 5 April
    2007.
Varley, Christopher. *Aba Bayefsky Revisited: A Retrospective Exhibition.* Toronto:
    Koffler Gallery, 1989.
Velleman, Leo. "Belsen." In *Flap: 39 Reconnaissance Wing*, n.p. Hamburg:
    Vollmer and Bentlin KG, 1945.
Verlome, Hetty. *The Children's House of Belsen.* London: Politico's, 2004.
Victory from Above: The 1st Canadian Parachute Battalion. Produced by Lance
    Goddard. Written by Peter Kent. Koch International, 2002. DVD, 88
    minutes.
"Volunteers Fight Battle of Winter in Germany." *Mercury* (Hobart Town), 7
    January 1946, 3.
War Diary of the 1st Canadian Parachute Battalion. Compiled and edited by
    Walter Romanow, Morris Romanow, Helene MacLean, Rosalie Hartigan,
    and Bill Dickson. Calgary: Bunker to Bunker, 2006.
Watson, Scott. *Jack Shadbolt.* Vancouver: Douglas and McIntyre, 1990.
Watts, Sybil. "Windsor Woman Saw Buchenwald, Belsen." *Windsor Daily Star*,
    4 September 1945, 16.
Weindling, Paul. "Belsenitis: Liberating Belsen, Its Hospitals, UNRRA, and
    Selection for Re-emigration, 1945–1948." *Science in Context* 19, no. 3 (2006):
    401–18. https://doi.org/10.1017/S0269889706000998.
– *John W. Thompson: Psychiatrist in the Shadow of the Holocaust.* Rochester:
    University of Rochester Press, 2010.
– "The Origins of Informed Consent: The International Scientific Commission
    on Medical War Crimes, and the Nuremberg Code." *Bulletin of the History of*

Medicine 75, no. 1 (Spring 2001): 37–71. https://doi.org/10.1353/bhm
.2001.0049.

– "Victims, Witnesses, and the Ethical Legacy of the Nuremberg Medical
Trial." In *Reassessing the Nuremberg Military Tribunals: Transitional Justice,
Trial Narratives, and Historiography,* edited by Kim C. Priemel and Alexa
Stiller, 74–103. New York: Berghahn, 2012.

Weintraub, Karl J. "Autobiography and Historical Consciousness." *Critical
Inquiry* 1, no. 4 (June 1975): 821–48. https://doi.org/10.1086/447818.

– *The Value of the Individual: Self and Circumstance in Autobiography.* Chicago:
University of Chicago Press, 1982.

White, Hayden. *The Content of the Form.* Baltimore: Johns Hopkins University
Press, 1987.

– "Historical Emplotment and the Problem of Truth." In *Probing the Limits of
Representation,*

– *Tropics of Discourse.* Baltimore: Johns Hopkins University Press, 1978.

Whitlam, George. "Palestinians Should Be Helped." *Toronto Star,* 7 January
1993, A16.

Whyte, King. *Letters Home, 1944–1946.* Edited by Tanya Nanavati and
Maureen Whyte. Toronto: Seraphim, 1996.

Wiesel, Elie. "In the Face of Barbarians a Victory of Spirit." *New York Times,* 27
October 1963, 266.

– *The Jews of Silence: A Personal Report on Soviet Jewry.* Translated by Neal
Kozodoy. New York: Holt, Rinehart and Winston, 1966.

Wieviorka, Annette. *The Era of the Witness.* Translated by Jared Stark. Ithaca:
Cornell University Press, 2006.

Williams, Jeffrey. *Far from Home: A Memoir of a Twentieth-Century Soldier.*
Calgary: University of Calgary Press, 2003.

Winfield, Stanley H. "Journey to Galicia – A Glimpse of the Past." *The Scribe*
11, no. 2 (Fall 1989): 15–16.

– "Ted Aplin – 'The Angel of Belsen.'" *Zachor* (newsletter, Vancouver
Holocaust Education Centre), May 1994, 5.

Wodlinger, David. "An UNRRA Field Supervisor Looks Back." *Canadian
Welfare,* April 1948, 12–16.

Wright, Stephen L. *The Last Drop: Operation Varsity, March 24–25, 1945.*
Mechanicsburg: Stackpole, 2008.

Yardley, William. "Alex Colville Dies at 92; Leading Canadian Painter." *New
York Times,* 22 July 2013, B7.

Young, James E. "Interpreting Literary Testimony: A Preface to Rereading
Holocaust Diaries and Memoirs." *New Literary History* 18, no. 2 (Winter
1987): 403–23. https://doi.org/10.2307/468737.

– "Toward a Received History of the Holocaust." *History and Theory* 36, no. 4
(December 1997): 21–43. https://doi.org/10.1111/0018-2656.00029.

– *Writing and Rewriting the Holocaust: Narrative and the Consequences of Interpretation*. Bloomington: Indiana University Press, 1988.

Zander, Ulf. "To Rescue or Be Rescued: The Liberation of Bergen-Belsen and the White Buses in British and Swedish Historical Cultures." In *The Holocaust on Post-War Battlefields: Genocide as Historical Culture*, edited by Klas-Göran Karlsson and Ulf Zander, 343–82. Malmö: Sekel, 2006.

Zemel, Carol. "Emblems of Atrocity." In *Image and Remembrance: Representation and the Holocaust*, edited by Shelley Hornstein and Florence Jacobowitz, 201–19. Bloomington: Indiana University Press, 2003.

Index